SPECIAL EDUCATIONAL NEEDS IN
THE ORDINARY SCHOOL: A SOURCEBOOK
FOR TEACHERS

Alan Cohen is Lecturer in Education at Durham University. He taught in primary and secondary schools in Britain and the USA and in Colleges of Education before taking up his appointment in the School of Education at Durham. His publications include: *Readings in the History of Educational Thought* (with N. Garner), *A Student's Guide to Teaching Practice* (with N. Garner), *Primary Education: a sourcebook for teachers* (with L. Cohen).

Louis Cohen is Professor of Education and Head of the Department of Education at Loughborough University of Technology. He, too, taught in primary and secondary schools in Britain and the USA and in Colleges of Education before taking up appointments at Bradford University and at Loughborough University of Technology. His publications include: *Educational Research Methods in Classrooms and Schools, Experiments in the Social Sciences* (with G. Brown and D. Cherrington), *Statistics for Social Scientists* (with M. Holliday), *Perspectives on Classrooms and Schools* (with L. Manion), *A Guide to Teaching Practice* (with L. Manion), *Multicultural Classrooms* (with L. Manion), *Linking Home and School* (with M. Craft and J. Raynor), *Educational Research and Development in Britain, 1970–1980* (with J.B. Thomas and L. Manion), *Multicultural Education: a sourcebook for teachers* (with A. Cohen).

SPECIAL EDUCATIONAL NEEDS IN THE ORDINARY SCHOOL: A SOURCEBOOK FOR TEACHERS

edited by
ALAN COHEN
University of Durham
and
LOUIS COHEN
Loughborough University of Technology

P·C·P
Paul Chapman
Publishing Ltd

First published 1986
Harper & Row Ltd

Reprinted by
Paul Chapman Publishing Ltd
144 Liverpool Road
London N1 1LA

British Library Cataloguing in Publication Data
Special educational needs in the ordinary
school : a sourcebook for teachers.
  1. Exceptional children - Education
  - Great Britain
  I. Cohen, Alan   II. Cohen, Louis
  371.9'0941   LC3986. G7

ISBN 1 85396 096 9

Typeset by Burns and Smith
Printed and bound in Great Britain by
Butler & Tanner Ltd, Frome and London
A B C D E F G   5 4 3 2 1 0 9

CONTENTS

INTRODUCTION

Special Educational Needs in the Ordinary School: a sourcebook for teachers aims to introduce student teachers and teachers to what the editors consider to be some of the most important problems and issues which face special education today. Although current prevailing perspectives in special education might variously be described as psychological, medical, administrative and educational, particularly prescriptive-educational (Tomlinson, 1982), the editors have deliberately chosen a 'sociological' perspective as a dominant theme in the selection of readings in spite of their awareness that there has been a curious absence of sociological theorizing about special education – indeed, sociology has tended to neglect special education as a central focus of its concern.[1]

For example, until comparatively recently there has been lacking a sociological dimension to the discussions about the concept of integration, which has tended to be seen as a moral, educational and more recently a political issue (Oliver, 1985). What seems obvious, however, is that *professionals* working or about to work in special education need to know much more than what Tomlinson describes as 'recipe' knowledge (pedagogical, clinical and psychological) – often presented to them as unproblematic in its range of what are, in fact, controversial concepts and notions. They need also, and probably more importantly, to acquire an understanding that what happens in special education, in its policies, practices and implementation, is deeply rooted in and influenced by wider social, economic, historical and political perspectives.

There is a danger in assuming that if theory and practice in special education have not been informed (at least until very recently) by sociological perspectives, they have nevertheless been well-served by other research perspectives. This would seem *not* to be the case.[2] Archer (1984) has commented that in the twentieth century the greatest stumbling-block to the explanation of educational achievement (or non-achievement) has been the assumption that the factors involved and responsible are properties of the individual child, be these psychogenic (intelligence, motivation or aspirations) or sociogenic (factors of home environment). Even social class, she asserts, has been reduced to a personal membership characteristic, an artificial aggregate of those similarly ranked on some occupational scale. Much of the investigative work has been characterized by this 'atomistic empiricism', producing research in special education which has operated within the 'unconscious assumptions' of the field's practitioners (Rist and Harrell, 1982). The assumptions are (a) that disability is a condition that individuals have; (b) that disabled/typical is a useful and objective distinction; (c) that special education is a rationally conceived and coordinated system of services that help children who are labelled disabled; (d) that progress in the field is made by improving diagnosis, intervention and technology. Put another way, a great deal of research to date has been *for* special education (serving the field as it conceived of itself), not *of* special education, which would necessitate looking at the field from alternative perspectives (Bogdan and Kugelmass, 1984.) In this sense, special education research has mainly functioned to ascribe an individualized, objective character to the concept of handicap and to exclude accounts of possible social factors and determinants. Thus the handicaps of children with special needs have been thought of primarily as defects or diseases of individuals rather than the products of social interactional processes (Bart, 1984). In terms of social policy then, special education becomes conceptualized as a problem best tackled by professionals, be they medical, psychological or educational. There may well have been a shift from considering children as having 'medical' to having educational problems, but the problems are seen as being best solved by the expertise of the professional, by substituting the educational psychologist for the doctor. In this way, much of the special education debate still tends to centre on how such problems are discovered and how they are best dealt with. The focus is on the child, but still on his or her difficulty (Kirp, 1982).[3]

An underlying theme which has influenced the choice of readings in this text is that definitions, diagnosis and treatment of children with special educational needs *must* be seen as a social process, very often to do with containment functions in society even though the rhetoric *suggests* that they are typically thought of as procedures performed for the benefit of the individuals served.[4] It follows, therefore, that some of the most pressing problems and issues in special education are those concerned with the rhetoric of special educational needs, the categorization, selection and assessment of children with 'special needs', the problems associated with the curriculum arrangements and offerings for children with 'special needs' and the integration–segregation debate. A recurring perspective in the text, deliberately emphasized, is that to do with the rhetoric of special educational needs: in essence largely interpreted, until recently, as being concerned with the definition of achievement or non-achievement on both psychogenic and sociogenic variables, usually concentrating on the negative properties of individual children, their failures, disabilities, lack of intelligence, their behavioural and emotional disturbances, whilst at the same time providing sometimes very suspect mechanisms for determining who has these properties, or lack of them. Until recent times there has been little evidence of a shift from attempting to question this unproblematic 'given' perspective to that of asking such questions as who defines special educational needs, by what procedures and processes, and in whose interest; in short, a move from identification and assessment of the characteristics of individuals to specifying and explaining the *social processes* through which and by which achievement or non-achievement is defined.

Thus, the rhetoric of special needs must be critically evaluated within the social-historical context in which special education has developed, a context which has fostered a climate in which social problems have been viewed as individual's problems treatable by the application of 'scientific' methods and control.[5] It is important, therefore, to examine closely the evidence from which the Warnock Report (DES, 1978) derived its conclusions, particularly with regard to the three broad areas of need which the committee identified. In brief, these were:

(a)   the need for provision of special means of access to the curriculum;
(b)   the need for provision of a special or modified curriculum;
(c)   the need to give particular attention to the social structure and emotional climate in which education takes place.

Most teachers, if questioned about the Warnock Committee recommendations, would perhaps most easily recall that 'one in six children at any one time and up to one in five children at some time in their school career will require some form of special educational provision.'

It is certainly the case that the great majority of the 20 per cent of children regarded by Warnock as having special educational needs are to be found in ordinary schools and classrooms, and further, that the majority of these pupils present behavioural problems and/or learning difficulties to their teachers. It is equally important, however, to balance this 'finding'[6] with the ample research evidence which demonstrates that schools themselves exert considerable influence over their pupils' behaviour, attitudes and educational progress, an influence which is particularly potent on children who are least able intellectually and least privileged socially. Indeed, the fact that some schools are almost submerged by problems of deviant and disturbing pupil behaviour whilst other schools, drawing pupils from similar catchment areas, experience few problems points to school factors as being very often the more important contributing causes (see Reading 15).

Thus, the teaching approaches and methods, the organizational structure and 'climate' of a school may create or aggravate a whole range of problems which may be taken as evidence of special needs. Similarly, pupils are usually recognized as having special educational needs when those who teach them become concerned about their behaviour or progress in school. But there is ample evidence to suggest that in many successful schools teachers see such children primarily as a *teaching problem* rather than having a behaviour or learning problem, and further, they recognize that it is their responsibility to teach the child rather than to transfer the responsibility to 'specialists'. This attitude is in marked contrast to viewing the pupil as having a learning or behaviour problem with the implication that the trouble resides 'in' the child and is therefore not the teacher's responsibility.[7]

In selecting readings for this text considerable attention has been given to the difficult problems associated with the categorization, selection and assessment of children with special educational needs. The fact that the terminology used in special education to categorize children is both complex and ever-changing is no mere accident, for it results from the competition between groups who have vested interests in defining weaker social groups where the winning party succeeds finally in applying the labels, categories and definitions (Tomlinson, 1982). Thus, we can trace the changes in educational thinking which questioned both the ideas about special education embodied in the 1944 Education Act and about their implementation in practice – changes from the emphasis on the separate nature of special education with its implicit assumption that ascertainment was a medical responsibility to the gradually emerging consensus that special education should be seen essentially as an educational matter and that the distinction between 'special' and 'ordinary' children was to a great extent arbitrary.[8]

It is only in the last decade that the dominance of medical and psychological models with their emphasis on deficits and individual disabilities has been challenged by alternative perspectives in special education, perspectives which have concentrated more upon examining the social interests served by the development and expansion of special education.[9] Thus, from a sociological stance, the characteristics, disabilities or deficits of a child are less the *centre* of interest than are the processes of definition, for it is the processes which *produce* the special child rather than anything which the child may or may not 'inherently' possess. The 'special' child is thus seen as 'the product of structured social forces which become focused on the definitional process' (Squibb, 1981).

Of crucial importance to any discussion on categorization and assessment is that to do with the very notion of children with 'special needs', a concept which conflates 'normative' conditions with 'non-normative'. Thus, although there is some *normative* agreement about various categories of handicap (blind, deaf, epileptic, severe mental handicap, etc.) usually defined within the medical sphere of competence, other categories (slow learning, educationally subnormal, disruptive, maladjusted, etc.) are not, and never can be normative categories simply because there are neither agreed criteria nor adequate measuring devices with which to accurately assess these categories. How we decide who has these conditions and to what degree depends upon the beliefs, values and interests of those making such judgements. In short, such decisions are products of prevailing social and cultural values. The importance of the problem of categorization is highlighted by the fact that by far the largest number of children ascertained as having 'special needs' are to be found within these crucial non-normative categories. For example, since 1945 the number of children classified as ESN(M) has always added up to half of *all* children judged to be handicapped. Furthermore, since the settlement of black immigrants into Britain, these non-normative categories have included quite disproportionate numbers of black children. A 'conflict' sociological perspective[10] would explain such 'imbalances' from the viewpoint that the selection process for special education acts as a societal mechanism of social control and its clients overwhelmingly share a propensity for school failure and, very often, membership in a low-status social group. Tomlinson (1982, p.67) comments that the new legislation based on the notion of special needs is likely to intensify the confusion of normative categories with non-normative, so that from a sociological point of view it becomes of the upmost importance to ask what sort of children, in terms of social class and background, are being selected for non-normative categories, whether they are statutory or merely descriptive. In short, the marked expansion in the classification of children with special needs in non-normative categories may be more of a solution to problems of social order and control than a blueprint for educational 'needs'.[11]

The 'curriculum' in normal schools has received but scant attention from sociologists and none at all with respect to 'special' education. As a result, the study of the curriculum has tended to lack any real consideration of the social and political forces that influence it and, in particular, the social implications of the kinds of curriculum which are offered to different social groups (Eggleston, 1977). Certainly the field of special education has produced a wealth of literature to do with practice and methods, what to teach and how to teach it, but in general, these 'practitioner' level offerings have lacked any real theoretical underpinning. Thus, advice to teachers of children with special needs on classroom practice and organization, teaching approaches, effective use of resources, recording progress and the like are to be found in abundance, but there is little evidence of either any deep examination of the overall aims and objectives of special provision or discussion about the values and beliefs which might be implicit in these aims (Tomlinson, 1982, p.134). This is in no sense a criticism of the practitioner who, after all, operates in a context which is markedly influenced by social and historical values and beliefs. Historically, the special education curriculum has functioned to subvert the lifechances of its clients, illustrated by the importance afforded to manual and vocational training in special education, with, for some, its eventual sheltered and limited goals of employment. Such 'limited' goals ostensibly have enabled handicapped pupils to maximize their limited abilities in a way that most closely approximates to 'normal' individuals. It is this 'approximation' that henceforth rules their lives, and it is to this approximation of normal life that handicapped children's 'special' education has been geared (Bart, 1984, p.87).[12]

The 'conflict' sociological viewpoint emphasizes the importance of critically examining the system of special education not so much in terms of meeting special needs in the most appropriate ways but in broader sociological and structuralist perspectives as serving to reproduce and perpetuate a particular social order. 'Special needs' are seen as socially constructed categories and their manifestation in the form of special provision and special schools exist largely to remove from ordinary schools those pupils whom teachers find unacceptable rather than to serve best the needs of children thus categorized.

It has been argued earlier that teachers need a deep understanding of the social/historical, political and economic forces which shape and influence values and beliefs about special education *as well as* the pedagogical skills and techniques with which to teach their pupils. From the perspective of the practitioner, however, it might well be argued that, whilst recognizing that the selection, assessment and allocation procedures *are* social constructs and that it *is* very necessary to consider factors other than the overt criteria for categorization, nevertheless, as an example, the removal of a highly disruptive and disturbed child from a particular class to a special unit may well be not only in the ordinary school's interest but also in the best interest of the child (Croll and Moses, 1985, p.19). Again, the fact that categorization, assessment and allocation techniques are not only socially constructed but imperfect does not mean that the difficulties to which they refer are not real – children *with* special needs are there, and have to be taught!

Designing appropriate curriculum experiences for children with special needs presents very complex problems for teachers. The wide range of special needs and the concomitant difficulties are highlighted by Brennan (see Reading 5):

There are pupils with special educational needs who do not require special curriculum; that does not mean their main curriculum should not be scrutinized in terms of their special needs. There are other pupils for whom special curriculum is essential, but it does not follow that they are unable to participate in main curriculum. A minority of pupils may be unable to participate in main curriculum; that does not necessarily mean that they cannot gain from the planned or hidden curriculum through interaction with other pupils. Such is the complexity encountered when considering design for special needs.

Special education arrangements and provisions in ordinary schools have, until recently, been planned with two main purposes in view – either that learning difficulties would be effectively diagnosed and cured (the 'remedial' department) or that children who presented particular special problems would be taken out of circulation in order to avoid disrupting the work of their 'ordinary' peers. In many schools today such 'solutions' are still in practice. Fish (1985) comments that problems arise because many schools either plan provision on the curing assumption or on the segregation assumption and that only recently have many schools recognized the need for a combination of short-term and long-term arrangements. Further, he argues, new legislation and current knowledge have redefined the purpose of special education in ordinary schools and the move towards integration reinforces this new formulation. As a result, the ordinary school can no longer plan programmes to cure short-term difficulties while expecting long-term ones to be solved elsewhere.

Because this text is addressed to future teachers as well as serving practitioners the choice of readings in this section is unashamedly biased towards 'recipe' knowledge.

Of all the current issues and foremost amongst debates relating to 'special educational needs' the topic of integration looms largest. Like the 'myth' of progressivism espoused by the Plowden Report (1967), integration has become somewhat of a slogan and 'banner' for action. It cannot be understood, as Gurney (1985) suggests, solely in terms of educational process or placement, for it is larger than life, expanding beyond the confines of schools and spilling over into the political arena. Indeed, Burden (1985) comments that historians of twentieth-century educational thought and practice will find it somewhat easy to relate the spirit of the times to particular catch-phrases and that it seems entirely appropriate that the catch-phrase of the 1980s should 'integration at all costs'. Or as he wryly asks, should it be 'integration at no cost'?

Rehearsing the arguments and complex issues in the debate about integration would be out of place in the introduction to this text. Instead, the reader is referred to authors who tackle this subject,[13] whilst at the same time being reminded that 'integration' is a constantly recurring theme in the readings which have been selected.

In brief, 'integration' is a concept most usually applied to the bringing of handicapped pupils from segregated special schools into ordinary schools. Increasingly, proponents of integration (e.g. Booth and Potts, 1983, p.1) have defined it as the process of developing the participation of children and young people in their communities, an integral part of this process being their involvement in the social and educational life of *comprehensive* nursery, primary and secondary schools as well as further and higher education. Thus the concept of integration is applied not just to handicapped children but to all pupils who have needs and interests to which schools do not respond, the argument being that children who are dispatched to special schools and classes are there, for the most part, because ordinary schools have failed to restructure their curricula and forms of organization to cater for diverse needs, interests and talents. In this sense, the integration debate has forced all who are concerned with special education to justify or attempt to legitimate their own views and interests, as well as allowing a discussion of special education in much wider terms than was possible when segregation was legitimated by an ideology of what Tomlinson describes as 'benevolent humanitarianism' (1982, p.76).

'Integration', at its core, is about social engineering, about changing societal values via the education system. It is essentially a political issue inextricably linked with the concept of comprehensive education, a political issue which has bedevilled the contradictory ideologies implicit in government policies, for on the one hand there is seen a need to control those with 'special needs' (like other minority groups) by not allowing them to have any deleterious effects in the spheres of culture and the economy, and at the same time there is a desire to protect the more severely handicapped, expressed in policies of community care and attempts to create equal opportunites (Barton and Tomlinson, 1984, p.78.).

Certainly the 1981 Education Act *purports* to support the general idea of integrating children with special educational needs in ordinary schools and it is likely that it may well succeed in this respect with those children whose special needs are to do with physical and sensory disabilities. However, for the great majority of children with special needs, that is, those with moderate learning difficulties and behavioural or emotional problems (formerly classified ESN(M) and maladjusted) it seems very probable that the Act's influence will be extremely limited.

There are several reasons to support this view. Government policies are both constrained by and dictated by competition over priorities and scarce resources. Thus, many of the official documents relating to the question of integration make reference to the problems of financial constraints. An example of this is the government White Paper on *Special Needs in Education* (DES, 1980) which concludes its discussion with the statement that 'only when the economic situation improves sufficiently will it be possible to bring to fruition all the committed efforts of those engaged in meeting special needs' (p.23). Furthermore, such 'scarce' financial resources as are available may be distributed at the discretion of local education authorities, since the relativity in the legislation of the 1981 Act makes each LEA able to operate the law to fit in with its previous practice and provision – accommodating the 'enabling' character of the Act to the wide variety of practice and level of provision in different local authorities (see Reading 2). Galloway (1985, p.38) comments that the Act's commitment to integration can be dismissed quickly, for we need look at only two of the 'escape clauses': children with special needs should be educated in ordinary schools subject to 'provision of efficient education[3] for the children in the school , and 'the efficient use of resources'. Since the 1981 Act requires local education authorities to obtain approval from the Secretary of State before closing special schools, existing special schools constitute an obvious resource – and must be used unless there is irrefutable evidence that the need no longer exists. Indeed, a number of local authorities have continued to open special schools after having introduced their integration policies. With the Warnock estimate of 20 per cent of pupils having special needs at some stage in their educational life it becomes highly improbable that schools will retain the 2 per cent of pupils, or fewer, who had hitherto been sent to separate special schools. In fact, segregation policies have flourished, for there has been a massive increase in the number of places in special schools for ESN(M) and maladjusted children since 1944 (Squibb, 1981). Given the extended definition of special needs proposed by Warnock and by the 1981 Education Act, there appears to be little doubt not only that separate schools can be self-maintaining but that they function to prevent and deter their clients' chances of being integrated into ordinary schools. Galloway (1985, p.39) explains this phenomenon in terms of a variety of Parkinson's Law which states that the number of children with learning or behavioural problems thought to need separate special educational help will continually increase to exceed the available supply.

The current emphasis and attention given by schools to special educational needs appears to be concentrated on the 2–6 per cent of pupils who are to be statemented, an emphasis which must certainly, to some degree, be at the expense of the other 18 per cent, most of whom will remain unstatemented. Peter (1984) argues that by allowing the 1981 Education Act to concentrate on time-consuming and costly procedures of assessing and making statements for the estimated 2 per cent of children with severe or complex learning difficulties, and at the same time refusing to give extra money for meeting the law's demands, the Government has virtually ensured that the Act's wider intentions go unmet. As a result, she claims, the needs of *most* of the children it was supposed to help are being submerged under a welter of bureaucracy. It goes without saying that this large group of unstatemented pupils will be the one for which schools have an urgent need to make fundamental changes both in curriculum offerings and organization and in teacher attitudes towards children with special needs. Brennan (1982, p.108) aptly comments:

[...] among the most disadvantaged children in our schools are those in ordinary schools who have special needs about which little is being done. Consequently, one of the first moves in ordinary schools should be to make proper arrangements for the education of pupils with special needs who are already in the schools.

This section has stressed that, although the 1981 Act undoubtedly has important implications for policy and practice in ordinary schools, its likely impact is very much open to question, most importantly because it contains nothing to ensure fundamental changes in special education practice. In contrast to other countries, the British approach to special education has emphasized 'professional concerns' and 'expertise' at the expense of legal norms or of the bureaucratic setting of standards. In fact, like much education law, the Act tends to reflect a broad consensus on what constitutes good practice and *requires* little if any significant change in the policy and practices which already exist in ordinary schools (see Kirp, 1982 and Reading 2). Welton *et al.* (1982, p. 48) reflect this view:

Fundamental change is unlikely to occur without simultaneous developments in the administrative structure, in relationships between professionals, administrators and users, and without changes in practice, attitudes and ideas. We have found in our research that the most specific aspects of the Special Education Procedures instituted following Circular 2/75 were not generally implemented as intended, but either became adapted to local use or ritualised as a *post hoc* means of recording or justifying decision making.[14]

There can be little argument that (to slightly alter a well-known educational phrase) 'at the heart of the integration process lies the teacher', for it is the teacher who, after all, has always been responsible for the education of the vast majority of children with special needs who have always been found in ordinary schools! It seems obvious, then, that the success or failure of integration schemes must depend very significantly, in the last resort, on the beliefs, values and attitudes of teachers. What, then, do teachers think about integration?

Firstly, it should be noted that since the 1981 Education Act some local authorities are interpreting its findings as a licence to close special schools, sending their former pupils to ordinary schools usually without providing the financial resources, extra equipment, facilities and teachers which are necessary for any integration prospects to have a reasonable chance of success. Such efforts to enforce 'integration on the cheap' have been both feared and vociferously resisted by the teachers' unions. It is also the case that the old 'categories of handicap' and the new 'children with special needs' categories encompass a considerable number of children whom the staff of normal schools wish to exclude at all levels of integration. Thus, the NUT (1979, p.14) discussed the problem of 'particular groups of pupils – particularly the severely maladjusted and those of extremely limited ability – who may present insuperable problems for teachers in the ordinary classroom situation' (see Reading 3). Research by Thomas (1982) reported in Gurney (1985) compared the attitudes towards integration of teachers in Tucson, Arizona, where there has been a long-established policy of mainstreaming, with those of teachers in Devon, where no such policy has been applied. Approximately 60 per cent of the 125 Devon primary school teachers interviewed were opposed or very opposed to the notion of integrating ESN(M) children in ordinary schools whilst only 7 per cent were strongly in favour. At the secondary level an even higher proportion (approximately 73 per cent) of the 78 teachers interviewed were opposed to integration. In Tucson, although a much more positive attitude prevailed, there were still as many teachers in ordinary schools opposed to integration as favouring it.[15]

Studies in Britain (Brennan, 1981; Hegarty and Pocklington with Lucas, 1982) following the Warnock Report's humanitarian assumption that integration *per se* is a 'good thing' have tended to focus their attention on optimum provision for successful integration schemes, documenting the various efforts by schools and LEAs to interpret and implement integration policies. An important recent research study (Croll and Moses, 1985) provides illuminating evidence on teachers' *experience* of children with handicaps, on teachers' *opinions* on integrating children with handicaps into their classrooms and on teachers' and headteachers' *attitudes* towards various handicaps in the ordinary school. Briefly, the research addresses itself to two major themes: the extension of the concept of special educational needs to include up to a fifth of the school population, and the central role of the ordinary classteacher in this process. More specifically, the project was particularly concerned with the ways in which junior-school teachers assess pupils in their classes as having special educational needs, and the incidence of special educational needs consequent upon these assessments. The research sample consisted of 428 junior-school teachers, 61 headteachers and 37 remedial teachers in 61 junior/primary schools randomly sampled in 10 LEAs. The study of children concentrated on 34 second-year junior classes (children aged 8 to 9). Some of the most important findings of the research are as follows.

Teachers recognize the special needs of a substantial minority of their pupils and see them, for the most part, as being the responsibility of the ordinary school. That these special needs are essentially of an educational kind is indicated by the way in which learning difficulties dominate the teachers' perspectives. The most commonly identified learning difficulty was a problem with reading. Behaviour problems formed the next largest category of special needs and such children often also had learning problems. Both assessment of and provision for the majority of children with special educational needs is, in large part, left to individual schools. Almost without exception, teachers view the difficulties of their pupils as arising from factors innate to the child or from elements in his home environment or from a combination of these. In the case of learning difficulties, innate factors are seen to predominate with home factors an important secondary influence. In the case of behaviour problems, this pattern is reversed; home and related factors are seen to predominate but innate characteristics are also seen as important. It was unusual for a teacher to view a child's difficulties as arising from factors within the control of the teacher or the school. When the teachers were asked how they would feel about having children with various types of handicap in the ordinary classroom, it was clear that they had a warmer welcome for the idea of children with physical and sensory disabilities than they had for the idea of children with severe learning problems and behaviour problems. For any particular type of handicap, having had experience of a child with that disability in the classroom was associated with an increased willingness to have a child of that sort in the future. But, overall, it was at the prospect of the types of problem with which teachers were most familiar, those associated with learning and behaviour, that enthusiasm for integration was at its lowest (Croll and Moses, 1985, pp 147-153).

The fact that teachers show least warmth and enthusiasm at the prospect of having children with severe learning disabilities or highly disturbed and maladjusted children integrated into their normal classroom is hardly surprising given that, very likely, the same teachers have for years had interests and a say in the removal of such troublesome pupils from their jurisdiction, assured by the knowledge that special school teachers, with skills and expertise in dealing with a variety of handicapped children have been equally anxious to retain a clientele in special schools. Probably Tomlinson (1982, p.80) very accurately sums up teachers' attitudes on this issue when she writes: 'Crudely, teachers in normal schools may be willing to accommodate the "ideal" child with special needs in their classrooms – the bright, brave child in a wheelchair – they will still want to be rid of the actual "average" child with special needs – the dull, disruptive child.' Furthermore, the current DES preoccupation with 'accountability' may be one of the many pressures which will dampen the prevailing enthusiasm for integration. Booth (1981, pp 309-310) comments: 'If teachers are to be held directly responsible for the progress of their pupils, then they may be increasingly willing to separate children they consider to have "real" intractable problems from those amenable to "ordinary" teaching.' Other pressures are concerned with the issues of resources – time, money and manpower, for in the present climate of deep mistrust that exists between teachers and their employers, moves by administrators towards integrating more children with special needs are more and more unlikely to be positively received by the teaching profession, especially if such administrative moves are seen as a way of cutting the education budget. The simple fact is that integration cannot take place at all on a 'no extra cost' basis – it cannot even take place on the cheap (Burden, 1985, p.26).

Provision for *prevention* in relation to special educational needs is another important consideration. The early years are a time of enormous importance in determining the chances that a child will have for his or her later life. During this period of major developmental changes the child learns to communicate linguistically and socially and to develop a massive array of cognitive skills. It is also a time of susceptibility to potentially hazardous experiences – common childhood illnesses, accidents, family trauma and environmental disadvantage (Lindsay, 1984, preface). Some children's handicaps become increasingly serious as they grow older and, if undetected, constitute an increasing impediment to their educational progress (Wedell and Raybould, 1976; Wall, 1979). The handicap of hearing impairment and its effects on language acquisition is a good example. Gurney (1985) comments that provision for prevention in relation to special educational needs appears to be extremely limited in most LEAs, many having recently cut back on their financial resources and staffing. As a result, fewer children can now be helped and are thus likely to be older when the hearing problem is identified and remediated. What is obviously needed is a screening programme initiated in the early *pre-school* years with the particular purpose of discriminating children with catarrhal problems.[16]

This section of the introduction has emphasized that the integration debate, as well as being concerned with philosophical, humanitarian and egalitarian ideas, is also a debate about resources, provision and the vested interests of professionals, and that it is the latter rather than the former issues which are more likely to determine the outcome. Barton and Tomlinson (see Reading 3) share this sobering perspective:

[...] our major criticism of the movement for integration is motivated by our belief that it is based on a totally unwarranted optimism. Despite the claims in the Warnock Report about the privileges and opportunities in our society in which the 'special' or the 'handicapped' should share, there is a vast amount of research evidence to show that our society, and in this instance the school system, are characterized by gross inequalities [...]. What we are seriously suggesting is that, given the inequalities within society at large, and given those dominant assumptions and practices that are firmly established in our school system, particularly at the secondary levels, if integration is to have any major significance, then the struggle for its realization must include a coherent, concentrated criticism of those unacceptable features of the education system and a demand for more fundamental social changes. To do less will mean that integration will lead to subordination in an already divisive system and be a further illustration of the way in which political rhetoric supercedes practice.

NOTES

1. Tomlinson (1982) suggests that, although sociology has developed a whole range of theoretical perspectives on ordinary education and recent social policy analysis, the sociological tradition in special education has tended to be 'functional', concentrating, for example, on the use of social surveys to discover 'how many' handicapped children or children with special educational needs there are, and that, by and large, theory and practice in special education have not been informed by sociological perspectives.

2. See Wedell (1985). Reporting on a recent survey of research in special education Wedell writes that 'it was apparent from the survey that descriptive research was still the area in which the largest number of projects were being carried out (41 per cent). Just over half of these studies were still concerned with investigations of children grouped by category of handicap or other diagnostic classifications . . . [and] that this could no longer be regarded as a meaningful basis for descriptive studies, quite apart from the fact that it was at variance with educational practice since the 1981 Act' (Wedell and Roberts, 1982, p.23).

3. Kirp (1982) argues that the British approach to special education has emphasized 'professional concerns' and 'expertise' at the expense of legal norms or of the bureaucratic setting of standards. Thus, the relativity in special education legislation allows each LEA to operate the law (in this case, the 1981 Act) to fit in with its previous practice and provision. See Reading 2.

4. Thompson (1984) discusses *ideology* as the study of the ways in which the meaning of particular words or ideas serves to sustain relations of dominance and describes its purpose as 'the linguistic legislature which defines what is available for public discussion and what is not'. It is in this sense that Tomlinson (see Reading 17) writes that 'the concept of "special needs" has become an ideological rationalization for those who have the power to shape and define the expanding special education system and have vested interests in this expansion. Those who can define the "needs" of others and give or withhold provision have great power, yet the benevolent image with which the notion of "catering for special needs" has become imbued precludes discussion of the supposed needs, or criticism of provision and practice.' Indeed, Tomlinson asserts, 'the whole concept of special needs is ambiguous and tautological. It has become part of a rhetoric that serves little educational purpose.' See also Reading 15.

5. See Reading 16.

6. See Reading 15 and Galloway (1982, 1983). It remains the case, however, that schools vary considerably in the number of children they appear to regard as having special needs. Galloway (see Reading 15) makes the point that 'successful' schools may well disguise the existence of children who would be regarded as problems in other schools. In such cases, meeting special needs effectively removes pupils from the limelight.

7. See Galloway (1983).

8. See Tomlinson (1982, chapter 3, 'Issues and dilemmas in special education', pp 58–88). Tomlinson traces the influence and outcome of the conflicting and competing medical and educational 'vested interests' in special education

during the postwar period of changing ideologies, showing clearly the *problematic* nature of categorization. She emphasizes the deliberate policy which has persisted from 1946 to the 1978 Warnock Committee Report of not tracing 'causes' of educational backwardness while implicitly attributing it to environmental and family deficiency.

9. For an account of the 'expansion' of special education, see Swann (1985) and Squibb (1981).

10. For useful discussions of the 'conflict' sociological perspective and its applications to the field of special education see Tomlinson (1982 chapter 1, 'Why a sociology of special education?' and chapter 3, 'Issues and dilemmas in special education') and Oliver (1985). For more detailed and comprehensive discussion of the 'conflict' perspective see Archer (1979) – chapter 2 provides a very useful discussion of the notion of 'dominant groups' in education – and Karabel and Halsey (1977).

11. Squibb (1981) analyses the annual statistics for the year 1961 and 1976 of the number of children categorized as handicapped, showing that in most cases (with the exception of the blind, partially sighted and epileptic) there were increases in the number of children in each handicapped category *greater* than the increase in the total population of schoolchildren. Squibb claims that, in part, this can be explained by the fact that structures set up to provide for a given phenomenon tend to work in ways that increase their legitimacy and territory. Thus, the greater the proven need for the service, the greater the power, status and career opportunity which accrue to it. Similarly, the greater the range and sophistication of the devices used to test for a handicap, the more widely will that handicap be discovered (p.47).

The largest non-normative categories (the maladjusted and the ESN) taken together constituted over two-thirds of *all* handicapped children. Squibb reports that they increased dramatically from 1961 to 1976, by 237 per cent and 150 per cent respectively.

See also Swann (1985). Swann provides an analysis of changes in the size of the special school population and in the proportion of children who attended special schools between 1978 and 1982. His findings are that, overall, there is no evidence of a trend towards integration. However, different results emerge for different statutory categories of handicap. For example, there is evidence of integration in the case of children with sensory handicaps, but for children with learning difficulties and those ascertained as maladjusted there is very clear evidence of a trend towards increasing segregation, especially in the primary age group.

12. Tomlinson (1982, pp 135–136) accounts for the lack of sociological interest in the special education curriculum by claiming that it appears to be negatively defined – it offers 'non-knowledge', since children who participate in a special curriculum have already been defined as not able to benefit from even the low-status knowledge of a normal curriculum. Thus, she affirms, it seems self-evident that what happens in special schools has little if any relevance to major sociological concerns such as social stratification and class, social equality and social mobility. Furthermore, since there is a pervasive benevolent humanitarianism implicit in the rhetoric of providing special educational

treatment for special needs, it becomes very difficult to subject the curriculum to critical scrutiny. In this sense, humanitarian and philosophical approaches tend to beg such questions as who has the power and the expertise to decide what form the 'good' special curriculum shall take, or who controls it, what its ultimate aims are, and who can give or withhold resources for its implementation.

13. For example, see Reading 3, Booth (1981), Booth and Potts (1983) and Tomlinson (1982, pp 76–81). For a very detailed critical appraisal of the Warnock Committee's 'evidence' and 'findings' see Reading 15 and Lewis and Vulliamy (1981).

14. Gurney (1985, p.4) makes the point that 'integration' as a term is often intended to rally support and create further pressure for change, but that, although such actions are worthy in that they relate to a goal considered to be socially desirable, an unfortunate by-product tends to be a seductive belief that desired change *is* taking place. Thus, the resulting mistaken assumption, in this case that integration is moving forward, is created as much by the proponents of integration as by the agencies who are being criticized: Government, DES, LEA and advisory services. As a result, these agencies, feeling themselves criticized and embattled, tend to direct attention to work already done and to schemes afoot, thus laying emphasis on the positive side and avoiding scrutiny of poor practice and woeful deficiencies in their provision for special needs. There is, therefore, he asserts, an unintentional 'conspiracy' which enhances the reality of the current situation.

15. All the teachers in Thomas's research felt inadequately prepared for slow-learning pupils at the initial training stage and few felt that wider curricular needs of such pupils could be adequately met in an integrated class. These findings tend to mirror those of other studies: Alexander and Strain (1978); Smart *et al.* (1980); Vandivier and Vandivier (1981).

16. Over the past 20 years or so there has been an increasing interest shown in the early identification of difficulties suffered by children. The rationale is simple: the earlier such problems can be identified or diagnosed the sooner appropriate action can be taken. The action can be curative or ameliorative. The range of problems and the number of young children involved has led to the development of simple and quick methods of identification – screening. Screening programmes are in use at various stages from before conception to about the 7 + age level and are concerned with the physical, psychological, linguistic and social development of children (Lindsay, 1984).

REFERENCES

Alexander, C. and Strain, P.S. (1978) A review of educators' attitudes towards handicapped children and the concept of mainstreaming, *Psychology in the Schools,* Vol. 15, No. 3, pp 390–396

Archer, M.S. (1979) *The Social Origins of Educational Systems,* Sage, London

Archer, M. (1984) *Foreword.* In L. Barton and S. Tomlinson (1984) Special Education and Social Interests, Croom Helm, London

Bart, D.S. (1984) *The differential diagnosis of special education: managing social pathology as individual disability.* In L. Barton and S. Tomlinson (Eds) (1984) op.cit.

Barton, L. and Tomlinson, S. (Eds) (1981) *Special Education: Policy, Practices and Social Issues,* Harper and Row, London

Barton, L. and Tomlinson, S. (Eds) (1984) *Special Education and Social Interests,* Croom Helm, London

Bogdan, R. and Kugelmass, J. (1984) *Case studies of mainstreaming: a symbolic interactionist approach to special schooling.* In L. Barton and S. Tomlinson (Eds) (1984) op.cit.

Booth, T. (1981) *Demystifying integration.* In W. Swann (Ed.) (1981) The Practice of Special Education, Basil Blackwell, Oxford

Booth, T. and Potts, P. (1983) *Integrating Special Education,* Basil Blackwell, Oxford

Brennan, W.K. (1981) *Special education in mainstream schools: the search for quality,* National Council for Special Education (NCSE), London

Brennan, W.K. (1982) *Changing Special Education,* Open University Press, Milton Keynes

Burden, R. (1985) *To integrate or not to integrate: is that the question?* In P. Gurney (Ed.) (1985) op.cit.

Croll, P. and Moses, D. (1985) *One in Five: the assessment and incidence of special educational needs,* Routledge and Kegan Paul, London

Dalzell, J. and Owrid, H.L. (1976) Children with conductive deafness: a follow-up study, *British Journal of Audiology,* No. 10, pp 87–90

Department of Education and Science (DES) (1978) *Special Educational Needs* (Warnock Report), Cmnd 7212, HMSO, London

Department of Education and Science (DES) (1980) *Special Needs in Education* (White Paper), Cmnd 7996, HMSO, London

Eggleston, J. (1977) *The Sociology of the School Curriculum,* Routledge and Kegan Paul, London

Fish, J. (1985) *Special Education: the way ahead,* Open University Press, Milton Keynes

Galloway, D. (1982) A study of pupils suspended from school, *British Journal of Educational Psychology,* No. 52, pp 205–212

Galloway, D. (1983) Disruptive pupils and effective pastoral care, *School Organisation,* No. 3, pp 245–254

Galloway, D. (1985) *Schools, Pupils and Special Educational Needs,* Croom Helm, London

Goodman, L. and Miller, H. (1980) Mainstreaming: how teachers can make it work, *Journal of Research and Development in Education,* Vol. 13, No. 4, pp 45–57

Gurney, P. (Ed.) (1985) *Special Educational Needs in the Ordinary School,* Perspectives 15, School of Education, University of Exeter

Hegarty, S. and Pocklington, K. with Lucas, D. (1981) *Educating Pupils with Special Needs in the Ordinary School,* NFER-Nelson, Windsor

Hegarty, S. and Pocklington, K. with Lucas, D. (1982) *Integration in Action,* NFER-Nelson, Windsor

Karabel, J. and Halsey, K. (1977) *Power and Ideology in Education,* Oxford University Press, Oxford

Kirp, D. (1982) Professionalisation as policy choice: British special education in comparative perspective, *World Politics,* Vol. 34, No. 2 pp 137-174

Lewis, I. and Vulliamy, G.I. (1981) *The social context of educational practice: the case of special education.* In L. Barton and S. Tomlinson (Eds) (1981) op.cit.

Lindsay, G. (Ed.) (1984) *Screening for Children with Special Needs,* Croom Helm, London

National Union of Teachers (NUT) (1979) Special educational needs: the NUT response to Warnock, NUT, London

Oliver, M. (1985) The integration-segregation debate: some sociological considerations, *British Journal of Sociology of Education,* Vol. 6, No. 1, pp 75-92

Peter, M. (1984) A hard act to follow *Times Educational Supplement,* No. 3535, 30 March, p.23

Quigley, S.P. (1978) *Effects of early hearing-impairment on normal language development.* In F.N. Martin (Ed.) (1978) Pediatric Audiology, Prentice-Hall, Englewood Cliffs, NJ

Rist, R. and Harrell, J. (1982) Labelling and the learning disabled child: the social ecology of educational practice, *American Journal of Orthopsychiatry,* Vol. 52, No. 1, pp 146-160

Smart, R. Wilton, K. and Keeling, B. (1980) Teacher factors and special class placement, *Journal of Special Education,* Vol. 14, No. 2, pp 217-229

Squibb, P. (1981) *A theoretical structuralist approach to special education* In L. Barton and S. Tomlinson (Eds) (1981) op.cit.

Swann, W. (1985) Is the integration of children with special needs happening?: an analysis of recent statistics of pupils in special schools, *Oxford Review of Education,* Vol. 11, No.1, pp 3-18

Thomas, D. (1982) Teachers' attitudes towards integrating educationally subnormal children in Devon, Flinders University, S. Australia

Tomlinson, S. (1982) *A Sociology of Special Education,* Routledge and Kegan Paul, London

Thompson, J. (1984) *Studies in the Theory of Ideology,* Polity Press, London

Vandivier, P.L. and Vandivier, S.C. (1981) Teacher attitudes towards mainstreaming exceptional students, *Journal of Special Education,* Vol. 17, No. 4, pp 381-388

Wall, W.D. (1979) *Constructive Education for Special Groups: handicapped and deviant children,* Harrap, London

Webster, A. and Ellwood, J. (1985) *The Hearing Impaired Child in the Ordinary School,* Croom Helm, London

Wedell, K. and Raybould, E.C. (1976) The early identification of educationally 'at risk' children, University of Birmingham 1, pp 22-26

Wedell, K. and Raybould, E.C. (1976) *The early identification of educationally 'at risk' children,* University of Birmingham

Wedell, K. and Roberts, J. (1982) Special education research; a recent survey, *Special Education: Forward Trends,* Vol. 9, No. 3, pp 19-25

Welton, J., Wedell, K. and Vorhaus, G. (1982) *Meeting Special Educational Needs: the 1981 Act and its implications,* Bedford Way Papers, No. 12, Heinemann, London

Wood, D.J. (1982) *Fostering language development in hearing-impaired children.* In M.M. Clark (Ed.) (1982) Special Educational Needs and Children under Five, Educational Review Occasional Publications No. 9, University of Birmingham

SECTION 1

POLICY, PROBLEMS AND PERSPECTIVES

INTRODUCTION

This part of the sourcebook consists of four readings, the first of which is a succinct yet comprehensive account of the main details embodied in the 1981 Education Act on Special Education. Russell traces the 'philosophy' behind the Act, discussing the influence of some of the Warnock Report's main recommendations and showing how they have become firmly incorporated in the new legislation. Of particular interest is the detailed discussion on parental rights and how these may herald a new role for parents. The suggested readings explore further the background to the 1981 Act, consider the implications for its implementation and probe some of its most significant anomalies.

Reading 2 provides a systematic examination of the passage of 'legislation', described as just one point in the process of negotiation and bargaining which continues throughout the period of policy implementation. Using the 1981 Education Act as a case study, Welton and Evans develop a conceptual framework which sees *legislation* as a significant reference point, a statement of government intent, but *implementation* as a political process involving negotiation, bargaining and compromise between different sectors of government, between central and local government, between education, health and social services, between administrators and professionals, and with parents. The suggestions for further reading provide additional support for the main arguments discussed in Reading 2, identifying those professional and administrative factors which will affect the development and implementation of the 1981 Act.

Barton and Tomlinson, in Reading 3, present a detailed sociological analysis of the motives behind the move towards integration in England. Their major thesis starts from the assumption that integration is not solely the product of benevolent and enlightened attitudes to children. Rather, they argue, the motives are rooted in economic, professional and political vested interests which may relate more to the 'needs' of the wider society, the whole education system and professionals working within the system than simply to the 'needs' of individual children. The suggested readings consider some of the most crucial issues which have emerged in the 'special education' debate–categorization and selection, the rhetoric of special needs and integration; and Swann's article provides clear evidence of a trend towards increasing segregation.

Reading 4 explores the concept of 'handicap' from a philosophical viewpoint. Wilson and Cowell maintain that the way we define handicap depends on the social values prevailing in our society. These, they claim, are likely to be: (1) physical ability, (2) social competence, and (3) intellectual performance. We attach much less importance and value to qualities of character, such as patience and kindness, even though we do believe in these. Instead of blindly accepting the three values and the criteria associated with them, the authors suggest that we should look for rational criteria on which to base our definition of 'handicap', and that if, instead, we based education on values of character, rather than only paying lip-service to them, we would define handicap differently. In the suggestions for further reading, Hargreaves depicts how competition and differentiation remain endemic to schools, and how ability labels carry rich connotations of pupils' *moral* worth. Two further suggested readings examine the assertion that the handicapped have a right to education by virtue of being human beings.

Reading 1
THE EDUCATION ACT 1981
P. Russell

The Education Act 1981, perhaps for the first time in special education legislation, embodies a broad concept of civil rights and a firm recognition of the role of parents in education decision making. Parental involvement will inevitably have considerable implications not only for the professionals involved in assessment and education decision making but for voluntary organizations and individuals concerned about parents rights and the development of strategies to ensure that these are recognized.

Like many other pieces of United Kingdom legislation, the Act has been greeted by diverse emotions ranging from enthusiasm for what could be seen as a 'parents' charter' to Neil Kinnock's much quoted adage that it was 'like Brighton Pier, good as far as it goes, but a poor way of getting to France'. Those who had perhaps expected that the Education Act 1981 would correspond to the USA Public Law 94.142 failed to understand that legislation in this country is usually *enabling* rather than prescriptive. The 1981 Act comes at a time of economic crisis and retrenchment in government expenditure. However, it embodies perhaps for the first time in

P. Russell (1983) The Education Act 1981, *Concern,* No. 49, pp 6-13

special education a broad concept of civil rights and a firm recognition of the role of parents in education decision making.

THE PHILOSOPHY BEHIND THE ACT

The Warnock Report (DES, 1978), which supplied the philosophy behind the Act, made some 250 recommendations. Some of these – in particular the abolition of the old categories of handicap – are firmly incorporated in the new legislation. The new broad concept of special educational needs will inevitably widen awareness of the variety of learning difficulties and special needs experienced by a range of children during their school years. It will also extend the availability of special educational provision for children already in ordinary schools, which must have considerable long-term effects upon subsequent placement of handicapped children in mainstream education.

Most importantly the Act formalizes parental involvement in assessment of their child. It recognizes the Warnock principle of a continuum of need, with LEAs able to carry out assessments for the under 2s. It also establishes new and formalized links with health and social services, as well as the voluntary sector, all of which may have major inputs into special education.

The passage of the Bill through Parliament was in itself a new exercise in consumerism. The voluntary sector demonstrated their capacity to work together and to provide an informed and committed perspective on the draft legislation. Consultation between the government department responsible for drafting and the consumer bodies is reflected not only in the Act but in the Circular which states its broad philosophy.

The 1981 Act represents one milestone in a succession of Acts to meet special needs. The 1944 Act was a precursor to the 1971 Act which brought mentally handicapped children into the education system. Circular 2/75, whilst not a statutory instrument, had profound effects upon professional attitudes to assessment and review and parental involvement. The 1980 Act, with its appeals procedures and requirements on LEAs to provide relevant information for parents, has direct links with the civil rights and consumer element running through the 1981 Act. Circular 1/83 in turn puts flesh upon the bones of the 1981 Act, stating the principle in Warnock terms of assessment as a continuous process and the emphasis in the new procedures on parental participation and professional perceptions of the child as a 'whole person'. The focus 'on the child himself rather than on his disability' is an important concept in special education and encouraging for parents who may have experienced negative feedback on their child's potential and development.

PARENTAL RIGHTS

Perhaps the most significant element of parental rights in the Act is the requirement that the individual professional reports (which make up the *Statement of Special Educational Needs* at the end of the new assessment procedures) should be made available to *parents* as well as to the relevant professionals.

Although confidentiality has been a major area of parental concern for many years, it should not be forgotten that professional codes of practice (or the lack of them) frequently create barriers between interested professionals concerned for the development of the child. Whilst it is possible that some professionals may write 'edited' reports for public consumption, decision making will at least now be carried out on the basis of generally circulated information. Parents in particular will have not only the right but a *duty* to contribute to this information-giving exercise and the problems of communicating accurately and adequately in an interdisciplinary context will no doubt be widely aired.

In the new and more open approach to assessment of special educational needs, Circular 1/83 rightly stresses that 'relations between professional advisers and parents during the process of assessment are of vital importance'. Although debate centred on the availability of *reports* during the passage of the Bill through Parliament, written reports represent the tip of the iceberg of parental–professional collaboration and consultation over a considerable period of time. The new assessment procedures must ensure that both parents and the professionals review their methods of working together with hopefully improved relationships as a result of the complex process of assessment. Indeed LEAs *must* further parental participation and ensure parental satisfaction that they have had a fair hearing if they are not to waste time and professional resources in protracted disputation.

THE ROLE OF THE ADMINISTRATOR

The new procedures outlined under the Education Act 1981 introduce an extra and important dimension to parent–professional relationships, namely the role of the education administrator. The new assessment procedures formally link parents with a *designated* official of the LEA. This officer not only informs and advises but in certain circumstances *interprets* parents' representations on their child and his special educational needs.

The critical role of the education administrator has been largely overlooked in professional analyses of changes in current special educational services. But a recent analysis of Public Law 94.142 (Sabbatini and Joiner, 1981) in the USA clearly identifies the administrator as a key agent in service development. Sabbatini and Joiner found that local administrators exercised considerable discretionary powers in implementing policy elements determined by professional agencies. If they did not share consensus on the overall *goals* of educational policy, such policy could be damaged almost inadvertently by 'passive sabotage'.

The same study highlighted the dilemmas faced by education administrators for ordinary schools required for the first time to take account of *special needs*. Sabbatini and Joiner highlighted five stages involved in the acceptance and active promotion of new procedures:

1. awareness of current good practice;
2. increasing interest by administrators in such new practices;
3. information on the consequences of new services;
4. publication of information material on good innovative work;
5. availability of credible data on acceptance of new procedures.

All five conditions imply heightened consciousness of the philosophy behind change and an awareness of other perspectives on such change. Legislation seldom achieves revolutions. Rather the 'drip and trickle' effect of slow progress characterizes UK legislative initiative. A constructive and mutually supportive dialogue between parents, administrators and professionals concerned with special education will be an integral part of changing the system.

A NEW ROLE FOR PARENTS

The ethos of the 1981 Act (as of the Warnock Report which preceded it) is participation and partnership with parents. Parents have traditionally seen themselves as *clients* of the education and related services. For some the move to the role of *agent* may be frightening as well as challenging. Not all parents will initially find the new broad concepts of special educational needs comfortable, since special education is still feared by those who only envisage it as institution-based provision with a narrow and sometimes stigmatizing remit.

However, the new procedures encourage a more open approach to parents from health and social services as well as education. Section 10 of the Act gives education and health services the opportunity to offer access to information, counselling, guidance and befriending *before* formal procedures have to begin.

The voluntary sector in particular has a major challenge in moving towards a more professional and specific service not only in acting on behalf of parents – perhaps in the role of the much debated 'named person' – but also as advocate on parents' wider rights with regard to provision in a particular authority. Partnership implies information and informed consent.

The provision of appropriate relevant and readable information material not only on the Act but on parent participation in terms of the statement and ultimately the appeals procedures will be vital.

Although there was some initial criticism of the 1981 Act in as much as it could be interpreted as offering a passive role to parents, there seems little doubt that the new procedures will certainly lead to a much broader concept of civil rights and due processes in special education. The USA experience through Public Law 94.142 clearly demonstrates how formal procedures for parental involvement in assessment and educational decision making lead to a major *advocacy* role for the voluntary sector, and a growth of self-advocacy amongst consumers of education services.

ADVOCACY AND PARENTS' RIGHTS

1. *'The named person'*

In the context of parental involvement, a number of new roles in special education have emerged during the creation and implementation of the Education Act 1981. Firstly, the Warnock concept of the 'named person – essentially counsellor and adviser' is incorporated in the Act but is undefined in function in the accompanying circular and regulations. The role of the 'named person' is broadly in line with the central Warnock philosophy of 'parents as partners'. Although the 'named person' could logically move from befriending and counselling to advocacy, the latter function is not a necessary function of the role.

2. *The expert witness*

There is evidence that even prior to the implementation of the Act, many parents have been turning to independent expert witnesses or to second opinions in the context of educational assessment of their child. Educational psychologists, in particular, are frequently requested to give considered judgements on a particular child and the move will be strengthened by the right of parents to make representations under the new legislation.

Privatization in assessment is in some respects a recognition of similar trends in other areas of family life, namely a desire to participate in important decisions and to be fully informed about children's educational progress. Similar moves can be observed in the emergence of the 'Independent Social Worker' in child care disputes. However, the growth of 'second opinions' in this field (and it should be remembered that BUPA has recently opened its first assessment centre for this purpose) will not be in the parents' or child's interests if there is misunderstanding about the nature of both LEA and private assessments and about the use of any such information material when it has been made available.

3. The advocate

The third emerging role is that of the *advocate*. The citizen advocate is clearly identified in some other Western European countries and in the United States. Whilst there is a potential advocacy role in that of the named person, it should be remembered that the independent expert witness is giving a *professional judgement* or assessment of a particular child at a particular time and is not an advocate except in the provision of specific and professionally accepted evidence which may be used by an advocate or the parent on his behalf.

A NEW ROLE FOR VOLUNTARY ORGANIZATIONS?

The idea of the 'citizen advocate' is relatively new in the United Kingdom. If the role of the 'named person' is developed to embody the broadly enabling concept of the USA 'parent counsellor' (as established under Public Law 94.142), it is possible that such a role in turn could become that of enabler, adviser and advocate. But it seems probable that we will follow the USA precedent and see a growing advocacy role by *voluntary organizations* who will act on behalf of parents and pursue their interests through a variety of channels.

Many of the issues on which parents are likely to seek advocates (as opposed to counsellors and advisers) will relate to *policy* issues wider than the needs of the individual child. Although parents may appeal on personal grounds, such as the preference for one local school rather than another, they may also question broader policy issues within the LEA. Policy issues could include integration, the allocation of resources and the provision of specialist services such as speech therapy and physiotherapy. In such circumstances support for parents is more likely to come from self-help groups or larger voluntary organizations. The voluntary sector, indeed, may find itself with a major role in recruiting and training advocates and in 'matching' them with parents.

Many parents already enjoy informal advocacy of their expressed interests through professionals or voluntary bodies with whom they are in contact. But some interest groups (such as the old categories of ESN(M) and the maladjusted) have no network of parent groups to help them. Some special educational needs have potentially socially stigmatizing labels (like maladjustment) and in these instances parents may lack the early counselling and advice which could avert the subsequent need for advocacy when things have gone wrong. The availability of appeals procedures should not divert attention from the much greater need to help parents work positively and successfully within the system from the earliest stage.

Four tasks

It seems likely, therefore, that voluntary organizations will perform a fourfold role, Firstly, they will provide information and support in the early days, when making the machine accessible may be a major problem. Secondly, they will provide a resource and training function for those already working in a professional or voluntary capacity with parents. Thirdly, they will provide an advocacy service and – in view of the specific needs and procedures to be followed – probably provide background information and training for representatives of parents' interests. Fourthly, and by no means least, they will enhance parents' capacity to be *self-advocates*. Thus, we may finally see the emergence of locally based 'parent coalitions' as in the USA, which are 'non-sectarian' in disability terms and which are literally watchdogs of the *local* education scene.

WHOSE RIGHTS?

It has been widely assumed that advocacy in the context of the Education Act 1981 will be wholly concerned with the rights of *parents* in determining their child's educational needs. However, the past decade has seen a movement parallel to that of advocacy for parents, namely the rights of disabled young people to have advocates and to acquire the skills of self-advocacy in order to participate in decision-making processes. The Advocacy Alliance's programmes in long-stay hospitals have clearly demonstrated this role in the United Kingdom, as does the 'People First' movement promoted by Paul Williams and others for teaching self-advocacy skills to people with mental and multiple handicaps.

The Education Act 1981 does not specify consumer involvement for children – although reference is made in the Education Act 1981 (Scotland) to consultation with the over-16s. But reference is made such consultation in

Section 6 of the Circular, which states that 'the feelings and perceptions of the child concerned should be taken into account and the concept of partnership should wherever possible be extended to older children and young people'. It seems likely therefore that one of the procedural implications of working with *parents* will be the recognition of a parallel set of rights for *children and young people.*

In such circumstances both child and parents may legitimately need representation and policy issues emerge for the voluntary sector about the extent to which it can provide an enabling advocacy service for individuals if the organization itself disagrees with the aims pursued.

THE APPEALS PROCEDURES

Although there has been considerable disquiet at the differentiation between parents of handicapped and non-handicapped children in terms of appeals, the new procedures do introduce a new civil rights perspective into special education which was formerly lacking. The White Paper stated that most children with special educational needs would be 'indistinguishable in law from the majority of the school population' and parents of children with statements will retain the overall right to go to the Secretary of State in cases of dispute.

Despite the limitations in terms of enforcing Appeal Committee decisions on LEAs, the new system does extend parental rights. Such committees will be required to have at least one member with 'relevant knowledge'. LEAs, like parents, would prefer not to enter into proceedings which must at times be contentious and expensive. The procedures will, it is hoped, encourage LEAs to develop the concept of a 'named person' to include acting as negotiator between themselves and dissatisfied parents (a role similar to that successfully developed by the 'parent counsellor' in Public Law 94.142). The procedures also introduce the idea of conciliation and informed negotiation based on shared information and responsible discussion.

INTEGRATION

The 1981 Act specifies that children should be educated in ordinary schools subject to certain conditions including the efficient use of resources.

As Hannon (1982) points out in the *Journal of Social Welfare Law,* the conditions so specified are 'framed so as to permit any LEA in the country to pursue a quite contrary policy' but it is generally true that legislation in this country tends to express the best of current practice rather than anticipate new developments.

The expertise which has developed in the past decade has largely been in response to legislation, which was in turn responding to existing trends in service provision and professional attitudes. The *professional* expertise required was largely lacking in 1971 although financial resources were more generally available. Integration is a *social* as well as an educational trend, reflecting more positive attitudes to disabled people and their families in the wider community as well as in professional services.

The 1981 Act, with its global approach to children's special educational needs and its move away from the 2 per cent of largely special-school-based children *must* take account of many children *already* integrated within the mainstream system. It seems inevitable that the expertise unquestionably available within many special schools will be extended into the wider community. Similarly teachers in ordinary schools will have to become acquainted with special educational procedures and provision. Since both parents and teachers will have to find solutions for many special educational needs within existing structures, time, mutual education and the extension of specialist support and advisory services will effect change with or without additional resources. Whilst the issue of resourcing is of course a crucial one in the wider development of special educational provision, it would be foolish to hide behind resources and ignore the possibility of change from within the system.

IN CONCLUSION

The Education Act 1981 must be seen as a challenge to provide better special education within diverse settings and in a way which is acceptable not only to parents but to the children and young people who are direct consumers of these services. Since all legislation tends to be an amalgam of what has gone before together with a formalization of current trends, the Act anticipates even if it does not statutorily require changes in the system. The formalization of parental rights and involvement in assessment and education decision making is an important step forward. The existence of an appeals procedure must produce commitment by LEAs to make the system accessible and acceptable. Parents, teachers and administrators will have new roles which can range from productive consultation to confrontation and disappointment.

The firm commitment to *interdisciplinary* services for children with special needs in the end has important implications for *professional* relationships in terms of inter-agency confidentiality and – hopefully – in the recognition of the importance of good record keeping and monitoring in making the new procedures work. Clearly the Act will need monitoring. Local authority responses will vary not only according to financial resources but in line with the philosophy of education, professional attitudes and *parental pressure*. In the last resort parents themselves must see the Act as a resource and machinery which must be made to work on behalf of children with special needs.

The principle of shared access to the information on which an educational decision is made must (however inadequate the individual reports) introduce a new perspective of accountability. The civil rights lobby will undoubtedly challenge the discretion of individual LEAs to develop local policy – and in turn may find that discretionary rights are not necessarily negative in as much as they enable or restrict according to the quality of the debate generated in the wider community. The Act can serve as a parents' charter only if the parents are willing to take up responsibilities as well as rights in maximizing its efficiency on their behalf.

REFERENCES

Department of Education and Science (DES) (1978) *Special Educational Needs* (Warnock Report), Cmnd 7212, HMSO, London
Department of Education and Science (DES) (1983) *Assessments and Statements of Special Educational Needs,* Joint Circular DES 1/83, LAC(83)2, HC(83)3, HMSO, London
Hannon, V. (1982) The Education Act 1981: new rights and duties in special education, *Journal of Social Welfare Law,* September, pp 257–320
Mental Health Law Project *et al.* (1980) *Report by the Education Advocates Coalition on Federal Compliance Activities to Implement the Education for All Handicapped Children Act (PL 94.142),* Washington DC
Sabbatini, D.A. and Joiner, C. (1981) *A Policy Study of Exceptional Children (PL 94.142),* Council for Exceptional Children, USA, September, pp 24–39
Voluntary Council for Handicapped Children (1982) The Education Act 1981: the role of the named person, Discussion Paper

TOPICS FOR DISCUSSION

1. Discuss the view that the 1981 Education Act, 'like Brighton Pier, is good as far as it goes, but a poor way of getting to France'.
2. In what sense could it be claimed that the 1981 Education Act is a 'parents' charter'?
3. 'The first thing to be said about Warnock's conclusion on the prevalence of special education need is that it could equally well have been reached on adequate research evidence at any time in the previous 50 years' (D. Galloway, 1986, *Schools, Pupils and Special Educational Needs,* Croom Helm, London, p.11). Discuss.

SUGGESTIONS FOR FURTHER READING

1. J. Welton *et al.* (1982) *Meeting Special Educational Needs: the 1981 Act and its implications,* Bedford Way Papers, No. 12, University of London, Institute of Education, Heinemann, London. This publication discusses the background to the 1981 Education Act, the Research Project on the Assessment of Special Educational Needs, and considers the implications of the research findings for the implementation of the 1981 Act.
2. D. Galloway (1985) *Schools, Pupils and Special Educational Needs,* Croom Helm, London. Chapter 2 'Administration and Legal Issues' discusses background factors to the 1981 Act, the Act itself and some of its most significant anomalies.
3. J. Fish (1985) *Special Education: the way ahead,* Open University Press, Milton Keynes. Chapter 1 of this book provides a useful perspective on international trends and developments and major ideas given expression by the 1981 Education Act.

Reading 2
THE DEVELOPMENT AND IMPLEMENTATION OF SPECIAL EDUCATION POLICY: WHERE DID THE 1981 ACT FIT IN?
J. Welton and J. Evans

INTRODUCTION

The White Paper on Special Needs in Education, the 1981 Education Act and its associated Regulations and Circulars may be seen as the definitive government statement of assumptions and intentions about the education of a section of the pupil population of England and Wales. In this sense they could be called 'government policy', and all actions consequent upon the passage of the legislation could be called 'implementation of government policy'. Such a simple view of the relationship between

J. Welton and J. Evans (1986) The development and implementation of special education policy: where did the 1981 Act fit in? *Public Administration,* Vol. 64, No. 7. This paper draws from the findings of the Pilot Project on Assessment of Special Educational Need, as well as from the current research project on the 1981 Education Act. The authors wish to acknowledge and thank Gwynne Vorhaus for her contribution to the Pilot Project; and Brian Goacher, Klaus Wedell and participants at a project research seminar for their comments on an earlier draft. While each of the two research projects has been funded by the Department of Education and Science, the views expressed in this paper are those of the authors, and are not necessarily those of the Department.

policy and implementation, and of the relationship between legislation and administrative and professional behaviour, presumes a linearity of cause and effect rather than a process which investigation shows to be inherently interactive and recursive. As Welton (1981) noted, 'New laws do not arise in a vacuum, nor do they create entirely new forms of practice.'

It is widely acknowledged that legislation is rarely implemented as its architects intended. British educational legislation is broadly enabling rather than minutely prescriptive. Where there is consensus such legislation enables and encourages the 'reasonable person', 'the enlightened local authority' – that is, one which implements policy along the lines promoted by the prevailing (government-sponsored) model of good practice. Where there is dissension, legislation inhibits the 'unreasonable person' or 'rebel local authority' (Welton, 1982).

Weatherley and Lipsky (1977), reporting on the implementation of equivalent special education legislation in the State of Massachusetts, described the way in which at the point of service delivery various school personnel (or 'street level bureaucrats') developed coping mechanisms to manage the demands of their job, which 'may in the aggregate, constrain and distort the implementation of the special-education reform'. However, while the power of the professionals and administrators who operate at the interface between an organization and its clients is difficult to control, nevertheless they are constrained by dependence on both the organization and their clients for the continued existence of their roles (Barrett and Hill, 1984).

All policy has a history and the 1981 Education Act can be seen as one point in the development of ideas about handicap and the management of handicap in the education system. The Act had its roots as far back as 1966 when various organizations asked the then Government to set up a committee of inquiry into special education – a committee which was established eight years later in 1974, eventually producing the Warnock Report on *Special Educational Needs* (DES, 1978). In the following year, not waiting for the Warnock Committee to report, the Government issued its Circular 2/75 (DES, 1975) which, through its recommended procedure for identifying and assessing children with special educational needs, formalized the changing relationship between education and health service personnel in the assessment and placement of children with various categories of handicap.

The Education Act which reached the statute book in 1981 and was brought into force on 1 April 1983 had a very long gestation period. Its principles were formed in a climate of educational thinking and government policies very different from those which prevailed at the time of its implementation. The changes in professional thought about the education of children with special educational needs were reflected in the shift of responsibility for severely subnormal children from Health to Education in 1970, and the espousal by the Warnock Committee of the relative principle of need. The policy of integrating children with special educational needs within ordinary schools had roots in the wider move to incorporate 'minority groups' within mainstream institutions and can be seen as a logical development of the principle of comprehensive education. Similarly, the right given to parents in the 1981 Act to see the written professional advice on which local education authorities make decisions about children's needs and provision had its origin in the broader movement for citizens' rights to information and to be involved in decision making about their own future. Even the way in which the Act failed to take any explicit account of resource provision reflects a style of education management reminiscent of the 1960s period of expansion rather than the financial stringencies which were to accompany the Act's implementation.

The point at which the main tenets of new government policy crystallize is unclear. The principal officer (civil servant) in the Department of Education and Science responsible for coordinating work on the Education Bill claimed in a radio interview that the White Paper could not be published until the Government had a broad idea about the framework of the legislation, although the details still needed to be filled in. Then draft instructions were given to parliamentary counsel as to the scope and detail of a Bill. Counsel and the Department then negotiated over the exact wording of clauses. The minister involved then sought approval of the draft by cabinet colleagues in committee.

Examination of the White Paper on Special Education, the Bill, Hansard, the Act, the Regulations and Circulars of Guidance to Local Authorities indicates that further developments took place on the basis as well as the detail of government policy during the passage of the legislation through Parliament, and between the granting of Royal Assent and the delayed publication of the Circulars of Guidance early in 1983. A further period of definition and redefinition followed as the Department responded to local education authority, professional, parent and pressure group requests for clarification of principles and procedures.

The then Minister of State for Education, Baroness Young, described the Education Bill as an important statement of intention since government policy intended to achieve a new legal framework, to cause everyone with responsibility for children with special educational needs to look again at their practices to see that each child got the maximum educational advantage, and to be a starting point for all LEAs to match the practice of the best (Barker, 1981). Elsewhere (Young, 1980) she noted the roots of the legislation and possible criticism that:

> somewhere on the long road leading from the Warnock Report towards legislation some of the spirit of the report appears to have been lost [. . .] this is not the case. It is simply that in translating recommendations into law we move into the dispassionate world of the lawyers, who like builders have to construct secure foundations on which the building can rise.

Later in the same speech, Baroness Young noted the limited power of the legislator over the process of implementation. The Warnock Report had emphasized the roles and rights of parents in decision making about a child's special educational needs, but as she said:

> The law is not the place [. . .] where feeling can be enshrined. Legislation can insist for example that the parents must be consulted over the provision made for their child, but it cannot ensure that this is always done with as much understanding as we all would like. As the Warnock Report so rightly recognized, nothing [. . .] would be fully effective without changes in attitudes [held by professionals and administrators] and that cannot be achieved by legislation.

The question arises as to how far the Warnock Committee recommendations were reflecting real trends in professional and administrative opinion or how far they were flying a kite for their preferred option from amongst a range of ideas and practices. In framing the 1981 Act, the Government clearly felt that the special education service was ready to move in the direction charted by Warnock. The history of previous education reports such as Plowden (Central Advisory Council for Education, 1967) indicates that the majority of practitioners may be much less ready to take on new attitudes, practices and arrangements than had been envisaged.

THE POLICY PROCESS

We agree with the critics of the notion that policy is a 'fix', and of a 'top-down' approach to the study of implementation, while recognizing its relevance for service managers, whether civil servants or local government officers, who are accountable for the delivery and protection as well as the development of policy. Barrett and Hill (1984) urge researchers to 'pay attention to the way in which the process of implementation is essentially a political process characterized by negotiation, bargaining and compromise between those groups seeking to influence (or change) the actions of others, and those upon whom influence is being brought to bear'. The two studies of the development and administration of special education policy directed by Welton and Wedell at the University of London Institute of Education indicate that very similar processes of negotiation, bargaining and compromise occur during the period leading to design of new legislation, during its passage through Parliament and in its implementation. A change of legislation may be seen as just one significant event in the general process of service and policy development. Barrett and Hill (1984) concur that 'the political processes by which policy is mediated, negotiated, and modified during its formulation and legitimation do not stop when initial policy decisions have been made: but continue to influence policy through the behaviour of those responsible for its implementation and those affected by policy acting to protect or enhance their own interests'.

As a starting point for understanding the development and implementation of policy Barrett and Hill (1984) suggest the study of the 'policy process' or, as Hill (1981) describes it, a 'policy implementation chain' within which issues are increasingly solidified. Evans (1984) summarized a multidimensional model for understanding the way in which local authorities adapt to new legislation such as the 1981 Education Act. Like Barrett and Hill (1984), Evans recognized the variety of actors and agencies involved and the linkages between them, their value systems, interests, relative autonomies and power bases, and the interactions taking place between them, in particular their negotiating and bargaining behaviour. She suggested that local authority departments should be viewed from four distinct, but related, perspectives:

1. the local education department as a formal organization set up for a specific purpose and accountable to the local authority, to central government and to the electorate;
2. the local authority as a decision-making body at all levels, from street level to political level, involving the exercise of political, administrative and professional power and authority;
3. the local authority as a collection of political, professional, officer and user interest groups;
4. the local authority as a collection of individuals seeking to fulfil their own as well as clients' needs.

Policy is made and implemented at all levels of welfare service activity. Government policy, such as that promoted by the 1981 Education Act, is just one factor shaping the relationships and behaviour which go to make up the service as delivered to and experienced by children with special education needs and their parents. The service which is delivered emerged as an outcome of interaction between central government legislation, local authority policy, administrative and professional policy and the coping behaviour of professionals and others working with children and families. Government policy backed by legislation is a special case in having potential power to modify arrangements and behaviour, to supply or remove resources or even to disband a tier of administration or service. However, as noted above, Baroness Young recognized that, in a field such as special education, legislation cannot easily change professional and, we might add, administrative attitudes and behaviour. Even where a government has legislative authority, it may be unwilling to exercise that authority coercively, lacking the means to ensure compliance. The fact that national educational policy is implemented through quasi-autonomous local education authorities determines the strategies which government adopts in seeking compliance to its policy priorities. Further, a policy issue such as special education involves the education, health and social services – separate – policy sectors at both central and local levels of government.

Whitmore (1984) has developed an approach to the analysis of policy and implementation based on Knoepfel and Weidner's (1982) model of a policy core embedded in programme shells. Whitmore identifies six aspects of policy formulation and implementation:

1. *the core dimesion* – in this case the problem of special education;
2. *the policy paradigm* – i.e. the way the problem and solutions to the problem are defined;
3. *the monitoring framework* – the 'policy' in the sense of Acts of Parliament, Regulations, Circulars etc.
4. *interorganization resource dependencies* – i.e. central-local government dependencies, and inter-agency relations;
5. *administrative structures and processes* – channels through which 'policies' are formulated and carried out;
6. *the professional interface with the consumer* – i.e. how 'policy' is carried out at the field worker/client level.

Whitmore describes the model not so much as a core surrounded by shells as the layers of an onion – a multidimensional model in which each of the layers comes in contact with and influences the other. The processes which led eventually to the Royal Assent to the 1981 Educational Act and which continued from that date reflect processes of adaptation between each of the components which Whitmore identifies:

1. changes in the core dimension, the policy issue – the emergence of a new way of conceptualizing the problem of the education of handicapped children;
2. changes in the policy paradigm – the way in which special educational need is defined and provision conceived, e.g. in relation to integration and the contribution of parents;
3. changes in the policy framework – the legislation and circulars of guidance;
4. changes in the relationship between organizations – between central government and local education, social service and health authorities and between each at local level;
5. changes in administrative structures and processes particularly in the 'statementing process' and resource allocation;
6. changes in the relationship between professionals and clients.

Studies in policy making and implementation which embrace 'top-down' models would see the passage of legislation as establishing a 'fix' from which subsequent action flows. However, the study of implementation must take account of the existence of many, sometimes conflicting, policies affecting the same area of activity. Meeting special educational needs involves a relationship between education, health and social service sector policies; forming a prime example of a policy area in which there are several conflicting and often confusing and unclear policies operating at the same time, affected by various paradigm shifts and by changes in the policy and administrative frameworks which alter the relationship between agencies, the whole being affected by overall economic policies.

POLICY FRAMEWORK

The process of policy formulation and the way in which policy emerges is not merely an exercise in corporatism. The dominant consensus which is established is rarely without its critics. The agenda for discussion and the people approached to give advice to a committee of inquiry such as Warnock illustrates Lukes's (1974) contention that power operates in such a way as to exclude certain points of view so completely that they are not seen as part of the debate. For example, although black Afro-Caribbean children were overrepresented in special schools, there was no representative of the black community on the Warnock Committee. In the context of social and educational awareness of the early 1970s, race was not seen as a significant issue in special education.

Kirp (1982) has suggested that there are several possible approaches to the conceptualization and evolution of a framework for social policy. He argues that the British approach to special education has emphasized 'professional concerns' and 'expertise' at the expense of legal norms or of the bureaucratic setting of standards. For example, in contrast to equivalent United States legislation, the legal rights given to parents under the 1981 Act are severely curtailed by the proviso that the appeals committee (chosen by the LEA) do not have the last word in decision making. Although the appeals machinery to be used is that of the 1980 Act, in the case of appeals against the 'statement of educational need' the rules are changed so that the recommendation of the appeals committee is not binding on a local education authority. However, Aldrich and Leighton (1985) and Hannon (1983) note the potentially constraining influence of the Commissioner for Local Administration (or Ombudsman) on the administrative but not policy-making behaviour of local authorities.

Kirp (1982) also suggests that bureaucratic standard setting cannot be practised either, since the relativity in the legislation makes each LEA able to operate the law to fit in with its previous practice and provision – accommodating the enabling character of the Act to the wide variety of practice and level of provision in different local authorities. In Kirp's view special education in England and Wales is conceptualized as a problem best tackled by professionals, whether medical, psychological or educational. Although there has been a shift from considering children as having what he calls 'medical' to having educational problems, those problems are seen as being best solved by the application of professional expertise, mainly by substituting educational psychologists for the medical profession. For Kirp, debate then centres on how such problems are discovered – ascertainment – and how they are to be overcome. The focus is on the child, but still on his or her difficulty.

The core of the policy process is the conceptualization of the policy issue and the emergence of a dominant consensus about the nature of the problem and how it should be approached. The emergence or protection of a consensus about the policy paradigm may be controlled by powerful interest groups which set the agenda for discussion and limit explanations and solutions to the problem within a narrow range of options. The negotiations and bargaining which go on as the policy is redefined take place against a background of constraints which limit the options open to policy makers.

These include, not only the control over the production of ideas by certain powerful interest groups, but also structural constraints such as the mutual dependencies of central and local government, and between services at a local level over the execution of government policy. Whitmore's model (1984) needs to take account of interpolicy resource dependencies across sectors of government and of social policy.

The dual government role of, on the one hand, providing the legislative framework to bring about change in the structure and processes of local education authorities and, on the other hand, making choices between priorities while seeking to manage the economy by imposing strict controls on local authority spending leads to the emergence of competing policies which local authorities find it difficult to reconcile. Baroness Young describes the Government's position on resources in a speech (1980):

> I readily acknowledge that additional resources for certain aspects of special education would help in achieving some of the Warnock Committee's goals, but I must say that I am a little horrified by the way in which a few people, who should know better, have read the White Paper and said that nothing can be changed without extra resources. This is simply not true. There is scope for some re-deployment of existing resources within the new statutory framework and over the next five years the total school population will fall dramatically. This demographic trend must be reflected in the number of children with special educational needs. I suggest to you, that those who say that now is not the time to make changes, run the risk that the change will never be made.

In the 1981 Education Act the Government recognized that local authorities have to respond to local need and left certain sections of the Act as enabling rather than prescriptive. For example, the section on integration is subject to three provisos, including one which safeguards the 'efficient use of resources'. Some pressure groups have argued that although integration is a central tenet of government policy, this part of the Act will ensure that integration will not develop as the norm for special education provision. Swann (1985) analysed the numbers of children in special schools in the four years prior to the Act's implementation, and found no evidence of an underlying trend towards integration. The apparent conflict between the Government's endorsement of the principle of integration and the practice within LEAs leads us to question whether this aspect of the 1981 Act is merely symbolic legislation which the Government knows will not necessarily be adhered to by LEAs. The implementation of such legislation may have been found impractical or there may never have been any real power or intention to carry it through. However, symbolic legislation may still be an important negative or positive influence on professional and administrative thinking and practice. An indication of which parts of the Act form the continuing core of government intention may become clear through the way in which it reacts to the declared or undeclared policies and practices of local education authorities over such issues as integration, or use of the 'statementing procedure'.

Another example of the dualism of government policy, and the tension between its functions for the economy and for social welfare, is exemplified by the Act's new definition of special educational need and provision. Lukes (1981) has argued that the relativistic definition of need and the removal of a duty on LEAs to provide special education for children with specific categories of handicap will have the effect of allowing LEAs to provide 'as much or as little as they want'. This may be an unintended effect of the legislation, but the introduction of such flexibility during a time of reduced public spending may have a different effect from that which would have occurred in a time of expansion. Welton (1982) has argued that the means of examining local authority decision making provided for parents by the statement and appeals procedures established in the Act could, as indeed its architects intended, protect children from the effect of economic cuts, or poor LEA provision. There is already some evidence of strain within local education authorities between the need to maintain spending on special education for children whose provision is protected by a statement, and the need to cut overall spending. An authority which espouses a policy of minimal statementing on educational grounds lays itself open to the accusation that it is protecting itself by denying children the protection from service cuts which the statement should provide. It can, however, be argued that government policies on local government spending will have at least as much impact on special education as will the 1981 Act. Shipman (1984) has argued that the tendency towards increasing centralization of decision making within the education service is not so much to control education as to control education spending: *'The substantial threat is not a conspiracy in Elizabeth House, but financial constraint exercised by the Treasury.'* Whether, as some commentators have suggested, the Act was designed to assist the Government and local authorities to control spending or genuinely to promote and protect the education of children with special needs, its implementation cannot be understood without reference to other government policies.

Policy making, and implementation at central government level, involves a process of negotiation between government departments (to attempt to reconcile conflicting objectives), negotiation with professions, interest and pressure groups, local authorities and their associations, government legal advisers, politicians, civil servants and professional advisers such as HMI. During this process issues become increasingly crystallized and the consensus which emerges is at best a compromise which it is hoped will enable those concerned with special education to fulfil their objectives and obligations without endangering other governmental priorities or placing an impossible burden on the administrators and professionals whose duty it is to provide for children's special educational needs.

The passage of the 1981 Act has become, therefore, a reference point for those involved in providing special education. It is easily identifiable, fixed in time and provided in written form. However, the way in which the Act is interpreted is open to negotiation and clarification. It is clear from our research that the process of negotiation and bargaining between and within central and local government, and involving the professions and parent groups, continues – after the Act, as before it and during its passage.

POLICY CONTEXTS

Once granted Royal Assent, the Act becomes a focus for policy making at the local level, since local authorities have to re-evaluate their policies, arrangements and procedures in the new light of the new monitoring framework. The complexity of the administrative response is compounded by the number of local agencies which are involved. Special education assessment and provision involve at a minimum three separate organizations: the local education authority, the district health authority and the social service department, not counting the contribution of voluntary organizations. Each has its own history, paradigms, policies, structures and procedures. District health authorities are funded directly by central government and have no direct accountability to the public through local ballot. LEAs and SSDs, on the other hand, are parts of the same local authority, competing for revenue which is in part raised locally from an electorate to whom they are directly accountable for spending and service provision. District health authorities and local authorities are not necessarily geographically coterminous; a fact which complicates coordination of practice and provision. These different structures of accountability, funding and administration cause difficulty in coordinating the system of assessment and provision for children with special educational needs envisaged in the Act.

The structural constraints outlined above provide the context within which negotiation between local implementers takes place in order to provide a framework for policy delivery, including the coordination of action across welfare sectors to provide education for children with special needs. The policy/action distinction becomes blurred here, since it is often unclear to what extent policies evolve through an incremental adaptation of existing practices rather than as a considered response to the demands of the new legislation. Our study of local authority response to the 1981 Education Act suggests a range of behaviours from (a) rationally considered change to (b) incremental reactive coping and (c) rejecting or ignoring the demands for change.

The difficulties of interagency cooperation and adaptation to change have been explored by many writers on welfare policy. Welton (1981) sees one of the major obstacles to coordinated planning and delivery of welfare services as the 'the inherited division of welfare' which (a) establishes and maintains the statutory and administrative frameworks and (b) creates, justifies and protects competing definitions of client needs and professional response. Whitmore (1984) points out that when interagency cooperation takes place it happens on a temporary *ad hoc* basis which does not undermine the autonomy of individual agencies and leaves the agency domains intact. There are powerful forces within the various welfare agencies seeking to prevent a blurring of boundaries between them, not least of which is the concern for professional status and autonomy. Education, health and social services departments are staffed by a large number of different professional groups, each with its own structure and hierarchy. Whittington (1983) identifies several factors which inhibit cooperation between professionals working with the same client groups. One is that professionalism is a strategy of job control in which one of the main prizes is the right to define and determine the situation in a given sphere of work. In the case of special education, we have seen a shift of dominance from one professional group (medical) to another (educational psychologist). This shift arose through a change in the way in which the policy issue (special educational need) was conceptualized and a change in the policy paradigm, particularly the way in which solutions to the problem were defined. A shift in the monitoring framework occurred both through the 1970 Act and through the recommendations of Circular 2/75 (DES, 1975) which put educational psychologists or educational advisers in the key position in the multiprofessional assessment of children's needs. The shift away from the terminology of handicap to that of educational difficulty reflected and reinforced the dominance of educational paradigms.

Negotiation and day-to-day cooperation across the boundaries of health, education and social services are constrained by several factors:

1. different geographical areas;
2. different funding priorities and arrangements – the term 'Cinderella services' applies to those peripheral activities which command low priority in the health services but are key inputs into the support of children with special educational needs;
3. differences in professional status and hierarchy;
4. different professional ideologies;
5. differences in the relationships between the various education, social service and medical professionals and their client groups.

The medical professions have high-status and rigid hierarchies which stress the preeminence of consultants and the low status of paramedical and nursing services. Consultants operate as independent practitioners and have shown themselves reluctant to relinquish their autonomy in assessing and prescribing for their patients. Doctors within the child health service are less inflexible and more accessible. The community health service, of which the child health service is often a part, has a relatively low priority within regional and district health authorities but it also has a history of links with local education authorities in respect of children with special needs. Even so, some doctors find it difficult to accept what they see as their diminished role and authority, particularly with respect to discussing placement or provision with parents. However, agreement between the local education and health authorities about working practices seems easier to achieve than does agreement over allocation of resources. Funding priorities in the health service lie elsewhere than with community health. There appears to be a shortage of almost every resource which the LEA might hope to obtain from the DHA. There is a tension implicit in the wording of the 1981 Act whereby the LEA is accountable for the provision of whatever is recommended in a 'statement of educational need', although the cost and control of some provision is the responsibility of an autonomous organization, the DHA. The 'statement procedure' requires teachers, medical officers, paramedicals, educational psychologists and other professionals to give written advice to the LEA without reference to known availability of resources. In principle the LEA is required to make a statement of need which is specific to the child's need and not affected by resource availability, but then go further and state how it intends the child's needs should be met. The statement procedure was designed to make explicit the process of decision making about a child's needs and provision, and the relationship between professional advice and administrative and political resource constraints. Where there are insufficient resources available to meet a child's need the gap should be examinable through the incongruence between different parts of the statement. The Act therefore provides a means for making LEAs accountable for decisions about providing for children's special educational needs, but leaves them in some circumstances powerless to deliver resources whose volume is limited by other central government policies or controlled by another welfare organization.

A prime example of this is speech therapy for which demand far exceeds supply. Speech therapists work with adults as well as with children, requiring DHAs to make a choice about priorities between patient populations. LEAs cannot directly influence the allocation of resources by a partner health authority. Under the 1981 Act parents who remain dissatisfied with the provision made in the statement can appeal, but even if their appeal is upheld, the LEA cannot force a DHA to provide. This is a dilemma of interorganizational resource dependency highlighted by the 1981 Education Act, and yet to be resolved.

Another example of the divergence between health and education authority interests concerns the integration of children with special needs into mainstream education. LEAs which make moves in this direction may find that such policy decisions have resource implications for the health authority. For example, the placement of physically handicapped children in mainstream schools may place an additional burden on health authorities in the provision of physiotherapy. If special education is concentrated in a special school or unit, the physiotherapy service may be provided in a more cost-effective way and with more specialist facilities. However, if physically handicapped children are in ordinary local schools, physiotherapists may have to spend much more time travelling to visit individual children in less specialist surroundings. Similar mismatches of objectives and resources are found between education and social service departments within the same local authority. For example, a social service department may have a policy of restricting the use of community homes and where possible returning children to their local area. This leads to pressure upon local schools who have to cater for children who may have severe behavioural or emotional problems which would previously have led to a residential placement. Similarly, the increasing practice by LEAs of returning severely physically or mentally handicapped children from expensive 'out-county' residential placements to educate them within the LEA puts extra pressure on social service departments to support their families. These examples illustrate the mutual interdependence of the agencies involved and the extent to which a policy decision which follows a change of policy paradigm in one sector may have resource implications and conflict with the policy paradigm in another sector.

The professional ideologies of those in health, social services and education need to be taken into account when formulating policy at both central and local government levels. The 1981 Act confirmed in statute the change in policy paradigm which makes the learning difficulties and special educational needs of the child the central focus of attention. It is possible that this *educational* definition may cut across the medical and social problems which are being dealt with elsewhere. For example, a residential placement for 'social reasons' may be resisted by education professionals or administrators because there are no compelling educational reasons to justify extra expenditure. Similarly, the medical needs of a physically handicapped child may be glossed over because his or her educational or social needs may be better met in an integrated setting. The multiprofessional assessment of children's need was incorporated into the 1981 Act with the intention of providing a means of resolving such interorganizational problems, but in the context of limited resources, separately controlled, the statement procedure highlights the difficulties inherent in the social division of welfare.

Attempts by administrators to alter the framework and to impose new working practices upon personnel both in education and other agencies are part of the process of adaptation where local arrangements are not in accord with the requirements of new legislation. Within the education system there may be a tension between professionals and administrators and between different professional groups as roles are redefined and new areas of responsibility delineated. The LEA will also try to influence working practices within health and social services, through negotiating new relationships with the other agencies involved, by reallocating resources or, if necessary, by imposing new procedures. From the point of view of central government, all this activity may be seen as 'implementation', but from the local perspective such activities are still at the level of policy making and the outcomes in terms of matching service delivery to government policy are problematic.

The outcome of the formulation of new administistative structures and procedures promoted by the 1981 Education Act within local authorities should be manifest in the changed working relationship between professionals and between professionals and administrators, and in their working relationships with children and families. These adaptations of behaviour and relationships may or may not be the intended outcome of the policies and guidelines issued by local authorities, or reflections of the policy intentions of the government which sought to shape structures and behaviour through legislation. Weatherley (1979) contends that the behaviour of 'street level bureaucrats' is highly discretionary. He maintains that individuals rather than organizations construct policy in order to survive and to continue to deliver to their clients such service as they are able in a new or changing situation. It is the service delivery workers who decide on priorities when resources are limited, undermining or circumventing new procedures in order to keep their workloads within manageable limits, to maintain the continued existence of their organizations, and to meet the need of their clients as experienced through day-to-day contact. The same processes which Welton *et al*, (1982) observed following Circular 2/75 are now found in the way local education authority administrators and professionals are adapting the 1981 Act to local circumstances. Those concerned with policy and administration at more central levels (in central government, and centrally within local government) may see such adaptations as 'policy failure'; it is difficult to identify which adaptive behaviour is (a) a genuinely exceptional and appropriate response to local circumstance, (b) bloody-minded or incompetent disregard of agreed policy, or (c) a creative development which eventually led to a wider change in consensus about the policy paradigm.

Given the financial, structural and ideological constraints built into policy making described in this paper, adaptation of policy at the level of service delivery may have an important role in reconciling conflicting policies. For instance, a shortage of resources will mean that decisions about limiting access to resources will have to be taken if the over-arching government policy of restricting local government spending is not to be breached. Decisions on resource allocation taken at the level of field workers are hidden or unofficial. The 1981 Act demands that the assessment and the statement of need for individual children is to be made without reference to resource implications, but there is evidence that statements of need are being framed to coincide with the resources available either from health, education or social services, and that professionals are being pressed to tailor their written advice to LEAs to meet the resources which they know to be available. In some cases professionals have justified their apparently unprofessional conduct by referring to the alleged harm which would be done to parents and children by advising the local authority of resource needs which are unlikely to be made available. However the knowledge that their written advice will be made available to the parents may be an even more significant influence on professional behaviour. This process of adaptation at street level to defuse conflict for the local authority was also evident in the way in which special education assessment was conducted under the Circular 2/75 procedure which preceded the 1981 Act. Significantly, it was just this kind of adaptation of the ascertainment procedure to meet professional, administrative and political needs which the 1981 Act statement procedure was designed to overcome. The difference lies in making the written evidence open to parents in the statement of need which can provide evidence for appeal against the local education authority.

The Circular of Guidance on *Assessments and Statements of Special Educational Needs* (DES, 1983a) promotes the view that parents should be treated as 'partners' in the process of assessment, and yet there are factors built into the system which make such a partnership unattainable for many parents: lack of knowledge (both professional and of organizations), degrees of articulateness, feelings of powerlessness, ignorance of rights under the Act. It is very easy for administrators and assessing professionals to manipulate and outmanoeuvre parents to achieve the outcome which they need administratively or which, despite the wishes of the parents, they genuinely believe to be in the best interest of the child. Parents who disagree with the LEA and insist on what they want may be seen as 'trouble-makers'. The aspect of the Act which makes the LEA ultimately accountable to parents is one which the built-in structural interest groups and organizational factors make most problematic. Even if parents manage to overcome pressures to conform to the wishes of the local authority and appeal against a statement of need, there is no obligation for the LEA to give way unless the parent is able to make a successful appeal to the Secretary of State.

CONCLUSION

In attempting to assess the contribution of the 1981 Education Act to the development of special education policy and practice we have indicated that we view the passage of the legislation as just one point in the interactive process of negotiation and bargaining; a process which pertains to the conditions which formed the will to legislate, throughout the passage of legislation in Parliament, and during its period of establishment in and adaptation by local authorities. Such negotiation can be seen in two ways: as either positive or zero sum activities. That is to say, the object of negotiation can be an outcome which is mutually advantageous to all parties (i.e. positive sum) or it can lead to a situation where if one group or individual achieves the outcome it wants then another group or individual sees that as a 'loss' (i.e. zero sum). Such an interpretation of the outcome of negotiations depends on whether one is adopting a consensus or a conflict model of organizational behaviour. The situation within local authorities and health authorities seems more complicated than such a simple dichotomy would allow. The mutual dependencies of the health, education and social services and a consensus about the object of their activities (i.e. to meet children's special needs) do not preclude conflict over the means of achieving this nor the desire of one group to prevail over another in order to influence the way in which the goals are achieved. In fact the mutual dependencies and the power relationships between the three services with respect to children with special needs have been changed by the 1981 Education Act, so that one could expect conflict to occur as one group tries to exert its newly created power over another.

Bacharach and Lawler (1980) see organizations as being divided into various overlapping groups – work groups and interest groups – which form coalitions to enhance their power base or to exert influence on decisions. They argue that most interactions betweens groups in organizational settings are neither positive sum nor zero sum but 'mixed motive': 'A mixed motive situation encompasses elements from both positive and zero sum situations. In other words parties are simultaneously confronted with incentives to cooperate and incentives to compete. However, Bacharach and Lawler see such cooperation and competition as part of the struggle to gain or retain power and influence and not as a result of conflict of perspectives or approach to a common task. Conflict and power struggles are not ends in themselves but are part of the process of achieving a common task so that within this framework the specific policy content and the formal organizational context will play a significant role in the way in which bargaining and negotiation take place.

Policy implementation cannot be seen as a simple linear top-down process, but as a political process involving negotiation, bargaining and compromise by those groups who are affected by it. The relative autonomy and the power of these groups are part of the wider structure of power relationships within central and local government, and between local-level agencies such as LEAs, DHAs and SSDs. Bachrach and Baratz (1962, 1970) stress the importance of power and the mobilization of bias in decision making. This process operates continuously, and at all levels: (a) on central government over the nature and interpretation of policy and choices about allocating resources between policy sectors; (b) on local government concerning the local policy and priorities; (c) on individual working decisions at the level of administrative, and professional practice with children and parents. Ultimately special education policy is made real (Weatherley would say made) by the action of individual workers within the authority – the doctors, teachers, psychologists and others – who together with local administrators make decisions about the way in which children's special needs are defined and met.

So our model of the policy process must take account of the impact of structural factors such as central local government relations, the powers and duties of local authorities, the influence of different and sometimes incompatible government policies (especially financial policy) together with the influence of local factors such as the political complexion of an authority, demography, and the historical pattern of service. It must also look at the negotiation and bargaining processes and the way in which policies are formulated within local authorities, where policies require new ways of working in order to implement or adapt to the directives of central government. It is necessary to identify decision makers and policy-making procedures within local authorities and health authorities and the levels at which decisions are made which effect the delivery of special education.

A key to understanding the way in which the policy process develops is the behaviour of interest groups which crystallize round common causes or needs. Ultimately the key indicator of the outcome of the policy process is the way in which individual clients experience the service, the way in which their needs are met. We therefore follow Whitmore (1984) in taking an 'action focus', whilst bearing in mind the influence of the interest structure and context within which interests operate. It is important to stress that a description of organizational structures, relationships and interest groups provides the background for the study of action – the decision making which establishes new administrative structures and procedures and the context for individual administrative and professional decisions relating to clients. None of these on its own would be sufficient to provide an overall model.

To understand the impact which the 1981 Education Act has had on the emergence and delivery of policy we must make sense of behaviour which occurred over time but did not occur in a simple process of cause and effect namely:

1. the developments in ideas and practices which led to changes in the dominant policy paradigm for special education;
2. the consultations (bargains and negotiations) between the Government and professional, local authority and parent/voluntary associations;

3. the process of design and the passage of the Act and associated Regulations and Circulars and Guidance through the civil service and Parliament;

4. the dissemination of government information, and the negotiated interpretation of the legislation with local authorities, professional associations and parent/voluntary groups;

5. the way in which local authorities, DHAs and professionals respond to the new legislative framework;

6. the dissemination of local authority information about its response to the legislation;
   possible adaptations in local authority and DHA arrangements and processes in response to the new framework of interorganization dependency;

8. the working practices of 'street level' administrators and professionals working with children and parents;

9. the way in which children and parents experience the special education service.

Table 2.1 illustrates the dimensions and stages involved as new policies emerge and are clarified, modified and implemented. What emerges from this process is a *progressive focusing* whereby the issues involved in the implementation of policy became *'increasingly solidified'*, to use Hill's (1981) term, in a sequence of clarification, *a policy–implementation chain*. There is no clear cut-off point where policy making stops and implementation begins. Government policy for special education is the product of definition and redefinition and the 1981 Act has become just one of the structural conditions or constraints within which local education authorities and professionals evolve their own policies about meeting special educational need. It is the continual negotiation between the actors and interest groups at all these levels which leads to changes in consensus about the policy paradigm and creates the conditions in which changes in government policy and legislation emerge. Could it be that somewhere in both the DES and the DHSS there are files marked 'The 1981 Education Act: Possible Amendments'; and will those putative amendments be the same in each Department?

Table 2.1 Progressive focusing and the development of special education policy, 1970–1985

Stages of policy development	Focus of activity	Interests involved	Constraints on action	Action
Changes in policy paradigm	local	professionals, administrators, voluntary organizations	present practice, ideas & provision	Warnock Committee set up
consultation prelegislation	local to central	professionals, administrators voluntary organizations, DES, DHSS	present practice LEA structures, professionals	Warnock Report; White Paper
legislation	central	civil service, government pressure groups	other government policies, LEA/DHA/SSD structures, Warnock Report, 'public' opinion	1981 Act
interpretation	central to local	ministers, civil servants, administrators, professionals	legislation, other government policies, LEA/DHA/SSD structures & funding, professional & public opinion	draft circulars & regulations
statutory instruments, circulars of guidance	central to local	DES, DHSS LEA, SSD, DHA	legislation, other government policies, local government practice & funding, professional & public opinion	issue regulations & circulars
dissemination & interpretation, negotiation	central and local	DES/HMI/ DHSS, LEA/DHA/ SSDs, voluntary organizations	1981 Act, regulations, circulars, local government structures, professional & public opinion	seminars, conferences, letters etc

LEA/SSD/ DHA policy appraisal and formulation	local	LEA, SSD, DHAs, professions, 'members', voluntary organizations,	legislation etc., local service structures, professions, public opinion	policy adaptation
local authority dissemination, interpretation, negotiation	local	'members' 'officers', professions, voluntary organizations schools, parents	legislation etc., local service structures & policies	directives, INSET etc.
structural and procedural change	local	'officers' professions, clients	legislation etc., other government & LEA policies	adaptation of structural procedures
professional/ client interface	'street'	professionals, administrators, clients	legislation local procedures, resources	service delivery

REFERENCES

Aldrich, R. and Leighton P. (1985) *Education: time for a new Act?* Bedford Way Papers, No. 23, Heinemann, London

Bacharach S.B. and Lawler E.S. (1980) *Power and Politics in Organisations,* Jossey Bass, London

Bachrach P. and Baratz M.S. (1962) The two faces of power, *American Political Science Review,* No. 56, 947–952

Bachrach P. and Baratz M.S. (1970) *Power and Poverty: theory and practice,* Oxford University Press, New York

Barker, A. (1981) *In on the Act,* BBC Radio programme, 17 November

Barrett, S. and Hill, M. (1984) Policy, bargaining and structure in implementation theory: towards an integrated perspective, *Policy and Politics* Vol. 12, No. 3, pp 219-240

Central Advisory Council for Education (1967) *Children and their Primary Schools* (Plowden Report), HMSO, London

Department of Education and Science (DES) (1975) *The Discovery of Children Requiring Special Education and an Assessment of their Needs,* Circular 2/75, HMSO, London

Department of Education and Science (DES) (1978) *Special Educational Needs* (Warnock Report), Cmnd 7212, HMSO, London

Department of Education and Science (DES) (1980) *Special Needs in Education* (White Paper), Cmnd 7996, HMSO, London

Department of Education and Science (DES) (1981) *Education Act 1981* Circular 8/81, HMSO, London

Department of Education and Science (DES) (1983a) *Assessments and Statements of Special Educational Needs,* Joint Circular DES 1/83, LAC (83)2, HC(83)3, HMSO, London
Department of Education and Science (DES) (1983b) *The Approval of Special Schools,* Circular 6/83, HMSO, London
Evans, J. (1984) Researching the welfare network. Paper given at the BERA Conference
Hannon V. (1983) Education: some forms of legal redress outside the courts, *British Journal of Educational Studies,* Vol. XXXI, No.3, October
Hill, M. (1981) *The policy–implementation distinction: a quest for rational control?* In S. Barrett and C. Fudge (Eds) (1981) Policy and Action, Methuen, London
Kirp, D. (1982) Professionalisation as policy choice: British special education in comparative perspective, *World Politics,* Vol. XXXIV, No. 2, pp 137–174.
Knoepfel, P. and Weidner, M. (1982) Formulation and implementation of air quality control programmes: patterns of interest consideration, *Policy and Politics,* Vol. 10, No. 1, pp 85–109
Lukes, J.R. (1981) *Finance and policy making.* In W. Swann. (Ed.) (1981) The Practice of Special Education, Oxford University Press, Oxford
Lukes, S. (1974) *Power – a radical view,* Macmillan, London
Shipman, M. (1984) *Education as a Public Service,* Harper & Row, London
Swann, W. (1985) Is the integration of children with special needs happening?: an analysis of recent statistics of pupils in special schools, *Oxford Review of Education,* Vol. 11, No.1
Weatherley, R. (1979) *Reforming Special Education: policy implementation from state level to street level,* M.I.T. Press, Cambridge, Mass. and London
Weatherley, R. and Lipsky, M. (1977) Street level bureaucrats and institutional innovation: implementing special education reform, *Harvard Educational Review,* Vol. 47, No. 2, pp 171–197
Welton, J. (1981) Two problems in the study of social policy with special reference to education, *Research in Educational Management and Administration,* BEMAS
Welton, J. (1982) Implementing the 1981 Education Act, *Higher Education,* Vol. 12, No. 5, pp 597–607
Welton, J., Wedell, K. and Vorhaus, G. (1982) *Meeting Special Educational Needs: the 1981 Education Act and its implications.* Bedford Way Papers, No. 12, Heinemann, London
Whitmore, R. (1984) Modelling the policy/implementation distinction: the case of child abuse, *Policy and Politics,* Vol. 12, No. 3, pp 241–267
Whittington, C. (1983) Social work in the welfare network: negotiating daily practice, *British Journal of Social Work.* Vol. 13, pp 265–286
Young, Baroness (1980) Address to the White Paper Conference, University of London Institute of Education, 28 November

TOPICS FOR DISCUSSION

1. With reference to the 1981 Education Act, discuss how its implementation may be seen as a political process involving negotiation bargaining and compromise between vested interests.

2. 'The question arises as to how far the Warnock Committee recommendations were reflecting real trends in professional and administrative opinion and how far they were flying a kite for their preferred option from amongst a range of ideas and practices.' Discuss with reference to the contention that 'power operates in such a way as to exclude certain points of view so completely that they are not seen as part of the debate' (Lukes, 1974).

3. 'In a field such as special education, legislation cannot easily change professional and, we might add, administrative attitudes and behaviour.' Discuss with reference to the range of local authority responses to the 1981 Education Act cited by the authors in their study.

SUGGESTIONS FOR FURTHER READING

1. M. Peter, (1984) A hard Act to follow, *Times Educational Supplement,* No. 3535, 30 March, p.23. The author argues that by allowing the 1981 Education Act to concentrate on time-consuming and costly procedures of assessing and making statements for the estimated 2 per cent of children with severe or complex learning difficulties, and at the same time refusing to give extra money for meeting the law's demands, the Government has virtually ensured that the Act's wider intentions go unmet. Indeed, she writes, the needs of *most* of the children it was supposed to help are being submerged under a welter of bureaucracy.

2. J. Welton, (1982) Implementing the 1981 Education Act, *Higher Education,* Vol. 12, No. 5, pp 597–607. The article examines factors affecting the development and implementation of policy with reference to the 1981 Act. The author identifies six professional and administrative factors: (1) the nature of the professional domain of special education assessment, (2) competing definitions of special educational need and good practice, (3) the concern for professional and administrative accountability, (4) the concern for the rights of users of special education provision, (5) the politicization of special education through the development of interest groups, and (6) the market relations between supply and demand in special education provision.

3. J. Welton, K. Wedell, and G. Vorhaus, (1982) *Meeting Special Educational Needs: the 1981 Education Act and its implications,* Bedford Way Papers, No. 12, Heinemann, London. A very useful account of the background to the 1981 Education Act which concentrates on the functions of special education legislation. Chapter 2 describes the authors' research project on the assessment of special educational needs and chapter 3 outlines the implications of the research findings for the implementation of the 1981 Education Act. Of particular interest is the discussion of the implications for the analysis of decision making.

Reading 3
THE POLITICS OF INTEGRATION IN ENGLAND
L. Barton and S. Tomlinson

In England the integration on mainstreaming of children previously categorized and transferred out of normal and into special education has currently created an important educational debate. In common with other Western industrial countries which initially developed segregated provision for those known as handicapped, exceptional or special, England now appears to be making moves to dismantle separate provision and educate both normal and special, if not in the same classroom, at least in the same building or on the same campus. The ideological justification for integration is, interestingly, exactly the same as the original justification for segregation – it is one of 'benevolent humanitarianism' or 'doing good to individual children'. Whereas only seven years ago the needs of handicapped children were apparently best served by separate provision (DES, 1975) now the children's needs are apparently best served by integrated provision (DES, 1980).

This chapter seeks to explore some of the motives behind the moves towards integration in England. It starts from the assumption that integration is not solely the product of benevolent and enlightened attitudes to children. The motives are rooted in economic, professional and political vested interests. The treatment meted out to those who, in post-Warnock Report terminology, are considered to have 'special educational needs' (DES, 1978) may well be enlightened, but it also involves the social categorization of a relatively weak or powerless social group whose lives are very much affected by professional and political decisions. The motives behind integration, just as those behind segregation, are a product of complex social, economic and political considerations which may relate more to the 'needs' of the wider society, the whole education system and professionals working within the system, rather than simply to the 'needs' of individual children.

This kind of analysis is currently not popular in England (see Warnock, 1982). There is considerable reluctance to examine special education as a social and political process rather than as an individualized process. But, more and more children will in the future be considered to have 'special needs'. The suggestion in the Warnock Report that in future some 20 per cent of school pupils may have 'special needs', rather than the 2 per cent officially in special education up to 1981, appears to have become an

L. Barton and S. Tomlinson (1984) *The politics of integration in England.* In L. Barton and S. Tomlinson (Eds) Special Education and Social Interests, Croom Helm, London

accepted 'truism' among many policy makers and practitioners. This means that, while in the past under 200,000 children were deemed suitable for a 'special' education, in the future some 1.5 million children may receive some kind of 'special' education. So it is important to move away from the individual to social perspectives. Changes in the forms, organization and provision in special education are not the result of mysterious processes of evolution nor benevolent adaptations; the changes in the law relating to special education (Education Act 1981), and in moves towards integrated provision, are the result of decisions by government and by professionals who may, as in most educational processes, have other interests in mind than the 'needs' of the children and their parents. The early 1980s have seen considerable political manoeuvring between central and local education authorities and between different professional groups involved in special education (particularly medical, psychological and teaching personnel), and the forms the new integrated provision will take will be a product of these manoeuvres.

To assist understanding as to why an 'integration debate' is occurring in Britain, this chapter first briefly documents the emergence of segregated provision and the 'categories of handicap'. The second section documents some different and contradicting conceptions of integration. The third section points to the naïveté and ambivalence present in the debate, and points out that special education, like other parts of the education system, is about social control and social engineering as much as about individual self-fulfilment. The final section argues the case that any pursuit of integration must also include an informed and sustained critique of those prevailing aspects of the education system that will impede the realization of such goals.

SOCIAL ORIGINS

The literature documenting the emergence of provision tends to stress the 'charitable' and the 'good' and often creates the impression of spontaneous development from humanitarian matters.

> As with ordinary education, education for the handicapped began with individual and charitable enterprise. There followed in time the intervention of government, first to support voluntary effort and make good deficiencies through state provision, and finally to create a national framework in which public and voluntary agencies could act in partnership to see that all children, whatever their disability, received a suitable education. (DES, 1978, p. 8)

In fact, the development of special education owed more to economic considerations, to professional vested interests and, from the beginnings of compulsory state education in 1870, to the needs of the normal education system to function unimpeded by 'troublesome' children (see Tomlinson, 1982, chapter 2).

Economic considerations have always been paramount in the development of special education. A permanent dilemma has been how to make sure that as many as possible of the handicapped grow up productive or, if that is not possible, how to provide as cheaply as possible for their care. Thus, the first Commission of Enquiry into the education of the handicapped in England, The Egerton Commission, 1884–89 had a frankly economic purpose:

The blind, deaf and educable class of imbeciles, if left uneducated become not only a burden to themselves but a weighty burden on the State. It is in the interests of the State to dry up the minor streams which must ultimately swell to a torrent of pauperism. (Egerton Commission, 1889, introduction)

The move towards segregating children in special schools came during the 1890s, but the Chancellor of the Exchequer himself expressed fears that, if too much money was made available for 'defective' children, too many local authorities 'especially in Ireland' would discover large numbers of such children (quoted in Pritchard, 1963). The same economic considerations which governed segregated provision now constrain integrated provision. A government White Paper on *Special Needs in Education* (DES, 1980) referred more often to 'present economic circumstances' than to special needs.

Professional vested interests have also shaped the development of special education in Britain. Its history is marked by professional rivalries and hostilities between medical, psychological, educational administrative and educational teaching personnel. The medical profession, struggling for recognition during the nineteenth century, enhanced its interests by claims to control the education of the 'defective'. The profession of psychology developed much of its professional mystique by claims to control the mental testing which developed post-1913 in Britain. Hostilities between medical and psychological personnel continued up to 1944, when medical officers were given the statutory right to 'diagnose' handicap and prescribe educational treatment, a right which they retain, although under the 1981 Education Act educational psychologists now have statutory duties in the assessment processes. The various needs and interests of the plethora of

Table 3.1 Statutory categories[a] of handicap, 1886–1981

1886	1899	1913	1945	1962	1970	1981 Suggested descriptive categories
Idiot	Idiot	Idiot	Severely subnormal (SSN)	Severely subnormal (SSN)	Educationally subnormal (severe) (ESN(S))	Child with learning difficulties (severe)
Imbecile	Imbecile	Imbecile				
		Moral imbecile		Psychopathic		
Blind		Blind	Blind		Blind	Blind
			Partially sighted		Partially sighted	Partially sighted
Deaf		Deaf	Deaf		Deaf	Deaf
			Partially deaf	Partially hearing	Partially hearing	Partially hearing
Epileptic		Epileptic	Epileptic		Epileptic	Epileptic
		Mental defective (feeble-minded)	Educationally subnormal		Educationally subnormal (mild or moderate) (ESN(M))	Child with learning difficulty (mild or moderate)
			Maladjusted		Maladjusted	Maladjusted
						Disruptive
					Special educational needs	
Defective		Physical defective	Physically handicapped		Physically handicapped	Physically handicapped
			Speech defect		Speech defect	Speech defect
			Delicate	Delicate	Delicate	Delicate
			Diabetic			
						Dyslexic? Autistic?

a. Categories suggested but never adopted include: the neuropathic child, the inconsequential child, the psychiatrically crippled child, the aphasic child and others. Autism and dyslexia were recognized under the 1970 Chronically Sick and Disabled Persons Act.
Source: Tomlinson (1982).

professional groups involved in special education can be clearly seen to operate in the current integration debate. Particularly, the teachers' unions are keen to defend the interests of their members. The National Union of Teachers does not want its members to have to face children who 'present insuperable problems in the normal school' (NUT, 1979).

But the crucial underpinning to the development of special education was the need for normal schools to function unimpeded by children who would not, or could not, conform to the normal routines of the classroom. Special education became a 'safety valve' for the normal system. The method of 'payment by results' to teachers, in operation until the end of the nineteenth century, ensured that children who could not or would not produce 'results' were excluded from normal schooling, and complex mechanisms of assessment and classification developed to rationalize the exclusion.

Table 3.1 illustrates the development of statutory categories of handicap from two in 1886, to eleven in 1945. The 1981 Special Education Act did officially abolish statutory categories, but the old labels appear to be remaining as descriptive categories. The Education Act of 1944 had, of course, enshrined the notion of selection by 'age, aptitude and ability' for particular types of schooling and this provided a continuing rationale for the segregation of handicapped children. During the period 1945–81 the numbers of children segregated in special schools increased dramatically. Booth (1981) provides an interesting discussion of this increase (from some 47,000 in 1950 to 135,000 in 1977), and points out the ambivalence of policy makers, who could insist that the 'planned and sensible integration of handicapped children in ordinary schools should continue' (DES, 1980, p. 9) while at the same time publishing statistics which showed that placements in special schools and classes had increased. Booth also points to the considerable increase in 'special' provision, which until the 1981 Act did not officially fall within the 'special' remit – for example, the growth of disruptive units. Categorizing more and more children out of the normal education system and into some form of special education is obviously functional for the normal education system and the question can be raised as to *why* an integration debate is taking place at all.

DILEMMAS OF INTEGRATION

Central government, represented by the Department of Education and Science (DES), has always demonstrated considerable ambivalence towards the idea of integration in England. This ambivalence reflects the political nature of decisions to segregate some children away from mainstream education, and thus exclude them from even attempting the kind of credential-oriented education which brings occupational success, mobility and advancement in industrial society. After all, the result of a 'special' education is that children are destined for a 'special' life-career in terms of employability, self-sufficiency and dependence. The rise of comprehensive education in the 1960s brought the dilemma into the open.

DES ambivalence is illustrated in Acts, Circulars and Recommendations over the past 30 years. A major claim in the recent integration debate is that 'integration is not new' – a clause in the 1944 Education Act enabled children to receive their special education in ordinary schools. However, as Parfitt pointed out in 1975, although 'the DES has always maintained that special education should be a second choice,. [...] the chances are at present that ordinary schools will not provide satisfactory (special) education' (Parfitt, 1975, p. 12). A year later, in 1976, a Labour government included in the 1976 Education Act a clause (in Section 10) requiring that pupils should only be given education in special schools in certain circumstances, but this clause was never implemented. DES ambivalence was further reflected in the White Paper of 1980, which preceded the 1981 Act: 'The Government takes as its starting point the principle that children and young people who have such needs should be educated in association with those who do not...' (DES, 1980, p. 13). However, later on the same page, this 'starting point' is qualified: 'For some children with special needs association, or full association, with other children is the wrong solution, and to impose it would be unfair to the child, his parents, other children and the taxpayer' (ibid.). This ambivalence results from contradictory educational, social and economic pressures. Egalitarian beliefs have, over the past 20 years, worked strongly in England towards the idea of educating all children within a common school – not selecting out for brightness or dullness, talent or handicap. Indeed, Mary Warnock herself was of the opinion that:

> It will gradually come to be expected that ordinary schools must expect to cater for very many more special needs, and that the whole concept of children with peculiar needs (or indeed peculiar talents) must be a natural part of the comprehensive ideal. (Warnock, 1980)

Lecturers who designed an Open University course on Special Educational Needs (Open University 1981) are also strongly committed to the development of comprehensive schools in which *all* children are educated regardless of 'capabilities, background, interests or handicap' (Booth and Potts, 1983, p. 26). But these beliefs are equally counterbalanced by traditional pressures for selecting out an elite for high-status education, or for selecting out those who are thought to impede the academic-type curriculum offered in comprehensive schools.

Similarly, the ambivalence can be traced to the familiar economic consideration that special education, whether offered in segregated or integrated provision, should not cost too much. There is certainly some indication, post-1981, that some local authorities are interpreting the 1981 Education Act as a licence to close special schools and place children in normal schools without offering money or resources, an 'integration on the cheap' feared by the teachers' unions (NUT, 1979, p. 12). The whole mechanism for the assessment of children with special needs – only children with severe difficulties being recorded via a statement – invites a rhetoric that the 'special needs' of large numbers of children are now being catered for in ordinary schools. The reality may be that no finance or resources are being offered to the schools either to 'discover' or to cater for these needs.

A further dilemma of integration which is implicit in the current debate at central and local level, and in the contributions by professionals and practitioners in both normal and special education, is that the old 'categories of handicap' and the new 'children with special needs' in fact include large numbers of children whom normal schools wish to exclude at all levels of integration. The NUT spoke of 'particular groups of pupils – particularly the severely maladjusted and those of extremely limited ability – who may present insuperable problems for teachers in the ordinary classroom situation' (ibid., p. 14).

The notion of 'children with special needs' conflates what we have here termed 'normative' conditions with 'non-normative'. That is, there can be some normative agreement about certain categories of handicap or need – such as blind, deaf, epileptic, severe mental handicap. These conditions affect children in families from all social classes and occupational groupings. On the other hand, categories such as educationally subnormal, maladjusted, disruptive are not normative. There are no adequate measuring instruments or agreed criteria to decide on these particular categories – for example, the inclusion of children in a category of 'disruptive' depends on value-judgements, and there can be legitimate arguments between professionals, parents and others as to what constitutes the category. Kennedy (1980) has pointed out that 'the normal state against which we measure abnormalities is a product of social and cultural values'.

In England these non-normative categories have always included the largest numbers of children in special education, the important point being that these children are predominantly of working-class origins, and, since the settlement of West Indian immigrants, have also included large numbers of black children. Thus, a major dilemma in the integration debate is that it is predominantly about the 'integration' of children who in England were known in the 1930s as 'the social problem class' (Burt, 1937), and this raises questions about the nature of special education – how far is it 'education' and how far is it 'social control'? The literature produced so far documenting 'integration' in England gives little indication that there are wider social and political implications. A visitor from abroad, coming uninformed, would receive the impression that an unproblematic, humanitarian process was taking place in the education system which was solely about provision and resources.

Underpinning the dilemmas as to whether and why integration is taking place, how expensive it will be, and who is being integrated or segregated are debates about the actual meaning of integration. Definitions of the term are numerous, but most recent ones start from the assertion in the Warnock Report that integration is 'directly in line with the principle that handicapped and non-handicapped children should be educated in a common setting as far as possible' (DES, 1978, p.100), and that there are 'three main forms of integration'. These forms are locational integration (special units or classes on the same site as an ordinary school, or in the same building); social integration (where locational integration takes place plus social interchange); and functional integration (in which special children join their peers on a part- or full-time basis). The Warnock Report was, of course, accepting the humanitarian assumption that integration *per se* is a 'good thing' and the major discussion should concern implementations, and indeed the Report described a range of alternative forms of provision ranging from complete segregation to short periods of 'exclusion' in ordinary schools.

Taking their cue from this assumption, two major recent research studies funded by the Government have focused on optimum provision for integration, and description of 'what is happening' (Brennan, 1981; Hegarty and Pocklington with Lucas, 1982). Brennan started from the assumption that 'the Warnock Report has identified the conditions associated with effective provision for children with special needs in ordinary schools' (p. 19) and his work was mainly concerned with documenting attempts by particular schools and LEAs to integrate. Similarly, special education journals in Britain, notably *Special Education – Forward Trends,* now routinely include articles describing attempts at 'integration'. Hegarty and his colleagues at the National Foundation for Educational Research (NFER) have reported a study as to how integration is being interpreted and put into practice in 17 LEAs. In a useful discussion they noted that the concept is complex and dynamic, and that 'it has evolved from simple opposition to placement, to encompassing a variety of arrangements in ordinary schools'. However, they also point out that 'integration is not a self-evident goal and must be justified in a rational way' (Hegarty and Pocklington with Lucas, 1981, p. 14). Although the NFER studies are of very real value in documenting the varieties of 'integration' currently being developed, descriptive studies do not give much scope for discussion of conflicts that may be inherent in the processes, and of the vested social and professional interests that various forms of integration or segregation may be serving.

There is, in existing literature, very little discussion as to why integration has become a popular process; any notion that the concept may be problematic – may be serving other interests than that of the 'good of the children' – is conspicuously absent. Conflict, difference of opinion, vested interests, have been laundered out of much of the writing on integration.

There are, however, some signs of a critical literature developing (see Barton and Tomlinson, 1981). Booth (1981) has provided a critique of what he calls 'the authorised version of events' (p. 290). He ironically observes that, while central government has made noises for 20 years concerning integration, segregated provision has grown dramatically, and certainly up to 1981 'indicated a general movement towards increasingly segregated forms of educational provision'. If the integration principle was really accepted 'we would anticipate teachers and policy makers trooping off to witness examples of good practice [...] We would find adminstrators eagerly reallocating money [...] We should be witnessing a careful costing of alternative schemes' (p. 300). Booth also examines some of the pressures which may work against the current enthusiasm for integration, notably the press for accountability: 'If teachers are to be held directly responsible for the progress of their pupils, then they may be increasingly willing to separate children they consider to have "real" intractable problems from those amenable to "ordinary" teaching' (pp 309-10). Thus Booth begins to probe some of the contradictions inherent in the notion of integration, and to point out that it is not an unproblematic concept. Dilemmas over the process of 'integration' are perhaps better recognized in other European countries, and even more so in the United States, where 'mainsteaming' has provided a focus for a large amount of critical literature (Sarason and Doris, 1979; Ysseldyke and Algozzine, 1982).

The 1981 OECD report on *The Education of the Handicapped Adolescent* maintains that, whilst there are many who agree in principle with the aims of integration, there are divisions of thought in terms of practical objections concerning its implementation, to the extent that:

> Some of them see the social objectives of integration as incompatible with providing high quality special education for children with disabilities and significant difficulties. Others see the degree of differentiation required of ordinary schools as impossible to achieve. Many see the social objectives as paramount and the achievement of educational standards of secondary importance. (p. 139)

In the United States, Sarason and Doris (1979) contend that many schools are unprepared to deal with mainstreaming; some undertake the minimal requirements and those pupils labelled mentally retarded are benefiting least from such programmes. Strain and Kerr (1981), in a major examination of research findings in the United States, argue that a careful survey of the literature indicates that, as far as mainstreaming is concerned, 'no operational definition exists' and they ask 'what types of educational practices actually do qualify as mainstreaming' (p. 77). Ysseldyke and Algozzine (1982) have considered some of the factors that impede mainstreaming, notably teacher attitudes and public funding. In the American literature there is certainly more recognition that integration, at the levels of both conceptualization and implementation, is characterized by ambiguity, contradiction and conflict.

A MISPLACED VISION?

Any adequate understanding and explanation of the issues relating to special education must look beyond the individuals who are considered as having 'special needs', to the types of institutional and political arrangements that fundamentally influence the ways in which such minority groups are treated. By critically examining some of the presuppositions that characterize a great deal of the approaches in this sphere of human experience, we can begin to identify limitations and hope to seek for more appropriate and inevitably fundamental changes.

Supporters of integration use a variety of arguments to justify their position. These include: a belief in an integrated society, one in which the handicapped, by right, share in the privileges and opportunities available; a belief that the educational system is one of the means that society provides for individual fulfilment and thus education is good for individuals; and a belief that successful processes of integration need not just sufficient resources but, more importantly, the right sorts of teachers in terms of skills and attitudes. The Warnock Report illustrates these beliefs, and in the chapter dealing with 'Special education in ordinary schools' the grounds for such practices are depicted as being part of a 'widely held and still growing conviction that, so far as is humanly possible, handicapped people should share the opportunities for self-fulfilment enjoyed by other people' (DES, 1978, p. 99) – in this instance, that which is allegedly enjoyed through participation in the normal educational system.

This claim may be part of a misplaced vision, the convictions of which demand closer inspection. It is a romanticism that ignores the inequalities and contradictions that are endemic not only to special education but, importantly, to both the educational system with which further association is being sought and the wider society in which it is located. Too much is being uncritically accepted.

Special education in England – its goals and development – cannot be analysed or understood in isolation from the ideologies and practices of comprehensive education. The abolition of the tripartite system of education which had developed out of the 1944 Education Act came about through strong egalitarian support for social and educational reform. This movement was based upon a number of important beliefs. First, education was seen in terms of an investment that would yield national and personal benefits, because a close relationship was envisaged between the products of the education system and the needs of industry (Dale, 1979). Second, in contrast to the tripartite system, comprehensive education would be involved in a greater development of talent which, importantly, would lead to greater wealth (Reynolds, 1981). Third, it was believed that the introduction of the comprehensive system of education would lead to the amelioration of inequalities of opportunity and thus reduce the social-class divisions within society (*Unpopular Education,* 1981). Even though for many pupils within the state system of education certain forms of early selection were removed with the introduction of the comprehensive school, competition and differentiation remained endemic to schooling. 'Ability' was still very narrowly conceived in terms of the cognitive with success via competitive, formal examinations legitimating such attitudes and ideology. The social and personal implications of such practices are powerfully brought out by Hargreaves in a discussion of the comprehensive school system:

> This very narrow definition of ability, grounded in the curricular evaluation of the cognitive-intellectual, has its effects on pupils. Ability labels are not seen by pupils as mere *descriptions* of part of their total set

of attributes as human beings; they are seen rather as generalized *judgements* upon them. Because the mastery of the cognitive-intellectual domain is so essential to success in school, ability labels carry rich connotations of pupils' moral worth. (1982, p. 62)

Examinations influence the nature of the curriculum and an essential part of the public accountability of teachers is viewed by many in terms of exam results, while the emphasis upon formal assessment is being strengthened via 'overt government and local authority initiatives [...] there is increasing pressure on schools from community and management alike for standards, for qualifications – for visible, quantifiable testimony of pupil achievement' (Broadfoot, 1981, p. 200). In the English school system success and failure are perceived in individualistic terms, with credentialism remaining a central feature of the school system. Some aspects of the curriculum are more highly valued than others, with high-status subjects being studied by the 'brightest', 'ablest' pupils, supported by the best staff and resources.

Social-class influence upon the quality and quantity of the education that pupils experience are still a potent force, and the vast majority of working-class children are amongst the failures or rejects of the school system. Discussing the way in which secondary schools fail abysmally to enrich the lives of these pupils, Hargreaves maintains that:

> To have dignity means to have a sense of being worthy, of possessing creative, inventive and critical capacities, of having the power to achieve personal and social change. When dignity is damaged, one's deepest experience is of being inferior, unable, and powerless. My argument is that our secondary schools inflict such damage, in varying degrees, on many of their pupils. (1982, p. 17)

Thus discrimination and stigmatization have become established within the formal school system. However, this should not be understood as a licence to blame teachers. They are under severe constraints themselves, particularly as schools (and thus their tasks) are constantly being expected to fulfil a very wide range of expectations (Grace, 1978). In addition, in a period of recession we are experiencing an increasing intervention on the part of the state, and this is not only at the ideological level in terms of a redefinition of educational goals (Salter and Tapper, 1981), but also in the sphere of cuts in public expenditure. Indeed a recent survey of schools by Her Majesty's Inspectorate (see *Times Educational Supplement*, 9 April 1982, p. 7) demonstrates clearly that the reductions in local authority spending are having their effect on teacher–pupil ratios, resources and general morale amongst staff, and the Report contends that:

To put it in a nutshell, many L.E.A's and schools are surviving financially by doing less; but they are often obliged to take the less in the form that comes easily to hand rather than shaping it to match educational priorities.

This type of decision making cannot be explained merely in terms of pragmatism and, even though there are inequalities in the actual allocation of cuts within and across local authorities and schools, a lesson to be drawn from such events is that educational values have little or no influence in such a process. The grounds for such decisions are to be found elsewhere, and the results of a cost-efficiency model in the reduction of teachers, the removal of certain subjects from the curriculum, as well as the lack of equipment and resources, have to be understood as part of the general encroachment and increased centralized control in the sphere of education. The state of the economy and the political will to support state schools are crucial determinants of needs, opportunities and resources.

Before attempting to draw out some applications to the issues of integration, this brief survey of some of the important aspects of 'ordinary' schooling needs to be viewed as supporting a major proposition with reference to the role of schools. In this analysis the educational system is seen as inevitably involved in a process of social engineering, and special education is crucially a part of this process. Teachers do contribute, consciously or unconsciously, to the reproduction of a particular form of society and the development of specific types of 'educated' people to meet the needs of such a society (Salter and Tapper, 1981). So, as Hargreaves (1982) notes, they must increasingly appreciate the social functions of schooling and be actively concerned with the sort of society they want to create or maintain.

THE POLITICS OF INTEGRATION

A great deal of the literature fails to offer any serious attempt to discuss the politics of integration. It is our contention that this must be given paramount attention because integration is inevitably concerned with social engineering via the education system.

Government policies for those with 'special needs', like other minority groups, are based upon contradictory ideologies. First, there is the need to control such groups by not allowing them to have any damaging effects in the spheres of culture and the economy. What constitutes the 'needs' of the 'special' is influenced by these intentions. At the same time there is the desire to protect the more severely 'handicapped' and this is expressed in policies of community care and equal opportunites – the handicapped supposedly experiencing the same rights and privileges as other members of the community or society. Policies are supposedly based on two principles, those of assimilation – the merging of a previously alien, rejected group into the wider society – and equality of opportunity – including the benefits that this affords. However, the policies are constrained by competition over priorities and competition over scarce resources. In the official documents on issues relating to integration the question of financial constraints is very evident, as can be seen from some of the concluding remarks in the government White Paper entitled *Special Needs in Education*: 'Only when the economic situation improves sufficiently will it be possible to bring to fruition all the committed efforts of those engaged in meeting special educational needs' (DES, 1980, p. 23). What is not acknowledged in this statement is that, given the arrival of economic recovery, special education will be but one group amongst a number competing for further financial support. It is also alarming to appreciate that, given the lack of financial resources, those that are available are distributed at the discretion of the local authorities, because, as Lukes points out, the 1981 Special Education Bill 'gives discretion to L.E.A.'s to provide *as much or as little as they want,* because the definitions of special educational needs and special educational provision are up to them' (1981, p. 319, our emphasis). There is now official legislative support to decide what is significant (and thus what is not) and to back that judgement with all the resources available that they feel are necessary. This will lead to inequalities of allocation within and across local authorities and thus the quality of the services available. Educational values may have little influence on future decisions made about 'special' education.

However, our major criticism of the movement for integration is motivated by our belief that it is based on a totally unwarranted optimism. Despite the claims in the Warnock Report about the privileges and opportunities in our society in which the 'special' or the 'handicapped' should share, there is a vast amount of research evidence to show that our society, and in this instance the school system, is characterized by gross inequalities. Historically, equality of opportunity has not and does not exist for large numbers of the populace, who both within and after school experience the personal, social and economic effects of failure.

We are not arguing here that integration is of no value, nor that there ought not to be demands for such practices. What we are seriously suggesting is that, given the inequalities within society at large, and given those dominant assumptions and practices that are firmly established in our school system, particularly at the secondary levels, if integration is to have any major significance, then the struggle for its realization must include a coherent, concentrated criticism of those unacceptable features of the education system and a demand for more fundamental social changes. To do less will mean that integration will lead to subordination in an already divisive system and be a further illustration of the way in which political rhetoric supercedes practice.

REFERENCES

Barton, L. and Tomlinson, S. (Eds) (1981) *Special Education: policies, practices and social issues,* Harper and Row, London

Barton, L. and Walker, S. (Eds) (1981) *Schools, Teachers and Teaching,* Falmer Press, Falmer

Booth, T. (1981) *Demystifying integration.* In W. Swann (Ed.) (1981) op.cit.

Booth, T. and Potts, P. (1983) *Integrating Special Education,* Basil Blackwell, Oxford

Brennan, W.K. (1981) Special education in mainstream schools: the search for quality, National Council for Special Education (NCSE), London

Broadfoot, T. (1981) *Towards a sociology of assessment.* In L. Barton and S. Walker (Eds) (1981) op.cit.

Burt, C. (1937) *The Backward Child,* London University Press, London

Dale, R. (1979) *The politicisation of school deviance: reactions to William Tyndale.* In L. Barton and R. Meighan (Eds) (1979) Schools, Pupils and Deviance, Nafferton Books, Driffield, England

Department of Education and Science (DES) (1975) *The Discovery of Children Requiring Special Education and an Assessment of Their Needs,* Circular 2/75, HMSO, London

Department of Education and Science (DES) (1978) *Special Educational Needs* (Warnock Report), Cmnd 7212, HMSO, London

Department of Education and Science (DES) (1980) *Special Needs in Education* (White Paper), Cmnd 7996, HMSO, London

Egerton Commission (1889) Report of the Royal Commission on the Blind-Deaf-Dumb and others, HMSO, London

Grace, G. (1978) *Teachers, Ideology and Control,* Routledge and Kegan Paul, London

Hargreaves, D. (1982) *The Challenge for the Comprehensive School,* Routledge and Kegan Paul, London

Hegarty, S. and Pocklington, K. with Lucas, D. (1981) *Educating Pupils with Special Needs in the Ordinary School,* NFER–Nelson, Windsor

Hegarty, S. and Pocklington, K. (1982) *Integration in Action,* NFER–Nelson, Windsor

Kennedy, I. (1980) Unmasking medicine, *The Listener,* 6 November

Lukes, J.R. (1981) *Finance and policy making in special education.* In W. Swann (Ed.) (1981) op.cit.

National Union of Teachers (NUT) (1979) Special educational needs: the NUT response to Warnock, NUT, London

OECD (1981) *The Education of the Handicapped Adolescent - Integration in the School,* OECD, Paris

Open University (1981) Special needs in education, Course E241, Open University Press, Milton Keynes

Parfitt, J. (1975) The integration of handicapped children in Greater London, Institute for Research into Mental and Multiple Handicap, London

Pritchard, D. (1963) *Education of the Handicapped, 1760-1960,* Routledge and Kegan Paul, London

Report of the Working Party on the Future of Special Education in Birmingham (1980) Education Committee, Birmingham

Reynolds, D. (1981) *The comprehensive experience.* In L. Barton and S. Walker (Eds) (1981) op.cit.

Salter, B. and Tapper, T. (1981) *Education, Politics and the State,* Grant McIntyre, London

Sarason, S. and Doris, J. (1979) *Educational Handicap, Public Policy and Social History,* Free Press, New York

Strain, P. and Kerr, M. (1981) *Mainstreaming of Children in Schools,* Academic Press, New York

Swann, W. (Ed.) (1981) *The Practice of Special Education,* Basil Blackwell, Oxford

Tomlinson, S. (1982) *A Sociology of Special Education,* Routledge and Kegan Paul, London

Unpopular Education (1981) Written by Members of the Centre for Contemporary Cultural Studies at the University of Birmingham, Hutchinson, London

Warnock, M. (1980) A flexible framework, *Times Educational Supplement,* 26 September p. 2

Warnock, M. (1982) Marxist spectacles, *New Society,* 11 March, p. 405

Ysseldyke, J.E. and Algozzine, B. (1982) *Critical Issues in Special and Remedial Education,* Houghton Mifflin, Boston

TOPICS FOR DISCUSSION

1. Discuss the authors' assertion that 'the *motives* behind integration, just as those behind segregation, are a product of complex social, economic and political considerations which may relate more to the "needs" of the wider society, the whole educational system and professionals working within the system than simply to the "needs" of individual children'.
2. In what ways may conceptions of 'integration' be different and contradictory?
3. What prevailing aspects of the present educational system will tend to impede the processes of integration?

SUGGESTIONS FOR FURTHER READING

1. S. Tomlinson (1982) *A Sociology of Special Education,* Routledge and Kegan Paul, London, chapter 3, 'Issues and dilemmas in special education'. The author examines important issues which have emerged in the 'special education' debate - categorization and selection, the rhetoric of special needs and integration.

2. R. Warner-Putnam (1979) Special education – some cross-sectional comparisons, *Comparative Education,* Vol. 15, No. 1. The article cites evidence to show that 'special education' tends to persist, in different ways, as a permanent subsystem of the educational system, and though appearing (by various forms of legislation) ready to be 'dismantled', the underlying functions and aims remain in spite of the changing rhetoric and ideologies.

3. W. Swann (1985) Is integration of children with special needs happening?: an analysis of recent statistics in special schools, *Oxford Review of Education,* Vol. 11, No. 1, pp 3-18. This research demonstrates that, whilst it is commonly supposed that there is an increasing trend towards the integration of children with special needs into ordinary schools, overall there is no evidence of a trend towards integration. There is evidence of integration in the case of children with sensory handicaps, but in the case of maladjusted children and those with learning difficulties there is clear evidence of a trend towards *increasing* segregation. The author also asserts that there is little indication that education authorities at either national or local level take the duty to integrate very seriously. This study examines figures for the years 1978-82 (the year of the publication of the Warnock Report to the year following the enactment of the 1981 Education Act).

    See also, W. Swann (1984) Statistics of segregation, *Childright,* No. 8, pp 18-19.

Reading 4
HOW SHOULD WE DEFINE 'HANDICAP'?
J. Wilson and B. Cowell

INTRODUCTION

In this article we want to put together two developments: first, some current assumptions of educational provision for children with special educational needs and, second, a style of research suggested by the work of some recent writers such as Harré (1974; Harré and Secord, 1972) Wilson (1972, 1981) and Winch (1958, 1970). We summarize below what we wish to say.

1. The way we define 'handicap' and similar terms depends on the social values prevailing in our society. These are likely to be (a) physical ability, (b) social competence and (c) intellectual performance. We attach much less value to qualities of character, such as patience and kindness, even though we do also believe in these.

J. Wilson and B. Cowell (1984) How should we define 'handicap'? *Special Education: Forward Trends,* Vol. 11, No. 2, pp 33-35

2. Instead of blindly accepting the three values and the criteria associated with them, we should look for rational criteria on which to base our definition of 'handicap'.

3. Education could be considered as such a criterion. However, the kind of education we provide is based on, and determined by, the same three values of physical ability, social competence and intellectual performance.

4. If, instead, we based education on values of character – rather than paying only lip-service to them – we would define 'handicap' differently. We would see it primarily in terms of emotional disability, instead of physical, social and intellectual impairment. It would be difficult – but not impossible – for teachers to establish and apply such criteria in schools.

5. Educational research has a role to play in identifying and making clear these, often hidden, values and criteria on which education provision is based and which influence policy makers, teachers and others. Unless educational research does this it will only reinforce our preconceived ideas about the ways children with special needs should be educated, or lead us to accept new assumptions which may not be more explicit than our existing ones.

CURRENT ASSUMPTIONS ABOUT 'HANDICAP' AND SPECIAL PROVISION

What counts as a handicap depends on the norms of the social group that uses the term and, in particular, on the activities or qualities which that group regards as normal or desirable. Most people do not question the prevailing criteria of success within their own milieu; they accept rather uncritically certain standards and prevailing social values. To find out exactly what these values are in our own society demands careful research but a useful starting point might be the following assumptions about values.

Physical ability is the criterion commonly used in relation to handicap since physical disadvantages are more obvious than others. More importantly, our society has no real belief in the greater value of the qualities of mind and spirit. A crippled body we understand; a crippled mind we understand in part; a crippled soul barely figures in our utilitarian terminology.

Social roles and competence will be valued – again, these are relatively obvious. We are concerned with whether or not a child can live a 'normal life' (determined in terms of social expectations), whether he is employable, whether he can 'mix well', whether he can take part in the activities current in our society.

Predictably *performance* or achievement is highly esteemed in our utilitarian culture. This may be self-evident, but we need to remember that states such as enjoying, contemplating, appreciating, loving or simply being content could also be used as criteria for being 'normal'. We think more naturally of academic success, careers and some kind of productive existence. Intellectual competence is our first criterion for the more able child; we may stretch this to performance in music and the arts but we do not stretch it much further. Ability to make friends, to care for others or to show patience towards others might be paid lip-service; but no more than that.

The use of any criteria can be challenged. But there are social defence mechanisms that might predispose us to dismiss such challenges to the values mentioned above. We can argue that it is much more difficult to identify advantages and disadvantages if we think of the mind, the heart and the soul than if we think only of the body, of if we try to rely on criteria which might be acceptable across cultures rather than those criteria of success which prevail in our own parochial society. We may point to the practical importance of achievement and of social competence, whatever our higher ideals may be. We may suggest that, to the child at least, such goals as physical achievement and having a job will – whatever our own values – count for more than anything else.

NEED FOR RATIONAL CRITERIA FOR 'HANDICAP'

There is some truth in all these responses but we should not blindly accept prevailing criteria or shirk the task of establishing the importance of some criteria as against others. We have to attempt to justify their importance on rational grounds, rather than blindly accepting the particular values current in our own society or social group. Unless we attempt to do this we simply reinforce social values acceptable at a particular time and impose them on the handicapped (who are the least capable of defending themselves from the consequences of such an imposition). We then need to ask whether or not culture-free criteria of 'normality' can be established on a rational basis rather than on the basis of what is acceptable in a particular society.

Our aim that we set out to *educate* all these children could be regarded as giving us some rational criteria at least. By contrast, if we lived in a primitive society we might be concerned with hunting animals in the forest and we might wish to single out the strong and swift as hunters and/or those who were likely to perish in the hunt unless given special support. But today we have the time, money and – apparently – the inclination to view children in a less obviously utilitarian light. We are concerned with their learning; not only with whether or not they have sound teeth, sufficient toys, colour television and non-polluted air. We ought to ask: 'Which children are "special" from an *educational* (not from a social, military, medical or economic) point of view?'

CONFLICTING VALUES IN WHAT WE TEACH

All this may seem obvious but it is a good deal less obvious than what we think the children ought to learn. We do not, when we think about it, actually believe that the criteria of social competence and achievement are as valid as we claim. In fact we would probably all admit that learning to make friends (very different from merely 'mixing well'), to love people, to enjoy the arts, to like some kind of work for its own sake (very different from accepting social criteria of employability) and similar achievements are much more worth learning than most of the stuff we put on timetables and in the curriculum. Thus our *actual* (and surely rational) beliefs about what is worth learning seem at odds with what we actually teach. We do not really think physical and social handicaps are of prime importance. The important handicaps are those which impede a child from learning (to put it briefly) to be a *person*, not from learning physical or social skills or academic or vocational achievements.

It may make little odds whether or not I have only one arm, whether or not I am paid for my work (I can still *work* – the concept of work is not tied to public or paid employment), or whether I can perform well at various academic or practical exercises. Those are not central to my personal, moral and spiritual qualities. Of course we can try to indoctrinate people into thinking that they are central; we can teach people (often by expressing the wrong kind of concern) that a person with only one arm or without a job is of less value than a person with only one friend or without a sense of humour. But that will depend on us and has little to do with being 'handicapped' in more important senses.

Our prejudices are compounded by the remarkable fact that most great educationalists in the past – and many today pay lip-service to this – have insisted that the education of character, personality, morality and the emotions are at least as important as either the 'academic' or the 'practical' side. But in practice most of our schools regard as 'normal' an educational regime in which pupils undergo a series of subject-based sessions throughout the day. This has the predictable result that, in so far as we identify pupils as handicapped or (sinister word) 'disturbed' in their emotions, character or mental health, we tend to pick on those pupils who find it hard to tolerate such an educational regime; those, in short, who cannot 'cope with' (another significant phrase) an educational system which we regard as 'normal'.

AN ALTERNATIVE APPROACH

If we could imagine an educational regime in which the development of character, the handling of emotions and personal interaction were genuinely valued as central, in which plenty of time was devoted to them and in which a serious attempt was made to foster and assess them, then what we should count as 'normal' and 'handicapped' would turn out very differently from what we do today. Emotional cripples would become identifiable, as physical cripples are now visible; different *kinds* of 'handicaps', 'advantages' and 'needs' would stand out from the ones we accept today.

It may be objected that identification of this kind is so much more difficult than the identification of more easily visible deficiencies of today's 'handicapped' children that we cannot be expected to change our attitudes. It may be argued that we can see well enough if a pupil is capable of playing games and doing his 'normal' school work but not if he is (say) unable to make friends or control his aggression or form relationships with the opposite sex. But, as these examples may suggest, our ability to apply such new criteria is quite adequate, provided we have enough opportunities in school life (and take them seriously enough) for these different qualities to become visible. Many teachers can recognize these qualities already but are short of time or energy to apply them as criteria because of curricular demands. The whole set-up may mask our own fears about the difficulties of educating pupils in any other way. These fears are largely groundless.

INFLUENCE OF SOCIAL VALUES ON INTEGRATION POLICY

The general ideas which guide our *treatment* of handicap flow from the socially acceptable criteria mentioned earlier. An illustration of how prevailing social (and questionable) values dominate what we do is the idea of integration. That it is good to 'integrate' is commonly accepted today. In a hierarchical society with established values and a highly visible class or status system, differences between one man and another are seen as inherently justified. When such a society comes under attack, or its individuals become disillusioned with its supposed justifications, *any* difference becomes tarred with the brush of unjustifiable privilege. There is a fear that, if A is distinguished from B by some criterion or other, the difference will be used to set up another hierarchy in which some are labelled as 'inferior' or 'failures' and others as the opposite; hence the only safe way seems to be to play down or mask or psychologically deny the differences. This is one of the main roots of egalitarianism; any division or separation is seen as threatening. The view that different classes and talents play different parts in a harmonious society – as envisaged, for instance, by Plato or illustrated by Menenius Agrippa's metaphor about the social body in Shakespeare's *Coriolanus* (I.1) – is taken as unsatisfactory, because of the potential conflict between parts. It is as if the only safe form of social justice ought to be based on equality and the rejection of any differences. The stress on 'society' and social competence (rather than on the autonomous and unique individual) contributes to these attitudes.

Plato may have been right, however, in so far as the placing of particular individuals in groups must logically depend on what the group is *for*. We select players for football teams by the criteria of football, university entrants by intellectual criteria, and so forth. If we are concerned with the education of children with special needs, the relevant criteria are educational; it is no good putting pupils who cannot add into a group learning advanced mathematics. What must count as a 'handicap' or 'advantage' here must depend on the purpose of the enterprise. Educational criteria are often vague and multiple, but they are not indefinitely flexible; when we want to mix or 'integrate' different types of individuals, we are still out to achieve some purpose – and that purpose will determine the type of 'mix'. Physical handicap is irrelevant to learning Greek but relevant to learning gymnastics; no sense, let alone justification, can be given to any general or overall ideal of 'integration' (or 'segregation').

THE ROLE OF EDUCATIONAL RESEARCH

If it is true, as we have argued, that what we in fact do with 'special' children – both in identifying them and in treating them – depends on our chosen values, what can educational research do about it? Clearly the chief task will be to clarify our assumptions about what is worth doing so that those who make and carry out policy and treatment will be more aware of and critical about the assumptions on which they are proceeding. But this clarification is a considerable task; it cannot be done from an armchair, and to that extent must be distinguished from the conceptual or linguistic analysis practised so vigorously at Oxford and elsewhere over the last half-century. It is more a kind of conceptual anthropology; we have to find out what principles and assumptions control the thinking (and hence the decisions) of those concerned; and that means interacting and conversing with them, not merely issuing them with questionnaires or seeing what they have to say in structured interviews. For, as we have said, the assumptions are often hidden, not only from the interviewer but from the person interviewed. Much time and effort are required to grasp the shape and style of a person's deepest thoughts, even on one particular issue or topic.

Enough research in the right direction has already been done to give grounds for confidence. Much of the appropriate methodology may best be worked out during the course of a particular project but it may be helpful here to comment on three strands of current work.

THREE RELEVANT APPROACHES

Clinical psychologists and psychiatrists, and some anthropologists, have been trying to discover their subjects' or patients' value assumptions. Their methods seem relevant although there are difficulties. For instance, in psychiatry or psychotherapy the therapist will try not only to understand but also to help the patient, which may often get in the way of a proper understanding of what we need to find out. Moreover, the data are too often fitted too hastily into some well known *theory* (e.g. Freudian). Perhaps most important of all for our purposes, there is no tradition of psychiatry dealing with patients' values or their attitudes to education or politics; it is concerned, as the therapists are, with the patients' close personal relations and their private lives, not with their views on education or handicap. It is this preoccupation, connected, understandably, with medical or curative interests, which has so far prevented psychiatry from bearing in any very direct way on lines of research that we consider useful.

Work inspired by Goffman (1959) and more recently by Harré (1974; Harré and Secord, 1972) often under the heading of 'ethnomethodology', seems to fit in better with what we have in mind. Harré makes the point that any serious research about human beings must pay great attention to how they conceptualize, to what goes on in their heads; they cannot be treated in the way that natural scientists treat their subject matter. Harré and his followers have been chiefly interested in social *behaviour*, however – what happens on the football terrace or in the classroom; they have, moreover, been strongly influenced by the idea that all or most social behaviour can be related to certain categories or models. Whatever the merits of these views, they do not fit our particular interests very well.

The work of one of the present authors and his followers, most evident in a recent investigation of how people think about discipline and moral education (Wilson, 1981), may be thought more obviously relevant; and so it is, in much of its general methodology. But Wilson's work seems to imply (1979, pp 71ff) that the researcher must first establish a 'proper' or 'rational' set of views and concepts about the research topic and collect opinions and concepts from his research subjects only in the light of that set. This works quite well where it is clear (as perhaps with 'discipline' it is) that there is a proper understanding of the concept. But there are many topics where this approach would be premature and might, indeed, be based on some socially accepted set of assumptions. In the case of handicap and 'special' children, it would be unwise to start from any *particular* view about identification and treatment; we need first to map out the views and concepts of people concerned with special education without any preconceived ideas about how they measure up, or fail to measure up, to the researcher's own pre-established picture.

This last point is central to any research of this kind, just as it is central to non-directive psychotherapy. If we are trying to find out how somebody else (even a particular author) thinks or feels, the only 'method' is to put ourselves in his shoes. Nothing is gained, and a lot lost, by seeing his thoughts and feelings in the light of certain extraneous standards (however reasonable); we have first to appreciate how thinking and feeling in the way he does is, from his viewpoint, understandable. We need virtually to take on his values and terminology, as a historian learns to speak with the voice of men of another age. Understanding depends on this and so does the possibility of communicating such understanding to the person himself. Research would indeed be in the worst sense 'academic' if it could not help people to see how they think, what presuppositions they are in the grip of, what concepts they are using (or abusing).

The whole process has a lot in common with the questioning and probing in Plato's Socratic dialogues and recent analytic philosophy, though we do need some psychological insight and understanding of what feelings underlie a person's concepts and commitments. The more orthodox, quasi-behaviouristic (or quasi-scientific) training and practice of so much educational research is not appropriate here. Unless research into special needs takes these methods seriously – in particular, the investigation of the *language* and *concepts* that we use – it is unlikely to do more than reinforce prevailing sets of social assumptions or – just as uselessly – unconsciously generate new ones.

REFERENCES

Goffman, E. (1959) *The Presentation of the Self in Everyday Life,* Doubleday, New York

Harré R. (1974) *Some remarks on 'rule' as a scientific concept.* In T. Mischel (Ed.) Understanding Other Persons. Blackwell, Oxford

Harré R. and Secord, P.F. (1972) *The Explanation of Social Behaviour,* Blackwell, Oxford

Wilson, J. (1972) *Philosophy and Educational Research,* NFER, Slough

Wilson, J. (1979) *Fantasy and Common Sense in Education,* M. Robertson, Oxford

Wilson, J. (1981) *Discipline and Moral Education,* NFER, Slough

Winch, P. (1958) *The Idea of a Social Science,* Routledge, London

TOPICS FOR DISCUSSION

1. The authors argue that if we based education on values of *character* we would define 'handicap' differently and see it primarily in terms of emotional disability instead of physical, social and intellectual impairment. What difficulties would face teachers trying to establish and apply such criteria in schools?
2. How far is it possible to establish 'culture-free' criteria of 'normality' on a rational basis rather than on what is acceptable in a particular society?
3. What are the implications for teachers of the authors' contention that 'no sense, let alone justification, can be given to any general or overall ideal of "integration" (or "segregation")'?

SUGGESTIONS FOR FURTHER READING

1. D. Hargreaves (1982) *The Challenge for the Comprehensive School,* Routledge and Kegan Paul, London. Hargreaves's book provides ample support for the contention that 'special education – its goals and development – cannot be analysed or understood in isolation from the ideologies and practices of comprehensive education' (see Reading 3). Hargreaves (p. 62) describes how competition and differentiation remain endemic to schooling and, because the mastery of the cognitive-intellectual is so essential to success in school, ability labels carry rich connotations of pupils' moral worth – an important underlying theme of Wilson and Cowell's argument.
2. D.N. Aspin (1982) Towards a concept of human being as a basis for a philosophy of special education, *Educational Review,* Vol. 34, pp 113-123. Aspin develops the assertion found in the Warnock Report that the handicapped have a right to education by virtue of being human beings.
3. R.A. Withers, (1983) Mary Warnock's 'doctrine of compassion' as a justification of special education, *Educational Review,* Vol. 35, No. 3 pp 220-224. In contrast to Aspin's discussion, the author argues that there is no 'doctrine of compassion' and that the most important consideration in deciding the treatment appropriate for many, though not all, handicapped persons is that they may attain a measure of independence.

THE CURRICULUM AND SPECIAL NEEDS

INTRODUCTION

Section 2 of the sourcebook addresses itself to the problems of designing appropriate curriculum and organizational structures for children with special needs. The difficulties involved are highlighted and emphasized by Brennan at the start of Reading 5:

There are pupils with special educational needs who do not require special curriculum; that does not mean their main curriculum should not be scrutinised in terms of their special needs. There are other pupils for whom special curriculum is essential, but it does not follow that they are unable to participate in main curriculum. A minority of pupils may be unable to participate in main curriculum; that does not necessarily mean that they cannot gain from the planned or hidden curriculum through interaction with other pupils. Such is the complexity encountered when considering design for special needs.

This reading consists of a detailed practical examination of the above quotation in which Brennan explores the various forms of handicap (defects of hearing, vision or mobility; educational disadvantage; significant learning difficulties; emotional or behavioural difficulties; multiply handicapped pupils) and very aptly poses a number of crucial questions with respect to each of the forms of handicap he discusses. This section is followed by a critical account of three approaches to general curriculum design for special needs: the objectives model, the process model and a model based upon situational analysis. Brennan reflects upon their particular strengths and weaknesses and is concerned with their applicability to the various kinds of special needs. The suggested further readings examine various aspects of curriculum provision for special needs dealing with academic organization, modification of curriculum content and classroom organization. The article by Swann takes a broader perspective and is particularly valuable for his critical appraisal of the 'behaviour objectives' model and the problems associated with this approach.

In Reading 6, Hegarty discusses the findings of an NFER study (1978–81) which was set up 'to examine in depth current provision for handicapped children in ordinary schools and to identify those factors which make for successful integration'. The article focuses on structural and organizational factors and the ways they impinge on the process of educating pupils with special needs in the ordinary school. Hegarty comments: 'The responding conclusion to emerge from this study is that integration *is* possible. Special educational needs can be met in the ordinary school, and to a far greater extent than is currently the practice.' The further readings suggested include the much more detailed full account of this research study by Hegarty *et al.* (1981), chapters 5–9 of which are particularly relevant to curriculum issues. Jones's article offers a very worthwhile discussion of the problems involved in setting up a resource department to cater for special needs, while Hodgson *et al.* consider the role of ancillaries and the effective planning involved to maximize liaison.

Reading 7, as its title indicates, presents a comprehensive checklist of practical questions to help schools and teachers who are considering the introduction of integration programmes. It covers, first, general questions and then seven specific areas: curriculum, staffing, school, child, family, social and physical considerations. The suggested readings in a sense 'answer' many of the questions raised in the NUT document by offering evidence of how teachers cope with the various problems which arise in attempting to initiate integration programmes. Of particular importance is Galloway's succinct exploration of the 'hidden curriculum' and the messages it conveys in relation to the school's policies and practices.

Reading 8 depicts the three most common forms of provision for low achievers in secondary schools: the 'special class', the extraction system and mixed-ability teaching. McCall proceeds to critically evaluate each form of provision, pointing out the suggested advantages and disadvantages for each type of arrangement. He argues that seldom is consideration given to more than one form of arrangement even though established information clearly suggests the need for a range of provision rather than any single dominant form. In the readings which support this article, Garnett argues that the Warnock concept of special educational need encourages the notion of a continuum of need rather than a series of pigeon-holes into which children have so far been uncomfortably and often inappropriately slotted. Such a radical change of emphasis, she asserts, demands an equally radical change of attitude across an educational system steeped in a tradition of selection and categorization. The other suggested readings support this viewpoint by a practical discussion of how curriculum principles need to be transformed in order that change can be effected.

Mary Warnock, in Reading 9, replies to the accusation that the authors of the Report deliberately included the phrase 'special needs' to cover up their conservatism and inertia with the veil of humanitarian-sounding claptrap. She maintains that the legislation concerned with the education of the handicapped must be ultimately humanitarian in its intention and spirit, rather than straightforwardly utilitarian. In retrospect, however, she finds the main reason for the newly apparent poverty of the concept of special needs is in its definition, or rather its lack of definition, since 'one of the main, indeed overwhelming difficulties is to decide *whose* needs are special, or *what* "special" means'. The suggested further readings are powerful counterblasts to this humanitarian perspective of special needs, written and lucidly argued from a 'conflict' sociological viewpoint.

Reading 5
DESIGN OF THE CURRICULUM
W. K. Brennan

DESIGN FOR SPECIAL NEEDS

There are pupils with special educational needs who do not require special curriculum; that does not mean their main curriculum should not be scrutinized in terms of their special needs. There are other pupils for whom special curriculum is essential, but it does not follow that they are unable to participate in main curriculum. A minority of pupils may be unable to participate in main curriculum; that does not necessarily mean that they cannot gain from the planned or hidden curriculum through interaction with other pupils. Such is the complexity encountered when considering design for special needs.

Defects of hearing, vision or mobility

In this group the assumption is that there are no complicating factors of serious intellectual or emotional problems, though there may be some retardation of educational progress and tension due to frustration arising from the additional learning demanded by the disability. Because their problems are considered to be the easiest the school may fail the pupils through too easy an assumption that they can find their own level in the main curriculum. In fact the answers to many questions are required if the balance of their curriculum is to be appropriate to their potential and realistically related to their anticipated future needs:

W. K. Brennan (1985) *Design of the curriculum.* In W. K. Brennan (1985) Curriculum for Special Needs, Open University Press, Milton Keynes

1. What would be the main curriculum balance in the absence of the disabilities?
2. What are the additional learning tasks involved in the management of the disability?
3. Does the disability involve any communication difficulty in the classroom?
4. How will the disability affect the time taken to complete any necessary written or practical work?
5. Will there be any problem of movement between learning situations?
6. What are the implications of questions 2, 3, 4 and 5 on the time available for learning the main curriculum?
7. If the time available involves main curriculum limitations, what is the possibility of restoring balance through extended education in school or college?
8. What are the long-term prospects for individual pupils in terms of career opportunities and are they likely to alter?
9. In the context of the answers to the above questions, what is the most desirable and practical curriculum balance?

A process of analysis similar to the above is essential if pupils in this group are to be appropriately and effectively educated. It is necessary at two levels – first, in terms of groups of pupils with similar needs, so that there is a framework available in the school; and second, in terms of individual pupils so that the necessary modifications of the framework may be identified relevant to each pupil. Some of the information required to answer the questions will be found in the records which follow pupils through education. Otherwise consultation may be necessary with previous schools, psychologists, specialist teachers, doctors or social workers, for good-quality information is essential if the questions are to be answered in a manner which will contribute to the formulation of an appropriate curriculum balance for each pupil.

Educational disadvantage

The psychological and social effects of the disadvantage are stressed for this group. However, the effect of inappropriate, inefficient or intermittent teaching cannot be overlooked as a source of educational failure which may also adversely affect attitudes to school. Specific teaching in basic subjects should attack the retardation and success there make a contribution to improving attitudes, though the latter will probably require attention to the organization and tone of the groups in which curriculum is delivered. Again there are questions which require answers:

1. What is the precise nature of the disadvantage and for how long has it operated?
2. How does it affect basic learning and what are the areas in which special needs are evident?
3. How are attitudes to school, teachers, learning and other pupils affected?
4. What previous efforts have been made to overcome the disadvantage and what was the degree of success?
5. What are the implications of answers to questions 1-4 for basic subject teaching, and to what extent will they require withdrawal from main teaching groups?
6. If withdrawal is necessary, how is it to be organized and how will it affect time available for main curriculum?
7. What is the arrangement necessary in order to secure the best balance between special needs teaching and main curriculum?
8. What changes, if any, are required in the organization or tone of teaching in order to improve attitudes to school?
9. What arrangements are necessary for monitoring or modifying curriculum and who is to be responsible for them?

The outcome of the analysis must gain the confidence of these pupils and demonstrate that they can be successful. To do this, basic teaching must be efficient as well as appropriate and must have the support of the broader planned curriculum. Hidden curriculum may have little influence at first, becoming influential only as the pupils' attitudes begin to change, self-concepts improve, and as they start to identify with the school and assimilate its values.

Significant learning difficulties

Pupils with significant learning difficulties may be usefully considered as two subgroups with different curriculum needs. First, there are pupils with extensive learning difficulties associated with general immaturity who require a curriculum continuously related to their developing special needs throughout their time in school: an *adaptive-developmental* curriculum (Brennan 1974, 1979). The final part of this chapter applies directly to that kind of curriculum, but what must be noted here is the importance of working out that special curriculum in detail so that it may be carefully related to main curriculum in order to identify special objectives attainable through main activities. The concept of a common core curriculum makes this procedure essential. Second, there are pupils without the immaturity of the first group, and with normal or near normal intellectual potential, who are at risk through specific difficulties affecting progress in basic academic skills or communication. Theirs is not the problem of educational disadvantage with psychological or social overlay; more a question of *learning disability*. Once that is realized, the questions posed for the educationally disadvantaged pupils are relevant to the needs of these pupils. In seeking the answers, the school will require access to refined assessment techniques closely related to specific, structured teaching techniques the definition of which should be the main purpose of the assessment. Most schools will require outside assistance with the assessment and possibly with the teaching procedure, but the responsibility for ensuring that specific teaching is conducted within an appropriate and balanced curriculum must remain within the school. Securing interaction with main curriculum should not be a major problem with these pupils, though in the early stages modified teaching may be required making allowance for their specific difficulties with reading and writing.

Emotional or behavioural difficulties

Pupils with emotional or behavioural difficulties raise the most serious problems for education because of the variety of causation, teaching and prognosis which they present. In terms of curriculum this is most marked, and it accounts for the limited literature on this aspect of their education (see Wilson and Evans, 1980, which contains an excellent review of literature; also Dawson, 1980, especially chapter 5). More than any other pupils these maladjusted children require what the Warnock Report (DES, 1978) identified as 'particular attention to the social structure and emotional climate in which education takes place'. Initially it is the extreme difficulty, if not impossibility, of teaching the pupils within the constraints of the ordinary classroom without detriment to other pupils which has led to their identification as pupils with special educational needs. At the heart of their problem is the degree of individualization necessary to meet their needs – individualization of adult–child relationships, of teaching methods of disciplinary demands, of pace and pattern of learning – yet within a context which maintains a sense of group cohesion sufficiently flexible to accommodate the changing moods of individual pupils. In this the teacher is paramount. Adults must be able to accommodate themselves to pupils without loss of control and guidance; be firm within friendship; chastise without rejection; apologize without loss of face; laugh without losing their sense of purpose: these qualities are essential if curriculum is to succeed. Whether or not the curriculum requires the same degree of individualization will depend on the range of learning potential and academic ability within the group, though there will be educational retardation at all levels. Even where a group curriculum is possible, fluctuations of mood and behaviour among pupils will require individualization of curriculum delivery and demand. Yet, even in the most varied and disturbed groups, there will be periods of relative calm and cohesion, however short, when pupils may be engaged in communal activities that contribute to group feeling and allow a gradual introduction of the kind of situation to which pupils must learn to accommodate if they are to participate in main curriculum.

The curriculum problem for these pupils is twofold, involving the objective of personal, emotional and social stability and then elimination of educational retardation. At one time it was thought that the personal–social aspects had to be resolved before basic learning could be attempted. More recently the therapeutic effects of successful learning have been recognized. and the result has been a broader approach to curriculum involving specific structured teaching (Haring and Phillips, 1962; Hewett, 1968). Thus the taught curriculum will concentrate on a carefully worked-out approach to basic skills utilizing small steps in order to ensure success, taking account of the short concentration periods of many pupils, and allowing work to be undertaken as and when individual pupils are receptive. It will go further: many pupils lack very basic, interpersonal social skills either because they fail to perceive other people in sufficient detail or because their perception is fluctuating and determined by their shifting moods. Perception can be improved and the basic skills can be taught through task analysis and prescriptive teaching of the type successful with basic academic subjects (Laslett, 1977, Tower *et al.,* 1978; Argyle, 1972; Flavell, 1968). In extreme cases the technique may be used to modify behaviour to the point where more open teaching and learning may begin. The scholastic and social skills established must then be generalized by the pupils in broad open situations.

These are tasks for the planned curriculum and for the aesthetic experiences of art, craft, music and movement, and the inspiration of the humanities and literature. Here, too, inputs may need to be of short duration and the background organization sufficiently flexible to allow teachers to take advantage of receptive phases of individual mood and group morale. Essential in this type of teaching is the accumulation of a wide variety of material for use in the classroom, in structured teaching or in more open sessions.

The hidden curriculum also presents problems when educating

maladjusted pupils. The egocentricity of individual pupils, together with fluctuating group morale, may introduce so great a lack of cohesion as to make the concept of a hidden curriculum inappropriate. Nevertheless the hidden curriculum can be a powerful influence for good which must not be abandoned. It may have to be planned for deliberately, either initially, or following breakdown of morale, or when new admissions to the group bring about qualitative changes. The probability is that the ethos of the group at any time will owe more to the adults involved than would be required or occur in a normal adult–child group. Consequently the pattern of adult relationships and behaviour will require close attention and analysis as part of overall curriculum input. Identical adult behaviour is not the objective – but adult consistency is necessary. Pupils should see adults behaving differently and yet become aware of consistent attitudes and values. Such a general model of relationships among adults may begin to transfer to the pupils, but it is also required as a consistent feature to which specific learning by the pupils may be referred as part of the process of generalization.

It is often argued that the wide individual differences among maladjusted pupils make the concept of the curriculum inappropriate. This is true only if the curriculum is seen as a structure determining the work of the teacher as he or she interacts with the pupils. If, on the contrary, the purpose of the curriculum is seen as ensuring the teacher is clear in mind about the aims and objectives appropriate for the pupils, then it assists the teacher in behaving with freedom in the classroom. It is the teacher who is clear in mind about what the pupils are to learn or assimilate who is best placed to react to their moods, motivations and interests in selecting appropriate materials and approaches while moving to clear objectives. With maladjusted pupils this is essential for successful education. Without it individualization loses its purpose and activity may lead nowhere.

Multiply handicapped pupils

The above groups are not independent or mutually exclusive. Blind pupils can have emotional or behavioural difficulties; pupils who require adaptive–developmental curriculum may also have specific learning difficulties; and among any of the major disabilities there will be pupils who are also educationally disadvantaged. Almost any serious disability generates secondary difficulties for the pupil which, though not sufficiently serious to rate as disability, interfere with learning to an extent to be taken account of when planning curriculum and teaching. The grouping of pupils is useful in facilitating discussion and in the developement of general curricula, but the interaction of disabilities and the secondary conditions generated by them make it essential that individual needs are carefully considered before curriculum is finalized and at each review.

Curricula intended to meet special educational needs must take account of different kinds of learning. Some learning can be considered as basic, essential and capable of definition in the precise terms that make it suitable for a behavioural approach. Other learning is more subtle, involving the emotions, judgement, or thought sequences leading to the solution of a problem. These are not simple 'can or cannot' entities but require to be approached, established, refined and generalized through interaction of mind and personality between the teacher and the taught. Other learning cannot be approached directly through the taught or indirectly through the planned curriculum: it must be assimilated through the pupils' total experience in the school, involving the hidden curriculum.

In relation to these varied forms of learning, pupils with special educational needs are no different from others. Where they differ is in the time taken from main curriculum by the necessity of meeting their special needs and the importance of maintaining a balance between these two aspects of curriculum. Further, because special needs are *personal,* meeting them shifts the balance between the personal and social aspects of curriculum, reducing the time available for the latter. So the special problem for teachers of pupils with special needs is one of how to establish and sustain the balance between main and special curriculum and between personal and social curriculum aims, plus, for some pupils, the question of ensuring that the hidden curriculum operates effectively. How this problem – one of curriculum priorities – might be approached is considered in the following section; a single solution is unlikely to be appropriate for all areas of the curriculum. The kind of learning required in different curriculum areas must be taken account of and may be an important factor in the identification of those areas where participation in main curriculum presents least problems. Among the areas identified will be those where mixed-ability teaching is a viable proposition presenting opportunities for full interaction between pupils with special needs and other pupils.

GENERAL DESIGN

Three approaches to general curriculum design are relevant to curriculum for special needs: the objectives model, the process model, and a model based upon situational analysis.

The objectives model

This model is based upon behaviourist psychology. In the model an intervening step is considered necessary if the aims of education are to be successfully translated into curriculum transactions in the classroom, and for this purpose objectives must be defined. The objectives consist of the knowledge, skills, attitudes and values which must be established by the pupil if the aims of his education are to be satisfied. Objectives need to be precisely defined in a manner which will allow the teacher to assess, through observation of the behaviour of the pupil, whether or not they are established; hence the frequently used term 'behavioural objectives'. Observation includes objective measurement wherever possible, and the precision of the process not only benefits the pupil but also allows for improved evaluation and refinement of the curriculum itself. In the curriculum model, *terminal objectives* are first defined as the end products of the curriculum; from these, *intermediate objectives* are proposed which accord with the development of the pupils and their acquisition of knowledge, skill, etc. as they move through the school. Curriculum *content* and *learning experiences* are selected appropriate to the objectives, and a *recording system* is designed through which the progress of the pupils may be monitored. The record is the basis of *evaluation* and ideally it should be possible to modify objectives, content or teaching methods at any point where the evaluation shows it to be necessary for individual pupils or groups of pupils. The process of curriculum or teaching modification is often referred to as 'feedback' (there is an extensive bibliography on the objectives model, mainly from the USA where the approach seems to have been generated: e.g. Tyler, 1950; Taba, 1962; Popham, 1977).

The objectives model is not without its critics (Stenhouse, 1971; Macdonal-Ross, 1973). In its extreme behaviourist form it is regarded as narrow, relevant only to instruction in rote knowledge or the teaching of basic scholastic, physical and social skills. There have, however, been modifications which move the model away from the extreme. Eisner (1969) saw behavioural objectives as limited to direct instruction, proposing *expressive objectives* which were to describe situations calculated to evoke personal responses from pupils without defining the response in advance, and what he named 'type III' objectives where pupils were placed in open-ended problem-solving situations. The broadening of the objectives approach opens considerable curriculum possibilities, as follows.

Behavioural (instructional) objectives

These are the objectives that seem to be most widely referred to in the schools. They are concerned with the details of what the pupil has achieved as a result of the teaching recieved. The outcome of the pupil's learning is specified *before* the learning is undertaken, in detail. The exact nature of the response, the conditions under which it is obtained, the standard to be achieved, and the number of trials that must produce the correct response are all specified in advance. The terms of specification must make it possible to observe and, ideally, measure the response on the basis of the pupil's behaviour. The objective *is* the specified behaviour and the teacher knows in advance what to look for from the pupil. To operate in these terms complex behaviours must be broken down into constituent subroutines by task analysis, and the intermediate behaviours must be defined and organized in a correct sequence. Terminal and intermediate behavioural objectives may be broadly specified in curriculum structure, but for teaching in the classroom specific definitions are required free from any ambiguity (Ainscow and Tweddle, 1979).

Expressive objectives

Expressive objectives describe educational encounters. Teachers organize situations that have within them the possibility of worthwhile experience for the pupil, but there is no attempt to define or prescribe the outcome for the pupil. The pupil acts freely, the thinking or feeling emerging being his own making. The situation is evocative, *not* prescriptive. In the expressive objective part of curriculum, the pupil has the opportunity to make personal use of skills learned through instructional objectives or type III objectives, and these free, personal outcomes constitute the expressive objective *for that pupil* (Eisner, 1969, 1972). At the level of curriculum structure there will be broad descriptions of situations selected for the possibilities that they hold for pupils, and these should be related to the development of the pupils and the organizational phases of the curriculum. Situations that gain more as pupils develop may be repeated in curriculum. At classroom level teachers will select and modify situations on the basis of their knowledge of the pupils.

Type III objectives

These objectives focus upon problem solving by the pupils. In setting out the problem the teacher provides a high degree of structure in identifying the situation, defining the conditions and parameters within which the pupils must work, and indicating the kind of problem which is to be resolved. Ideally the situations should lend themsleves to more than one solution, but however much information is given to the pupils it does not include solutions. Pupils approach the problem freely, working things out for themselves. The teacher does not assess pupil performance on any predetermined relationship between the problem and the solution but on the ingenuity of the solution worked out by the pupil (Eisner, 1972). Curriculum structure could include problems with variables progressively increasing to match the development and maturity of the pupils and to embrace different subjects or experiences, as well as collective group approaches to problems. Again this will be a broad structure, offering guidance to teachers about the type of situation to be presented yet allowing the teacher to shape the details to interest and motivate pupils. In these problem situations there will be opportunity for pupils to apply knowledge acquired through the instructional objectives curriculum in ordered and applied thought processes, which could assist in integrating their knowledge and extend and enrich their insights.

The three types of objective imply different kinds of curriculum activities, creating a variety which acts as a safeguard against the limitation of curriculum through excessive or 'trivial' use of instructional objectives with behavioural outcomes. They go further: the teacher becomes involved in different kinds of evaluation, in the process observing wider aspects of the pupils' learning. Many of the skills and procedures that make thinking and problem solving possible are established through instructional objectives and the same is true about many means of self-expression. Using the skills in those ways gives retrospective purpose to the learning of them, motivating the pupils for further instructional learning. Positive feelings which accompany the resolution of problems or satisfactory self-expression incorporate the purpose of expressive objectives.

What, it may be asked, is the principal contribution of the extended objectives model? The answer is *precision*. Instructional behavioural objectives alone establish precision only in a narrow band of curriculum activities. With expressive and type III objectives, the precision applies in the construction of the situations selected and prepared for the pupils, though outcomes are left open. The curriculum constructor is compelled to plan more rigorously, as a result of which curriculum becomes more effective, better sequenced and more attractively varied.

The process model

In the process model there is no attempt to define the outcome of the curriculum in behavioural terms. Curriculum is shaped by the selection of content as knowledge which is intrinsically worth while and such that will facilitate the procedures, criteria and concepts appropriate to the particular kind of human experience it represents. If this is achieved, it is argued, no other extrinsic justification is required. The aim is that pupils should think themselves through to positions of understanding, insight and appreciation, establishing forms of discussion appropriate to situations under consideration. Planning the curriculum involves selecting the content and devising teaching methods to achieve the aims; evaluation becomes part of the process, not dependent on behaviour specified in advance. The model was worked out through the Schools Council Humanities Curriculum project which had a topic approach, for example 'war', 'poverty', 'relations between the sexes'. Pupils discussed the material presented with a teacher-chairman who sought to play neutral role in the enterprise, free from any particular point of view which might influence the conclusions of the pupils. Broadening of view, tolerance of opposition, critical attitudes to evidence and deepening of insight were to emerge from the experience of the pupils (Stenhouse, 1970, 1975).

In one sense the model does seek ends, though in process rather than behavioural terms, and one criticism has been about the difficulty of assessing pupils' work and the value to them of the experience. The concept of teacher impartiality has been challenged on the basis that teachers should have positive attitudes on moral questions. Another limitation arises from the sophistication of the humanities materials, in terms of reading level and procedures. If the basic skills do not exist then the material is not necessarily the most efficient approach to teaching them. The technique has validity for pupils with special needs, though it may require the production of appropriate presentation material (Gulliford and Widlake, 1975).

The situation model

The starting point is an *analysis of the existing situation* on the assumption that something is going on which it may be possible to improve – not unusual in schools. External factors for assessment include: social changes and ideological shifts; parent and community expectations; development in academic disciplines; the level of support available for the teachers. Internal factors such as pupil attitudes, teaching-staff skills and interests, availability of resources and school ethos are examined in order to identify possible problem areas.

Next comes *goal formulation* though not necessarily in behavioural terms. Statements of teacher and pupil actions desired are related to the situational analysis in areas where change or modification might operate.

From here arises *programme assembly* involving selection of subject matter and arrangement in teaching sequence related to organization of materials and equipment and the deployment of staff. At this point there can be a survey of *application and interpretation*, including identification of any practical problems likely to arise from the introduction of new procedures or modification of existing practice, with forward planning calculated to overcome the problems.

Finally there is *operational assessment*. This is broad and ongoing, related to classroom experience, recording the responses of pupils and teachers, determining the extent to which curriculum objectives are achieved, and concerned also with wider issues such as school organization, morale of staff and pupils, and possible implications for future situation change. If necessary this leads to reanalysis of the curriculum situation or parts of it (Skilbeck, 1976; see also Sockett, 1976).

These features of general curriculum design appear most directly applicable to curricula for special needs. The situational model highlights the importance of a broad analytical approach to curriculum. Behavioural objectives are efficient in the learning of physical and social skills and in the rote aspects of basic subjects. The process model stresses the need for logical and sequential thought in approaching problems and for the education of the emotions, though without the concern for precision which is a feature of Eisner's expressive and type III objectives. No one of these approaches will meet all curricular needs. They must, therefore, be combined in designing a balanced curriculum for special needs.

APPROACHING THE BALANCE

Teachers of children with special educational needs face the problem of accommodating within a limited time both the learning made necessary by special needs and the broader aspects of education through which the pupil is enabled to relate to the natural and social environment. The more time-consuming the special curriculum, the less time is available for the wider curriculum; the more personal the special needs, the more difficult it becomes to provide a balance through the social objectives of curriculum. For teachers of pupils with learning difficulties the problem is the more serious. They work with pupils whose special needs affect learning over *the whole of the curriculum* with time and balance as ever-present, continuing pressures. It is not surprising, therefore, to find that the literature on curriculum for special needs abounds with work relating to pupils with learning difficulties, which is heavily drawn upon in the following discussion (Tansley and Gulliford, 1960; Stephens, 1977; Lerner, 1976; Brennan, 1974, 1979).

An instructional approach

The instructional approach arises from a combination of traditional curriculum organization into subjects allied to teaching methods based upon a class or group and is usually associated with specialist subject teaching. The subject matter to be taught is considered in relation to the time available for teaching it and the assumed learning potential of the pupils who are to be taught (Taylor, 1970). On this basis curriculum content is organized according to a hierarchy of importance into three categories:

The instructional priorities:
1. *Must* be learned. This is the core of curriculum, the imperative essential minimum to be mastered by the learners.
2. *Should* be learned. The next category of importance; content in this category is to be learned only if the *must* category learning is firmly established.
3. *Could* be learned. The least important category, to be attempted only by learners who master the content of the *must* and *should* categories.

The three categories constitute the whole curriculum to be learned by those in the group with normal learning potential. For these pupils, and where subject matter is consistent with the logic of the hierarchy, the approach may be relatively efficient. But where there are special needs that impede learning the result is frequently ineffective. Such pupils may learn the core in a satisfactory manner only to be left in possession of knowledge or skills which they are unable to make use of outside the learning situation due to their inadequate frame of reference and inability to generalize to everyday situations.

The instructional approach has a heavy responsibility for many pupils with learning difficulties who leave school with very few mathematical concepts; the result of time expended on a core imperative of the four basic rules of number. On the practical side are boys who have not experienced all woodworking tools because they failed to work through models designed to provide the experience in the time available, or girls who did not know how their cheese straws were to be cooked because they had not finished their preparation in time. In a science lesson slower pupils listened to the lecture and demonstration but, while others then engaged in individual experiments, they were set to copy notes from a blackboard as 'otherwise they will not finish them', to quote the teacher. These situations are still far too common; they occur most frequently in mixed-ability classes in ordinary schools but are not unknown in special schools, from which two of the above examples are taken. In part they result from teaching methods where a single curriculum meets the needs of most of the class but has little logical basis for others. Yet, as will be shown later, the categories of the instructional approach may be useful in another context.

An experience approach

The experience approach starts from the premise that in the limited time available the priority rests with bringing the pupils in contact with the maximum number of 'experiences' likely to be of value to them in 'life' or in the post-school world. The curriculum tends to be outward looking and organized on topic or centre-of-interest lines with emphasis on what can be done outside the school. It is often assumed that the interest generated by the activity will be sufficient to ensure learning in basic subject skills, and as a consequence direct teaching of these may not form part of the curriculum. The assumption may be justified where the pupils have established early skills, have no learning difficulties and are subject only to time limitation. But where the learning is not established, or there are general or specific learning difficulties, the assumption does a disservice to the pupils. The situation is often encountered in the higher classes of junior and secondary schools where the emphasis is on providing common experience. Children with special needs for whom special curriculum or teaching has been arranged in the lower part of the school are often 'integrated' into classes in the upper school without continuation of the special arrangements; so for some pupils the foundations of learning are not developed, while for others established learning is allowed to deteriorate. Even where the experience approach is appropriate it does not evade the necessity to select carefully the experiences to be included in the curriculum.

Neither of the above approaches alone will sustain a balanced curriculum. The instructional approach is adequate for basic skills but may establish them without the necessary transfer to open situations, while the experience approach ensures that the pupil has a broad background, but may generate interest and motivation in pupils not utilized in the learning of basic skills. One approach is too 'closed' to provide for broad and rich education; the other is too 'open' to provide the structure required by some pupils if they are to master the basic skills. However, both approaches share a limitation, for neither considers 'levels' of learning when establishing the priorities which govern curriculum selection. They both assume a constant level of learning in the curriculum and there seems little place for the concept of differential learning according to the nature of subject material or the needs of individual pupils.

Core and periphery

This approach was developed by Tansley and Gulliford (1960) in their work with slow learners. They postulated a curriculum based upon (i) a central core of language and number and (ii) a periphery of useful knowledge about the environment, aesthetic activities and practical interests:

> As the core develops, so the periphery widens, and as the child achieves command of the essential tools of learning he realizes their usefulness. The interplay between core and periphery becomes more sensitive and apparent.

There is fluidity here, interaction between the areas; skills are applied in the periphery with the excitement feeding back to motivate learning in the core; the instructional closed approach increases potential in the open experience area while gaining purpose from it. Also present in this approach is the beginning of differential learning with the idea of 'awareness' in the periphery, especially 'social awareness'. Later work by Ainscow and Tweddle (1979) developed a more precise approach to the core or closed curriculum by applying behavioural objectives methods in the area, thereby improving the model, though their work adds little to the concept of the periphery or 'open curriculum' as they termed it. This aspect of the approach was elaborated by Tansley and Gulliford (1960):

> The periphery subjects can be integrated or correlated and used at all levels to encourage the development of basic subjects. There is no need for detailed syllabuses which so often result in an atomistic, subject-centred approach to learning. What is wanted is an approach which emphasizes the relationship between the various elements in knowledge and results in broad rather than detailed experiences.

The curriculum was to be approached from three points of view: the logical, based on the internal logic of subjects and order of presentation; the psychological, taking account of child development and pupil motivation; and the social, contemporary in terms of the pupils' relationships but also taking account of the social demands to be made in the future. Both core and periphery were to be subjected to this analysis and from the balance among the viewpoints would emerge the priorities governing curriculum selection and presentation. In what manner was the curriculum to be organized and presented – subjects or experiences? The answer was a compromise, or in terms of this discussion, a balance.

The core and periphery approach has much to commend it and has been widely applied in the education of children with learning difficulties, but there are limitations. As stated, it is biased to knowledge rather than skill and the concept of differential learning is only beginning to emerge in the reference to social awareness. Nor is it made clear what the relative importance is between core and periphery curriculum or whether expansion in the latter is to be entirely governed by progress in the former.

Broad-based approach

The broad-based approach has emerged from a Schools Council seminar on curriculum for special schools reported by Wilson (1981). In Figure 5.1 the rectangle represents the whole of the curriculum with the different aspects represented by the capitalized (upper-case) labels on the diagonals.

As knowledge is wider than subjects, it has been inserted in brackets on the original SUBJECT diagonal. Looking at the diagonals in Figure 5.1, it

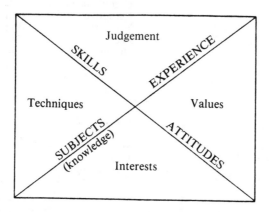

Figure 5.1   Broad-based approach to curriculum balance

is possible to conceptualize the areas between them as representing combinations indicated by the lower-case labels. Thus a combination of knowledge and skills is seen as technique; skills and experience as judgement; experience and attitudes as values; and knowledge and attitudes as interests. The left side of the figure (knowledge, skills and techniques)

Table 5.1 Broad-based curriculum. The range of the broad-based approach is seen if the skills and attitudes to be established by the pupils are set against the experiences and subjects that are to form the curriculum

Skills	Attitudes	Experiences	Subjects
Perceptive	Self-confidence	*Aesthetic/creative*	Arts
Seeing	Self-awareness	Appreciative	Crafts
Hearing	Self-discipline	Expressive	Music
Touching	Honesty		Home economics
Smelling	Integrity	*Ethical/spiritual*	Dance and
	Sensitivity	Humanitarian	movement
Manipulative	Consideration	Religious	Drama
Dexterity	Compassion		Literature
Agility	Adaptability	*Social/political*	English
Handwriting	Perseverence	Historical	Second language
Tool/Material	Initiative	Contemporary	Religious
control	Imagination	Projective	education
Movement	Objectivity		History
	Concentration	*Physical*	Geography
Communication	Helpfulness	Individual	Social science
Listening	Accepting of	Collective	Physical science
Speaking	help	Cooperative	Arithmetic
Reading		Competitive	Mathematics
Writing			Physical
Using technical		*Communication*	education
equipment		Receptive	Health education
Non-verbal/		Expressive	Preparation for
artistic		Face-to-face	work and
expression		Distant	leisure
			Preparation for
Intellectual		*Mathematical*	family/
Observing		Computive	community life
Investingating		Conceptual	
Estimating			
Measuring		*Scientific*	
Computing		Physical	
Assessing		Social	
Problem solving		Proof/	
		hypotheses	

Social	*Industrial*
Self-care	Working
Self-regulation	conditions
Accepting others	Working
Assisting others	procedures
Interaction	Work choice
Travelling	Worklessness
Using leisure	
Working	*Leisure*
Caring for living	Range
animals and	Assessment
plants	Choice
Aesthetic	*Economic*
Judging	Income
Discriminatung	Expenditure
Selecting	Budgeting
Conserving	

would certainly focus on the core curriculum involving the instructional approach and use of behavioural objectives. Experience, attitudes and values (the right of the figure) offer scope for the process model, expressive objectives, and the experience approach. The areas of judgement and interests may be regarded as operating over both sides of the figure, and though this takes the figure beyond its original purpose it appears consistent with the broad-based approach.

These are helpful techniques of curriculum survey which stress the broader aspects of school subjects and should prevent the common weakness where knowledge is allowed to dominate teaching. They are a logical outcome of the broad-based curriculum, one advantage of which is that they are aimed at broadening work in special schools, thus acting on the Warnock Report criticism that special school curricula were generally too narrow (see Tables 5.1 and 5.2).

The weakness of the broad-based approach is the absence of any indication of priorities among the aspects of curriculum considered. Nor does it take into account that there might be different levels of learning in the curriculum. Consequently the approach offers little guidance towards a solution of the time limitation problem so central for children with special educational needs. Such a solution requires the establishment of curriculum priorities in all the attributes of the broad-based approach – not just in skills and knowledge, where it is not possible to include everything desirable in the time available; the same is true of the more intrinsic attributes of values and judgement. Without such priorities there is danger that the broad approach may dissipate effort over the whole curriculum without bringing

Table 5.2 Broad-based curriculum and development. Another way to analyse and assess the broad-based approach is to chart curriculum subjects against aspects of pupil development as in this profile.

Development	Arts	Crafts	Music	Home economics	Dance/movement	Drama	Physical education	Literature	English	Second language	Religious education	History	Geography	Social science	Physical science	Arithmetic	Mathematics	Health education	Work experience	Leisure experience	Community experience	Preparation for family life	Gardening/rural studies	Safety/traffic education	Disability management	Disability support
Personal																										
Physical			×		×	×	×											×						×	×	
Self-concept						×	×	×	×	×	×	×	×	×				×	×	×	×	×		×	×	×
Self-regulation	×	×	×		×	×			×									×	×			×		×	×	×
Independence					×	×			×															×	×	×
Moral behaviour						×					×	×	×									×				
Social																										
Perspective							×		×		×	×	×	×	×			×	×	×		×			×	×
Competence									×	×																
Judgement						×					×			×	×			×	×	×					×	×
Intellectual																										
Perception	×	×	×		×	×	×							×	×										×	×
Observation	×	×			×	×								×	×	×		×	×	×	×		×	×		
Memory	×	×	×		×	×			×																	
Problem solving	×	×	×				×	×	×					×	×	×	×								×	×
Language	×	×	×	×	×	×	×	×	×	×	×	×	×	×	×	×	×	×	×	×	×		×	×	×	×
Reading			×					×	×	×	×	×	×	×	×			×	×	×	×	×		×	×	×
Writing																										
Numeracy/maths			×											×	×	×	×		×		×		×			
Social concepts																										
Environmental concepts	×	×	×									×	×	×	×				×	×	×		×	×	×	×
Objectivity																										
Aesthetic																										
Artistic	×	×	×	×	×																					
Musical			×		×	×														×						
Dramatic																										
Literary						×		×	×	×	×	×														
Imaginative	×	×	×		×	×		×	×			×								×						
Practical																										
Dexterity	×	×	×																							
Agility					×		×																			
Craft/domestic		×																								
Handwriting								×	×	×	×	×	×	×	×	×	×									
Vocational/leisure																										
Attitudes											×	×		×	×	×		×	×		×		×	×	×	×
Knowledge																										
Skills																										

any aspects to an operational level in the behaviour of the pupils. The priorities themselves will not resolve the time dilemma unless they can be associated with the idea of levels of learning appropriate to the needs of the pupils. This is attempted in the next approach to balanced curriculum.

Differential learning

The differential approach has been gradually developed out of the idea of social awareness suggested by Tansley and Gulliford (1960; see also Brennan, 1974, 1979). Though worked out mainly in curriculum for pupils with learning difficulties, the principles apply wherever the time available for education imposes upon teachers the task of curriculum selection in order to ensure that what the pupils are required to learn will be relevant to the tasks and roles of later life.

Knowledge and skills

The problem of securing balance in the curriculum is approached in differential learning by stipulating that knowledge and skills may be included at two levels, designated at *function* and *context*, as illustrated in Figure 5.2.

	KNOWLEDGE	SKILLS	
Function	Thoroughness	Proficiency	Accurate Permanent Integrated Generalized
Context	Awareness	Familiarity	Recognized Appreciated Associated

Figure 5.2 Differential learning approach to curriculum balance – knowledge and skills

Function learning is essential learning which must be established in the behaviour of the pupils if they are to face the problems of later life with a reasonable level of success. Learning at this functional level must incorporate some critical qualities: it must be accurate, permanent, integrated and generalized. Accuracy and permanency require no comment. Integration is necessary to ensure that knowledge and skill do not consist of isolated, splinter achievements, while generalization ensures that they operate in the everyday behaviour of the pupils.

Context learning does not require the precise, thorough qualities defined above, for it serves a different purpose. It is the assimilated learning which is the background or context of pupils' behaviours and allows them to relate to and maintain contact with the natural, social, emotional and aesthetic aspects of their environment. Through it pupils are aware of or familiar with many things which they may be unable to make explicit.

Function level in curriculum

The term *thoroughness* is used for knowledge at the functional level, with *proficiency* identifying that level of skill. In considering pupils with special needs, two factors are considered: first, what is entered in the curriculum at the functional level must be learned with the qualities noted above; second, the time it will take to establish that level of learning is such that it must be limited to absolute essentials if broader aspects of curriculum are to be negotiated successfully. It will be possible to design general curricula at this level where there are pupils with similar special needs, though it will always be necessary to make evaluation of this aspect of curriculum in terms of the needs of individual pupils, individualizing curriculum and teaching for small groups or single pupils whenever that is seen to be necessary.

This part of the curriculum has about it some aspects of the 'core' discussed earlier. Large parts of it will consist of basic subjects and social skills for some pupils, with, for others, the essential foundation knowledge and skills for a wider range of studies where higher-order learning is seen to be possible and appropriate. For example, except for pupils for whom the study of chemistry to higher level was a feasible and appropriate curriculum possibility, there would be little point in entering the table of elements and laws of proportion in the functional level; similarily, certain basic skills in arts or crafts would be appropriate at this level only where pupil aptitude and interest indicated a major curriculum component. As will shortly become apparent, exclusion of knowledge or skill from the functional level does not imply total exclusion from the curriculum. Conversely, for pupils with moderate or severe learning difficulites, the functional level will include fundamental linguistic, social and self-care knowledge and skills which other pupils bring to school with them and about which the school curriculum need not be concerned.

Context level in curriculum

At the context level knowledge is labelled by *awareness* and skill by *familiarity*. The key concepts at this level are recognition, appreciation and association, for the purpose of learning is that the pupils should acquire a broad background which will enable them to relate to people, conversation and events in the environment in a manner acceptable to other persons and within the broad norm of their social group. For pupils with moderate or severe learning difficulties it will be sufficient if the knowledge/background guards them against attracting unwelcome attention or ridicule through exposing ignorance of common topics, language, sport, entertainment or news items, and their contact with skills enables them to appreciate expertise when they see it and enter into everyday discussions about it. Other pupils will require wider backgrounds which include areas ranking for this level of curriculum only because shortage of time has excluded them from the functional level. This is made clear by considering the examples used previously in discussing knowledge: pupils for whom tables of elements and laws of proportion are inappropriate will nevertheless need some context awareness of chemistry as a particular subject within a general classification of science, or as a way of dealing with the properties of substances, or even as a way of knowing that some 'chemicals' are poisonous; and though functional skills of art or craft may be unsuitable for some pupils, there is no doubt that all should experience the activities, gain the satisfaction that comes from them and acquire familiarity which enables them to appreciate as many forms of artistic expression as possible.

An important aspect of the context curriculum is that it does *not* require the precision of the functional. It can be more relaxed; it is conducive to an activity approach, and it can gain greatly from the 'planned' aspect of the curriculum.

Relation of function and context

The purpose of the differential learning approach is that of securing balance in the curriculum, so there is a continuing relationship between the function and context levels. The more restricted the functional curriculum, the broader and more important the context curriculum becomes if the pupils concerned are to demonstrate their limited function within a general awareness and familiarity that allows them to relate successfully to life around them. An extensive curriculum at functional level reduces the importance of the context but does not eliminate it. All normal people have areas of expertise where they operate at functional level but few maintain it over the whole of their behaviour, relying for general orientation on broad background at the context level. For example, most people today are aware that at a certain point in a space vehicle the occupants experience 'weightlessness' – yet they have never experienced it and would be unable to explain it; but for a limited number of people it *is* important that they should understand the physical laws which govern weightlessness at the functional level as a part of a whole complex of knowledge that has made possible the reality of the space vehicle. Knowledge at the latter level is clearly unnecessary for all people. In terms of skills, sports provide a good example, for it is the familiarity with sporting skills established in the physical education curriculum that allows a multitude of people to appreciate and enjoy the performance of those sportsmen and women who have established skills at the proficiency level.

The proposal that the curriculum should operate with different levels of learning for pupils with special needs, then, is perfectly consistent with the way that almost all normal people behave in our culture, where the astrophysicist requires a broad context background if he is not to make a fool of himself in more mundane political or social matters or be regarded as a philistine in the arts. There must be balance in the relative content of functional and context curricula for pupils with special needs which are similar, and the balance will require assessment for individuals within the groups. The *relative, complementary importance* of the two aspects of curriculum should not be overlooked: where the functional curriculum is limited, for whatever reason (sensory, social, emotional or intellectual), the context assumes more importance than the functional in enabling the individual to accommodate himself to his social situation. This is well known to teachers of pupils with moderate learning difficulties. They know from many research studies that where their pupils fail in the postschool world it is not usually because they lack the basic skills of the functional curriculum (which they often do), but because they are unable to relate in an acceptable manner to the everyday behaviours and topics of the workplace and the street which are the concern of the context curriculum. The implication is clear: if the balance between function and context is to be achieved, the relationship must be evaluated in terms of relative importance as well as in curriculum content, and to achieve this the needs of individuals must be taken into account.

Priorities in curriculum

The differential learning approach has introduced the useful concept of different levels of learning in curricula, but it has not gone beyond this in terms of curriculum priorities. The problem remains that it will not be possible to include all beneficial learning at either of the levels, and therefore selection will continue to be necessary. Here a useful framework is provided by introducing the priorities defined above in the instructional approach, as illustrated in Figure 5.3.

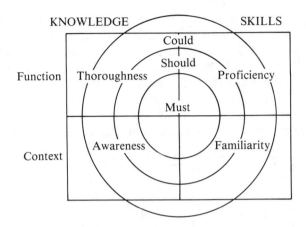

Figure 5.3 Differential learning – knowledge and skills – with priorities

Figure 5.3. emphasizes that selection may be necessary in all areas of curriculum at both levels if a balance is to be achieved appropriate for the needs of individual pupils. In practice this may be approached through the construction of a general curriculum calculated to meet the needs of groups of pupils with similar special needs. The general curriculum has a number of advantages when seen in an appropriate context:

1. provides purpose and direction for curriculum transactions;
2. clarifies the teacher's role and contribution in curriculum;
3. provides structure for observation of pupil progress;
4. allows for rapid and accurate identification of failure to progress;
5. information on breakdown becomes the starting point for modification of curriculum/teaching.

Through this framework the general curriculum becomes diagnostic in the true sense as the failure of the pupil attracts attention and directs it to his special needs with a starting point for modification.

Experience and attitudes
The principles of the differential approach may also be applied in the curriculum areas of experience and attitudes, as Figure 5.4 illustrates. Because experience and attitudes are concerned with internalized matters, the figure lacks the precision of that for knowledge and skills. Nevertheless it is possible to stipulate levels of learning. Function learning is now postulated as the effects of experience and attitudes incorporated in the behaviour of the pupil. Context learning is not incorporated in behaviour

but recognized by the pupil as a 'norm' or expectancy in his social situation.

The nature of the learning in this area of curriculum will mean that criteria for curriculum inclusion will also differ from those of knowledge and skills. However, it would be wrong to consider the knowledge/skills and experience/attitudes aspects of curriculum as separate, for teaching in the former areas may take important contributions to the latter – not necessarily in terms of what is taught but more from the style of teaching and learning and the relationships that inform classroom communication.

	EXPERIENCE	ATTITUDES	
Function	Direct & Personal	Operational in Self	Incorporated in Behaviour
Context	Communicated Awareness	Appreciated in Others	Recognized as 'norms'

Figure 5.4 Differential learning approach to curriculum balance – experience and attitudes

Experiences included in curriculum at the function level are those which *must* be incorporated in the behaviour of pupils as essential to their education. Time pressures make the restriction necessary and the nature of the learning requires that the experiences be direct and personal, the outcome of situations planned for the purpose. Similar restriction will be necessary for attitudes included in curriculum at this level. Those to be worked for should be absolutely essential as support for appropriate and acceptable behaviour to the extent that they constitute the moral basis from which pupils will judge their own and others' actions. Criteria for curriculum inclusion are not so rigorous at the context level. Here the purpose is to establish a background that will enable pupils to generalize and regulate established behaviour to accord with the social environment. Thus experience may be indirect, communicated through literature, drama, social or religious studies, and through the planned and hidden curriculum. From these activities pupils will also derive a general familiarity with or awareness of attitudes – a context of expectancies wider than the attitudes which inform their own functional behaviour.

Attitudes and experiences and the values which emerge from them are of particular importance in curriculum for children with special educational needs. The importance derives from their having more to contend with than their more fortunate contemporaries through the additional demands, constraints and frustrations generated by their disabilities. Pupils with special needs require a broader curriculum to compensate for the additional demands, yet it will not be possible to include all that is desirable in a curriculum limited by time. There is increased pressure on their teachers as they seek to achieve appropriate priorities for experiences and attitudes at both function and context levels in the curriculum. The priorities from the instructional approach again serve a useful purpose as they focus attention on the problem.

Figure 5.5. emphasizes that priority choices are necessary in all the aspects of curriculum represented by the quadrants, though there is not a fixed degree of importance between the function and context levels. The importance is relative and compensatory, and must be determined by a close study of the needs of pupils and an equally careful assessment of their life situations and the demands likely to be made on them in the future. Of first importance is knowledge of the pupils' previous experience and its effect on their contemporary behaviour, especially where special needs arise from emotional or behaviour difficulties – see the discussion earlier in this chapter.

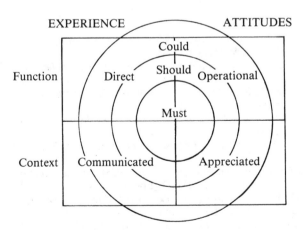

Figure 5.5 Differential learning – experience and attitudes – with priorities

THE BALANCED CURRICULUM

No single model or approach is capable of sustaining a full curriculum for children with special educational needs, though all have some contribution which is valuable. So here again pupils with special needs are *not* different from other pupils. In aspects of curriculum where learning with accuracy and permanency are necessary, the behavioural objectives model and the instructional approach offer a high degree of learning efficiency with optimal expenditure of time. The process model, together with expressive and type III objectives, combines with the experience or, better, broad-based approach as the basis for those aspects of curriculum concerned with emotional and aesthetic development or knowledge utilized in the process of thinking and problem solving. The differential learning approach, growing out of the core–periphery concept, offers a structure able to accommodate the above curricular suggestions and adds to them the levels-of-learning idea which ensures that precision is achieved where necessary while maintaining a broadly based curriculum closely related to the needs of pupils. It also offers a useful approach to the problem of a common or core curriculum. Situational analysis directs attention to the many factors, in school and in the broader environment, which must be examined and taken account of in reaching the necessary decisions about curriculum priorities and their implications for curriculum development.

REFERENCES

Ainscow, M. and Tweddle, D.A. (1979) *Preventing Classroom Failure: an objectives approach,* John Wiley, Chichester

Argyle, M. (1972) *The Psychology of Inter-personal Behaviour,* Penguin, Harmondsworth

Brennan, W. K. (1974) *Shaping the Education of Slow Learners,* Routledge and Kegan Paul, London

Brennan, W. K. (1979) *The Curricular Needs of Slow Learners,* Evans–Methuen Educational, London

Dawson, R. L. (1980) *Special Provision for Disturbed Pupils,* Macmillam Education, London

Department of Education and Science (DES) (1978) *Special Educational Needs* (Warnock Report), Cmnd 7212, HMSO, London

Eisner, E. W. (1969) *Instructional and expressive objectives.* In M. Golby *et al.* (1975) Curriculum Design, Croom Helm, London

Eisner, E. W. (1972) Emerging models for educational evaluation, *School Review,* August

Flavell, J. H. (1968) *The Development of Role-Taking and Communication Skills in Children*, Wiley, New York

Gulliford, R. and Widlake, P. (1975) *Teaching Materials for Disadvantaged Children,* Evans–Methuen Educational, London

Haring, N. G. and Phillips, E. L. (1962) *Educating Emotionally Disturbed Children*, McGraw Hill, New York

Hewett, F. M. (1968) *The Emotionally Disturbed Child in the Classroom*, Allyn and Bacon, Boston

Laslett, R. (1977) *Educating Maladjusted Children,* Crosby Lockwood Staples, London

Lerner, J. W. (1976) *Children with Learning Disabilities,* Houghton Mifflin, Boston

Macdonal-Ross, M. (1973) *Behavioural objectives: a critical review.* In M. Golby *et al.* (1975) Curriculum Design, Croom Helm, London

Popham, W. J. (1977) *Objectives 72.* In L. Rubin (Ed.) (1977) Curriculum Handbook: the disciplines, current movements and instructional methodology, Allyn and Bacon, Boston

Skilbeck, M. (1976) The curriculum development process: a model for school use. In Open University (1976) Styles of curriculum development, Course E203, Unit 8, Open University Press, Milton Keynes

Sockett, H. (1976) *Design in the Curriculum*, Open Books, London

Stenhouse, L. (1970) *The Humanities Project: an introduction,* Heinemann Educational, London

Stenhouse, L. (1971) Some limitations on the use of objectives in the curriculum, *Paedagogica Europaea,* pp 78-83

Stenhouse, L. (1975) *An Introduction to Curriculum Research and Development*, Heinemann Educational, London

Stephens, T. M. (1977) *Teaching Skills to Children with Learning and Behaviour Disorders*, Merrill, Columbus

Taba, H. (1962) *Curriculum Development: theory and practice*, Harcourt Brace Jovanovich, New York

Tansley, A. E. and Gulliford, R. (1960) *The Education of Slow Learning Children,* Routledge and Kegan Paul, London

Taylor, P. (1970) *How Teachers Plan their Courses*, NFER, Windsor

Tower, P. *et al.* (1978) *Social Skills and Mental Health,* Methuen Educational, London

Tyler, R.W. (1950) *Basic Principles of Curriculum and Instruction,* University of Chicago Press, Chicago

Wilson, M. D. (1981) *The Curriculum in Special Schools,* Schools Council – Longman, London and Harlow

Wilson, M. and Evans, M. (1980) *Education of Disturbed Pupils*, Methuen Educational, London

TOPICS FOR DISCUSSION

1. The author suggests three approaches to general curriculum design which are relevant to curriculum for special needs: the objectives model, the process model and a model based upon situational analysis. Discuss the advantages and disadvantages of each model in relation to: (a) children with defects of hearing, vision or mobility without serious intellectual or emotional problems; (b) children who are educationally disadvantaged; (c) children with significant learning difficulties; (d) pupils with emotional or behavioural difficulties.

2. Discuss the strengths and weaknesses of the 'broad-based approach to curriculum for special educational needs. In what way does the 'differential learning' approach attempt to counteract the deficiencies of the 'broad-based' method of curriculum development?
3. Distinguish between function learning and context learning and describe how they are related.

SUGGESTIONS FOR FURTHER READING

1. A. Hodgson, L. Clunies-Ross and S. Hegarty (1984) *Learning Together: teaching pupils with special educational needs in the ordinary school,* NFER – Nelson, Windsor. Part I of this study deals with academic organization (pupil grouping, supplementary teaching and timetabling); part 2 discusses the modification of curriculum content (models of curriculum content and individual programmes of work); part 4 examines teaching (classroom organization and practice, monitoring progress, use of second adult and pupil helpers, and guidelines for classroom practice).
2. S. Hegarty *et al.* (1982) *Curriculum Development in Special Education,* Schools Council–Longman, London and Harlow. This survey of the curriculum describes various school approaches to curriculum development.
3. W. Swann (1983) *Curriculum principles for integration.* In T. Booth and P. Potts (Eds) (1983) *Integrating Special Education*, Basil Blackwell, Oxford. Swann argues that prevalent conceptions of the special curriculum impede integration. He examines the current emphasis given to the use of behavioural objectives as a basis for the special curriculum and some of the problems associated with this approach. The chapter ends with a description of some principles for an integrated curriculum.

Reading 6
MEETING SPECIAL EDUCATIONAL NEEDS IN THE ORDINARY SCHOOL
S. Hegarty

Educating pupils with special needs in the ordinary school has become a major concern of educators in recent years. The Warnock Report (DES, 1978) described the topic as 'the central contemporary issue in special education'. Since the ramifications of integrated provision extend throughout the school system, it is to be expected that there will be a wide range of practice, opinion and conviction associated with it.

S. Hegarty (1982) Meeting special educational needs in the ordinary school, *Educational Research*, Vol. 24, No. 3, pp 174–181

The present study sought to shed some light on all this by documenting and analysing current practice. It was conducted at the National Foundation for Educational Research, to a commission from the Department of Education and Science, over the period 1978–81. The formal brief was 'to examine in depth current provision for handicapped children in ordinary schools and to identify those factors which make for successful integration [...]'.

Unlike most of the research conducted into this topic, the study did not seek to make comparisons between integrated and segregated provisions. Many of the so-called efficacy studies are beset with methodological difficulties and offer little to inform practice. The focus rather was on structural and organizational factors and the ways in which they impinge on the process of educating pupils with special needs in the ordinary school.

To carry out this work 17 integration programmes in 14 LEAs were selected for detailed study. The programmes varied greatly in terms of type of special needs catered for, age and number of pupils, organization and number of schools involved. Special needs were categorized in terms of the statutory categories of handicap which prevailed at the time, since this was how LEA'S generally described provision. The main categories of handicap were represented, excepting maladjusted (which was the subject of other studies at the time), with particular emphasis on the educationally subnormal and physically handicapped. Pupils' ages ranged from preschool to 16-plus, with a slight preponderance in favour of the primary sector. The number of pupils involved in a programme ranged from 8–10 in a small special class to 100 or more in a large special centre or spread over several locations. The organization of programmes involved links between special schools and ordinary schools, special arrangements made for a *group* of pupils with special needs in an ordinary school, and the individual integration of single pupils. Some programmes were confined entirely to a single school, though mostly drawing on a broader catchment area. Others involved a number of schools, sometimes covering an entire LEA. Detailed descriptions of 14 of these integration programmes are given in *Integration in Action* (Hegarty and Pocklington, 1982).

The main research technique used was interviewing, initially loosely structured but becoming more focused as specific areas of concern and questions about them emerged. Initial visits to locations were essentially introductory and fact-finding at a comprehensive level. They entailed introducing the study and securing effective cooperation, obtaining an outline account of the programme and the context within which it operated, identifying key individuals for subsequent interviewing and generally laying the groundwork for later fieldwork. Subsequent visits led to more specific questioning as a picture of the provision built up. Also, the emerging data from the different programmes interacted with and illuminated each other: issues raised in one location sometimes led to fruitful lines of inquiry in other locations that might not have arisen otherwise.

Interviews were held with teachers and ancillary staff in the schools, educational psychologists, advisers and education officers where they were involved, speech therapists, physiotherapists, medical officers and consultants, as appropriate. Other professionals consulted briefly included careers officers, social workers and school nurses. Opportunities were taken to talk with pupils, generally on an informal one-to-one basis; some formal interviews were held, as well as a number of structured group discussions.

Information gathering was not confined to interviewing, and other research tools were used as appropriate. Thus, most though not all of the teachers interviewed had a major involvement with pupils with special needs. In order to get a wide range of perceptions and opinions a questionnaire was developed for completion by main school teachers. This sought information on the extent and nature of their contact with pupils with special needs, their attitudes toward them, their knowledge of special needs and perceived competence in teaching these pupils, and the information and support they received. A further questionnaire sent to integration programmes consisting of special centres in ordinary schools sought factual information on the service they received from educational psychologists, speech therapists and physiotherapists. In addition to informal observations by the project team throughout the period of study, a further researcher was engaged to carry out structured observations in four of the integration programmes. This entailed a week's observation in each location covering both classroom and playground.

Detailed case studies were conducted on 42 pupils selected from the different programmes to give a range of special needs, ages and extent of integration. Information was sought from their parents, by both questionnaire and interview, on their attitude to the integrated placement, their contact with the school and other agencies, and other factors. A social development profile was devised for these pupils, covering various aspects of adjustment, independence, relationships with others and personal presentation. This was completed twice by teachers with a nine-month interval to give information on pupils' social and emotional development.

The resounding conclusion to emerge from this study is that integration *is* possible. Special educational needs can be met in the ordinary school, and to a far greater extent than is currently the practice. There are many pupils in special schools at the moment who could be educated satisfactorily in ordinary schools, given the requisite commitment and resources. So far from damaging the ordinary school in any way, this process can add to its educational strength and enhance the provision made for all its pupils. The difficulties and drawbacks must not be minimized since that would be to sacrifice pupils' educational well-being on the altar of principle. If an ordinary school cannot accommodate given pupils without educational loss, then special schools may well continue to be the preferred placement. Such situations, however, pose a considerable challenge to both special schools and ordinary schools. As long as some pupils attend special schools when their peers with comparable special needs elsewhere receive satisfactory education in ordinary schools, there are grounds for disquiet.

This general conclusion subsumes a host of data about the process of integration. These are discussed in detailed in the main report emerging from the study *Educating Pupils with Special Needs in the Ordinary School* (Hegarty and Pocklington, 1981). Six broad headings are used to structure the discussion: setting up integration programmes; staffing; practical considerations of accommodation, resources and cost; the content and nature of teaching; social considerations; and parents.

SETTING UP PROVISION

When setting up an integration programme there are various steps that can be taken to maximize the likelihood of success and avoid potential pitfalls. Where there is an element of choice, care should be taken in selecting a school. There can be pressure to use schools which have spare space or to opt for sites that will necessitate a minimum of alterations. These pressures should be resisted if the result is a location which is unsuitable in other respects. New building may be difficult to justify at a time when falling rolls make spare classrooms available, but adaptation costs should be kept in perspective – unless major, they are trivial in relation to other costs when spread over a number of years.

One of the most crucial factors in the choice of school would seem to be the enthusiasm of the headteacher and his or her capacity to enlist the cooperation of staff. A related indicator is the extent to which a school is responding to the needs of pupils with educational difficulties already at the school. Numerous other factors relating to the ethos of the school, its location and the fabric of the building can usefully be taken into account. A decision in practice will usually entail balancing positive and negative features since it is rare for all the desired features to be available. When compromise is necessary, staff-related factors should be accorded highest priority. While some integration programmes flourished despite premises that were grossly unsuited, persistent lack of enthusiasm on the part of head and/or other staff was an enormous obstacle.

Teacher attitudes can be affected in significant ways by the initial overtures to the school when an integration programme is first mooted and by any preparation made. Heads were generally involved in the early discussions, but other staff were not usually informed, much less consulted, until the matter was a *fait accompli.* Unduly protracted consultation can waste a great deal of time and perhaps serve no good purpose. If there is any acknowledgement, however, of the fact that an integration programme is a matter for the whole school and will effect major changes there, staff must be involved as early as possible. It is remarkable to find staff not being given a say or consulted in some measure on a major development in the life of a school.

Views on preparing a school beforehand varied. Preparation of staff was generally acknowledged to be important – and generally not provided. Failure to prepare staff can result in negative attitudes and damaging stereotypes persisting longer than they need. It can also mean that staff are insufficiently aware of individual pupils' special needs and what they can do to meet them. This is all the more regrettable in view of the relative ease with which available resources were deployed to provide effective preparation in a few instances. Preparing parents of pupils already at the school was done carefully and extensively in some schools, whereas other schools deliberately refrained from overt preparation on the grounds that this would only serve to single out the pupils being integrated and hinder their assimilation into the school. In point of fact, no objections to the integration programme, other than very minor ones, were reported from main school parents; indeed there was a fairly widespread endorsement. Preparation of pupils already at the school tended to be limited.

STAFFING

The central resource for an integration programme is its staff – teachers and ancillaries with a particular responsibility for pupils with special needs, other teachers, and professional staff from outside the school. Staffing ratios in the special centres visited were generally good. Approximate ratios only could be calculated in some locations since staff were deployed outside the special centre or provided a service for pupils not formally assigned to it. This highlights the inadequacy of pupil–teacher ratios in determining appropriate staffing levels. Integration is not simply a question of educating those pupils formally assigned to the integration programme. New roles are required, and there is often an associated extension or improvement in the service offered; staffing provision must be set at a level to allow for all of this.

There seemed to be no clear career route for staff into integration programmes. Under individual integration, ordinary class and subject teachers simply had pupils with special needs thrust upon them. Teachers working in special centres had a wide variety of teaching experience in both special and ordinary schools. About a quarter had had no teaching experience. Most of these teachers had received little or no specialist input on handicap during initial teacher training. Rather more than half had subsequently taken courses of at least a year's duration covering different aspects of remedial and special education. Most had taken one or more – frequently many more – short courses relating to special needs. Two-thirds of ancillary staff had some professional training, generally the NNEB qualification; though its relevance was strictly limited, a number of LEAs insisted on the NNEB qualification for appointment as classroom assistant.

Teachers appointed to special centres typically carry out a multifaceted role that in terms of daily routine and professional demands is quite different from that of mainstream colleagues. Other specific roles that may be necessitated by integration include: working in a support role to enable pupils to follow the mainstream curriculum; transferring pupils from a special school or special centre to the mainstream; providing specialist help for individual pupils in conjunction with their class teacher; and maintaining oversight of an integration programme.

The role of ancillary staff is critical in integration. Their availability can determine the feasibility of a programme, and the way in which they are deployed its success or failure. Ancillary staff are usually engaged initially to provide physical care but they can be effectively deployed also in an educational role or as paraprofessionals to implement speech therapy or physiotherapy programmes. They can form relationships of familiarity and friendship that can be helpful for some pupils with special needs. A general finding was that ancilliary staff were underutilized in terms of the complexity of the demands made on them: some were restricted to purely caring roles when they could have contributed much more to meeting the needs of pupils in their charge.

One of the most striking findings to emerge was the extent to which ordinary teachers endorsed the presence of pupils with special needs in their schools. Ninety-seven per cent of those responding to a questionnaire item affirmed that it was appropriate for handicapped pupils to be placed at their school. Many of these had been reluctant if not actually opposed to the idea when the integration programme was first mooted but had come to change their minds after seeing it at work. Most teachers were quite willing to have pupils with special needs in their classes, though some did not take them seriously for teaching purposes, pointing to the social benefits which constituted sufficient justification for having them in an ordinary class. This was particularly likely to happen with pupils who had moderate learning difficulties. This entails a considerable risk of 'patronizing' pupils. Their need of carefully judged teaching is no less, and probably greater, than that of their peers, and inclusion in a teaching group for social rather than pedagogical reasons is a questionable practice.

Over half of the ordinary teachers described their knowledge of handicap at the outset of the integration programme as non-existent or poor. Most claimed a considerable increase in their knowledge with the passage of time, partly through direct experience of pupils with special needs and partly through informal contact with other staff who were better informed. A majority felt that they knew enough about handicap to deal with the pupils they came across but many added that this was only because of the support available within the school and because their responsibility for pupils with special needs was limited. In point of fact, it would seem that teachers could contribute more to their education if they were better informed and possessed the requisite skills. Formal liaison between specialist teachers and their colleagues was generally weak. Some staff liaised very effectively as individuals but adequate *systems* of liaison and support were the exception rather than the rule.

Integration programmes involve a wide range of professionals from outside the school. The account here focused particularly on LEA advisory staff, educational psychologists, speech therapists and physiotherapists. A recurrent theme for all of these was the pressures caused by understaffing and the fact that involvement in an integration programme might come at the end of a long list of other priorities. As far as the schools were concerned, this was unsatisfactory – the more so as they were often in particular need of the specialist advice and support that these professionals could have supplied. Teachers working in small special centres do not have the resources of a special school at hand or even colleagues who share their professional concerns. They depend on outside agencies for specialist advice and support and are vulnerable in their absence.

Integration requires new ways of working on the part of many professionals. There is need to collaborate with colleagues, share information, view pupils' problems in a comprehensive light, disseminate skills and generally move toward interdisciplinary working. These new ways of working have to be developed in the context of staff shortages – which may be exacerbated by the demands of integration programmes. Interdisciplinary working is particularly important but also very difficult to achieve. Aside from the obstacles set by territoriality and traditions of isolated professionalism, there is a considerable conceptual problem: locating contributions from different disciplinary backgrounds within a common conceptual framework can be a challenging intellectual task, and unless resolved can defeat efforts at interdisciplinary working. The examples encountered were few in number and relatively limited in scope. Emphasis was almost exclusively on assessment with very little in the way of joint treatment or other working.

The need for more training emerged plainly and was recognized by many teachers and ancillaries. There were clear implications for initial and early in-service training. The focus in the study was on what can be done at local level using readily available resources. There is no question of making good the deficiencies of initial training or providing a substitute for formal full-time in-service courses (or their part-time equivalents). Much can be done to supplement these courses, however, and also promote awareness among those who are unlikely to take a formal course. Custom-built local courses can be organized and are generally much appreciated. Numerous training possibilities are offered by different aspects of professional interaction: formal collaboration; working together on a common professional task; having contact with expertise; team teaching; visits and meetings.

PRACTICALITIES

There is a practical side to integration that must not be ignored since mundane realities can sink high-minded ideals. This is particularly evident in the matter of school buildings. The problem for integration is that it entails educating pupils with special needs in buildings that must cater for all pupils. Generally, the buildings will not have been designed with their needs in mind and a degree of adaptation is required. Such adaptation must serve various functions: meeting basic physical needs – access, mobility, toileting; facilitating access to the curriculum; and furthering pupils' social assimilation. It was our impression that, beyond dealing with the essentials of ramping and making suitable toileting provision, staff paid little attention otherwise to the physical environment. This is to be regretted since attitudes toward a special provision and its assimilation into the school as well as the suitability of the educational programme can all be influenced by the attention paid to the physical environment.

A major determinant of what is feasible is the amount of money available for spending. The majority of staff interviewed were quite uninformed about the financial aspects of the provisions they worked in. This seemed to reflect the complexity of educational finances, lack of accounting competence and, quite commonly, an attitude toward costs that was a mixture of disdain, fatalism and lack of interest. Staff in senior positions were regularly unable to produce quite specific pieces of information on costs. There was a very common view in any case that this was not their concern: they were educationists and their concern was to promote the educational well-being of pupils. Others could see to the finances. Moreover, even if a full costing could be produced, it would so reflect the particular local situation as to be valueless for any more general purpose.

We take issue with this view. While acknowledging the enormous difficulty of assigning costs with any precision, we hold that teachers and other staff are in a better position to argue for the resources they need if they can be specific about the financial implications. There are notable problems in costing integration programmes: identifying what is to count as a cost; taking account of non-quantifiable factors; apportioning costs between the integration programme and the main school; and interpreting any results obtained. We have proposed a simple accountancy structure for looking at the monetary costs of integration programmes. This is not intended to replace the detailed treatment of costs that an accountant might provide. Its use is as an adjunct to a detailed description of a programme, to sensitize educators to the cost-incurring elements and their order of significance. This should help them to monitor their use of resources and specify the resource implications of proposed innovations.

Costs vary enormously for different integration programmes. There are common threads however which can be picked out by examining the different forms of provision in terms of staff and professional services, premises, resources and transport. One conclusion that emerges from doing this is that comparisons between integrated and segregated provision in terms of costs are at least as problematic as any of the other comparisons that are made. In particular, some of the popularly held beliefs about the relative cheapness of integration do not have a sound basis.

CURRICULUM

Whatever their other special needs, pupils' educational needs must remain paramount as far as schools are concerned. This underlines the importance of curriculum in integration. It is important to distinguish between the entire curriculum of a school and the effective curriculum for pupils with special needs from which their programmes of work are selected. It is vacuous to speak of pupils with moderate learning difficulties, say, having full access to the curriculum in a secondary school if they spend most of their time on basic skills work and receive only token teaching in science or music.

The curriculum in integration rests on two opposing principles: giving pupils the same or similar access to the curriculum as their peers; and providing appropriate help to meet their special needs. Applying these principles and finding a balance between them occasioned much difficulty. The particular problem was how to capitalize on the curricular opportunities of the main school while providing programmes of work that were differentiated according to individual need. Once again, the root of the difficulty was that integration was seen as a matter for the special centre and any necessary curriculum development was the responsibility of special education staff. In point of fact, if curricular access is to be expanded, subject specialists from the main school have to be involved; it is for them in conjunction with special education staff, rather than the latter working on their own, to work out how to make the full range of the curriculum available to pupils with special needs. Guidelines may be drawn from special school practice but only to a limited extent. Meeting special educational needs in the ordinary school is a different enterprise from meeting them in the special school, and new curricular offerings – different both from those of the special school and from those already available in the ordinary school – must be devised.

Preparation for adult life was assigned high priority in the curricular provision of the programmes we studied at secondary level. In some cases numbers were still building up and provision was embryonic. This provision was not generally made on an integrated basis. Main school resources were utilized, but the common view was that these pupils' needs were too specific and distinct from their peers in the mainstream and were best met separately. In some locations this took the shape of formal leavers' courses while in others the aim was to have an informal orientation toward adult life throughout the curriculum in the later years of schooling. The content of this preparation had two broad strands: one related to the world of work and post-school education, and one dealing with adult living in a more general way. Preparation for work was provided through careers education and guidance and through work experience. The latter proved difficult to set up in some instances but was found to be extremely valuable when it did take place. The more general preparation for adult living included a wide range of personal and domestic skills, dealing with society's institutions and use of leisure time.

As well as devising appropriate curricula, integration programmes entail modifying teaching practice. Ordinary teachers must be able to cope with a wide ability range, selecting appropriate learning strategies and resources and managing pupils' learning in the context of the ordinary class. Some pedagogical approaches can be borrowed from special schools, but the difference in the learning environment leads to different constraints and opportunities. We encountered some innovative practice for supporting pupils with special needs within ordinary classes but there is need of much development in this area. The problem is to provide the necessary support in an unobtrusive and cost-effective way; the pupil must have access to the lesson without being isolated from peers. The numerous difficulties reported in this area stem in part from the lack of training and in part from the general ignorance of appropriate strategies for managing the learning of pupils with special needs in ordinary classes.

Monitoring pupils' progress is an aspect of pedagogical practice that assumes particular importance in integration since pupils are receiving inputs from different sources and there can be a danger of their education being uncoordinated if not fragmented. The standard of record keeping generally leaves much to be desired. Teachers may know a great deal about their pupils without being able to articulate this knowledge for curricular purposes or for passing on to colleagues. There is need of more systematic approaches to record keeping, and also to draw on teachers' tacit knowledge of their pupils and make it accessible in usable form. Records that are devised and maintained with pupils' educational programmes in mind are a means of monitoring their educational progress and ensuring that diverse inputs come together into coherent educational programmes.

THE SOCIAL DIMENSION

Integration programmes provide numerous opportunities for interaction between pupils with special needs and their peers at the different stages of the school day: before and after school; assembly; registration and form periods; classroom; breaks; lunch; and extracurricular activities. These are only opportunities, however, and it must not be assumed that sheer physical proximity automatically leads to meaningful encounters. There is a great deal that can be done both indirectly and directly to promote interaction between those with special needs and their peers. Indirect moves include removing obstacles that hinder contact and instituting structures and procedures that promote it. This can be something as trivial as changing the time of assembly or ensuring that all pupils have a common playtime or it can entail restructuring the school's registration arrangements and system of pastoral care.

Direct interventions to promote interaction were rare. This would accord with the general reluctance to interfere in relationships between pupils. Approaches such as peer tutoring which are in widespread use in America have had little application in Britain. One use of peer tutoring was reported to have been very successful in promoting playtime interactions between junior age pupils with severe learning difficulties and their peers.

What of pupils' social and emotional development? There was a broad consensus among teachers, parents and pupils themselves that they had benefited in terms of social and emotional development from taking part in the integration programmes. There were gains in self-confidence and independence, while being in an ordinary school promoted a realistic acceptance of the individual's handicapping condition. Friendly relationships between pupils with special needs and their peers did occur but they tended to be limited and often involved outgroups in the school. Negative relationships such as teasing were comparatively rare. The incidence of untoward behaviour and bizarre mannerisms was considered to have greatly lessened.

This picture is an encouraging one even if it cannot claim to be based on a representative sample. It is of interest primarily for the information it gives on the factors that bear on pupils' social and emotional development in integration programmes. Numerous factors come into play – age, nature of special needs, kind of interactions taking place, level of supervision and staff support, opportunities for independent action, and many more. These factors interact in a complex way with each other and with the characteristics of the individual location and pupils in it. Identifying them does not lead to prescriptions for action but it does focus attention on the determinants of social and emotional development, and may serve to sharpen the analysis of the social milieu of integration programmes.

Attitudes toward pupils with special needs were generally positive, to an extent beyond what the literature on mainstreaming would suggest. Teachers' thoroughgoing endorsement of the integration programme in their school has been noted, while other pupils generally accepted peers with special needs though not necessarily as fully fledged members of the school community. Among the various factors that govern the formation and evolution of attitudes, pupils' ages and their communication capacity stood out as having major relevance where peers were concerned. The way the integration programme was introduced was important for teachers: informing them and having due consultation with them were crucial in evoking positive attitudes. Particular considerations flowed too from the fact that some integration programmes involved a *grouping* of pupils with special needs: the group should not be too large in relation to the rest of the school; its identity as a group should not be too clearly marked; and care must be taken that individuals are not stereotyped through group membership or alternatively, that the group as a whole is not ascribed a handicapped or deviant identity because of a few individuals within it.

PARENTS

It emerged very clearly that parents wanted their children to be educated at ordinary schools. They were also more concerned about the nature and quality of the education on offer than some of the professionals realized or were prepared to acknowledge. Some sought an active role in this education while others eagerly accepted the opportunity to be involved when it was given them. Many more parents would play an active part in educating their children if their cooperation was enlisted effectively and they were given tasks to do which were meaningful and feasible for them.

Contact between home and school can be organized in various ways and serves different functions. Seeing their children at work was a particularly motivating experience for a number of parents while others benefited from seeing how teachers handled their children or dealt with untoward behaviour. Informal meetings such as coffee mornings helped parents to feel more at ease within the school, while being included in the open day arrangements, school plays and so on reinforced the sense of belonging to the normal community. Home–school books were used to convey messages and maintain a sort of running dialogue between parents and teachers. Home visits helped to form relationships and sometimes gave useful information in planning and carrying out pupil's programmes or work.

Much of this contact was at a general level of befriending and fostering good relations, sometimes intervening with various agencies on parents' behalf and in effect carrying out a social work role. Formal involvement of parents in their children's education was comparatively rare, despite the importance currently attached to it and the numerous exhortations toward it. If parents are to be actively involved, there are three essential steps. First, they must be made to feel at ease within the school and in the company of its staff. Then, unless they are already strongly motivated, they must be encouraged and led to believe that they can make an important contribution to their children's education. Finally, they must be given specific tasks to do which make sense to them and appear relevant to their children's needs.

When parents have a child their lives are changed forever. When that child is not 'normal' it comes as a heavy load. They may feel their lives are blighted and may face years of difficult and painful readjustment to expectation. Many parents do make a successful adjustment and come to recognize and cherish their child's individuality. Society often makes it more difficult for them to achieve this, however. When major institutions such as schooling remove their children from the local community and provide for them apart from the mainstream, the effect is to underline their specialness. If opinion leaders such as doctors and teachers concur with the man in the street in saying that these children must be segregated and indeed are better off that way, parents cannot easily stand against the tide.

One of the contributions of integration is that it helps parents in this regard. Their children attend an ordinary school, often the neighbourhood school, along with peers and are part of the local community. This does not remove the special needs but it does place them in perspective. Parents are all too aware of the need for specialist attention. They can benefit from having this provided in a context of normality where their child engages in some activities alongside peers. When this happens they are less likely to perceive their child in terms of the handicapped identity ascribed by society and may be helped to see him or her as a precious individual who happens to have special needs.

REFERENCES

Department of Education and Science (DES) (1978) *Special Educational Needs* (Warnock Report), Cmnd 7212, HMSO, London

Hegarty, S. and Pocklington, K. (1981) *Educating Pupils with Special Needs in the Ordinary Schools,* NFER–Nelson, Windsor

Hegarty, S. and Pocklington, K. (1982) *Integration in Action,* NFER-Nelson, Windsor

TOPICS FOR DISCUSSION

1. In what ways do structural and organizational factors impinge on the process of educating pupils with special needs in the ordinary school?
2. Discuss the factors involved in setting up an integration programme which are likely to maximize success and avoid pitfalls.
3. 'One of the most striking findings to emerge was the extent to which ordinary teachers endorsed the presence of pupils with special needs in their schools. [...] Many of these had been reluctant if not actually opposed to the idea when the integration programme was first mooted [...]' What pre- and post-conceptions about children with special educational needs might account for this change in attitude on the part of teachers?

SUGGESTIONS FOR FURTHER READING

1   S. Hegarty and K. Pocklington with D. Lucas (1981) *Educating Pupils with Special Needs in the Ordinary School,* NFER–Nelson, Windsor. Part 3 of this book (chapters 5–9) considers the factors involved in staffing: staffing levels, characteristics of teachers, ancillaries and specialist teachers, integration and the ordinary teacher, the role of external specialists, and the training needs of teachers involved.

2. E. Jones (1983) *Resources for meeting special needs in secondary schools.* In T. Booth and P. Potts (Eds) (1983) Integrating Special Education, Basil Blackwell, Oxford. In chapter 9 the author attempts to outline a model for resourcing comprehensive schools in response to the special educational needs of pupils. She considers barriers to change and the problems and principles involved in setting up resource departments.

3. A. Hodgson, L. Clunies-Ross and S. Hegarty (1984) *Learning Together: teaching pupils with special educational needs in the ordinary school,* NFER–Nelson, Windsor. Chapter 7, 'Teachers, Ancillaries and Liaison', deals with problems of changes in the staffing establishments of schools, extending the role of mainstream staff, recruiting specialist teachers, supporting mainstream teachers, and the deployment of ancillaries.

Reading 7
INTEGRATION: SOME PRACTICAL CONSIDERATIONS
National Union of Teachers

INTRODUCTION

The purpose of the following is to identify questions that may need to be considered before integration takes place. They should be asked by LEAs, professionals and parents at an early stage in the planning of integration, preferably before a final decision on placement is made. Teachers from the schools being considered for involvement in the scheme should be included in these discussions.

The list of questions is *not* to be used as an exhaustive checklist for evaluating integration schemes. The relevance of each question will vary according to the needs of each child and the nature of each school. They are

National Union of Teachers (NUT) (1984) *Integration: some practical considerations.* In NUT (1984) Meeting Special Educational Needs in Ordinary Schools, NUT, London. This section is written with reference to 'the child'. It is obvious that in many instances more than one child may be involved.

based on the premise that integration (and the meeting of special needs in general) has implications for all aspects of the life of the school and for all members of staff. The response must therefore come from the whole school if the social and educational benefits of integration are to be secured. To achieve this, teachers will need extra time, training and support.

First general questions are covered, and then seven specific areas: curriculum, staffing, child, family, school, social and physical.

GENERAL QUESTIONS TO CONSIDER

1. What level of integration is envisaged?
    (a) Education in a special class or unit with periods of attendance in an ordinary class and full involvement in the general community life and activities of the school?
    (b) Full-time education in an ordinary school with periods of withdrawal for special help?
    (c) Full-time education in an ordinary class with appropriate help and support?
2. If the integration scheme is as outlined in (a) or (b) above, how can the pupils and teachers in that unit/withdrawal group be involved fully in the life of the school?
3. (a) How is the curriculum for the child with special educational needs to be planned?
    (b) How are decisions on the form, content and delivery of the curriculum to be made?
    (c) How are the innovations or modifications to be planned for, agreed and introduced?
4. (a) Is there an immediate plan for integration for each child?
    (b) Is there a medium-term plan for integration for each child?
    (c) Is there a longer-term plan for integration for each child?
5. In looking at 1–4 above, have the factors listed under the seven subheadings below been considered and fully discussed with all those who are or could become involved: teachers, non-teaching staff, other specialists, the child's family, others involved in the school?

SPECIFIC AREAS TO FOCUS ON

The curriculum

1. How is the curriculum of the school to be made accessible?

2. (a) How can this child be given the same opportunities for the acquisition of knowledge, skills and understanding as other children in the school?
    (b) What changes would be required to achieve this in relation to, for example, each of the following areas: Arts; Craft, Design and Technology; Communication; Numeracy; Environmental Studies; Humanities; Languages; Living Skills; Music; PE/Games; Science?
3. Does there need to be any reconsideration of the ways in which each of these areas is taught? For example:
    (a) What is the usual balance between class, smaller group, individual teaching? How will the child's needs be met by the present system? Are changes required?
    (b) How is teaching organized now for other children with special needs?
    (c) Does the curriculum rely on methods of delivery that need adapting? Does it rely on access to certain resources?
    (d) How is the timetable now organized? Is the day broken up, do children move from room to room, does one group see several teachers in a day? Can this child cope with this? If not, what modifications are realistic?
    (e) Are there times when different groups meet: for example, year assemblies, sports for several classes, mixed-age teaching? Will this suit the child?
    (f) What areas not covered by the present curriculum will need to be introduced? Will this be for this child or also for others now at the school?
4. *The hidden curriculum*: careful thought needs to be given to the hidden curriculum for children with special needs.
    (a) Will the child need to be taught to acquire living skills which others have acquired already?
    (b) Will the curriculum need adapting to cover explicitly areas that are currently implicit?

The staff

1. Do the staff welcome the principle of integration:
    (a) in general?
    (b) in relation to this particular child, its needs and the school?

2. Has consideration been given by staff to ways in which they can best:
   (a) work together for the child with special needs?
   (b) adapt their teaching methods?
   (c) introduce the proposed record-keeping system?
3. What thought needs to be given by the staff to the proposed scheme in terms of:
   (a) the curriculum?
   (b) the child's need?
   (c) particular problems that need full consideration?
   (d) the sources of specialist help?
4. (a) Is integration *planned* in such a way that all staff involved can express both their enthusiasm and any doubts without feeling threatened or feeling that their professional skills are inadequate?
   (b) Do the review procedures allow for them to do this?
5. (a) Has one teacher been given responsibility for considering integration schemes and for looking at special educational needs throughout the school?
   (b) Is this person of sufficient status to carry weight with all others in the school?
   (c) Is his/her post part of the school's management structure?
   (d) If such a post does not exist at present, is one planned? Will the person appointed be in the post in time to play a full part in schemes now being considered?
6. (a) Is the school sufficiently well staffed to enable all teachers to give the integration programme the attention that it requires?
   (b) Do pupil–teacher ratios take account of the extra teacher requirements of schools integrating a child with special needs?
7. (a) Has one ancillary been given specific responsibility for special educational needs?
   (b) Have the ancillary staff who will be directly involved with this child been fully informed and consulted?
8. (a) Are other extra staff needed for the scheme proposed?
   (b) Does this allow proper cover for any necessary training and for any planning meetings?
   (c) When will any extra staff planned be in post?
9. (a) What training for teaching and non-teaching staff is planned now? Have future training requirements been assessed?
   (b) Do these plans cover all the staff involved? Do they cover specialist and peripatetic teachers?

(c)   What other staff need informing about the child's particular needs: for example, school technicians, office staff, dinner helpers, the crossing keeper, the school caretaker, the school nurse?

The child

1. (a)   Can the child cope with the integration proposed now? Will this child cope later?
    (b)   Has consideration been given to the child's view of what is planned? If not, would this be appropriate?
2. (a)   What difficulties or frustrations could this child face?
    (b)   Has consideration been given to this child's intellectual, social and physical needs both at the time of transfer and later?
3.   What are the gains for this child and what are the disadvantages for this child of this scheme?
4.   How will the integration proposed give this child confidence and ensure progress?
5.   Is there a need to consider a completely individual curriculum? If 'yes' how does this fit in with the proposal to integrate this child in other ways?
6. (a)   Has consideration been given to the child's needs if he or she has to be disciplined?
    (b)   What rewards or sanctions are most appropriate?
    (c)   Will these rewards or sanctions be seen as reasonable by other children and by the staff?
7.   Is there a system for counselling that needs modifying to suit this child? For example, is there a need for the child to see only one counsellor over several years?
8. (a)   Is there someone who fully understands the educational, social and physical needs of this child?
    (b)   How is this information to be disseminated to all involved and in time for them to take in the details?
    (c)   Are the likely medical demands understood: for example, coping with fits, the need for, and the effects of, drugs?
    (d)   Are other possibilities, for example, the need to repair hearing aids, fully planned for?
9.   Has consideration been given to the timing of the child's transfer from year to year within the school and from school to school?
10.   Can travel be arranged to and from school?

The child's family

1. (a) Are the family enthusiastic?
2. (a) Has the scheme been fully discussed with them, including all possible advantages and disadvantages?
   (b) Have their views been incorporated, their doubts and worries noted?
   (c) What steps are necessary to alleviate any reservations they may have?
3. (a) Is there a record-keeping system in which the child's family (or friends) should participate: for example, a reading programme?
   (b) Are there particular schemes for their child in which they can play a part?
4. (a) Can the family feel a welcome part of the whole school?
   (b) Are there other children whose experiences they can learn from or families they can contact?
5. (a) Is the relevant documentation copied for families?
   (b) Is it easy to understand?
6. (a) How will the review system involve the child's family?
   (b) Who will explain any changes planned and how long in advance?
7. (a) Has provision been made for home-school liaison visits? If these are appropriate, should they involve one teacher or each teacher who is involved with the child? Will non-teaching staff take part?
   (b) If there are such visits planned, are they reported fully to those working with the child?
8. Is there scope for support in the holidays from the immediate family or from neighbours or other children, so that the process of integration continues smoothly and the child does not lose ground gained?

The school

1. Is there enthusiasm for integration in the chosen school?
2. Is there experience of integration?
3. Is there a school policy towards integration?
4. Is there a coherent approach to the proposals for integration, including acceptance of the idea and a willingness to carry through the changes that may be needed?

5. (a) Does the school's policy for integration include an analysis of how each child can be integrated, and a system of review and recording procedures to monitor the needs of the child?
   (b) Are all relevant parties involved in this process so that the discussion is positive and open?
   (c) If there is no policy, is one planned? What procedures for analysis and review are proposed?
6. What range of children is now taught?
7. How flexible an approach is being developed in the school for all children as individuals?
8. How many children are to be integrated and what are their special educational needs?
9. (a) Are there already children in the school with similar or related needs?
   (b) How are they coping? Will this affect this child?
10. (a) How large is the school? Could this pose problems?
    (b) How large are the classes? Could this pose problems?
    (c) How large are the teaching groups? Could this pose problems?
11. Are there close working relationships with other agencies and relevant professionals: for example, educational psychologists, education welfare officers, advisers, voluntary agencies?
12. Is the local education authority fully informed and supportive? Is it likely to allocate extra staff and extra resources?

The social background

1. (a) Is the school timetable organized to promote social integration?
   (b) Are children who have extra help taught in class or withdrawn?
   (c) Is the focus mainly on group work or on individual work?
2. (a) Can children with special needs have access to all rooms that their class/group uses?
   (b) Can they go on all outings and visits?
   (c) Is there a possibility of using ancillary help to overcome any difficulties?
3. (a) Are children with special needs seen as a separate group?
   (b) Does the layout of the rooms demand that they work together away from the rest of the class: for example, if children are in wheelchairs or are visually handicapped? Can this be modified?
4. Are school clubs accessible to all children?

5. (a) At breaks, can a less mobile child get to all play areas?
   (b) Can he or she use the outside equipment and the equipment provided for wet playtimes?
6. (a) Are there other ways of involving this child with others socially? For example, are new children all looked after by older children?
   (b) Are there forms of help with which other children could be reasonably and safely involved?

The physical environment

1. *Access*
   (a) To the buildings
      (i)   Are there steps or ramps?
      (ii) Is there a gate? Can this be opened?
      (iii) Are there rails? Can this child use these?
   (b) Within the buildings:
      (i) Are there stairs or ramps?
      (ii) Are there rails? Can this child use them?
2. *Classrooms; library, science areas, etc.*
   (a) How are these laid out?
   (b) Does the layout presuppose mobility, normal vision, normal hearing? Are adaptations required to take account of children with special needs?
3. (a) How complex is the layout of the building? Is it single or split-site?
   (b) Are there clear and visible signs which the child can follow easily?
   (c) How far do children move in the day?
   (d) Is there a place where a child can rest?
4. *Lighting*
   Are all areas adequately lit, including classrooms, the library, science areas, changing rooms, corridors, toilets? (Lighting affects children who need to lip-read as well as those who are visually handicapped.)
5. *Noise*
   (a) Is the building noisy?
   (b) Are there lights as well as a bell?
   (c) Is there background noise, like traffic, that could interfere with hearing aids?
   (d) Is there reverberation that could cause problems?
6. *Doors*
   (a) How do they open?

(b)   How wide are they?

(c)   How fast do they close?

7.   Is there adequate access to the main school for transport? Is this also true for any sports area or swimming pool used, and for any other visits that the school arranges (both regularly and occasionally)?

8.   Is the equipment used in the classrooms, dining-rooms, science and sports areas appropriate for the child? Are there ways the equipment needs to be modified or changed?

9.   How are the floors and playgrounds covered? Could this affect the child's mobility?

10.   Are canteen and dining facilities suitably arranged? Is there space for a wheelchair? Is there access to serving hatches and counters?

11.   Are items like tables, desks, chairs, clothes hooks and lockers of appropriate design?

12.   Are all basins, showers and toilets used accesible? Are they easy to use? Are there rails if needed?

TOPICS FOR DISCUSSION

1.   'Careful thought needs to be given to the hidden curriculum for children with special needs.' What is the hidden curriculum and in what ways might it be different for children with special needs?

2.   'Has consideration been given to the child's view of what is planned? If not, would this be appropriate?' Discuss.

3.   'Are children with special needs seen as a separate group?' In what ways may this question be seen as appropriate and in what ways as inappropriate?

SUGGESTIONS FOR FURTHER READING

1.   S. Hegarty and K. Pocklington with D. Lucas (1981) *Educating Pupils with Special Needs in the Ordinary School,* NFER–Nelson, Windsor. Particularly relevant are: chapter 6, 'Specialist Teachers and Ancillaries in Integration'; chapter 7, 'Integration and the Ordinary Teacher', which discusses research findings concerning how competent ordinary teachers feel about catering for pupils with special needs; and chapter 8, 'External Specialists'.

2.   W.K. Brennan (1985) *Curriculum for Special Needs,* Open University Press, Milton Keynes. In chapter 5, 'Resources', the author discusses the teacher's role in curriculum planning and development, the school as a curriculum resource and the role of outside agencies.

3.   D. Galloway (1985) *Schools, Pupils and Special Educational Needs,* Croom Helm, London, chapter 6, 'The Hidden Curriculum, the guidance network and provision for special needs'. This very useful chapter discusses the relationships between a school's policy and practice and messages which may be conveyed through the hidden curriculum.

Reading 8
WAYS OF PROVIDING FOR THE LOW ACHIEVER IN THE SECONDARY SCHOOL: SUGGESTED ADVANTAGES, DISADVANTAGES AND ALTERNATIVES
C. McCall

Traditional arrangements for helping low achievers in secondary schools have developed amid a period of rapid educational change. Currently, therefore, the only certainty is that many general uncertainties are apparent, both in the educational philosophy held concerning the low achiever, and in the best means of providing for him. Most decisions are made at the local level after reviewing – via assessment procedures varying considerably in range and efficiency – the educational problems of each intake of pupils. The level at which children with difficulties are accepted by the school (that is, some schools seem capable of catering for a much 'lower low achiever' than other schools), the specific adaptability of the school itself, and the willingness of the school to expend the effort and money dictated by certain choices show that present practice is parochial. One thing, then, to be held clear at the outset is that present provision for low achievers and attitudes toward them extend to considerable patterns of diversity.

Certainly there are many patterns of organization to be seen, ranging from 'streamed' to 'unstreamed' schools, with virtually every intermediate kind of arrangement. Some schools have only one form of provision whilst others may demonstrate several distinct forms in an attempt to obtain the maximum degree of flexibility. Thus, while some schools continue only to offer educational support in respect of a 'bottom set' or 'special class', other schools reflect a variety of arrangements of a fixed or temporary nature such as a compensatory class, an extraction group for general help, an extraction group for specific help, individual tuition opportunities, and so on. Still more radical, some schools, in an attempt to ensure a good social mix and to alleviate the often difficult problems presented by the older low achiever, operate mixed-ability teaching with some age ranges of pupils or in some selected areas of the curriculum. That is, they take a conscious decision to reduce, as far as is considered prudent, separate arrangements for the education of low achievers.

C. McCall (1980) Ways of providing for the low achiever in the secondary school: suggested advantages, disadvantages and alternatives, *Educational Review,* Occasional Publications No. 7, pp 59–67

Each of the forms of provision so far described has disciples and opponents. Often the pros and cons of each particular arrangement are expressed more emotionally than rationally, and often in a manner that suggests the notion of either-or. Seldom is consideration given to more than one form of arrangement even though established information suggests the need for a range of provision rather than any single dominant form. Indeed, the likelihood of this statement being a truism can be illustrated by considering the following questions and their relation to the range of educational problems subsumed under the portmanteau expression 'low achiever'.

1. Rationally considered, what are the likely advantages and disadvantages of current forms of provision for the child with low academic achievement?
2. How far does each arrangement meet the needs of particular types of problem requiring extra educational help? How flexible is each arrangement *vis-à-vis* heterogeneity often found in designated low-achiever groups?
3. Are there other ways of arranging provision, including possible different combinations of traditional patterns, that permit greater flexibility and comprehensiveness of support?

Space permits no more than the briefest consideration of these questions and the coverage that is given is by no means exhaustive, but one hopes it may serve as the basis for further thought and discussion.

CURRENT FORMS OF PROVIDING FOR LOW ACHIEVERS IN SECONDARY SCHOOLS – LIKELY ADVANTAGES AND DISADVANTAGES

Only the three most common forms of provision are considered in this paper: the 'special class', the extraction system, and mixed-ability teaching. Most schools operate one or more of these arrangements whilst some schools are at present considering them in relation to their present arrangements. What follows is therefore likely to have relevance for many schools.

The suggested advantages and disadvantages of each type of arrangement are summarized in Tables 8.1, 8.2 and 8.3. Polarized

Table 8.1 The 'special' class *

Advantages	Disadvantages
Allows the child with marked difficulties to spend a good proportion of his time in one class with one teacher.	◄─────► May collect 'stigma', i.e. negative attitude on the part of other pupils and staff.
A useful form of provision for the very weak, immature or very timid child.	◄─────► May mean that some low achievers spend too much time apart from able children and the total school community life.
May offer an 'optimal situation' for on-going diagnosis/treatment of educational handicap.	◄─────► Collected diagnosis information from such a situation may be too specific to have easy, apparent meaning for general curriculum studies.
Offers maximum opportunity for work exclusively designed for the child with learning difficulties.	◄─────► 'Curriculum distancing' may occur.
	The arrangement can be wrongly used, e.g. pupils whom ordinary class teachers do not want are conveniently 'put out of sight'.
	Such arrangements tend to be filled by children from lower socio-economic groups.

* Such a class may have one of a variety of titles – 'remedial class', 'opportunity class', 'progress group', 'lower set' and so on.

Table 8.2 The extraction system

Advantages	Disadvantages
Children with low academic attainments are integrated more intensively within the general curriculum.	◄─────► Amount of 'remediation' an individual can receive is limited.
Group size can vary.	◄─────► Groups can be too large or too varied to be a realistic workload. Often extracted to inadequate facilities.

(continued)

(Table 8.2 continued)

Specific extraction is possible, i.e. withdrawal from particular subjects.	←——→ Open to referral misuse.
Extraction sessions can be aligned with main timetable subjects, e.g. all first-year children doing 'English' at the same time.	←——→ 'Curriculum distancing' may occur.
Groups can be more easily related to 'diagnosed needs'.	←——→ Opinion suggests it is a good system for children with mild or specific difficulties but bad for 'hard-core' learning problems.
	Needs a set timetable, hence level of flexibility for remedial specialist is reduced.
	Can highlight a child with difficulties to other children.
	Large campus makes for difficulties.

Table 8.3 Mixed-ability teaching

Advantages	Disadvantages
Theoretically, offers most integrated approach.	←——→ Weaker/bright child may suffer.
Can lead to flexible, varied teaching styles, and extend individual teacher's skills.	←——→ Requires extensive preparation and resourcing to be effective – is often badly resourced and organized.
Many incline to the belief that 'social benefits' accrue from this system of teaching.	←——→ Many still require some form of support provision – this needs careful consideration if the overall aim of integration is not to be defeated.
Dictates to the specialist subject teacher that he has responsibility for the educational welfare of all children.	←——→ Difficult to maintain effectively beyond lower school in many subjects.
Attitude to staff may be very positive.	←——→ Attitude to staff may be very negative.

(continued)

(Table 8.3 continued)

Puts the remedial specialist in the main classroom rather than taking the children out. ◄———►	Traditional training of remedial specialists has not readily equipped them for giving remedial help via general curriculum studies.
If remedial specialist operates in ordinary classroom, requires him to be very flexible and confident – and specialist teachers to consider carefully their participation with him.	

observations or comments are placed side by side for ease of comparison and linked via double-headed arrows.

I have written at more length on some of the issues emanating from these arrangements elsewhere (McCall, 1977) and I would also refer the reader to the work of Haigh (1977), Griffin (1978) and Cooper (1978). Suffice it here to extract the main intended comment, that is, that any of these arrangements if too rigidly adopted would be unlikely to meet the wide variety of educational problems found from a close inspection of the term low achiever. Such close inspection is apparent in the Warnock Report which serves to remind secondary schools that they may well be dealing with nearly the full range of children with special needs:

At present "remedial" groups include children with a variety of difficulties which, though different in origin, are frequently treated alike. There are children who have been absent from school and need to make up work which they have missed; children with physical or sensory disabilities, sometimes temporary, sometimes permanent; children with varying degrees of learning difficulties and children who need to be temporarily withdrawn from the normal class for specific purposes. The term "remedial", like the term "treatment", suggests that these children have something wrong with them that can be put right. It is true that some of them are suffering only a temporary learning difficulty and, given appropriate help, are able to return rapidly to their previous classes having completely overcome their disability. Others, however, require special help and support throughout their school lives and to say that these children require "remedial" education is misleading. Children in these so-called "remedial" groups have a wide variety of individual needs, sometimes linked to psychological or physical factors, which call for skilled and discriminating attention by staff – in assessment, the devising of suitable programmes and the organisation of group or individual teaching, whether in ordinary or special classes. For these children the provision of special support is just as important as for those who have been ascertained as requiring special education. We conclude that a meaningful distinction between remedial and special education can no longer be maintained. (DES, 1978, 3.39)

THE HETEROGENEITY OF 'LOW ACHIEVEMENT'

Given this range of learning difficulties we need the most extensive and flexible provision that is feasible and such provision can be arranged with the fullest efficiency only where senior management staff in secondary schools are prepared to examine more thoroughly their routines of assessment administered on entry. Edwards (1975) and Thompson and Hinson (1978) have written perceptively on a system of initial screening assessment for secondary schools. The system offers a comprehensive assessment programme which, by relating attainment measures via a scattergraph, offers a visual and lucid inspection of the likely range and type of learning difficulties to be provided for. From such an assessment procedure each school is likely to find that it faces *at least* three types of low achievement:

(a) those youngsters with low achievements in all the tested areas probably coupled with low verbal reasoning or low general ability scores – accepting the limitations of standardized tests and remembering the problems of the predictive validity of tests and the disadvantages of too rigidly applying labels, etc., it nevertheless seems fair to comment that such youngsters exist and, irrespective of current titles and provision, we can be certain that for most schools they will present a problem of long-term support;

(b) those youngsters whose related attainment/ability measures would suggest that they need support more along the lines of traditional remedial work, i.e. intensive early support with a view to enabling them ultimately to undertake the curriculum of the school without further additional help;

(c) youngsters whose restriction is within a particular subject (perhaps in mathematics only, or basic English skills only) – the causation for such selective restriction is open to a range of possibilities, e.g. a specific learning difficulty more apparent via that subject material, poor or restricted teaching within that subject area in the primary school, motivational block for that type of work.

We can add to this selection problems of more complex difficulty: youngsters whose low achievement is coupled with obvious immaturities in perceptual, language, motor or emotional development, often of a quite severe or complex nature. Such problems might well fall within the divisions already outlined or be so severe as to constitute a separate type of learning problem. Whatever the range of problems, one point is clear: a school cannot begin to direct adequate systems of provision unless it determines for its unique population of pupils the *type, range,* and *extent of learning difficulties* it needs to cater for.

ALTERNATIVE WAYS OF ARRANGING PROVISION

From this matrix of forms of low achievement it seems clear that support provision which is too limited to one form, or is restricted only to certain members of the school staff, the 'remedial specialists' trained or otherwise, is most likely to be too meagre. Provision is needed that embraces at least the following features:

(a) flexibility in allowing for a range of types of problem to be supported;
(b) provision that is tied closely to support and development in liaison with the general school curriculum and not separate from it;
(c) wide provision that involves all members of the school staff on a remediation/compensation basis, i.e. all staff having some role in extending basic learning skills;
(d) provision that is flexible enough to be altered as demand changes – incoming populations of children will vary in the types of learning difficulties they present;
(e) provision that continues throughout the school and is not confined only to the early stages of secondary schooling.

In respect of these features I would like to offer the following forms of provision for consideration. I have not seen these models operating fully in any particular school but I have seen features of them in many schools. They seem to me to offer more flexibility than some of the traditional approaches, to link the work of remedial and subject specialists more closely, and, in the case of the third form of provision suggested, to ease the transition from the primary stage to the secondary.

The forms of provision are arranged in an order of increasing radicalism to conventional arrangements.

Example I: extraction system and departmental link figures

This form of support is a slight extension of conventional systems. It offers the possibility of educational help being remediation plus compensatory work within a subject area, rather than being simply remedial work of the traditional kind. It fits easily into a general arrangement pattern whereby subject departments operate a 'setting' procedure. Remedial specialists extract the youngsters most in need of small-group help and these are fed back into the lowest 'set', in which operates a departmental link-figure whose role is to t.ansmit the subject content for those pupils with least attainment in the subject (or to modify the content offered) with as much compensation for their restricted attainment as is feasible. In this manner subject departments elect their own 'subject specialist for low attainment' or, if the role is shared on a rotational basis, all members of a given department might acquire experience in this area and bring their own unique talents to bear. Joint lessons with the remedial specialist might be a natural extension and an enterprising subject enthusiast with empathy for those youngsters with low attainment might ultimately become a source of in-service training for his departmental team, offering valuable ideas of compensating for low achievement within a subject context.

Example II: a centre for basic learning

Ideally this would be a permanent resource base from which would operate a conventional extraction system but which might provide the centre for more varied groups than current practice allows. Groups of children (including some formed across a wide ability and age range) based on diagnosed needs would spend time with remedial specialists and possibly subject specialists as well, undertaking support activities specifically designed in respect of their diagnosed needs. Such groups might comprise any or all of the following:

(a) a motor training group – there are considerable possibilities here for linked work with a physical education or drama/movement specialist;
(b) a group for children with specific learning difficulties;
(c) a group for defined help in one area, e.g. handwriting, spelling, basic number;

(d) a 'counselling' group – those children requiring a more therapeutic approach to learning, e.g. in respect of reading, as indicated by Lawrence (1973);
(e) a language development group.

These arrangements might be staffed by free timetabling to the remedial specialists, offering them opportunities to arrange their work on a combined system: say, extraction for a third of the week plus specific training groups for two-thirds of the week. Additionally, they might be supported by specific subject specialists being timetabled to assist particular groups for some allotted time. This arrangement could also lead to the production of useful resources that might form the basis of a school-based in-service training programme. Specialist subject teachers could be encouraged to visit the centre for basic learning during non-teaching time and to observe/participate in the work going on there.

The intention of such an arrangement would be to start from a broad base and to move through a 'core curriculum' in the subject areas with departments having free decision as to how they wish to group pupils, eventually culminating in another broad range of academic/practical activities in the closing years of school life. A central course for *all* pupils would link the two strands.

Example III: a more radical organizational arrangement

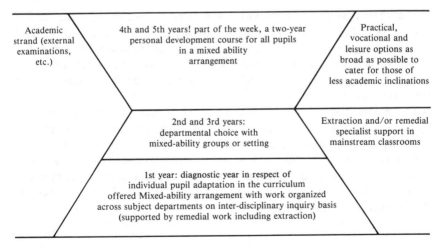

Figure 8.1

Figure 8.1 shows how remedial support would operate from year 1 to year 5, mainly via support within general curriculum areas. The first year would serve as a period of extended diagnosis of individual pupil need. From such extended diagnosis, better use might be made of remedial support and services in the second and third years.

The model is proposed as a direct alternative to a traditional organizational pattern still dominant in many secondary schools, that is the 'funnel-down curriculum'. With such an arrangement external examination syllabuses and associated teaching constraints are funnelled down to the first-year intake, the stem of the funnel being as broad or narrow as departmental or school tradition dictates. It generally operates as a subject-biased curriculum with a consequent dismembering of timetable and learning experiences into many rigid compartments. For the child with low achievements it represents (a) the most severe transitional arrangement from primary to secondary school and (b) the most difficult learning arrangement for them to have to adapt to. As the DES Education Survey 15 (DES, 1971) indicated:

> Exposure of the slow learners to a full programme of specialist teaching is unfortunately all too common. At a time when the suitability of this type of approach is being questioned for the more able pupils, its appropriateness for those without academic interests is even more questionable; their learning is fragmented, and seems to them unrelated to the world of things and people they know.

The alternative forms of provision presented are not the best ones or the only ones. They are offered merely as ideas to stimulate thought and discussion regarding the essence of arrangements for low achievers in the secondary school, that is, flexible patterns of provision to cater for varied needs. To imagine that the needs of low achievers are homogeneous and static is to ignore established facts.

This paper has dealt with aspects of provision for low achievers in secondary schools. Provision is only one element for consideration. Organizational formats do not of themselves remove or compensate for individual differences. Instruction and organization are interrelated, and progress in one demands progress in the other. Teachers, particularly in the secondary school, must be helped to give room to individual differences in the instructional framework they adopt.

REFERENCES

Cooper R. (1978) *Organization*. In M. Hinson (Ed.) (1978) Encouraging Results: helping children with learning difficulties in the secondary school, Macdonald Educational, London

Department of Education and Science (DES) (1971) *Slow Learners in Secondary Schools,* Education Survey, 15, HMSO, London

Department of Education and Science (DES) (1978) *Special Educational Needs* (The Warnock Report), Cmnd 7212, HMSO, London

Edwards R. (1975) *A remedial department in the West Midlands.* In C. Jones-Davies (Ed.) (1975) The Slow Learner in the Secondary School, Ward Lock Educational, London

Griffin D. (1978) *Slow Learners – A Break in the Circle: a practical guide for teachers in secondary schools,* Woburn Press, London

Haigh G. (1977) *Slow Learners,* Temple Smith, London

Lawrence D. (1973) *Improved Reading through Counselling,* Ward Lock Educational, London

McCall C. (1977) Remedial strategies in secondary schools, *Forum,* Vol. 19, No. 2.

Thompson G. and Hinson M. (1978) *Assessment.* In M. Hinson (Ed.) (1978) Encouraging Results: helping children with learning difficulties in the secondary school, Macdonald Educational, London

TOPICS FOR DISCUSSION

1. What other ways might there be of arranging provision, including possible different combinations of existing patterns which could permit greater flexibility and comprehensiveness in the support of low achievers?
2. With reference to the 'special class', the 'extraction system' and 'mixed-ability' teaching, how flexible is each arrangement considering the heterogeneity often found in designated low-achiever groups?
3. Critically discuss the 'model' offered as an alternative to the traditional 'funnel-down curriculum' pattern. What are the implications for general school curriculum and the involvement of school staff in attempting to adopt the author's model?

SUGGESTIONS FOR FURTHER READING

1. J. Garnett (1983) *Providing access to the mainstream curriculum in secondary schools.* In T. Booth and P. Potts (Eds) (1983) Integrating Special Education, Basil Blackwell, Oxford. The author argues that the Warnock concept of special educational need 'encourages the notion of a continuum of need rather than a series of pigeon-holes into which children have so far been uncomfortably and often inappropriately slotted'. She examines the need to begin at the point where attitudes and school ethos can accommodate change and discusses the organizational problems in making the mainstream curriculum accessible to pupils with special needs.

2. M. Wilson (1983) The curriculum for special needs, *Secondary Education Journal,* Vol. 13, No. 2, pp 17-19. Wilson's article considers various types of special needs, the content of the curriculum, the restricted curriculum and principles of organization with particular references to special needs.
3. P. Widlake (1983) *How to Reach the Hard to Teach,* Open University Press, Milton Keynes. Chapter 2, 'Changing Schools to Reach the Hard to Teach', discusses in a very practical way how the curriculum for pupils with special needs should be transformed, and the curriculum principles involved in ensuring that 'change' should stand a realistic chance of success.

Reading 9

CHILDREN WITH SPECIAL NEEDS IN ORDINARY SCHOOLS: INTEGRATION REVISITED
M. Warnock

There are fashions in thoughts as surely as there are in clothes. When you buy a new dress or a new suit, it is not always because the old ones are totally worn out, but rather that you have an instinct that something new is needed. The old dress won't do any more; it doesn't express what you meant. When you buy something new, you may fall in love with it when you see it in the shop. It seems perfect, both aesthetically and from the standpoint of utility. It is impossible that you could ever have got on without it. For a bit, this relationship lasts. You are still in love. But after a time (a time of varied length), you look at the thing you bought with new eyes, and think, 'That's it; I need a new dress.' Of course, at this stage you may enter a new phase of love. You may hold onto the old because it is comfortable, and you cease to notice it. But with ideas, this is a danger signal. You may need to be jolted out of the cosiness.

I believe that, in 1978, when the so-called Warnock Report (a name I dislike because, if ever there was a cooperative effort, that was) was published, the concept of special needs was exactly what was demanded by the circumstances. We wanted very much to get away from the statutory categories of handicap, within the confines of which the provision of special education had been contained. We wanted to widen the scope of any new legislation there might be so that it could cover provision not only for the 2

M. Warnock (1982) Children with special needs in ordinary schools: integration revisited, *Education Today,* Vol. 32, No. 3, pp 56-62

per cent of children who, at the time we wrote, were being educated in special schools, but for something more like 20 per cent of all children at school. We wanted to deflect people from thinking of special education as a peculiar form of education, carried out in special institutions. We wanted to ensure that educationalists and teachers concentrated not on what was *wrong* with children but on what, positively , they must have, if they were to benefit from education (which, after all, for the most severely handicapped had only recently become their right). Finally we wanted to go beyond the faction-dominated, highly political question of integration, the question whether there should be just one local school for all children, by raising the more pragmatic question, apparently less ideological, of how to ensure that all children, whether at school or at home, in special school or in hospital, could get what they needed.

I remember that, when I was still in love with the phrase 'special needs', I was mildly put out when some educational writer spoke slightingly of 'the rhetoric of special needs'. My new clothes had been seen as unsuitable, dowdy or, even worse, vulgar and pretentious. I still don't agree with the implication that we, the authors of the Report, deliberately introduced the phrase to cover up our conservatism and inertia with the veil of humanitarian-sounding claptrap.

I thought then, and still think, that legislation concerned with the education of the handicapped must be ultimately humanitarian in its intention and spirit, rather than straightforwardly utilitarian. But then, I also believed that one could demonstrate, on fairly solid grounds, what counted as an educational need. I thought one could distinguish between what was a *need* and what was something nice and agreeable, but an optional extra. I argued that, if there is an intelligible goal for education, then an educational need is that which must be provided if a particular child is to make progress along the road towards this distant goal. The more formidable the obstacles along the way, the more difficult the progress, and therefore the more numerous and manifest the needs. If I am to walk along a road I need shoes; but there are those who need a wheel-chair, or a pair of crutches, or a guide dog, or other things besides. These needs could be identified and met, and then off we could all go together. I still see that there was a kind of simplicity in the concept which made it attractive; and it was useful in so far as it at least departed from the medical model based on diagnosis of defects, and turned attention to a service model, based on delivering the goods. And it might have worn better, this smart little number, if it hadn't been for the recession. Suddenly in the cold wind, it began to look pitifully inadequate.

Perhaps the main reason for the newly apparent poverty of the concept of special needs is in its definition – or rather its lack of definition. In the 1981 Bill (English) the definition is negative. A special need is a need that cannot be met in the normal school within the limits of normal resources. This definition is absolutely all right in certain fairly extreme, and therefore clear, cases. If all the children, except one, in the school can get to the biology laboratory, but that one child can't because he is in a wheel-chair, then what he needs is a ramp. The provision of a ramp can be exactly costed; the need is indisputably special; and once the ramp is provided, the wheel-chair child is, as far as access to the biology laboratory goes, equal with his fellows. But suppose a more complicated case.

Here is a class of children – too many to a class – and some of them can understand what they are taught very easily, so easily that they are clamouring for more, and if they don't get it they will be bored and disaffected. A middle group can just about understand, and, if they work hard and are undistracted, they may be quite successful. But even within this group there may be many whose success is fairly meaningless to them; the goals of the lesson are of no particular long-term interest or value to them. And then there is another group who really have very little idea what is going on, and who achieve nothing, either passively riding on the back of the rest of the class, thinking their own thoughts, or, in boredom and frustration, chucking the furniture around. Which of these class members has a special need? For whom are extra resources beyond the normal provision of the school necessary? The terrible danger is that we shall say, 'They *all* need extra.' My love-affair with the expression 'special needs' came to an end the first time I heard someone say, 'All children are special: they all have special needs.'

Rather than attempting to analyse exactly what is so hopeless, indeed so repellent, about that statement, I want to digress, to discuss briefly the educational scene in Norway. The reason to pick on Norway, apart from the purely autobiographical fact that I have just been there looking at schools, is that the OECD has recently been asked by the Norwegians to produce a report on the education of the handicapped, and in particular on the way that the integration of children with special needs into ordinary schools is working out in practice. This report may be the first of several; and perhaps we in the UK would greatly benefit from such a detached assessment of the effect of legislation, after a few more years. It would be then that the robustness or otherwise of our policy of integration, and the viability of the concept of special needs on which it seems to be founded, would be put to the test.

INTEGRATION IN NORWAY

Norwegian legislation, bringing special and ordinary education together under one Act, dates from 1976. Parents now have a right to demand that their children be educated in ordinary schools, however severe their handicap. We were told that 99 per cent of all children are now being educated in ordinary schools. But the position is complicated. There still exist a fair number of special schools, and there appears to be no shortage of children to fill them. In addition, there are some institutions run by the social and medical services, but each containing a special school run by the educational service (and a prey to the kind of interprofessional conflicts that are not unknown in this country). Often the special schools seem to be extraordinarily well funded; and most of the children who attend them are there for primarily social reasons – they need boarding provision, or a longer school day than all of the ordinary schools can provide. But even if the 99 per cent claim is exaggerated, the Norwegians have come a long way towards integration.

Schools are funded by local authorities – the school boards of the local 'commune'. But every school has in addition a 10 per cent grant from central government for its disadvantaged pupils. Besides this, if a school agrees to accept a child with a specific need, the need can be exactly described, and the school can put in for what are called 'B-funds' for that child. The local authority receives the B-fund money from central government, and distributes it to its own schools. Of course schools claim more B-fund money than they get (and there is, equally unsurprisingly, a tendency to exaggerate the handicaps of 'special need' pupils in order to get more funds). No school receives more than about 50 per cent of the money it applies for. But still there is, by our standards, a great deal of money about. Sometimes, indeed, the provision seems almost wantonly extravagant. We saw a school where there was one very severely mentally retarded and psychotic boy for whom a special room had been allocated, and a special teacher, all to himself. There were two or three other mentally handicapped children in the same school, but he did not fit in with them, and had practically no contact with them. He was, it is true, geographically 'in' an ordinary school, but he was not, and could hardly have been, in any sense integrated with the other children, since his behaviour was too bizarre to allow him to attend ordinary classes even with his own special teacher beside him. But he was in the school because his parents wanted him to be there; and they were satisfied with the provision. Of course the paradox is that, when this particular boy reaches the age when compulsory education ends, he will go into a hospital or some other institution and probably stay there for the rest of his life. But still his education will have been 'integrated'.

There is a certain reticence in Norway about possible conflict between parents demanding their rights and local school boards with their psychologists and other advisers. In the extreme case I've mentioned, the parents won. But, in fact, I doubt if there was a conflict. The affluent and fairly radical school board in question acceded to the parents' wishes as a matter of principle. There is no provision in Norwegian legislation that the integration should be 'reasonable' in cost. But as recession begins to bite, and money for education is slowly reduced, no doubt conflicts will occur. However, Norwegian parents are law-abiding and, on the whole, biddable; they may quite readily fall in with the advice of the professionals. The key question that the professionals ask is: 'What is best for the child?' This is the Norwegian rhetoric. And people talk as if there were something that was, quite objectively and determinately, 'best' to be discovered by psychologists, advisers and school boards. Such spurious objectivity can be criticized. Nevertheless, there is in Norway a real and very strongly shared feeling that a child ought to go to his local school. Over and over again we heard the claim: 'He must go to the school *where he belongs*.' The whole idea of the *community* (the local authority area which has its own school board) is deeply felt.

None of the horrors of reorganization has been inflicted on people in Norway. But though decentralization is the rule, it is tempered by central control. The funds for children with special needs are centrally provided, but distributed locally. The curriculum is, in detail, a matter for local decision, as, for the most part, are teaching methods and the organization of the school day. But central government has laid down the broad lines of the curriculum – so many hours of mathematics, Norwegian, religion and English. What is best for the individual handicapped child is that, being where he belongs, he should have as much of the regular and normal curriculum as he possibly can, and that his segregation should be progressively diminished.

In Norway, then, we saw some extreme cases of integration, or of non-segregation. And I am completely persuaded that the overall benefits, both to the normal and the handicapped child, are in practically every case overwhelming. We saw Down's Syndrome children working alongside their contemporaries, fully accepted and functioning at a far higher level than they could ever have achieved in a 'special' setting with contemporaries who were themselves all mentally handicapped. Behaviour is largely a matter of imitation, and these children were behaving like the rest of the class. Their contemporaries treated them as real people, not expecting them to be other than they were, different from themselves, but part of the school. Even very severely disabled and mentally retarded children were accepted. No one thought it odd that they should be there; and the system of having more than one teacher in the class, even if one of the teachers was supposed to be working mainly with the disabled child, seemed, on the whole, to operate for the general good. Other children than the 'special' child tended to turn to each of the teachers equally, if they wanted to know something or needed help. We saw some remarkable examples of collaborative or team teaching.

But problems remain. First, it is, relatively speaking, easy to end the segregation of children, however severely handicapped, at primary school level. But what about secondary school? It is unthinkable that one should educate a child with his contemporaries up to the age of 11 or 12, or whenever the changeover comes, and then put him in with only the disabled in a special school. Or so it seems to me. It would be an intolerable disappointment and constant reminder of his disability. But at the secondary stage, even in Norway, difficulties begin to spring up. Norwegian schools are obliged by law to engage only in mixed-ability teaching (though there were some signs of surreptitious 'setting'). Teachers are trained and accustomed to a wide range of ability in the class. But how far down the ability range can they go without sacrificing the able to the less able? Norwegian parents are increasingly prone to raise this question, now that unemployment is beginning to rise above the accustomed 2 per cent and the school-leaving examination (the only examination there is), as well as the system of school marks, takes on a new significance. There is a new feeling that it would be rash to abolish special schools. Perhaps some children will always *have* to be segregated *for the sake of the rest*. There is a contradiction in a policy which apparently gives heart-felt priority to desegregtion, yet pours vast sums of money into special schools. The theory that these schools are to 'resource centres' (common to the Warnock Report and to Norwegian law) seems, at least in practice, to be a not very successful attempt to conceal the contradiction. I believe the same attempt, the same refusal to face the contradiction, is to be found, less obviously, both in our Report and in the consequent legislation.

Then there is the question of *who* is eligible for extra funds? These funds bring entitlement not only to special equipment but to extra teaching hours. It is manifestly easier to justify expenditure on the integration of a pupil whose disabilities can be described in terms that are both exact and dramatic than of one who is only mildly retarded or who has temporarily fallen behind with his work. No school board is likely to give extra funds for this kind of child.

UK PROBLEMS

I believe that these problems, perhaps only just appearing in Norway, are the very same that we have to face here. In our case, too, the concept of 'special need' carries a fake objectivity. For one of the main, indeed almost overwhelming, difficulties is to decide *whose* needs are special, or what 'special' means.

But, in addition, we in the UK have to decide whether we are *really* prepared to envisage the progressive desegregation of the handicapped in school, It is easy to pay lip-service to this principle, without really believing in it for one's own school, or one's own child's school.

As far as the physically handicapped are concerned, I suppose that there is no one who would now doubt the rightness of integration. And the only difficulties in the way are the various physical changes which have to be made to the school (or college) environment. To make these changes may be dauntingly expensive at the moment, but the principle cannot be in doubt; and even if the changes have to be made slowly, there is no doubt that they will come, and will be welcomed. The inclusion of the blind and partially-sighted, and of the profoundly deaf, present more complex but, I believe, not insoluble problems.

The policy decision becomes controversial when we consider those who are severely mentally retarded, those with complex multiple handicaps and, perhaps above all, those whose disability is 'maladjustment', a specific incapacity to get on in a normal school. How, it may be asked, can a child be integrated whose handicap consists of being unable to integrate himself? It seems clear to me that, if we really intend to try as far as possible to desegregate these children (and I am convinced that we should), then we shall have to do so by means of something like a 'unit' system, though, if possible, a unit not stuck on at the end of the school grounds but one which is literally a part of the main school building. The advantage of the unit is that several handicapped children with the same sort of needs can be educated in the same place. I cannot envisage our ever adopting the Norwegian system and establishing a special class and a special teacher for just one single psychotic child. Even the Norwegians themselves seem mildly surprised to find that this has happened; and, quite apart from the cost, the efficiency of such an arrangement is suspect. If either the teacher or the pupil is absent, the system breaks down. A unit may, of course, be nothing but a special school thinly disguised; and it will be as expensive to set up as a new special school. We cannot afford at the present time to envisage the dismantling of all the special schools for the severely handicapped that already exist, even if we build no new ones. I personally doubt whether we shall see this kind of dismantling and consequent integration in our lifetime; but I also believe that already the average pupil in the special school is much more severely handicapped than of old. The less handicapped are already in ordinary schools. And this is right. The more we understand how to educate the mentally retarded, the less need there is to segregate them. For example, there will not, I hope and believe, be many Down's Syndrome children left in special schools in a few years' time.

We must also remember that, if desegregation is our overall aim, there is a great deal to be done in preparation for it. We urgently need more teachers who *both* train in special education *and* teach in ordinary schools, and who are prepared to teach *both* handicapped *and* non-handicapped children. Before pupils can be properly desegregated, teachers must integrate themselves.

To some people it would sound like an absurd paradox to suggest that what was wrong with our schools was that they were too academic. How could an inner-city comprehensive school, say in dockside Liverpool, be thought to be *academic,* especially if it is compared with Winchester or St Pauls? But the point is not that the *schools* are too academic but that the curriculum is; so that there is a constant mismatch between what the pupils can do, and ought to be encouraged to do, and what is officially expected of them. And the worst of all the failing children will be those who would have succeeded if they had been at an old-fashioned ESN(M) school. For in a good ESN(M) school, children did not fail. They were set tasks at which, if they worked hard, they could succeed. Their education was firmly directed to an understanding of their immediate environment, and an ability increasingly to function efficiently within it. They were encouraged to work at the practical, not the theoretical, and in the best of the schools they ended up with pride in their own achievements and even the prospects of a job. (Of course it must be added that not all ESN(M) schools were good schools, and that the bad were very bad, with extremely low expectations of the pupils, normally self-fulfilling.)

I certainly do not advocate the retention, or the reopening, of special schools for the ESN(M). Such a policy would be totally incompatible with the 1981 legislation, as well as with the more general spirit of the age. But I do believe that, in order to accommodate those children who would have been their pupils (as well as many other children, as a matter of fact), we have most urgently to rethink the whole curriculum. I suggest that, instead of the present dichotomy between Arts and Sciences (a totally outmoded dichotomy in any case), there should be a fundamental division in the curriculum between the practical and the theoretical. Thus any subject – history, biology, music, art, mathematics – could be studied in either way.

No one should leave school with examination passes *only* in theoretical subjects. But some could leave with passes *only* in the practical, and these, of course, at various levels. Even reading and writing could be taught to the really slow learners in connection with practical subjects, and so could mathematics (the way most people learn and use mathematics, in any case, once they have left the classroom). I believe that this way of structuring the curriculum would prove beneficial to everyone. For it is not only the slow learners who suffer from the theoretical and abstract bias of the present curriculum. Who among those who attended even the most enlightened comprehensive school does not, for example, regret the non-practical manner in which he was taught modern languages? Who does not wish that he had spent less time learning the periodic table or various chemical formulae and more time learning to mend a fuse or correct the faults in his car? We all know that the choices to be made between arts and science subjects in English schools (things are not so bad in Scotland) are damaging to the country as a whole. But both arts and sciences could, with advantage, be subdivided into the practical and the theoretical. If this were done, I believe that we should see many more pupils who actually benefited from school, and who came to regard it as their own resource centre, where they could practise what they wanted to do. And among these pupils would be those who hitherto have necessarily failed. Unless we make some such change, we cannot seriously pretend to be interested in integration. I would far rather now press forward towards some such change than, within the bounds of the present curriculum structure, try to satisfy each pupil's special needs. I for one have grown tired of my old dress. I am sick of special needs. It is time to move on to the next idea.

TOPICS FOR DISCUSSION

1. Discuss the following statements:
    'I thought then, and still think, that legislation concerned with the education of the handicapped must be ultimately humanitarian in its intention and spirit, rather than straightforwardly utilitarian.' (M. Warnock, 1982)
    'It is resources and vested interests, rather than egalitarianism, which are more likely to determine the outcome of the integration debate.' (S. Tomlinson, 1982)

2. By removing children from positions of segregation do we ipso facto render them integrated?
3. 'We assumed that a special need could be defined in terms of help a child must have if he was to gain access to *'the curriculum'* [...]. Only occasionally did we think that the curriculum must be changed to suit the child.' (M. Warnock, 1982) Discuss.

SUGGESTIONS FOR FURTHER READING

1. S. Tomlinson (1982) *A Sociology of Special Education,* Routledge and Kegan Paul, London. In chapter 3, 'Issues and Dilemmas in Special Education', the author discusses the problems which arise as a result of the complex and ever-changing terminology employed in special education to describe and categorize children, and attributes such problems to the competing vested interests involved. She argues that the expedient solution to the problem of the continued creation of new categories of handicap has been the substitution of the notion of special educational needs as a rationalization for special education.
2. T. Booth (1983) Integration and participation in comprehensive schools, *Forum,* Vol. 25, No. 2, Spring, pp 40–42. The author links the integration issue to the reform of comprehensive education, claiming that the children who are sent to special schools and classes are there, for the most part, because ordinary schools have not adapted their curricula and forms of organization to diverse needs, interests and talents. He argues that, because integration and comprehensive education were not linked within the Warnock Report, the integration issue, as Mary Warnock put it, was 'fudged deliberately'.
3. J. Sayer (1983) *A comprehensive school for all.* In T. Booth and P. Potts (Eds) (1983) Integrating Special Education, Basil Blackwell, Oxford. In chapter 5 the author argues that most educators and most critics of secondary schooling agree that comprehensive development has not yet gone far enough to justify its inelegant description, and that it is rare to find a comprehensive school unaffected by social stratification. He discusses, in this context, the problems of determining the strategies required to integrate special and normal provision in comprehensive education.

INTEGRATION: SPECIFIC LEARNING DIFFICULTIES

INTRODUCTION

In Section 3 of the sourcebook Reading 10 examines the problems involved in integrating hearing-impaired children into ordinary classrooms. We know that children affected by relatively mild conductive hearing losses have learning difficulties in school, usually to do with speech and language development, listening skills, behaviour, reading attainment and general achievement. Hearing impairments caused by some kind of permanent damage to the sensori-neural systems we know to have much more serious effects on the child, for, as well as the difficulties described above pertaining to restricted auditory experience, the problems here are much greater, leading often to wider implications for social adjustment and emotional development (Webster and Ellwood, 1985). Thus, deafness is not just simply a deprivation of sensory input, but also a disruption of adult–child interactions and relationships. Hodgson outlines a number of conditions which she emphasizes *should be met* before a hearing-impaired or profoundly deaf pupil comes into the ordinary classroom. The conditions she specifies are concerned with school organization, the child and the classroom. Of particular value in the suggested further readings is the text by Webster and Ellwood which, the authors state, has been written primarily for the ordinary class-teacher who has no specialist qualifications or experience in teaching the hearing-impaired child. Reed provides a valuable account of the psychological, emotional and social consequences of hearing loss on children. Finally, Wadd adds a dissenting viewpoint, bringing to our attention that for the hearing impaired the question of integration is more complex that it seems. Many people handicapped by severe deafness come to identify themselves as a community. Thus, in an integrated educational programme where no special methods such as sign language are used, the aim is to prepare children for life in a *hearing* community, not a *deaf* one.

Reading 11, again by Hodgson, is concerned with factors involved in integrating physically handicapped children into ordinary schools. In planning for satisfactory integration in the school she discusses factors of school organization, the pupil, the classroom and the main conditions of handicap likely to be met by teachers in ordinary schools. The suggested further readings develop in more detail many of the points raised in the article.

Reading 12 focuses on the problem of visual handicap, and in doing so provides a microcosm of many of the opportunities and difficulties associated with the integration of handicapped children generally. Low begins the article with a comprehensive discussion of 'the shape of the problem', using DES official statistics to show that special educational provision for the visually handicapped *overwhelmingly* means separate or segregated provision, and, so far as the blind are concerned, separate provision very largely means boarding provision as well. Low critically evaluates the official, comparatively self-contained 'blind education system' and contrasts this with the significant number of children with a visual handicap being educated in a variety of settings outside these schools. The author propounds some very compelling arguments for integration and discusses the views of the opposition lobby in the section entitled 'Institutional resistance'. Of particular relevance to the topic of 'integration' in general is the close examination of 'ideological factors'. The suggested further readings by Hodgson and by Hegarty *et al.* concern themselves with the practical problems of integrating visually handicapped pupils, while the DES document discusses the implications of integration in the light of declining rolls for the special schools.

The last reading in this section (Reading 13) provides a fascinating account of four case studies which examines the importance of the *audience* when appropriate schooling for children with special needs is discussed. Two of the case studies demonstrate instances of children being transferred to special schools, one where there was a positive and concerted effort to 'integrate' and another where a move to segregate was allowed to lapse. The author explores how, between them, they illustrate the power and preoccupations of teacher, headmaster, psychologist and parent. Sewell suggests also that they all demonstrate that the outcome of such processes would have been difficult, if not impossible, to predict, if only because of the reflexive aspects of special educational needs. In the suggested further readings, Tomlinson's article adds weight to Sewell's thesis. She argues that all professionals involved in special education bring their own particular vested interests to the problems of selection, categorization and selection as well as their concern for individual children. Bart's scholarly analysis explains the role of special education and its management procedures as a societal 'sorting agency'. Rowitz contributes an important and comprehensive discussion of 'labelling theory' which is one of the themes examined by Sewell in the early part of his paper.

Reading 10
HOW TO INTEGRATE THE HEARING IMPAIRED
A. Hodgson

A survey conducted in 1983 (British Association of Teachers of the Deaf, 1984) indicates that the number of hearing-impaired children catered for in special schools and units has remained stable although there is a continued trend to educate pupils within units rather than special schools. Unit education, which has increased rapidly over the last few years, enables the hearing-impaired pupil to be given as much time in ordinary classes as he/she can benefit from, and to get as much specialist help as needed within the unit.

Table 10.1   Education of hearing-impaired pupils, 1981–1983

Pupils	1981	1983	% change
In special schools	3,722	3,469	− 6.9
In units	3,782	4,049	+ 7.5
In local schools	23,072	19,231	− 16.5

As can be seen from Table 10.1, there also appears to be a reduction in the numbers of hearing-impaired pupils being catered for in ordinary schools. An allowance must be made for the different criteria used by local authorities when defining hearing impairment in response to a survey questionnaire. The term generally includes a wide range of impairment, from profoundly deaf children to mildly hearing impaired. Some authorities will include all those with conductive deafness while others only those with sensori-neural losses; yet others only those pupils with hearing aids. The numbers may also reflect only those hearing-impaired pupils in ordinary schools receiving some form of specialist help and may not therefore be fully representative of all pupils with hearing impairment in ordinary schools.

The lower incidence (nearly 4,000 fewer in 1983) of hearing-impaired pupils in ordinary schools may also relate to additional factors. Firstly, there are indications of a lower incidence of hearing impairment in the population because of improved health care (i.e. fewer rubella syndrome pupils), Secondly, better hearing-aid technology and improved screening techniques leading to early identification of hearing impairments offer the

A. Hodgson (1984) How to integrate the hearing impaired, *Special Education: Forward Trends*, Vol. 11, No. 4, pp 27-29

opportunity for preschool intervention. With such help many pupils are later able to benefit from mainstream education without needing special help.

As numbers decrease and as desegregation has become part of the new orthodoxy, unit education for hearing-impaired pupils has gained in popularity. From such unit bases many pupils can receive part or all of their education in ordinary clasrooms (Wood and Hirshoren, 1981) although the indications are that at present only a small percentage of unit-based pupils receive all their education in ordinary classrooms. However, the responsibility for their progress is going to be increasingly with the ordinary class-teacher. It is extremely important, therefore, that such teachers are adequately prepared to help hearing-impaired pupils participate fully in class activities.

A principal aim in the education of hearing-impaired pupils is to develop their use and understanding of the spoken language so necessary for full participation in society. The question, then, is which educational environment is most likely to develop this: the special school, unit or ordinary class. A handicap of any sort is relative to context and it is important when considering placement for hearing-impaired pupils to distinguish those constraints and limitations imposed by the handicap itself from those which may arise out of the educational environment (Lynas, 1978, 1981).

If ordinary classes are considered, another important question is how far the ordinary teacher and hearing pupils should (or can) accommodate the special needs of the hearing-impaired pupil or, conversely, how far the hearing-impaired pupil can reasonably be expected to accommodate the demands of the ordinary classroom. Certainly awareness of the implications of different teaching systems and classroom practices is important when consideration is being given to placement of the hearing-impaired pupil in the mainstream.

FACILITATING INTEGRATION

To ensure satisfactory integration the following conditions should be met before a hearing-impaired or profoundly deaf pupil comes into the ordinary classroom.

School organization

1. Classroom teachers concerned should have a basic understanding of the nature of hearing impairment and its relation to learning. They should

be aware, for example, that hearing impairment leads to delay in speech and language development and that this will influence the child's ability to develop other communicative skills, of which reading is probably the most difficult. The retardation tends to be directly related to hearing loss (Jensema, 1975; Jensema and Trybus, 1978).

2. Before being introduced into ordinary classrooms, hearing-impaired pupils should have some training in developing their listening skills. Most deaf individuals have some residual hearing and the educational environment should make the most of this.

3. Classroom teachers should be (a) *au fait* with hearing aids and able to check they are properly functioning, (b) know that the aid amplifies all sounds, therefore loud background noise can frustrate the progress of the hearing-impaired pupil, (c) keep an extra battery/cord in the classroom.

4. Classroom teachers should be helped not to prejudge a hearing-impaired pupil. They should be made fully aware that the severity of hearing loss is not indicative of the likely success of an integration programme.

5. Classmates should be introduced to the consequences of hearing impairment and to helpful techniques to improve communication. In many schools visited it was reported that classmates had quickly become 'masters' at communicating with their hearing-impaired peers and could provide valuable help to the class-teacher in this respect.

The pupil

There are several academic and social qualities which should be optimally possessed by hearing-impaired pupils for whom ordinary schooling is being considered.

1. The pupil is able to use any residual hearing and can cope with full-time use of a hearing aid.

2. The pupil's language and speech skills are not too significantly below those of the class groups.

3. The pupil's age is within two years of the class average; otherwise he or she may find difficulty in fitting in with classmates.

4. The social/emotional maturity is equal, or nearly equal, to that of hearing classmates.

5. The pupil is sufficiently self-confident, independent and determined to function in the ordinary class.

6. The ability and concentration of the pupil is within the range for the proposed class.

(from Griffing, 1970, and Northcott, 1973)

It has been shown that the closer the hearing-impaired child's academic abilities are to those of his or her peers, the greater the chances for academic success in integration, and that the amount of hearing loss is not a reliable pointer to success here (Gonzales, 1980).

The classroom

Once in the classroom, the following guidelines will help the hearing-impaired pupil to function to his or her maximum potential.

1. Find the best seating arrangement for the hearing-impaired pupil where he or she can hear and lip-read best. The teacher may need to experiment, remembering that it becomes difficult to lip-read beyond 8–10 feet.

   In some activities (for example, classroom discussions) the hearing-impaired pupil is naturally at a disadvantage – unable to predict the next speaker and losing valuable visual cues whilst trying to locate him or her. It is often during such exchanges that the hearing-impaired pupil becomes 'lost', and may withdraw from the situation mentally or become disruptive in an effort to control it. Hearing-impaired pupils should be allowed to move to a position where they can best observe all their peers and, with some teacher control of the discussion, may be able to pick up some of the points. Although class discussions always put the hearing-impaired pupil at a great disadvantage, they are nevertheless an important part of class activities and should not be abandoned because of the presence of a hearing-impaired pupil. Simply summarizing the major points of the discussion at the end can provide the hearing-impaired pupil with an adequate alternative.

2. Teacher and peer speech should be normal and the speech rate moderate. Exaggerated mouth movements and incomplete sentences can be misleading.

3. To aid lip-reading, speakers should always face the hearing-impaired pupil and avoid standing with their backs to a window or light source. The light source should always be behind the hearing-impaired pupil.

4. Gestures, if used, should be natural, not exaggerated, as excessive movement can be distracting.

5. Of the many technical aids available to the classroom teacher, only a few will be of benefit to the hearing-impaired pupil. For instance, use of the overhead projector can be of enormous benefit as the teacher can face the class whilst the projected slides are on view. Later the slides could be made available to the hearing-impaired pupil to copy. However, material presented on tape audio-cassette and much material on video may be difficult, if not impossible, for the pupil to follow.

6. It is helpful when teaching to use as many visual cues as possible, such as pointing to objects or diagrams being spoken about. 'Those who cannot hear must use eyes instead of ears to receive information and in this respect are very different from hearing persons' (Stokoe, 1976).

   Although adapting a teaching style may be necessary to maintain progress, suggested alterations must not be misunderstood. They do not imply criticism of the way a teacher works but simply that, as a hearing person, the teacher may not be wholly aware of all the difficulties a hearing-impaired pupil has in normal, everyday situations. In presenting material the teacher must take care to use language consistent with the material taught, not to be overly complex or go too quickly through the material. Indeed, we observed that it was often helpful to other pupils as well as the hearing-impaired pupil for the teacher to paraphrase, simplify and repeat those points critical to the concept being taught.

   Use of visual aids such as written instructions and summaries is extremely important and, when combined with good oral presentation and periodic verification, should be enough to enable the hearing-impaired pupil to follow the main thrust of the lesson. If a hearing-impaired pupil who normally tries hard starts to withdraw or becomes difficult, this indicates a lack of understanding. The pupil must be encouraged to ask questions but from our observations this is something that hearing-impaired pupils are very reluctant to do.

7. It is almost impossible for a hearing-impaired pupil to look at material like maps and books and simultaneously listen to what the teacher is saying. Wherever possible, such teaching styles should be modified to take into account the hearing-impaired pupil. Where such techniques may be necessary, as for example in map reading, it may be possible to use a 'friend' to provide special help as necessary. The 'friend' could be a classmate or welfare assistant.

8. A hearing-impaired pupil has difficulty in localizing sound and would therefore find it hard to follow a questions-and-answers session

around the class. Such a problem is overcome if the teacher repeats such questions and answers.

9. It is not advisable to assume that the hearing-impaired pupil is getting the same information from a class as his/her normal hearing peers (Hedgecock, 1974). It is helpful to summarize lesson points on the blackboard and to put up key words and homework. It also helps the hearing-impaired pupil to have lesson notes to take away at the end of each session, if possible.

10. Class teachers should watch out for signs of fatigue, remembering that lip-reading is extremely tiring over long periods. It is important to determine why a pupil may not be paying attention. The aid itself may not be working efficiently or the ambient noise may be too high; there may have been insufficient back-up support or the pupil may simply be tired.

    This last point is particularly critical, as trying to comprehend verbal messages all day with an imperfect linguistic and auditory system is extremely tiring and by early afternoon many hearing-impaired pupils are unable to cope. It is desirable that as many of the language-based subjects as possible should be scheduled for the morning, although with complex timetabling this may not always be possible in secondary schools. If it is impossible to reschedule lessons, class-teachers may have to be made aware that hearing-impaired pupils may not function fully in the afternoons and may require more help than usual in class to maintain progress.

11. Cooperative working arrangements with the specialist teacher of the deaf and the classroom teacher can greatly aid integration. Such arrangements may include a specialist teacher modifying or adapting class materials and giving back-up support at the end of a topic or prior to the introduction of a new topic – remembering most deaf pupils do not read as well as their peers (Culthane and Curwin, 1978).

12. The class-teacher should make sure of the hearing-impaired pupil's attention before speaking – a 'helper' may be of use here.

13. It must be remembered that a hearing-impaired pupil is likely to require support throughout his or her school career (see Gearheart and Weishahn, 1980; Pasanella and Volkmor, 1981).

14. It is most useful to observe hearing-impaired pupils in unstructured situations (for example, breaks and lunchtimes) to ascertain their status within the peer group, and whether or not they take part fully in the group's activities. Acceptance within the peer group has a direct and important bearing on the pupil's education, as an unhappy,

isolated pupil is unlikely to be fully receptive to mainstream teaching. Once aware of the situation, the class-teacher may be able to help the pupil improve his or her status within the group if this proves necessary.

SUMMARY

To ensure that a hearing-impaired pupil integrates as fully as possible, all the above points must be taken into account adequately. To expect the classroom teacher to cope without some form of in-service training may hinder the process of integration. Such training would give the teachers the knowledge and information necessary to understand the educational problems of hearing-impaired pupils, and the confidence to begin to cope with them.

Our observation in schools suggest that the hearing-impaired pupil is expected to follow the curriculum for the mainstream class. He or she should be able to perform adequately within the group if placement is correct and if he or she receives extra assistance to enable progress to be maintained.

One very effective programme observed was the preview, teach and review paradigm, in which the specialist teacher previewed prospective lessons by discussing content, new concepts and language. The class-teacher then presented the lesson (the 'teach' component) after which the specialist teacher reviewed the material to ensure understanding. Such support was not needed in all subject areas but the indications were that support would be necessary for most language-based subjects such as English and history, and would be needed throughout the pupil's school career. Continued support throughout the pupil's career is likely to be necessary because hearing is unlikely to improve and the pupil will continue to miss some of the words intended for his or her ears.

REFERENCES

British Association of Teachers of the Deaf (1984) 1983 survey on salaries, staffing, numbers of hearing impaired children and use of manual communication, *The Teacher of the Deaf,* Vol. 8, No. 1, pp 11–15

Culthane, B. and Curwin, R. (1978) There's a deaf child in my class, *Learning,* Vol. 7, No. 2, pp 111–113

Gearheart, B.R. and Weishahn, M.W. (1980) *The Handicapped Student in the Regular Classroom,* C.V. Mosby, St Louis

Gonzales, R. (1980) Mainstreaming your hearing impaired child in 1980: still an oversimplification, *Journal of Research and Development in Education,* Vol. 13, No. 4, pp 15–21

Griffing, B.L. (1970) *Planning education programmes and services for the hard of hearing.* In F Berg and S.G. Fletcher (Eds) (1970) The Hard of Hearing Child: clinical and educational management, Grune and Stratton, New York

Hedgecock, D. (1974) Facilitating integration at the junior high level, *Volta Review,* Vol. 76, No. 3, pp 182–188

Jensema, C.J. (1975) *The relationship between academic achievement and the demographic characteristics of hearing impaired children and youth.* In Series R, N.2, Office of Demographic Studies, Gallaudet College, Washington DC

Jensema, C.J. and Trybus, R.J. (1978) *Communication patterns and educational achievement of hearing impaired students.* In Series T, N.2, Office of Demographic Studies, Gallaudet College, Washington DC

Lynas, W. (1978) Integration and the education of hearing impaired children, *The Teacher of the Deaf,* Vol. 3, No. 1, pp 7–15

Lynas, W. (1981) Integration and teaching styles, *Special Education: Forward Trends,* Vol. 8, No. 3, pp 11–14

Northcott, W.H. (1973) *The Hearing Impaired Child in a Regular Classroom: pre-school, elementary and secondary years,* Alexander Graham Bell Association for the Deaf, Washington DC

Pasanella, A.L. and Volkmor, C.B. (Eds) (1981) *Teaching Handicapped Students in Mainstream,* Charles E. Merrill, Columbus, Ohio

Stokoe, W. (1976) The study and use of sign language, *Sign Language Studies,* Vol. 10, pp 1–36

Wood, F. and Hirshoren, A. (1981) The hearing impaired in the mainstream: the problem and some successful practices, *Journal for Special Educators,* Vol. 17, No. 3, pp 291–302

TOPICS FOR DISCUSSION

1. Discuss the major considerations involved in deciding how far the hearing-impaired child can reasonably be expected to accommodate the demands of the ordinary classroom.
2. 'Severity of hearing loss is not indicative of the likely success of an integration programme.' What might be more important factors?
3. What are the implications for teaching style and curriculum organization of the fact that 'trying to comprehend verbal messages all day with an imperfect linguistic and auditory system is extremely tiring'?

SUGGESTIONS FOR FURTHER READING

1. A. Webster and J. Ellwood (1985) *The Hearing-Impaired Child in the Ordinary School,* Croom Helm, London. This book, the authors state, has been specifically written for the ordinary class-teacher who has no specialist qualification or experience in teaching hearing-impaired children. The authors provide a very readable and comprehensive guide to deafness (chapter 2,

'Deafness: some basic facts') and explain the developmental, social and psychological implications for hearing-impaired children of the classroom experiences likely to be encountered in the ordinary school.

2. M. Reed (1984) *Educating Hearing-Impaired Children in Ordinary and Special Schools,* Open University Press, Milton Keynes. The author considers the nature and consequences of the many different varieties of impaired hearing and the psychological, emotional and social consequences of hearing loss on children. He discusses the controversial question of the communication methods (oral and manual) which are used, the processes involved in developing language skills and the kind of curriculum needed for hearing-impaired children in ordinary schools.

3. For a dissenting view on the topic of integration and the hearing impaired, read P. Wadd, (1981) *The erosion of social and self-identity by the mainstream: a personal experience.* In G. Montgomery (Ed.) (1981) The Integration and Disintegration of the Deaf in Society, Scottish Workshop Publications. The author provides a vivid account of his own experience of mainstreaming, describing it as 'the most dangerous move yet against the early development of a deaf person's character, confidence and basic sense of identity' (p. 405).

Reading 11
INTEGRATING PHYSICALLY HANDICAPPED PUPILS
A. Hodgson

The principle of integration, now enshrined in legislation, encourages placement in mainstream schools for pupils with special needs. A project, funded jointly by the National Foundation for Educational Research and the Schools Council, focused on the tasks faced by schools and class-teachers as a result of increased integration. This project, Special Educational Needs in the Ordinary School, carried out by research officers at NFER, ran for a period of two years from January 1982. The project investigated over 70 primary and secondary schools in which pupils with special educational needs were being taught in mainstream classes.

By means of interview, classroom observation and discussion with groups of teachers, the team has been able to identify a range of approaches and methods on which teachers draw in meeting the needs of pupils with a variety of sensory or physical handicaps or pronounced learning

A. Hodgson (1984) Integrating physically handicapped pupils, *Special Education: Forward Trends,* Vol. 11, No. 1, pp 27–29

difficulties. We were able to detail the teaching strategies used and the process by which the curriculum is modified to take account of the needs of these pupils. It is hoped that the report will assist teachers at all levels of appointment in ordinary schools in planning and implementing learning programmes and teaching strategies for a wide range of pupils with special educational needs.

This paper, however, seeks to offer some guidelines and teaching tips to the mainstream teacher concerned with meeting the needs of physically handicapped pupils in a mainstream setting. These guidelines comprise a combination of points taken from areas of good practice uncovered by project fieldwork and others cited in recent literature.

FACTORS TO CONSIDER

Planning is a key word in the integration of physically handicapped pupils as both physical and social factors may limit the extent to which they can join in class activities. Unnecessary hardships can be caused by lack of adequate transport or unsuitability of the school building (Spencer, 1980). Other factors affect the pupil's acceptance by his or her peers – for instance incontinence (when effective toileting assistance is not given), social immaturity and interrupted attendance due to repeated hospitalization. We must remember that there are three levels of integration (physical proximity, social and academic) and that one level does not automatically lead on to the next. Total integration requires functioning at all three levels (societal integration) with the handicapped pupil becoming a naturally accepted member of the school community. Such integration requires positive attitudes and adjustments by *all* members of the school community. With physically handicapped pupils the physical environment of the classroom and school has to be even more carefully considered (Gearheart and Weishahn, 1976) than modification of teaching strategies. Acceptability of pupils in the ordinary classroom appears to depend upon their being academically able (Cope and Anderson, 1977; Anderson, 1973).

PLANNING FOR SATISFACTORY INTEGRATION IN THE SCHOOL

School organization

1. As much pupil history must be accumulated as possible. Receiver staff should be able to see the pupil at home or at the feeder school. This

contact should alleviate many fears. Reciprocally, the pupil should meet receiving staff.

2. Staff should be aware of the ways and at what level the pupil communicates both verbally and in written work.

Several schools in the study were able to make arrangements for the teacher in charge of pupils with special needs at the receiving ordinary school to visit pupils at work in the feeder schools in advance of their enrolment at the receiving school. The arrangement included a minimum of a day's visit to the feeder school to observe pupils and talk with staff concerned with each pupil. In this way the teacher in charge gained first-hand experience of how the pupils could cope in mainstream and, by discussion with their teachers, was able to gain information about materials and teaching strategies which had proved most useful. Staff felt that the information gained in this way was far more pertinent to the task of ensuring an adequate programme was provided at the receiving school than anything that could be transmitted through written reports. Although such arrangements were time-consuming initially, in the long term time was saved. It ensured a smoother integration of pupils at the receiving schools as special needs and problems were made known and acted upon prior to each pupil's arrival.

3. In-service training is essential to acquaint staff with the handicap question: the most common handicapping conditions and the psycho-physical and academic factors associated with them; and also to convince staff that beyond an unattractive body lies a real child who thinks and acts like other children (Allsop, 1980).

4. Physical adaptations should be decided. Is it, for instance, necessary to install or arrange (a) special toileting facilities, (b) ramps, (c) grab rails, (d) a lift (or modification in classroom usage), (e) safe storage space for crutches, etc. within reach of users? Freedom of movement, whether assisted or independent, is of greatest importance.

5. Any special emergency procedures should be anticipated and made known to the staff concerned (Bigge and Sirvis, 1978).

6. Help, support and advice from specialist personnel should be encouraged, for example from specialist teachers, physiotherapists and speech therapists.

7. Class-teachers should be prepared to work in the classroom with support staff such as welfare assistants and physiotherapists, and to collaborate with colleagues in order to share information and skills (Allsop, 1980; Gearheart and Weishahn, 1976; Johnson and Johnson 1980; Schultz, 1982).

The pupil

If physically handicapped pupils are to integrate into mainstream schooling as fully as possible, several academic and social conditions should be met.

1. The mobility of the pupil should be fully assessed; how and when physical help will be needed, what physical position and postures are to be encouraged or discouraged, what physiotherapy is necessary.
2. The physically handicapped pupil may have less energy than a non-handicapped one, thus reducing his or her ability to cope with the full school day. The class-teacher needs to be alert to signs of fatigue, to provide opportunities for rest and reduce work volume where necessary.
3. Often, because of handicap, the pupil uses muscles with abnormal tone to perform necessary tasks. All available adaptive methods and/or aids must be used in order to increase independence and efficiency of working.
4. Teachers should be ready to cope with specialized equipment and be aware of signs that it is not working properly.
5. Teachers should remember that electric typewriters do not increase speed but are useful for pupils whose writing is illegible or who have limited energy.
6. A welfare helper should be available when necessary, for example to take a pupil to the lavatory (Allsop, 1980; Gearheart and Weishahn, 1976; Johnson and Johnson, 1980; Schultz, 1982).
7. The age of the pupil should be within two years of the class average.
8. Social and emotional maturity needs to be more or less equal to that of non-handicapped classmates.

The classroom

What happens inside the classroom affects pupils' learning most immediately and it is the element of school life that is under the class-teacher's control. Once a pupil enters the classroom the following points can usefully be considered.

1. Advice on classroom management should be at hand – for instance on the durability and suitability of certain furniture since some items are less stable (Greer and Allsop, 1978) and on adaptations to help the pupil manage books, pencils and other materials (Hoben, 1980).
2. Suitable seating must be provided. Physically handicapped pupils must have stable, secure seating at the right height, and may also need tables so that wheelchairs can get under them. Pupils can outgrow

furniture and several teachers remarked on the need to monitor the arrangements.

3. The teacher should be ready to organize the classroom to accommodate specialized equipment such as an electric typewriter or book holders.

4. The pupil must be allowed to be as independent as possible and it is important that the teaching space allow the pupil to move around as independently as possible and become an accepted social member of the group. Many staff from project schools recommended that any equipment needed by pupils is as unobtrusive as possible and does not constitute a physical barrier between handicapped pupils and their peers.

5. If pupils have poor coordination, be prepared to tape paper to the desk or provide large pencils. Similarly, a slant board, providing a correctly angled surface, is useful for pupils who find horizontal surfaces impossible or difficult to work on.

6. A 'helper' or welfare assistant can be of great use in note taking for severely handicapped pupils; extra help should only be given, however, if it is clearly needed.

7. If writing is particularly difficult, maybe a helper or a tape-recorder can be used during tests.

8. Teachers must be prepared to deal with the asthmatic, epileptic or diabetic pupil in case of emergency – to cope with a seizure, to have sugar available for diabetics, for instance.

9. Classmates should be made familiar with the pupils' disabilities and special needs.

10. Teachers must give priority to organizing the classroom in such a way that the handicapped pupil's social and emotional development, as well as academic progress, is encouraged as much as possible.

11. Furniture should be arranged in such a way that the pupil can move about freely and see all of the room in its different perspectives. This encourages incidental learning and makes the pupil feel that he or she is part of the class.

    Some teachers reported very good results from discussing the problem with the class. Such discussions reinforced the pupils' awareness of the need for tidiness, for instance pushing in chairs when not in use, not leaving bags or books blocking aisles so as to allow freedom of movement for a wheelchair pupil or a pupil on crutches.

12. Crutches, wheelchairs and similar aids tend to get in the way when they are not in use. A storage area should be provided and pupils

trained to keep the aids in it.

13. The handling of books may be difficult for some physically handicapped pupils and can consume much energy. A slant board or book holder can be of great benefit; many kinds are commercially available.

14. Talking books can aid learning for pupils who are physically exhausted by traditional methods of reading.

15. Tag board or paper strips clipped to a board can be an invaluable aid as place keepers for pupils with erratic head movements. Helping the pupil to keep his or her place, or presenting material in small segments, can often make the difference between independent learning and time-consuming one-to-one tutoring.

16. Do not accept different standards of behaviour or work from handicapped pupils. They should be expected to be as clean and tidy in their workplace as their classmates. If they are mobile, with or without aids, they can be asked to run errands as often as other pupils.

17. Most physically handicapped pupils are able to take part in some form of physical education. A programme may require specialist help to begin with.

18. Important notices must be within easy sight, perhaps placed lower than normal, particularly if the pupil is wheelchair-bound. Several teachers remarked on the degree of independence this gave pupils, enhancing their feelings of being part of the class.

19. Physically handicapped pupils should have an equal chance to take part in the school's extracurricular activities. Advance planning may be necessary, particularly if the pupil is taken to school by taxi.

    One school encouraged parents to collect pupils on days they wished to stay later to participate in extracurricular activity. Sometimes parents are unable to do this but arrangements may be made with other parents collecting children from the same class. The fact that some pupils do have to come to school by taxi should not prevent pupils taking part in extracurricular activities if at all possible.

20. While basic teaching methods will probably not need to be changed for physically handicapped pupils, teachers will need to be flexible as to volume (but not quality) of work and the way it is produced.

SUMMARY OF NEEDS

Physically handicapped pupils attending ordinary classes will need few modifications of the education programme. However, teachers and other professionals must always maintain a positive attitude and encourage a similar response in the pupil's friends and peer groups. The literature suggests that ordinary class-teachers are not always prepared to work effectively with pupils who have special needs (Baum and Brazita, 1979; Middleton *et al.,* 1979; Byford, 1979; Schultz, 1982), but possibly this is because they do not know at first how to work effectively with such pupils.

From our study it would appear that, once initial anxiety about having a handicapped pupil in class is overcome, teachers are most concerned to ensure the full participation of these pupils in class activities. However, teacher expectations were often lower for handicapped pupils than for their non-handicapped peers.

Physically handicapped pupils are able to participate in all aspects of the curriculum although limitations may arise in physical education. Class-teachers, it has been suggested, should know about the purpose, care and maintenance of general equipment such as braces, crutches and wheelchairs, but – it must be stressed – this will not be their prime responsibility. Preparation of staff is generally acknowledged to be vital and yet is often not provided (Hegarty, 1982). Insufficient staffing, including support staff, or unsuitable staff deployment are other important factors which may limit an integration programme.

The main conditions likely to be met by teachers in ordinary schools are given below, together with their likely effects on education.

Allergies

These are fairly common and should be noted. Occasionally a pupil may miss school but allergies should not greatly interfere with his or her education.

Asthma

Pupils with asthma should be treated as normally as possible. Again, interference with education is unlikely.

Arthritis

The educational modifications here, particularly for juvenile arthritis (Stills disease), depend on age, severity of condition, general mobility and the range of mobility in arms and fingers. Education may be interrupted if the pupil misses a considerable amount of school time during an attack or needs hospitalization.

Amputation

Pupils with a prosthesis are usually able to function at nearly normal capacity and require little additional support except immediately after an operation when they are experiencing the greatest psychological effects.

Diabetes

Class-teachers should be aware of insulin reactions and diabetic comas but pupils should be expected to take part in all normal school activities unless specifically restricted by a doctor.

Epilepsy

All three common types of seizures are serious and the teacher should be aware and able to cope. Minor modifications and adjustments to the educational programme may need to be made for the pupil, particularly if the drugs used to control the epilepsy limit the pupil's learning ability.

Cerebral palsy

Of the serious crippling conditions, cerebral palsy is the most common. The severity of the condition may vary considerably and a full range of educational services may be needed. The severity will dictate whether the student would best be served in a segregated or an ordinary class.

Spina bifida

These pupils usually have normal intelligence but may have multiple handicaps resulting from varying damage to the central nervous system such as varying degrees of paralysis, sensory loss, bowel and bladder incontinence and often hydrocephalus. Most pupils profit from ordinary class attendance with only minor modifications to the curriculum if suitable care and support are available.

Muscular dystrophy

During the early stages very few adjustments are necessary but as the condition progresses some modification will be essential. The pupil should be regularly reviewed and modification and support made available when necessary so that he or she is maintained in the ordinary class for as long as possible. It is to be remembered that the pupil may have to receive education at home or hospital eventually (Gearheart and Weishahn, 1976).

REFERENCES

Allsop, J. (1980) Mainstreaming physically handicapped students, *Journal of Research and Development,* Vol. 13, No. 4, pp 37-44

Anderson, E.M. (1973) *The Disabled School Child,* Methuen, London

Baum, H.R. and Brazita, R.F. (1979) Educating the exceptional child in the regular classroom, *Journal of Teacher Education,* Vol. 30, pp 20-21

Bigge, J. and Sirvis, B. (1978) *Children with physical and multiple disabilities.* In N.G. Haring (Ed.) Behaviour of Exceptional Children, Charles E. Merrill, Columbus, Ohio

Byford, E.M. (1979) Mainstreaming: the effect of regular teacher training programmes, *Journal of Teacher Education,* Vol. 30, pp 23-24

Cope, C. and Anderson, E.M. (1977) *Special Units in Ordinary Schools: an exploratory study of special provision for disabled children,* University of London Institute of Education

Gearheart, B.R. and Weishahn, M.W. (Eds.) (1976) *The Handicapped Student in the Regular Classroom,* C.V. Mosby, St Louis

Greer, J.G. and Allsop, J. (1978) *Adapting the learning environment for hearing impaired, visually impaired and physically handicapped.* In R.M. Anderson, J.G. Greer and S.J. Odle (Eds.) (1978) Individualising Materials for Special Children in Mainstream, University Park Press, Baltimore

Hegarty, S. (1982) Meeting special educational needs in the ordinary school, *Educational Research,* Vol. 24, No. 3, pp 174-181

Hegarty, S. and Pocklington, K. with Lucas, D. (1981) *Educating Pupils with Special Needs in the Ordinary School,* NFER-Nelson, Windsor

Hoben, M. (1980) Toward integration in the mainstream, *Exceptional Children,* Vol. 47, No. 2, pp 100-105

Johnson, D.W. and Johnson, R.T. (1980) Integrating students into the mainstream, *Exceptional Children,* Vol. 47, No. 2, pp 90-98

Middleton, E., Morsink, C. and Cohen, S. (1979) Programme graduates' perception of need for training in mainstreaming, *Exceptional Children,* Vol. 45, pp 256-271

Pasanella, A.L. and Volkmor, C.B. (Eds) (1981) *Teaching Handicapped Students in Mainstream,* Charles. E. Merrill, Columbus, Ohio

Schultz, L.R. (1982) Educating the special needs student in the regular classroom, *Exceptional Children,* Vol. 48, No. 4, pp 366-368

Spencer, M. (1980) Wheelchairs in a primary school, *Special Education: Forward Trends,* Vol. 7, No. 1, pp 18-20

TOPICS FOR DISCUSSION

1. Discuss the author's remark that with regard to physically handicapped pupils there are three levels of integration (physical proximity, social and academic) and one level does not automatically lead on to the next.
2. What are some of the major factors of school organization to consider for the satifactory integration of physically handicapped children into the ordinary school?

3. How can teachers organize their classrooms to ensure that the handicapped pupil's social and emotional development, as well as academic progress, is encouraged as much as possible?

SUGGESTIONS FOR FURTHER READING

1. J. Allsop, (1980) Mainstreaming physically handicapped students, *Journal of Research and Development,* Vol. 13, No. 4, pp 37–44. A useful discussion of the problems of curriculum, physical environment, adjustment, peer group and general school organization in the integration (mainstreaming) of physically handicapped pupils.
2. S. Hegarty and K. Pocklington with D. Lucas (1981) *Educating Pupils with Special Needs in the Ordinary School,* NFER-Nelson, Windsor. Chapter 18 discusses in detail various factors which impinge on the social and emotional development of pupils with special needs. Of particular relevance is the discussion of 'maturity' under the three subheadings: self-confidence, independence and adjustment to handicap. This very useful reading is based largely on teachers' judgements of particular pupils but amplified in some instances by interviews with the pupils and their parents.
3. S. Hegarty and K. Pocklington with D. Lucas (1982) *Integration in Action,* NFER-Nelson, Windsor. Chapter 5, 'Individual Integration of Physically Handicapped Pupils', considers organization and aims, pupils, staffing, ancillary help, accommodation and resources, the curriculum, monitoring progress, and the role of parents with respect to the physically handicapped child in the ordinary school.

Reading 12
INTEGRATING THE VISUALLY HANDICAPPED
C. Low

This chapter considers the problems associated with integrating children with a particular handicap: visual handicap. This is worth doing for several reasons: first, it provides a microcosm of many of the opportunities and difficulties associated with the integration of handicapped children generally. In this connection, given the amount of systematic and well-directed pressure that has been brought to bear over a considerable period of time in support of greater integration for the visually handicapped (so far with only very limited success), it vividly illustrates the kind of resistance

C. Low (1983) *Integrating the visually handicapped.* In T. Booth and P. Potts (Eds) (1983) Integrating Special Education, Basil Blackwell, Oxford

integrationists often have to face. But second, by highlighting those aspects that are peculiar to a particular handicap group – what might be termed the 'handicap specific' as opposed to the 'common core' elements of the problem – it focuses attention on the need for a strategy which is sensitive to the needs of particular subgroups within the overall category of the handicapped as a whole. Finally, it is particularly worth looking at the visually handicapped at the present time since in May 1982 the Department of Education and Science called on local authorities, in regional conferences, to carry out, as the first of a series of reviews of provision for different groups of handicapped children, a review of their provision for the visually handicapped to culminate in the promulgation of a national plan by the summer of 1983. This is something for which the Vernon Report (DES, 1972) had called a decade earlier. Regional conferences were reactivated for the purpose in 1975, but nothing much seems to have happened as a result. It is to be hoped that the stimulus of declining numbers may possibly have injected the necessary fluidity into the situation to make a restatement of the integrationist position timely and a reorientation of provision possible.

THE SHAPE OF THE PROBLEM

According to DES official statistics, there were in January 1981, 975 blind and 2098 partially sighted children attending special schools, hospital schools, independent schools or special classes at maintained schools, receiving education otherwise than at school or awaiting admission to special school. These figures represent prevalence rates of 1.12 and 2.41 per 10,000 school population respectively. These 'officially identified' visually handicapped children are catered for principally in 32 inevitably small special schools – half run by local education authorities, and half (chiefly those for the blind) by voluntary bodies. Of these, 12, all boarding, cater for the blind alone; 16, of which 3 are boarding, for the partially sighted; and 4, all boarding, for blind and partially sighted children together.

Thus, special educational provision for the visually handicapped overwhelmingly means separate or segregated provision. Moreover, at least so far as the blind are concerned, separate provision very largely means boarding provision as well. The figure of 80 per cent for pupils boarding at schools for the blind appears low only in comparison with the staggeringly high figure of 97 per cent given by the Vernon Report a decade ago (the comparable figures for the partially sighted are 1971, 42 per cent; 1981, 35 per cent). Tony Booth (1981), arguing from the dropping proportions of the total school population in special schools for the visually handicapped since

1950, has suggested that visually handicapped children appear to be less likely to attend a special school now than in the past. But he himself acknowledges the possibility that this might be due to a fall in the proportion of children with sight difficulties as much as to any change of policy with regard to school placement. This would appear to be what has happened over the last ten years, at the beginning of which time the Vernon Report gave prevalence rates of 1.37 (blind) and 2.66 (partially sighted). Certainly the proportions of 'officially identified' visually handicapped children placed in special schools – have hardly altered at all since the publication of the Vernon Report a decade ago, and this is surely the relevant statistic to take.

The Warnock Committee (DES, 1978) stated that there has been a steady increase over time in the number of handicapped children placed in designated special classes and units in ordinary schools, rising from 11,027 in 1973 to 21,245 in 1977, i.e. from 6.8 per cent to 12 per cent of all children ascertained as requiring separate special provision. The children placed in these classes and units, the committee makes clear, have been mainly those with moderate rather than severe disabilities, but all categories of handicap are represented. So far as the visually handicapped are concerned, the partially sighted have felt the benefit of this trend to some extent, their numbers attending special classes in ordinary schools having risen from 81 in 1973, the first year when such statistics were given, to 205 in 1981. But the blind have hardly been touched by this development at all: no blind children were in special classes in ordinary schools when such information first became available in 1973, and by 1981 there were still only 7.

Warnock also states that placements of children with disabilities in ordinary classes are becoming more frequent, though statistics of these are not available. For some time now, it has been recognized that there are almost certainly a considerable number of children with a visual handicap of some sort in ordinary schools, in addition to those recorded in the statistics as receiving special education; increasing numbers have also been coming to light in hospitals for the mentally subnormal and similar institutions. Only lately, however, have we begun to gain some idea of the size of these groups, at least so far as the educationally blind are concerned. In 1982 Colborne Brown and Tobin were able to identify at least 1093 such children who were being educated in a variety of units and schools throughout the country outside what might be termed the 'official' blind education system. This finding that there are as many blind children being educated outside the 'blind education system' as in it accords with the picture derived from local authority social services statistics by Jamieson *et al.* (1977). But it would be a mistake to regard many of these placements as representing integration in the sense of full functional integration into the ordinary life and classes of ordinary schools. From this point of view, Colborne Brown and Tobin's description of their study as one of the 'integration of the educationally blind' is really rather misleading, and their liberal use of inverted commas round the word 'integration' shows some awareness of this. Their more neutral formulation, 'not attending special schools for the visually handicapped', which they use elsewhere, would perhaps be nearer the mark. In fact only 144 or 14.4 per cent of their discoveries were in mainstream schools or some sort of unit attached thereto. Almost all of the 114 children placed in a mainstream school directly were one-off placements. Some were sixth-formers having moved from schools for the visually handicapped. A substantial number were at infant school, so might not necessarily remain in integrated provision; and the authors surmise that it is probable that some were placed in mainstream schools for other than strictly educational reasons. None of this bespeaks a particularly vigorous growth of integration schemes throughout the land. The great majority of the children identified by Colborne Brown and Tobin (nearly 700 or 69 per cent) were in schools or units for the ESN(S), ESN(M/S) or physically handicapped, or in special care, hospital or hospital school – some in residential placement, but most on a daily basis; and closer analysis of a subsample of 411 cases showed that almost half (47 per cent) had a mental as well as a visual handicap, and three-quarters could accurately be described as multiply handicapped.

What kind of a picture, then, is presented by this diversity of circumstances in which visually handicapped children are being educated? On the one hand, we would seem to have an official, comparatively self-contained, 'blind education system', in which about 3000 visually handicapped children are being educated, very largely in special, often residential, schools specifically for the visually handicapped. On the other hand, there are also a significant number of children with a visual handicap being educated in a variety of settings outside these schools – settings which, by virtue of being outside the officially sponsored blind education system, all too easily give rise to the misconception that the children being educated in them are in fact being integrated into the community. So far as the partially sighted are concerned the contention of integration is probably correct. Colborne Brown and Tobin did not study this group, but Jamieson *et al.*, in their 1972 study, cited local authority social services figures showing that 29.8 per cent of registered partially sighted children aged 5–15 were in ordinary schools. The only questions, then, that arise concern the adequacy of the support they receive and the means of moving more of them from the comparative isolation of the closed official system towards the more open system of provision in the community. But so far as the educationally blind are concerned, there is real reason to question whether the system has not become skewed so as to make for a serious mismatch between provision and need – those who could safely take their place in the ordinary school, where the requisite systems of support exist, being educated away from the community in the official blindness system, and those who need the services that system has to offer being cut off from it with inadequate support, at least so far as their visual handicap is concerned.

In the rest of this chapter, bearing in mind that it is the education of the blind as opposed to the partially sighted that is usually thought to give rise to problems of such an intractable nature that the only thing to do with them is to sweep them under the carpet, I shall concentrate largely on the problems of the self-contained blindness system, on the rigidity in the system which gives it so much staying power despite those problems, and in particular on what is needed to make the official 'blind education system' more open-ended, capable of releasing people into the community at one end while at the other end it draws in those who can best benefit from the particular resources that it has to offer.

FURTHER DIMENSIONS OF THE PROBLEM

I do not intend to argue the full case for integration here. This has been done many times before, and no one not already convinced is likely to be converted by mere repetition. This chapter is essentially concerned with the question 'how?' not 'whether?'. But it may just be worth observing that the general case for integration has two aspects. The first, insufficiently stressed, is expressive or symbolic in character. Unnecessary segregation from the community represents a derogation from full humanity and citizenship. Secondly, integration also has an instrumental function. Separate socialization breeds attitudes of prejudice, intolerance and self-denigration; and integration, particularly at the formative stage of development, can do much to sweep away the barriers of ignorance and misunderstanding that keep the handicapped and unhandicapped apart, and ultimately lead to discrimination, dependency and an inability to cope.

These considerations apply in full measure to the visually handicapped. Going to an ordinary school helps a visually handicapped child to grow up and learn to cope with life as a member of a sighted and not a self-enclosed 'blind' world in the most practical way possible – by living in it. It also fosters in the sighted an appreciation of visual handicap as a wholly normal incident of human diversity instead of something alien, to be at best uneasy about or at worst to reject. But integration holds several other quite specific advantages – indeed imperative –so far as the visually handicapped are concerned. The chronically small numbers inevitably mean that the self-contained 'blind education system' has certain inherent limitations: it is forced to operate at a regional or even a national level. We have already seen that this entails an extremely high proportion of children having to board away from home for the whole of their schooling. Even so, many of the schools involved, especially those for the partially sighted, still have to cover the entire age range to attain viability; and in order to mobilize the resources necessary for more advanced work, a rigorous system of 11 + selection is more or less obligatory. The very fact of being a self-contained system also has serious drawbacks: as the National Federation of the Blind and Association of Blind and Partially Sighted Teachers and Students (1973) have shown, the special school, particularly the residential special school, has major disadvantages as a setting for the coeducation of the sexes, for educating blind and partially sighted children together, and for educating visually handicapped children in conjunction with children suffering from other kinds of handicap.

Much of this is often thought to be unavoidable on account of the extremely small numbers involved – there simply are not enough children to make viable primary, let alone comprehensive, schools on anything remotely approaching a neighbourhood basis. And the problems will become acute as numbers decline still further. The DES (1983) has projected numbers for the 'official' system of no more than 700 blind and 1600 partially sighted by the end of the decade. But as can readily be seen, this is only a problem as long as it is decided to retain a self-contained system of schools for the visually handicapped alone, more or less completely separated from the rest of the education system. If blind and partially sighted children were educated in ordinary local authority schools, it becomes immediately obvious that it would be possible for them to receive a normal primary and comprehensive secondary education much closer to home. Indeed the National Federation of the Blind and the Association of Blind and Partially Sighted Teachers and Students (1973) have estimated that if resource centres for the visually handicapped were established in as few as 40 primary and 40 related secondary schools strategically located throughout the country, 82 per cent of the visually handicapped school population could live well within daily travelling distance of their homes – a figure that rises to 95 per cent if 52 centres of each type could be established. It is obvious, too, that by bringing visually handicapped education much more into the educational mainstream, visually handicapped children could benefit from the greater resources and range and diversity of subjects and staff available in the ordinary school. Indeed the system of integration outlined here offers the only viable model, consonant with other objectives, for providing visually handicapped children with a fully comprehensive secondary education with direct access to higher education.

Is this practical? Many would say not, but there has been quite sufficient experience of integrating both blind and partially sighted children into ordinary schools both here and abroad to put it beyond doubt that it is entirely practical *so long as the necessary arrangements are made for providing within the ordinary school itself the specialist teaching and support which visually handicapped children clearly need.* The National Federation of the Blind and Association of Blind and Partially Sighted Teachers and Students (1973, 1977, 1980 and 1982) have devoted extensive study to the practical aspects of implementing a system of integrated special education for the visually handicapped, and the next section outlines their proposals in the context of the total range of provision required for visually handicapped children generally.

THE MAIN FEATURES OF A SYSTEM OF SPECIAL EDUCATION FOR THE VISUALLY HANDICAPPED

Special education for the visually handicapped, like special education generally, should aim to make available a range, continuum or diversity of provision. Only thus can the much talked-of individualization of provision be achieved or anything like a real choice provided. To comprehend the variety of needs evident among the visually handicapped school population, three main types of provision need to be made: for the seriously additionally handicapped, provision in residential special schools; at the other end of the scale, for those with comparatively mild visual handicaps, peripatetic support in the local ordinary school; for those in between, the educationally blind and those more seriously partially sighted, as already indicated, a network of resource centres in selected ordinary schools throughout the country.

The National Federation of the Blind and Association of Blind and Partially Sighted Teachers and Students (1982) have summarized the function, characteristics and resource requirements of such centres as follows:

1. The centres should provide specialist teaching in the skills required by visually handicapped pupils, and also back-up support, materials and advice for those pupils and the members of staff who will teach them in the ordinary classes of the school. In particular, after initially concentrating on the teaching of special skills within the resource centre, particularly in the early years at primary level, the objective would be to promote the progressive integration of each blind or partially sighted child into the ordinary classes of the school.

2. Each resource centre would provide for both blind and partially sighted children together, as recommended by the Vernon Committee, and cater for up to 5–10 blind and 10–20 partially sighted children.

3. Each resource centre would occupy about four or five small rooms at the heart of the ordinary school, and would be staffed by specially trained teachers, together with non-teaching assistants. The staffing ratios would be of the order of, in a primary school, 1 teacher for every 5 or less blind pupils, and 1 teacher for every 10 or less partially sighted pupils, plus 1 non-teaching assistant for every 2 teachers in the resource centre; in a secondary school, 2 teachers for the first 15 pupils, whether blind or partially sighted, plus 1 teacher for every 15 or less thereafter, plus 1 non-teaching assistant for every teacher.

4. Each centre would also have all the necessary equipment and materials, including books and materials in Braille and large print, and the resources to produce and duplicate them, plus tape-recording equipment, aids to low vision, mobility aids, and so on.

Although the schools in which resource centres are established should be very carefully selected, in particular for their all-round quality of educational provision, motivation towards the integration scheme and location, they would not need as a rule to be specially adapted in their physical structure. Visually handicapped children have no difficulty in coping physically in special schools that have not been specially adapted for them in any way and, given that one of the functions of the resource centre would be to provide or secure mobility training and aids, this should not present any particular problem in the ordinary school either. Nor should there be any great difficulty in making available in the ordinary school whatever in the way of resources is currently made available in special schools. Indeed the ordinary school will probably have a larger stock of 'general' resources from which the visually handicapped child will be able to benefit. Provided, too, that specialist teaching assistance is made available for the visually handicapped children as indicated above, there should be no problem over providing ordinary class teachers with the back-up support, guidance and advice which they will need in order to be able to cope with visually handicapped children in their classes. Home–school transport services would need to be considerably geared up to meet the needs of visually handicapped children attending ordinary schools with a resource centre, but savings on the cost of sending children away to residential special schools out-county would more than offset the cost of this.

In areas with a particularly small and far-flung visually handicapped population, peripatetic support in local schools may be the only alternative to boarding special education. It is not as good as support from a resource centre within the school, but it operates satisfactorily in sparsely populated parts of the United States, and is generally to be preferred to boarding special education.

If the official 'blind education system' is afflicted by so many problems, and an alternative blueprint without such drawbacks not only lies ready to hand but has actually been implemented successfully in many parts of the world, why should the 'blind education system', with all its difficulties, have displayed such resilience, and the alternative special educational strategy have been taken up in so few quarters here? The answer to this question must, at least in part, lie with the institutional resistance and ideological factors to which I now turn.

INSTITUTIONAL RESISTANCE

It is sometimes suggested that if integration has such a compelling logic for the official 'blind education system', nothing much needs to be done in order to bring it about. But if this is not actually disingenuous, it is extremely politically naive. As Booth (1981) has pointed out, the special education system has a momentum of its own. So long as special schools continue to exist and we continue to carry on running them, there will be places to be filled and people with an interest in filling them. At a time when space is at a discount, even single individuals can make a difference to viability. There will be pressure to retain the less handicapped within the system as a leaven for the other children and the staff. We can soon end up reaching the point where the children are meeting the needs of the institutions instead of the other way about. At the very least, the forces of inertia tell heavily in favour of the special school sector. A major redeployment of resources requires planning, effort, commitment and will. People have to change their established practices and modes of working. How much simpler just to carry on operating the well-tried procedures!

There are practical problems in integrating some handicapped children in some parts of the country. But often the practical difficulties have more to do with the reorganisation of jobs and occupational aspirations, with the reallocation of money and resources, than with the needs of children. This inertia within the system is an important human issue, and any change requires skill, sense and sensitivity. (Booth, 1981, p.308)

These points are well illustrated by the particular problem posed by the special grammar schools for the blind run by the Royal National Institute for the Blind for boys and girls respectively at Worcester and Chorleywood. In order to enhance their effectiveness and assure their viability, the Institute is presently seeking to merge the two schools, either on one of the existing sites or on a third site altogether, possibly in conjunction with another school for the blind. Some special schools for visually handicapped children with serious additional handicaps will continue to be needed, but if the integration is going to take place on any scale at all among the blind, the children who have typically gone to Worcester and Chorleywood in the past will be prime candidates for making the transition. Thus the two schools present a key impediment to structural reorganization. At a time when one is trying to redeploy resources for special education towards the ordinary school sector, it makes no sense to be making a major new investment in the special school sector such as the reconstitution of Worcester and Chorleywood would unquestionably represent. The creaming off of all the most suitable candidates would throw up a stumbling block to the development of properly designed projects for supporting the integration of blind children into ordinary schools at a local level of the kind discussed above. With all the institutional pressures that inevitably exist to fill special school places once they have been created, rather than going to the considerable trouble of developing support systems in ordinary schools of their own, it would be a natural temptation for local education authorities simply to send blind children to the residential schools where they know that provision has traditionally been made for them. Furthermore, given the present very general lack of proper provision for visually handicapped children in ordinary schools, those with responsibility for advising on placement have little alternative but to steer children towards this special school sector.

To the extent that the merger of Worcester and Chorleywood does not have the consequences feared above, and local schemes of integration do begin to blossom, then by contrast it will tend to lead to a wasteful overprovision of special school places. If the trend towards integration gathers pace, there would in fact be serious danger of creating a costly white elephant if the residential sector of secondary education for the blind was continued in the manner proposed. We have already seen that the number of blind children of secondary school age may be as low as 350 by the end of the decade. As many as a third of these could require the special provison reserved for those with serious additional handicaps, and not all the rest will be of Worcester–Chorleywood standard. A merged selective school providing 150 places, i.e. the size of the two existing schools combined, would thus be bound either to 'scoop the pool' or end up as a half-empty mausoleum. Instead of attempting to shore up an honourable but essentially outmoded tradition, the RNIB would be better putting its resources into helping to promote good schemes of integration at local level.

IDEOLOGICAL FACTORS

Special education, like most mysteries, is too important to be left to the professionals – they mystify things too much. Certainly the sort of institutional resistance just described is powerfully buttressed by a series of plausible misconceptions and misrepresentations that may be said to amount to an ideology of special education. The fact that much of this rests on an extremely insecure foundation of confusion and distortion is not to the point: the power of an ideology has much more to do with its value in supporting a particular view of the world than with the rationality of its specific propositions. A fuller account of these can be found in Low (1981). Space permits only the following summary here:

1. The essential slipperyness of the notion of integration, its convenient ability to mean all things to all men, make it a veritable godsend to the practitioners of mystification. Integration is portrayed as treating everyone handicapped and unhandicapped alike, exactly the same. The opponents of integration are thus enabled to argue that integration is incompatible with providing the kind of special help that handicapped children clearly need. But such an antithesis is wholly false. As we have seen, responsible advocates of integration for the visually handicapped are at considerable pains to specify how the necessary help can be made available. For them, 'integration' essentially means 'supported integration'. The only difference that separates them from their critics is their concern to see help mobilized in the ordinary school at the heart instead of on the periphery of the community.

2. We have already remarked the tendency to talk of anything other than education in a special school for the visually handicapped as

integration, regardless of the level of support provided. From there it is but a short step to pointing to the children who have not fared well in ordinary schools that did not have properly constituted resource centres, and who have perhaps had to move into the special school sector, as the 'casualties' or 'failures' of integration. But as will be clear, it would be quite wrong to write off the whole idea of integration in this way, given the almost total absence of properly supported schemes of integration in this country at the present time.

3.   It is often said that the mere fact of being educated in an ordinary school does not of itself constitute integration. The same point is made another way when people insist that it is the quality of provision that counts, not where it is made. But other things being equal, the ordinary school must be better as a base for integration than the special school. Though presence in an ordinary school may not be a sufficient condition of full integration, it is certainly a necessary one. The point was perhaps put most sharply for the visually handicapped by the Vernon Committee (DES, 1972, para. 5.30):

> We are deeply impressed by the argument that, if visually handicapped children are to be fitted through their education to live in the world with sighted people, the best way for them to acquire the necessary ability and confidence is to mix as freely as possible with sighted children during their schooldays. Social events arranged with neighbouring sighted schools may help a little, but contacts tend to be artificial or at least superficial; in order to get to know sighted children and to feel at home with them, a visually handicapped child needs to be in the same school as they are.

4.   Finally, calls for integration are frequently presented as too 'dogmatic', 'doctrinaire' or 'extreme'. Provision needs to be made, it is said, not according to some abstract principle, but according to the differing needs of each individual child. Those who can benefit from integration should certainly be integrated, but for those who need the sheltering care of the special school, this option should still be retained. All this sounds eminently reasonable, but again it caricatures the integrationists' position. For they, no less than their segregationist critics, recognize the need for a properly individualized range of provision, not excluding placement in a special school in cases of appropriate severity. But in a situation where the special school sector has a virtual monopoly this argument points entirely in the direction of extending systems of support within the framework of the ordinary school.

THE NEED FOR A PLANNED APPROACH

There needs to be planning for supported integration. It is not enough simply to impose, as the 1981 Education Act does, a general obligation to integrate, subject to considerations of educational suitability and efficiency. Without establishing any mechanism for ensuring that the support necessary to make integration a practical proposition is made available in ordinary schools, nothing very much is likely to happen. Given the current absence of facilities in ordinary schools for children with special needs, the educational criteria are seldom likely to be met. In these circumstances, the possibilities of integration will simply be bounded by the limitations inherent in existing arrangements.

The Act is far too individualistic in its approach. It imposes certain obligations to provide the necessary support if a handicapped child should happen to turn up in an ordinary school, but the crucial point is that, without the making of systematic arrangements that might make this more likely to happen in the first place, the arrival of a handicapped child in an ordinary school will be a happy accident at best, but will more probably be ruled out altogether by the inadequacy of existing provision.

Imagine the situation in concrete terms: in the face of a specific request to integrate, one of two things must necessarily occur – either integration will not be attempted for want of the necessary support, or it will, but with disastrous results for the same reason. Many authorities profess a commitment to integration in principle, but demonstrate little awareness of the implications of such a commitment in practice. That being so, the most likely response will probably be simply to drift along with the existing pattern of special schools by sending children away *faute de mieux*. If this is to be avoided, there needs to be a planned development at local authority level of the necessary systems for meeting special educational needs in ordinary schools.

What should be the locus of planning? Every LEA should have a plan, but should it always be a plan for making the necessary provision itself? If the optimum number of resource centres for visually handicapped children is only some 40 or 50 each at primary and secondary level, the answer to this question would seem to be 'no', indicating the desirability of a degree of regional planning; each region should probably have a specialist adviser on the visually handicapped. But the outcome of regional planning has, as we have seen, been disappointing. Nor do local education authorities seem very good at cooperating with one another at subregional level. In these circumstances, pinpointing a number of key authorities, strategic in terms of their size and location, and attempting to persuade them to implement a plan for integration, would seem to afford the best prospect of advance. There is some evidence to suggest that neighbouring authorities would then be more than happy to ride on the back of such a plan, just as they ride now on the backs of the special schools. In this way the original authority could also probably be assured of recouping a fair proportion of its costs.

A problem that authorities often come up with is that of the small number of visually handicapped children in relation to the total school population, or even to that of children with other types of handicap. Would it be acceptable, they often ask, to achieve economies of scale by setting up support units for the visually handicapped in conjunction with units for children suffering from different types of handicap? To this, the answer seems fairly clearly to be that it is certainly acceptable to establish units for children suffering from more than one type of handicap in a single school. But separate units need to be established, and there probably should not be too many of them – probably not more than a couple, in fact – if handicap is not to impose a disproportionate burden on the school and stretch the staff beyond its limit. There is clearly a limit to the range of problems that any given staff can be expected to deal with. At all events, the most important point is that a special support unit must specialize in the distinct problems that are undeniably still thrown up by at least some of the traditional categories of handicap, of which the visually handicapped are certainly one.

CONCLUSION

The conception of integration advanced in this chapter represents an essentially moderate form of the proposal, 'making ordinary schools special', a substantial redeployment of resources from the special to the ordinary school sector but on a selective basis to selected 'centres of excellence' specializing to some degree in the education of the visually handicapped. Such a model would not commend itself to all integrationists, some of whom, it seems, rightly seeing integration as a logical extension of the comprehensive principle, would regard even this as subjecting the children concerned to too much invidious differentiation, and would prefer to see all schools being able to respond sympathetically to the individual needs of all types of children.

Integration is not an all-or-nothing matter. The situation is both fluid and dynamic. A few pioneering ventures in supported integration have begun to be undertaken, but the special school system is under pressure and will unquestionably try to fight back. Things could well go either way. Realistically, one cannot effect a total transformation, even of a subsystem such as the education system, all at once. I prefer a more dialectical approach. The tender shoots of new integration schemes that have already put down their roots need nurturing and extending. That way we can hope to gain some purchase on the education system that could pave the way for more far-reaching developments later on. By attempting everything at once we could well fail.

REFERENCES

Booth, T. (1981) *Demystifying integration.* In W. Swann, (Ed.) (1981) The Practice of Special Education, Blackwell, Oxford

Colborne Brown, M.S. and Tobin, M.J. (1982) Integration of the educationally blind: numbers and placement, *New Beacon,* Vol. 66, No. 781, pp 113-17

Department of Education and Science (DES) (1972) *The Education of the Visually Handicapped* (The Vernon Report), HMSO, London

Department of Education and Science (DES) (1978) *Special Educational Needs* (Warnock Report) Cmnd 7212, HMSO, London

Department of Education and Science (DES) (1983) *Assessments and Statements of Special Educational Needs,* Circular 1/83 HMSO, London

Jamieson, M., Parlett, M., and Pocklington, K. (1977) *Towards Integration: a study of blind and partially sighted children in ordinary schools,* NFER, Slough

Low, C. (1981) Handicaps in the classroom, *New Society,* Vol. 55, No. 966, pp 460-461

National Federation of the Blind in the United Kingdom and Association of Blind and Partially Sighted Teachers and Students

(1973) *Educational provision for the visually handicapped,* Comments on the Vernon Report

(1977) Response to the Consultative Document on the Implementation of Section 10 of the Education Act 1976

(1980) Response to *Special Educational Needs,* Consultative Document on the Report of the Committee of Enquiry into the Education of Handicapped Children and Young People (Warnock Report)

(1982) *Regional planning of educational provision for visually handicapped children*

TOPICS FOR DISCUSSION

1. What are the main features of a system of special education for the visually handicapped proposed by the author?
2. What does the author suggest are the inherent limitations of the self-contained 'blind education system'?
3. 'The power of an ideology has much more to do with its value in supporting a particular view of the world than with the rationality of its specific propositions.' Discuss this statement with reference to the institutional resistance and ideological factors mounted against the integrationist perspective.

SUGGESTIONS FOR FURTHER READING

1. A. Hodgson, (1985) How to integrate the visually impaired, *British Journal of Special Education*, Vol. 12, No. 1, March, pp 35–37. Hodgson's article shows that the total number of visually impaired children who need additional support or special education, whether in mainstream or special school, has always been small and is presently declining. Declining rolls and the trend towards increased integration have wider implications for the mainstream sector. Hodgson's study indicates that the integration of visually impaired children is not a cheap option.
2. Department of Education and Science (May, 1984) *Proposals for the Future Provision in Special Schools for Children with Visual Handicaps*, DES, London. This DES document discusses the implications of integration and declining rolls for the special school.
3. S. Hegarty and K. Pocklington with D. Lucas (1982) *Integration in Action*, NFER-Nelson, Windsor. In chapter 10, 'Resource Area for the Visually Impaired', the authors discuss aims and organization, pupils, staffing, accommodation and resources, curriculum, monitoring progress, the social context and parental involvement with regard to integrating visually impaired pupils into ordinary schools.

Reading 13

THE MICRO-SOCIOLOGY OF SEGREGATION: CASE STUDIES IN THE EXCLUSION OF CHILDREN WITH SPECIAL NEEDS FROM ORDINARY SCHOOLS
G. Sewell

For micro-sociologists, the labelling of deviants cannot be clearly understood except with reference to the social context in which the act of labelling takes place. The emphasis is not so much on the sociological concomitants of those defined as deviant as on the social process through which definitions are constructed. As a seminal figure in the generation of labelling theory, John Kitsuse summarized the approach in these terms:

I propose to shift the focus of theory and research from the forms of deviant behaviour to the processes by which persons come to be defined as deviant by others. Such a shift requires that the Sociologist view as

G. Sewell (1981) *The micro-sociology of segregation: case studies in the exclusion of children with special needs from ordinary schools*. In L. Barton and S. Tomlinson (Eds) (1981) Special Education: policy practices and social issues, Harper and Row, London

problematic what he generally assumes as given – namely that certain forms of behaviour are per se deviant and are so defined by the conventional or conforming members of the group. (1962, pp 87-88)

The 'facts' of deviance, how it is caused, the effects it had and how it could be treated are of secondary importance to the micro-sociologist. Of greater concern is the way such attitudes came to be conceived as they did. Attitudes towards the 'abnormal' differ between social contexts. In her study of young adults released from mental subnormality hospitals in California, Mercer (1965) found considerable variation in parents' willingness to accept their children into the home again. In a later study (Mercer, 1973), she found that referral rates for psychological examination varied fivefold between schools.

The attitudes of the labellers and the role of supposedly irrelevant contingencies have come under closer critical scrutiny. Those who deal with deviants in a routine way – policemen, magistrates, psychologists and so forth – are thought to develop their own preferred ways of working and 'common-sense' stereotyping. This produces its own ideology, a mental set appropriate for performing the role. This shared approach will determine the kinds of people perceived and treated as deviant.

The effect of labelling on the deviant's sense of identity has also become a source of greater concern. The act of being perceived to be abnormal may well bring about changes in the way the individual conceives of himself. In a study of partially sighted adults entering rehabilitation agencies in the United States, Scott (1969) found that the solicitous attitudes of the staff made life more difficult for their clients. They were treated as if they were blind and encouraged to develop more dependent relationships.

Strong pressures are often exerted upon them to begin to think of themselves as blind. These pressures sometimes take the form of admonitions to 'face the facts'. More often, however, they are insidious, resulting subtly from the reactions of medical and welfare specialists, friends, family members and even the impaired person himself to the new label that has been applied to him. (p. 71)

In this way, the attitudes of the individual may become more handicapping than the original disability.

Recent evaluative studies in the mainstreaming of mentally retarded pupils have emphasized these reflexive aspects of special educational needs (Jones *et al.*, 1977; Gottlieb, 1980). The teacher and the social context he creates are seen as crucial to the adjustment and achievements of the child.

The Warnock Committee (DES, 1978) acknowledge that the knowledge and interpersonal skills of the teacher play an important part in the development of a child with special needs. In examining the assessment procedure, they recommend that the relationship of the child and teacher should be investigated in certain circumstances. Yet the main tenor of their recommendations is that the needs of the child should be of prime consideration.

According to my research, classroom observation by psychologists is almost non-existent, especially with older pupils.

Neither profession is enthusiastic about the idea. Many psychologists operate what they refer to as a 'Fire Brigade' service, attending to crises and giving objective tests. They may recently have been under pressure to spend more time liaising with headteachers, and giving them support on a preventive basis. But they find teachers suspicious and entry into the classroom difficult.

Though a few teachers expect psychologists to give an objective view and so indirectly help the child, most want their aid in making the child more manageable. They think of psychologists as secretive and are dismissive of their reports. They dislike the prospect of being observed dealing with difficult children. There is a widespread feeling that 'problem children', children who are 'really abnormal', 'really thick' and so on, should not be the concern of the ordinary teacher. They take up too much time, and the teachers argue that they were never trained to work with them. It thus seems 'unfair' that their competence in this area should be assessed. They would not want to utilize the period of ascertainment to re-evaluate their own skills and attitudes. The prime object of referral is getting rid of a child who does not fit into the working routines of the school or who otherwise threatens its smooth running. They know little of the methods or populations of the schools to which the children are sent. Referral is 'an act of blind faith' so far as the future of the child is concerned, 'another weapon in the armoury' for the schools. From this perspective, psychologists, doctors, social workers and 'the man from county hall' are perceived as a series of 'blocks' on justified teacher initiatives. The last thing many of them would want is that these outsiders should actively investigate their classroom behaviour.

As a result, many important details of teacher–pupil relations are withheld from the official assessment. This may be because the teacher is genuinely unaware of the social context he is creating. There may be a gulf between what he intends to happen and the effect he is actually having on a class and the teacher might never realize. It could also be that, in writing a report that concentrates on the needs of the child, the teacher is simply playing language games with the psychologist. Unless the psychologist knows what the classroom reality of the child is like, he has little way of checking. For their part, the heads would like to retain all possible freedom of manoeuvre in their dealings with troublesome children. And psychologists who have built up 'good relations' with the staff may find themselves implicated in the teachers' role as agents of social control. In order to preserve their own power as legitimators of definitions, psychologists might want to reduce areas of ambiguity rather than widen them through independent observation.

In cases where teachers and psychologists concur in wanting a child to be transferred to a special school but the parents object, there is considerable variation in the parents' ability to withstand official pressures. The more articulate probably have a greater advantage, and the psychologists might even bring them into some of the decision-making procedures. For others, there is hardly even an attempt to treat them as the 'partners' that Warnock recommended. This suggests further inconsistencies in the processing of these children.

Teachers, headteachers, psychologists and parents act as an 'audience' to the labelling of the child. They are rarely passive or impartial and they all play a part in the way the child learns about his identity. In this sense, labels like 'partially sighted', 'maladjusted' and so on cannot be considered objective statements, indicating some sort of unitary phenomenon to be located within the child. They are aspects of the social groups that provide them. These four case studies examine the importance of the audience when appropriate schooling for children with special needs is discussed. Two show instances of where children were transferred to special schools, one where there was a positive effort to 'integrate' and another where a move to segregate was allowed to lapse. Between them, they illustrate the power and preoccupations of teacher, headteacher, psychologist and parent. And they all demonstrate that the outcome of such processes would have been difficult, if not impossible, to predict, if only because of the reflexive aspects of special educational needs.

FIRST CASE STUDY: PHILIP

The first case study would seem to illustrate the point made by some writers (e.g. Meighan, 1981) that teachers are more likely to tolerate sensory impairment than deviant behaviour or low attainment, but that would be somewhat of an oversimplification. There are wide variations of response to the whole range of special educational needs. As one partially sighted adult remarked, 'Teachers like to think they are bothered.[...] Except for one or two they are not really bothered.' An assistant education officer would seem to have corroborated this when he suggested that many teachers felt untrained and so unable to help those with severe sight problems. Yet in most cases, he found it possible to talk them into making an attempt. The form that teacher response takes would seem to be crucial to effective integration, yet so far there have been few attempts to chart the effects of teacher–pupil interaction in the classroom on pupil handicap.

Philip was an able 9-year-old who suffered from congenital cataracts. He had had eight operations on each eye and, though sight in one was sufficient for him to read ink print, an infection in the other had caused complete impairment. He was resilient and outgoing. His parents had bought him his own child-sized motorbike and they were insistent that he should stay at the local junior school. The assistant education officer responsible for special education concurred. There were no units or residential schools in the county and the cost of out-of-county provision had risen sharply. Following Warnock, he had made his own survey of schooling for the 'severely partially sighted' and had concluded that all children who could read ink print and who were neither exceptionally able nor ESN should be integrated. This would benefit the children socially and, even in cases where expensive electronic aids and peripatetic teachers were required, it would save the county a considerable amount of money. The numbers of visually impaired children would be small enough to permit the assistant education officer to monitor each case individually.

In the event, Philip's teacher had been lent the electronic aid, but while his classroom was being rebuilt the class was temporarily rehoused in the gym, and the aid was in its original cardboard box. There were no plugs near the working area and Philip's teacher, Mr Black, assured me that Philip had not wanted to use it after the first month. The teacher had not heard of any teacher for the partially sighted and he had never made use of the peripatetic teacher in remedial reading for Philip. This teacher called at the school for half an hour, once a week, but the service was due to be withdrawn altogether at the end of the year, due to 'cut-backs'. Mr Black thought that Philip was 'very bright', but he did not know about county policy for able partially sighted children and had never requested an intelligence test. It would have appeared that there had been a culpable failure of communications and that resources were not being used as they had been intended. But this draws attention to the social context of the classroom and the importance of the teacher.

Mr Black was a large, confident man who had entered teaching in middle life. He had a booming voice and his presence dominated the school hall. He had an open classroom and allowed the children to wander around, even when addressing them as a group. The class worked to an integrated day and they had individual programmes. It was rare for neighbours or members of the same small group to be using the same book at any one time. Yet there were definite limits to pupil freedom. The class was divided into four mixed-ability groups – green, yellow, pink and blue – which each worked on a subject for a 30-minute block of time. Blue would be on arithmetic assignments, while pink used their writing workbooks and so forth. The programme each child followed was prepared in advance, so when Philip had finished exercise 10, he would be directed to exercise 12. Reading was managed by a class library arranged according to another colour scheme. White stickers corresponded to a reading age between 7 and 8, red stickers to one between 8 and 9. The book that Philip had chosen to read was too difficult for him technically, but it was about the Wright brothers, and Mr Black had let him attempt it because he knew of Philip's interest in machines.

All the children in the class had their own folders. Inside were duplicated sheets with a block of number squares. Philip would normally be on 'white' books and when he started the book he turned to the 'white' page and put a line round the number of the book. When he had finished it, he put a line through the number. In this way, books could be chosen by the children according to their interests and yet within their reading ability. With reading ages tested termly and each child listened to once a week or more, Mr Black kept a firm check on progress. The movement round the classroom was far from random. It had developed a pattern or routine which would incorporate exceptional needs.

This was also true of the kind of group activity referred to by most teachers as 'chalk and talk'. On discovering the extent of Philip's difficulties, Mr Black had abandoned the use of a blackboard. He had had an overhead projector installed in his room and, while the rest of the children sat in front of the screen, Philip stood by the projector and watched Mr Black as he wrote on the celluloid. If there were notes to be copied, Philip was free to move to a different table, so he could sit next to someone whose writing he could read. As Mr Black said, 'Philip arrived in this class a handicapped child, but now he's the same as all the rest, except for his sight.'

Philip had in fact arrived with no reading abilities at all and Mr Black had protested to his headteacher about having to teach him. He described himself as a 'bolshie character' and he persuaded the head to contact

County Hall. The response had been immediate and encouraging. A letter was sent from the assistant education officer promising an electronic aid and his continued support if the school attempted to 'integrate' Philip. As it happened, Mr Black had just started an Open University reading course and he started an individual course of reading for Philip. With the parents' blessing, he kept Philip behind after school for ten minutes every night for a year and a half, and his reading was now at about the age of 8. He had been a good student who picked up ideas quickly, and when a book interested him he could manage something harder.

The relationship had been far from simple, even so, especially at the beginning. As by chance again, though, Mr Black's previous career had been a social worker. He had worked with handicapped people 'for twenty years' and, if ever Philip threw a tantrum or said he could not do a piece of work 'because he couldn't see', Mr Black refused to give way. At times there had been 'bloody confrontations' and Mr Black had often threatened Philip with a smack if he wanted to give up, but the relationship had never been put in serious jeopardy.

The electronic aid – a closed circuit TV scanner which could magnify print and convert it from black on white to white on black – did not arrive for a whole year. In that time, the foundations had been laid. But when it did arrive Philip used it for every possible kind of assignment and the progress, in terms of his improved reading age and his confidence, was remarkable. After a month, Philip realized how far he had come and how much more he could do without it. He told Mr Black that he now felt it 'showed him up' among the other children. So it was put back in its box and had stayed there. Philip knew he could get it out again whenever he wanted, but he felt some stigma attached to its use and wanted to be independent of it. Mr Black had read Goffman's *Stigma* (1968) and knew enough about 'the moral career' and handicapped adults to encourage this step.

Mr Black and the head were aware of the progress Philip had made and of the responsibility Mr Black had had for this. Yet in focusing on Philip's reading age, his visual defects, his strengths of character and so forth, they had not realized the effect of the classroom context. Even within the same school, there was not another teacher who had taken a specialized course in reading or who had extensive experience of handicap. In a different school there would not have been a head who had organized a reading experience scheme or an individualized maths and writing structure. This gave the children permission to show their individual differences and preferences without stigma. Philip's two previous teachers had not realized that the corollary of such freedom was that a teacher should check up on children and do something for them on an individualized basis if they were failing. Mr Black was a teacher who could permit 'irregularities' like children moving round the classroom 'if they couldn't see', and who would also impose definite boundaries in terms of time, space and academic standards, where these were appropriate.

Philip had been a 'good pupil' and in concentrating on the child's capabilities Mr Black and the head felt quite confident that, provided his sight did not deteriorate further, he would continue to do as well. Yet just as Philip's previous teachers had failed to provide Philip with a satisfactory education, it was possible that his next ones might feel insufficiently trained or confident to help. Peripatetic remedial help was being withdrawn from the school and a comprehensive school might not have staff capable of stimulating an able child with particular learning difficulties.

Mr Black said, 'If Philip had been a dimbo, I would never have tried. It would not have been worth the effort.' In the class he was to take over the following year, there was a child with learning and behavioural difficulties. Previously, this child had been having daily support from a part-time teacher and she could have looked forward to peripatetic help in the junior department. But because of the 'cut-backs' such auxiliary help was being withdrawn. The head had therefore referred the child for psychological assessment, with Mr Black's approval. The psychologist had come to the school, met the parents and assessed the child, and the child was now to be sent to an ESN(M) school in the city almost 20 miles away. The psychologist had not spoken to Mr Black or observed the kind of classroom he might have been able to construct for this retarded child. Thus, a teacher with particular interests, attitudes and capabilities had been able to create a classroom setting which had provided one child with a genuine experience of 'normalization'; under pressure from wider political and financial changes, he had been a party to the segregation of another. Boundaries between the normal and abnormal had been redrawn at a local level and in neither case had there been a critical examination of how much the teacher could benefit the child.

SECOND CASE STUDY: GILLIAN

In formal administrative terms, the power of the head to remove children with special needs is hedged about with a number of restrictions. It is no longer legal for a child to be expelled. The head may suspend and may set no time limit to his return. But he is normally required to advise parents of their power of appeal to the governors or managers. He himself must inform the board and have their support. On the board, there will probably be a representative from County Hall. If a child is suspended *sine die,* it becomes the LEA's responsibility to find suitable provision. It is also the LEA's responsibility to provide special education and their legal terms of reference have always been very broad. If the administrators or psychologists feel that the reason for a suspension reflects inadequacies in the school, it is possible for them to call for an inspection. This is rarely done, however.

Recently, it has become more common for psychologists to discuss children who have special needs before the formal referral process is b oached. This is one of the main recommendations of Warnock. In cases w iere the head presses for a child to be removed, it is quite possible for psychologists to block or delay this. They may suggest alternative strategies and say they will follow the case up in six months' time. This makes it more difficult for the head to press for suspension as he has still not exhausted all the other possibilities. But it may commit the psychologist to more definitive action once six months have passed. This ensures that the exclusion of these children is a time-consuming and an apparently well thought-out process.

In practical terms, however, the head is left with considerable latitude. He makes the formal referral. He writes or at least countersigns the school's referral sheet, the SE1. And there is much he can do in a covert way to increase the pressure on the child and the school's psychological services. If his staff are under pressure, and he himself finds that his own sense of control is threatened, there is a great deal he can do to precipitate a crisis. How crucial his role can be is illustrated in the second case study.

Gillian presented as a shy girl of average ability when she arrived in the second year of a comprehensive. Two weeks after the start of the third year, her mother informed the school that she had spent the weekend in hospital after taking an overdose. Although the girl was discharged with no follow-up from the hospital, the school counsellor, educational psychologist, family therapy unit, two social workers and her doctor were subsequently involved with Gillian and her family. It appeared to the head that, as soon as significant progress was made with any agency, her mother withdrew Gillian and applied to another. Half-way through the third year, her concentration and behaviour began to deteriorate in school. She began to throw tantrums. The first of these took place when her class was taken by a student teacher. The whole group had got out of hand and in these circumstances, the behaviour of individual children would normally have been 'explained' in terms of the teacher's inexperience. Gillian was too 'visible' for this to happen. She was sent to the head following such misbehaviour and, while most children could be induced to accept responsibility for their actions or at least cry, Gillian disconcerted the head by 'looking blank and saying nothing'. The head was too sophisticated to pass judgement on this response and her journey from counsellor to psychologist to family therapy, but he did feel, 'You just can't get through to her. I get children in here who've been up before the courts, and they all give in. But she just looks straight through you.'

By the start of the fourth year, a rather bulky file had begun to accumulate in the head's office. Among the information it contained was a psychologist's assessment. This stated that she was a child of above-average ability with a Wechsler Intelligence Scale for Children score of 135. Yet she was put in the lowest maths set alongside children who had difficulties with subtraction and multiplication. The reason for this was of course strategic. She had missed a lot of school and was disruptive, so she was not considered for the upper sets. The teachers in the other low-ability sets could not manage her. The teacher of the bottom set had a small group and a reputation for being experienced and sympathetic. In his relationship with Gillian, he proved also to be obstinate. For a term everything went well, with Gillian doing the same simple sums the rest of the class did. Then an argument blew up about some writing on the desk. Writing on desks was endemic in the school. Elvis had just died and his name appeared in the violet ink that Gillian used. Gillian refused to admit she had done this and refused to rub the words off the desk. For a week the argument persisted. Then Gillian ran out of the lesson. She was sent to the head and he too was unable to get a 'reasonable' answer out of her. He reminded her of how she had had a lot of problems at the school in the past and that she could always rely on him, but if she ran out of lessons again she would have to be expelled. She was excused the maths teacher's lessons for a week. At the end of that period, the same argument blew up with the same teacher and he insisted she clean the handwriting off the table. She refused and she was sent to stand outside the head's office. Rather than face the consequences, she truanted and stayed out all night. She was expelled. She was taken into care and sent to a social services assessment centre. She ran away several times and stayed out overnight. While she had been at the comprehensive the psychologist had explicitly stated she was not maladjusted. After her stay at the assessment centre, it was decided she was. She stayed in a maladjusted school for a term and they found her too difficult to cope with. So she ended her schooling in a community home.

If Gillian's mother had not seen fit to move her from one agency to another, she might have had some chance of appearing 'normal' to the head. As it was, misdemeanours for which other children would have been given a telling off or a detention were magnified out of all proportion. And at the time of the handwriting incident, Gillian's mother had at last exhausted all outside help. Her mother had previously informed the head that Gillian was 'epileptic' or 'schizophrenic'. There was now no one with whom the head could share responsibility. Unable to develop a productive relationship, he had retreated to making threats. And when she stayed out all night, the head felt he had thereby been relieved of all responsibility. He could carry out his threat with impunity.

The staff only got to hear about the suspension indirectly. The head was not alone in not being able to 'get through to her', but several staff had in fact been able to form quite strong relationships with her. Yet it would have been unthinkable for them to have openly questioned his decision. Their authority was implicated in the struggle. The governors could not have objected. Gillian had had a history of unsuccessful psychiatric treatment and her tantrums and suicide attempt made her appear plainly disturbed. The psychologist would not have heard about the behaviour of the head or the maths teacher except from Gillian, and few psychologists seem to take the child's view of such matters seriously. Even if the psychologist had objected, there was little she could do. The child might have been subject to an unreasonable degree of pressure, but by running away, she had put herself in the wrong. Her exclusion was a *fait accompli*, and it was abetted by the swift action of the education welfare officer and social worker in placing her on a care order. An inspection would have revealed little wrong in the school's general organization. When social organizations draw the line between normal and abnormal behaviour, they often do so for strategic reasons. These may include the peace of mind of those who lead those organizations. The head may have felt himself to be powerless in this situation but in reality he had an unreasonable amount of power. And the outcome for Gillian was harmful.

THIRD CASE STUDY: SIMON

Aaron Cicourel (1974) refers to the group of professions that control access to deviant identities as 'gatekeepers'. He characterizes them as constituting a special mutually dependent relationship with deviants. If no one was defined as a criminal, there would be no policemen. If no one was defined as ESN, there would be no need for psychologists. This sounds a superficial argument, for if there were no criminal codes or policemen, all stable social groups would probably have to invent some other way of labelling behaviour it considered antisocial. Yet the force of Cicourel's argument is that the approach of each gatekeeper group conditions the kind of deviance they typically perceive as such. And it also influences the way official records are kept. With police and registrars these are there merely for the official's protection, and where details of a case have no bearing on this they are often neglected.

In the case of children being 'processed' through the special education assessment procedure, the appearance of a proper examination into the child's needs may be more important than a thorough investigation into practical outcomes. The motives of teacher, head and psychologist in pursuing a referral could then legitimately seem irrelevant. Recently the twists and turns in public policy about special schools have put the psychologists into an overtly political position. From having to keep children on long waiting lists, they have had to lead public relations exercises in persuading heads and teachers to keep more children with special needs. Then, as the cut-backs have threatened remedial teaching and the fall in the birth rate has menaced the infants department of special schools, they have had to win back support for them.

Few psychologists would seem to enjoy an explicitly political position and their power has more often been exercised through their role as experts in labelling. Warnock encouraged them to reject the idea that children could be categorized according to handicap, but those few who have tried this have found that it diminishes their power. In a fraught case conference the ability to stereotype this child as 'ESN(M)', that child as 'not maladjusted' is a very useful weapon. And it reflects well on the profession. Yet it does hide the fact that psychologists can and do disagree about the criteria on which they take their decisions. Some place a great deal of faith in IQ scores, others very little. Some look for underlying pathology, others for measurable behaviour. Yet while ideological differences within the profession are well known, this is rarely considered in specific assessment decisions. For the teachers and heads, beset by the ambiguities involved in relationships with exceptional children, the expert judgement of the psychologist comes as a release. Whether or not it accurately predicts the best outcome for the child as much as it helps the teaching staff is open to doubt.

Simon certainly appeared to have benefited from the exercise of this sort of power by the psychologist. He entered the comprehensive with no score on the NFER Group Intelligence Test C.D. (NFER, 1977) and a reading age of 6.7. The year-tutor and headteacher had an unusually advanced understanding of group-test reliability and of the conditions that obtain for some backward readers in some primary schools. Like most of his peers, Simon reacted positively to the new range of subjects offered, and it was not until the second term that he began to stand out. He had some low-effort grades and was withdrawn for a weekly session with the counsellor. The home was visited, and the parents informed that Simon might see a psychologist. They were asked if they would help with homework and reading. Simon was tested and the psychologist told the head at a liaison meeting that he was ' a typical ESN(M) pupil'. Simon went to a special school for two years where he became 'much more confident'. He then returned to the comprehensive and is at present preparing to take CSEs. During this time, the head of the special school visited the comprehensive twice and the head of the comprehensive spent a morning at the special school.

This account would correspond with much that is in the written records of Simon's case and it represents a heartening account of a liaison system that is sensitive to changing needs. Yet there are aspects of the case which appear on no records, which show how much of the outcome rested on hidden contingencies. Firstly, Simon had had a very unpleasant time in the last year of his junior school and this seems to have conditioned the view Simon's parents took of his identity. His teacher made the children feel:

> if you were in this teacher's good books, that was fine; but if you weren't, he didn't want to know. (Parent)

Simon was kept on the same reading primer all year. When he told his mother, it was not until a few days before the end-of-year parents' evening:

> So I went down when Simon was moving up to the senior school. And I asked him why Simon had been kept on the same book all year and he could give me no answer. He said, 'I've done my best, Simon's either downright lazy or stupid.' I was very upset.

The mother was obviously aware of the possibility that this teacher's attitude had handicapped her son. She decided not to complain, but the words had made a deep impression on her. When she was told about the referral, she was shocked, but she did not make any difficulties:

> I honestly thought this teacher from the Junior School was right all along. There was back-up there.

Even when the doctor told her there was little medical reason for Simon's 'abnormality', she still did not protest:

The doctor couldn't see any reason why Simon was like this. He thought it was lack of confidence, because he was quite a healthy child and when he was speaking to him, he didn't get the impression there was anything wrong, you know, anything lacking. I got the impression that the psychologist and doctor were there to help him. It was too much for him at school.

The official records would not show that there was disagreement among the teachers as well. Some saw him as 'definitely unhappy', a boy with 'tremendous problems' who did not have the 'personal resources' to overcome them. Others had quite a different relationship, but because of the political structure of the school, their comments, were not invited:

My particular involvement was in the terms of a subject. The power rests with the Head and the Pastoral Team and the SPS. I expressed reservations but they weren't taken note of. (Teacher)

After a few weeks' counselling, Simon's efforts grades improved and his reading age rose one and half years to 8.3 (Schonell). The headteacher was informed and he began to think that, though Simon was a shy lad, without many friends, his problem seemed to have been a temporary one, caused by changing schools. This explanation might have satisfied another psychologist who had less faith in IQ scores and different political pressures on her. But these aspects of the psychologist's role were hidden from the other actors. This case coincided with the publication of Section 10 of the 1976 Education Act and the area education offices, schools' psychological services and special school heads had good reason to fear that the Education Committee might take immediate action to cut special education funding. The psychologist informed the counsellor, with whom there was a very good relationship, that it was imperative to show long waiting lists. When Simon was discovered to be having extreme difficulties, the counsellor suggested referral. So, because of decisions taken at County Hall and Westminster and the school's good liaison with SPS, a child who in another 'less caring' school might have been left to 'sink or swim' was referred and quickly seen.

When, a few weeks later, the head suggested that Simon stay on at the comprehensive, the psychologist had already tested him and arranged a visit to the special school. She did not dispute the head's definition directly but she openly categorized Simon as 'a typical ESN(M) child'.

In point of fact, this projection turned out to have been misleading, but not for any reason that a formal examination could have predicted. Simon was among the top three or four children in his class. He had always objected to the idea of going to a school for 'dopes' and, though he allowed his mother to override his judgement, he worked hard to 'neutralize' the label (Sykes and Matza, 1957). It could be argued the psychologist's certainty about Simon's abnormality acted with the teachers' needs to have their own uncertainties about Simon's identity resolved, and that this coincidence of personal and political needs played a stronger part in the referral decision than any consideration of Simon's needs. Even had these needs been discovered, any predication would have been unable to cope with the reflexive aspect of special needs. Luckily the episode turned out well and Simon was able to 'neutralize' his deviant identity. Yet if he had reacted to the placement with despair, as so many children do (Younghusband, 1970), there would probably have been little question of his return.

FOURTH CASE STUDY: ADRIAN

The Warnock Report explicitly invokes the concept of 'Parents as Partners' and it would seem that psychologists spend more time with parents than they used to. Ten years ago, it was not unknown for parents to be told to attend a meeting at the school, whose purpose they did not understand, to be interviewed by a panel and informed that attendance by their child at a special school might only be for a year, while in fact such temporary stays were quite rare. Nowadays, parents have to grant their permission before psychologists examine a child and they are often told that notes of this meeting will be taken and a further case conference held. In some instances, parents are shown the SE4 form, though I have never met anyone to whom this has happened. In others, parents are invited to attend the case conference. These are not always all they appear, though. The issues may already have been decided at an earlier meeting by the professionals, and all the parents see is a 'performance'.

If parents reject the first suggestion about an examination, further pressure may be put on them by others, including the education welfare officer, and suspension might be threatened. If the parents agree to examination and reject findings, similar pressures may be brought to bear. In this case it takes determination and an inside knowledge of the rules for parents to carry on their fight. This might not be too difficult for a doctor or another articulate member of the dominant social groups, as this head illustrates:

I must say he was a very lovable little lad, but his learning was very, very poor and the whole reflection was bad. The parents went to their own child psychologist, privately. They spend quite a considerable amount of money. He said the boy was university material. They were a little dissatisfied and they moved house. Now he's at a private school.

Without these advantages, the parents' power to pursue definitions of their child's normality in opposition to the school and its gatekeepers might be considerably more circumscribed, but it still exists, as this last case study illustrates.

Even before Adrian left his primary school, the comprehensive had been notified that he was an immature, slow-learning pupil, who had been disruptive in his last year. He failed to score on the NFER Group Verbal Reading Quotient and his reading age was more than four years lower than his chronological age. Both his parents had been at special school and, as one had risen to the board of his firm by studying hard at night school after he had left, they both felt suspicious of assessment procedures.

Adrian broke his arm in his first term of comprehensive. This made it difficult for teachers to keep him occupied and this factor often makes it easy for a pupil to drift into deviance (Sharp and Green, 1975). He could not read independently, write or draw, and he had already learned how to disrupt lessons. When challenged about his misbehaviour, he reacted with a series of temper tantrums. Misbehaviour by Adrian and his friends in the lesson of one notably incompetent teacher culminated in song books being thrown about the room. It was decided that Adrian probably 'needed' a less demanding environment with a less complex timetable, fewer staff and a smaller pupil–teacher ratio. This was agreed at an informal level with the psychologist, who suggested either an ESN(M) school or the local unit for disruptive pupils, whichever proved the more suitable after a full examination.

Adrian's behaviour did not improve after this decision had been taken and a teacher visited the home to ask the parents' permission for a full examination. Mrs Smith said she did not like the idea of him going to a special school because she had not been happy at hers, but if this was for the best, she would agree. A letter was then sent asking her to meet the psychologist with Adrian at a certain time. Mrs Smith did not reply and she did not come. Another teacher visited, on the assumption that Mrs Smith might not be able to read. Mrs Smith said she would help Adrian with his homework and tell him to mend his behaviour, and that she would definitely attend the next meeting. Meanwhile his behaviour grew even worse and this time the deputy head was subjected to a tantrum. Mrs Smith did not attend the next meeting. The education welfare officer visited, pointed out the seriousness of the position, and got her to sign a written document giving her permission for Adrian to go to the disruptive unit. This would not have required the full special education assessment procedure. The head of the unit stipulated that all parents visited the unit before their child would be accepted, and Mrs Smith failed to keep the appointment made for her. Adrian kept coming to the comprehensive. But from that time, there was a slight improvement in Adrian's behaviour. The arm came out of plaster and he started to join in the 'normal' class activities. He began to wear school uniform. And his tantrums declined. He settled to work and the referral was allowed to lapse.

Two years later, Adrian was described by one of his teachers as, 'One of the lads. There's no difference between him and the others.' His reading age had improved considerably and, though much of his work was probably beyond him, this did not make him unusual. He was, at least in some minimal sense, 'coping'. His parents never explicitly resisted the referral. But as so much of the procedure rests on active consent, if not sincere cooperation, the parents could enforce their view of Adrian's normality simply by stonewalling.

CONCLUSION

When teachers and heads initiate referrals, it may be for a number of different reasons. They might perceive a child to be plainly unhappy or obviously 'abnormal'. They might think there is strong medical evidence that there is 'something wrong', and feel unable to help. They might feel that the child is a menace to the stability of the social system for which they are responsible. Micro-sociology emphasizes the diversity of audience responses. Structural explanations which show segregation as a form of class or ethnic repression might have a general validity, but they do not do justice to the full complexity of individual cases. Direct observation of the role of the audience would suggest that, even if there is no consistent prejudice at work, heads and teachers can hardly be trusted to be impartial. The SE procedure rests on written evidence from the professionals alone. It focuses on the needs of the child and it allows the needs of the heads, teachers and psychologists to remain hidden.

The head will almost inevitably have other organizational interests to be considered. Erikson (1964) draws attention to the possibility that, when labels are being considered, the social system is in effect determining the precise form of its boundaries. There are limits to acceptable pupil behaviour and teacher responsibility and labelling re-establishes the lines these will take. As the highest authority in a particular social system, this is a moment of great political importance for the headteacher, and through his decisions he indicates his own policy and his support for his staff.

Psychologists do not make routine investigations of teacher behaviour. They do not examine the way everyday working conditions and discipline are structured in the classroom. Instead they liaise with the teachers, and through their objective tests and written evidence they legitimate the idea that the child is and should be the first consideration. How accurate their predictions are is open to doubt. It seems strange that the justification for segregating pupils is that this is to satisfy special needs, when so many comparative studies of children with special needs in ordinary and special schools have been lukewarm about the value of special schools (e.g. Goldstein *et al.*, 1965; Jamieson *et al.*, 1977).

Parents who can be trusted to be 'intelligent' and 'not make a fuss' are offered 'performances' in the name of partnership. Those who are not to be trusted can often be persuaded. Those who object are subjected to visits from a succession of forceful and articulate members of the gatekeeping professions. Even so, it is still possible for those who possess inside knowledge to resist.

In these circumstances, the suggestion of the Warnock Committee that headteachers and psychologists are suitable candidates for the role of 'Named Persons' to parents of school-aged children seem either naive or conspiratorial. The supposedly hypocritical Victorians at least recognized that teachers might show bias in getting rid of their slow children. The Report of the Department Committee on Defective and Epileptic Children in 1898 recommended that a medical certificate be the *sine qua non* of segregated schooling, so that medical officers could provide some sort of check on teachers' powers. Doctors would seem to play a much less significant part in the transfer of school-age children and, where matters of educational need are supposed to be considered, this sounds only reasonable. But psychologists, who are being encouraged to disregard categories of handicap and who may feel unease about the iatrogenic aspects of concepts like IQ and maladjustment, hardly seem in a strong enough position to defend the child's interests against those of its school.

In the last ten years, various alternatives to the concept of 'Named Persons' have been suggested. Instead of the professionals choosing among themselves, Dr John Cash and 'Miff' wanted the parents to have someone they felt they could trust (Face to Face Conference, Warwick University,

1980). Wolf Wolfensberger initiated the idea of 'citizen advocates', who could befriend an individual who was mentally handicapped and also help them fight for their civil and welfare rights, should the need arise (Gottlieb, 1980). Szasz (1970) argued that placement in mental hospitals and special schools was often a cynical exercise in dumping unwanted people. He suggested that decisions should be made by a tribunal, with a 'prosecuting psychiatrist' who would argue on behalf of the state or an official institution and a 'defence psychiatrist' who would be paid to secure the least onerous 'result' for his client. And one Midlands psychiatrist has dismantled his local child guidance service, making a clear division between child psychiatry and educational psychology. He has also closed a local psychiatric unit and made allowance for children between the ages of 12 and 16 to refer themselves, providing their doctor agrees to this (P. McTurk, private communication, 1980).

All these schemes suffer the same disadvantage: they depend on the goodwill of people who may not be directly affected by the outcome. Many of the parents and children might never get to hear of their rights unless this were made mandatory. Parents should be informed of the date and place of the case conference and invited to bring along a friend or advocate, who would be allowed to ask questions on their behalf. This friend or advocate should also be allowed access to written evidence like the SE4 and previous school reports, and also bring along 'witnesses' of his own.

It was not the intention of this chapter to suggest that segregation from mainstream education is always wrong for the child. It may be the lesser of two evils. And it may provide the child with access to educational experiences and relationships that really are special. Yet it seems a point neglected by psychological approaches to assessment procedure that such is the diversity of reactions to 'deviant' pupils that selection for special schools and the outcome of a special education can be quite arbitrary. The professionals have an almost complete monopoly of the linguistic and symbolic power. They could act in good faith and still harm the child. The could act in defence of their own interests and neither parents nor children need ever know. The use of advocates will not affect the underlying disability. But it would enable someone with a private concern for the well-being of an individual child to investigate the personal bias and the public needs of the rest of the audience. If handicap and deviance relate as much to the micro context of the school and the family as they do to the child, this would at least make the procedures for excluding children with special needs from ordinary schools less haphazard and less hypocritical.

REFERENCES

Cicourel, A.V. (1974) *Police practices and official records.* In R. Turner (Ed.) (1974) Ethnomethodology: Selected Readings, Penguin, Harmondsworth

Department of Education and Science (DES) (1978) *Special Educational Needs* (Warnock Report), Cmnd 7212, HMSO, London

Erikson, K.T. (1964) *Notes on the study of deviance.* In H.S. Becker (Ed.) (1964) The Other Side: perspectives on deviance, The Free Press, New York

Goffman, E. (1968) *Stigma,* Penguin, Harmondsworth

Goldstein, H., Moss, J. W. and Jordon L. J., (1965) *Efficacy of Special Class Training in the Development of Mentally Retarded Children,* University of Illinois Press, Champaign, Illinois

Gottlieb, J. (1980) *Educating Mentally Retarded Persons in the Mainstream,* University Park Press, Baltimore

Jamieson, M., Parlett, M.R. and Pocklington, K. (1977) *Towards Integration,* NFER, Slough

Jones, R.L., Gottlieb, J. Gaskin, S. and Yoshida, R.K. (1977) Evaluating mainstreaming programmes: models, caveats, considerations, guidelines, *Exceptional Children,* Vol. 44, pp 588-604

Kitsuse, J.I. (1962) *Societal reaction to deviant behaviour.* In H.S. Becker (Ed.) (1964) The Other Side: perspectives on deviance, The Free Press, New York

Meighan, R. (1981) (Ed.) *A Sociology of Educating,* Holt-Saunders, Eastbourne

Mercer, J.R. (1965) *Career patterns of persons labelled as mentally retarded.* In E. Rubington and M.S. Weinburg (Eds) (1977) Deviance: the interactionist perspective (2nd edn), Macmillan, London

Mercer, J.R. (1973) *Labelling the Mentally Retarded,* University of California Press, Berkeley

Scott, R.A. (1969) *The Making of Blind Men,* Russell Sage Foundation, New York

Sharp, R. and Green, A. (1975) *Education and Social Control,* Routledge and Kegan Paul, London

Sykes, G.M. and Matza, D. (1957) Techniques of neutralization: a theory of delinquency, *American Sociological Review,* Vol. 22, pp 667-670

Szasz, T.S. (1970) *Ideology and Insanity,* Calder and Boyars, London

Younghusband, E. (1970) *Living with Handicap,* National Childrens Bureau, London

TOPICS FOR DISCUSSION

1. 'The act of being perceived to be abnormal may well bring about changes in the way the individual conceives of himself.' 'Discuss implications of this statement for children with special educational needs from the perspective of labelling theory.

2. Discuss the author's statement that 'referral is "an act of blind faith" so far as the future of the child is concerned, "another weapon in the armoury" for the schools'.

3. '[...] labels like "partially sighted", "maladjusted" and so on cannot be considered objective statements, indicating some sort of unitary phenomenon to be located within the child. They are aspects of the social groups that provide them.' Discuss.

SUGGESTIONS FOR FURTHER READING

1. S. Tomlinson (1981) *Professionals and ESN(M) education*. In W. Swann (Ed.) The Practice of Special Education, Basil Blackwell, Oxford. The author argues that all professionals involved in special education should recognize that, despite their concern for individual children, a great deal of what happens in special education is related directly to their own particular vested interests as well as the 'needs' of their clients. It is also the case that present professional roles and activities may be shaped and influenced by the legacy of an inherited and largely unquestioned philosophy.

2. D.S. Bart, (1984) *The differential diagnosis of special education: managing social pathology as individual disability*. In L. Barton and S. Tomlinson (1984) Special Education and Social Interests, Croom Helm, London. The author conceptualizes and explains the role of special education as one sorting process for 'normal' education and society. She analyses the effects of medical and psychological models and management practices stemming from such models in special education, particularly on the professionalization and curricular content of the field, and on the relationship of these models and management practices to special education's role as a sorting agency. Of particular relevance to Reading 13 is the author's comprehensive discussion of labelling theory.

3. L. Rowitz (1981) A sociological perspective on labelling in mental retardation, *Mental Retardation,* Vol. 19, No. 2, pp 47-51. A very thorough account of labelling as a social process. The author argues that as we move to moderate retardation, the reliability of diagnosis declines, and as we move to mild retardation, diagnostic reliability is very low. He offers evidence from American research to suggest that, for mild retardation, diagnostic reliability seems directly related to socio-economic status. Positive as well as negative aspects of 'labelling' are discussed and the author presents a number of hypotheses to suggest a relationship between labelling and social control.

INTEGRATION: DISADVANTAGED CHILDREN, CHILDREN WITH MODERATE LEARNING DIFFICULTIES, CHILDREN WITH EMOTIONAL AND/OR BEHAVIOURAL PROBLEMS

INTRODUCTION

Section 4 of the sourcebook consists of five readings, the first of which, Reading 14, examines in a very practical way some of the causes of problem behaviour which confront teachers in their day-to-day contact with pupils. Pik discusses a number of 'confrontation' situations, tense 'showdowns' which occur when, in response to what the *teacher* considers to be reasonable requests, the pupil 'digs in his heels' and shows open defiance and hostility. The author considers why such confrontations provoke strong and uncomfortable feelings in teachers and examines these feelings during and after such episodes. He assesses both the measures teachers usually take to reduce uncomfortable feelings and the strategies which are available to the class-teacher, offering a number of sensible and practical rules to do with *preventing* and *handling* confrontations when they arise. Pik's concluding suggestions are concerned with the strategies available to the in-school support network and those which are available to the support services (for example, the role of the educational psychologist).

Reading 15 is a masterly examination of the 'evidence' and 'findings' of the Warnock Report and a searching evaluation of various aspects of its implementation in the 1981 Education Act. Galloway questions a number of the Warnock Committee's main conclusions in a closely argued account of the evidence they relied on for their findings. For example, the instruments used in most of the research on children's behaviour on which the Warnock Committee based its conclusions were the Rutter A2 scale (Rutter, 1967) and Stott's Bristol Social Adjustment Guides (Stott, 1963, 1971). Both instruments, Galloway asserts, prejudge the issue, for they ensure that a substantial minority of children will be regarded as deviant, maladjusted, disturbed or just disturbing, depending on the preferred label. Moreover, the Warnock Committee's interpretation of the results is just as political, for, having decided what proportion of children whose progress deviated from some arbitrary and rather ill-defined concept of normality could be considered to have special educational needs (learning difficulties and/or behaviour problems), the research evidence was at hand to justify the conclusion. Galloway proceeds to argue the case that many children have special needs, even though these may not necessarily constitute educational needs, and that, largely, these needs arise from a range of personal, family and social circumstances. Of particular relevance to the topic under discussion in this section is the very comprehensive consideration which Galloway gives to the influence of the school on children's behaviour and progress. The suggested further readings echo the importance of this theme. Galloway discusses the effects of the hidden curriculum on both pupils and teachers and in the final reading describes the characteristics of 'successful' schools. Tomlinson's contribution is particularly relevant for its account of the 'social problem classes' and their identification with behavioural problems and underachievement.

In Reading 16 Tomlinson questions the status of the category and the concept of ESN(M), asking, 'What exactly is, or was, an ESN(M) child?' Although the 1981 Act on special educational needs abolished statutory categories of handicap, descriptive labels similar to the former categories have, in effect, replaced them. It is important to note that the category of educational subnormality, created in 1945, encompassed over half of all children designated as handicapped. The recently created 'children with learning difficulties', a very large subgroup of children with special educational needs, will encompass, Tomlinson asserts, even more working-class and black children, since they comprise a *majority* of children in remedial classes in ordinary schools. The author considers the problems which arise in categorization and selection with regard to the use of non-normative categories and critically evaluates the criteria by which children are referred, assessed and 'placed'. She discusses various accounts of educational subnormality, demonstrating how the apparently logical, rational accounts of subnormality are, to say the very least, suspect, and arrives at the conclusion (after very convincing arguments) that the whole concept of special educational needs is tautological. The paper concludes with a fascinating study of the accounts given by various professionals (headteachers, doctors, educational psychologists, special school headteachers and parents) of ESN(M) children, demonstrating clearly that the 'official' picture of smooth teamwork, cooperation and consensus is very much an ideology, for, in practice, accounts differ and conflict, and there are a variety of other conflicts, anxieties and serious problems of communication between professionals. The suggested readings add weight to Tomlinson's paper, providing perspectives on the development of special education with particular reference to prevailing social, economic and professional interests rather than in terms of ideological considerations of humanitarianism. Potts's useful article shows how professionals, by their patterns of work and training, may impede processes of integration.

Reading 17 is concerned with an examination of the evidence for the claim that special education is expanding. It discusses three reasons for the expansion: professional vested interests, comprehensive school dilemmas and the declining youth labour market. Tomlinson's major thesis is that the ideology of 'special needs' directs attention away from the social, economic and political concerns which have led to this expansion. She shows that this expansion is linked to enhanced definitions of 'achievement' which put more pressure on schools to raise standards and credential more pupils whilst at the same time forcing schools to devise courses for lower-level credentials and to separate out those who are either unable or unwilling to achieve even these lower-level qualifications. As a result, the author asserts, the subsystem of special education appears capable of seemingly indefinite expansion! Rather than ascribing the expansion of special education to accident, spontaneous adjustments, progress and benevolence, Tomlinson develops Archer's (1979) contention that educational structures are the result of the *interests* of those social groups who manage, as a result of conflicts, to achieve educational control. Thus, an understanding of the competition and alliances among interest groups in special education is crucial to understanding its expansion. Of particular relevance to this section is the discussion of 'comprehensive school dilemmas'. Tomlinson traces the pathways and outcomes of a number of dilemmas: the dilemma (only realized in the 1970s) that, if selection by ability was inadmissible, so was selection by disability or inability; the dilemma of the promise to offer equality of opportunity; the dilemma of raising standards and credentials by expanding the examination system while offering a suitable curriculum to the less able; the dilemma of incorporating a subject-oriented traditional grammar-school-type curriculum while at the same time admitting secondary-modern-type pupils. The ensuing response to the dilemmas posed by the less able and unwilling was to segregate them internally within the schools, to develop large remedial departments in schools, and to send disruptive pupils to the rapidly developing number of behavioural units. Tomlinson comments that up to the beginning of the 1980s there was little evidence that comprehensive schools had solved the dilemma of providing curriculum for the 'less able' or the 'remedial-special'. After a consideration of the social and political consequences of the disappearance of the youth labour market for less able and special leavers, the author ends the paper with a succinct criticism of the ideology of special needs, asserting that it has become part of a rhetoric that serves little educational purpose. The suggested readings echo the main points raised by Tomlinson. For example, Atkinson *et al.* examine how the growth in youth unemployment has been matched by an increase in state intervention measures to manage the 'social problems' thought to be an inevitable and direct consequence.

Topping's paper, Reading 18, concentrates firstly on the effectiveness of 'additions' to curriculum arrangements and offerings for children with learning difficulties. He reviews a number of research studies which have attempted to incorporate various 'extras' into their programmes for children with behavioural and emotional problems and suggests that there is some evidence that, where a school is able to be highly flexible in devising individual curricula for disruptive pupils, disruption and absenteeism are reduced. Giving pupils specific work targets and free time on target achievement has reduced disruptiveness in adolescents, and teaching children psychological concepts can produce more understanding and tolerance of the behaviour of others. The greater part of Topping's paper is devoted to an examination of a substantial number of studies to do with the variety of 'routine sanctions' widely used in schools to control pupils' behaviour. A useful summary of the main findings of the numerous research studies cited indicate, perhaps not surprisingly, that reward systems are much more effective in producing good behaviour than punishment, which often makes little difference. Nevertheless, punishment is usually much more frequently employed in schools than rewards, and further, what teachers intend to be punishing may not be so perceived by pupils, and increased disruption can result therefrom. The suggestions for further reading include a paper by Presland (1981) which examines the long-term and wider effects of using behaviour-modification techniques to bring about change in unwanted classroom behaviour. Merrett (1981) provides a useful review of behaviour-modification studies in British schools, while Olweus (1980) investigates personality factors and aspects of the home backgrounds of children rated as having habitual levels of aggressive behaviour.

Reading 14

CONFRONTATION SITUATIONS AND TEACHER SUPPORT SYSTEMS
R. Pik

By a confrontation situation I mean the tense 'showdown' that occurs when, in response to what the *teacher* considers to be a reasonable request for a pupil to either do something or stop doing something, he 'digs in his

R. Pik (1981) *Confrontation situations and teacher support systems.* In B. Gilham (Ed.) (1981) Problem Behaviour in the Secondary School, Croom Helm, London

heels', shows open defiance and communicates either verbally or non-verbally 'I won't, you can't make me and I dare you to try'.

The following are examples of confrontations drawn from suspension letters sent to a local education authority:

I asked Mark [aged 15] in a quiet and friendly manner to sit down and get to work. He continued to run around the classroom [...] I asked him, still very quietly, to leave the room [...] but all he did say was 'Piss off' and 'I'm not going'.

Denise [aged 14] screwed up [her] paper and threw her book on the floor. I replaced the book back on her desk and reopened the paper and told her that she would have to write on it. Denise screwed up the paper and threw the book on the floor again [...]

Steven said he wouldn't go to detention [for an incomplete homework assignment]. I said, Very well then, you will come with me to see Mr B. (Deputy Head) right now!' He then sat down in his seat and replied, 'I'm fucking not going anywhere!'

Talking to teachers, it is apparent to me that confrontations such as these have an intense and unforgettable quality which makes them very difficult to dismiss at the end of the school day. Although the slow learner in the classroom can be the source of endless frustration for the teacher, most teachers are able to 'switch off' from the slow learner's problems when the teaching sessions are over. The teacher feels that he has given his professional best and will try again tomorrow. There is seldom a feeling of apprehension about having to face the slow learner and his class again. By contrast, a teacher who has had a confrontation with a pupil usually experiences great anxiety about the prospect of having to face that child and his class the next day and possibly for the rest of the term. The incident may be replayed many times in the teacher's mind.

There are three related questions which are seldom discussed with teachers by the professionals who are meant to be offering support and advice either as part of the in-school support network or as members of the support services available to schools, for example educational psychologists. The questions are: Why do confrontations provoke such strong, uncomfortable feelings in teachers? What precisely are these feelings? What measures do teachers usually take to reduce these feelings? By failing to tackle these questions with teachers, professionals have failed to understand or appreciate the pressures on teachers, or they have failed to communicate to teachers that they really understand and appreciate these pressures. It is therefore hardly surprising that many teachers are often unable or unwilling to implement the advice being offered – because the tone of the advice is unsympathetic, or because the actual content of the advice is judged to be irrelevant, ineffective or impractical.

Before going on to outline specific management strategies I should like to explore the three questions in turn.

WHY DO CONFRONTATIONS PROVOKE SUCH STRONG, UNCOMFORTABLE FEELINGS IN TEACHERS?

I suggest that it is because in a confrontation there is more of the teacher *as a person* 'on the line', that is, exposed and vulnerable. The slow learner may sometimes cause the teacher to question his own expertise as a master purveyor of his subject; the openly defiant student challenges the teacher's authority *and* severely dents the image the adult has of himself as a reasonable and sensitive person. He puts a strong doubt in the teacher's mind about his ability to cope.

The following example illustrates this notion of the teacher as a person feeling devalued during a confrontation.

This incident began around 11.45 a.m. Denise was provided with paper and a text for a writing exercise after a discussion period (in which she participated sensibly).

(1) Denise screwed up her paper and threw her book on the floor.

(2) I replaced the book back on the desk and reopened the paper and told her she would have to write on it.

(3) Denise screwed up the paper and threw the book on the floor again. I replaced it again and explained she was being asked to do something and should learn to do what she was told without getting angry about it. Denise's response to this was a chain of swear words ending in a clenched fist swung towards my face. But Denise's action at this point was clearly not intended to hurt me as she stopped her fist before it made contact with my face.

(4) I walked away at this point in order to give my attention to the rest of the class. A book thrown by Denise hit my back, followed by several screwed balls of paper.

(5) I picked up the book and returned it to Denise, taking the opportunity to explain to her she could not behave in this way or do whatever she wanted to do when she felt like it. She replied that I couldn't make her

do anything and I insisted that she had to learn to do what she was told to do. She threw the book at me again. I said that there was no point in being aggressive as it would not achieve anything. She swore at me again and I said I did not have conversations with people in that sort of language. I asked her whether she *wanted* me to hit her and I explained that I don't talk to people in that way. She replied that I wouldn't dare hit her, and I replied that I didn't want to. I explained to the class that hitting someone did not achieve anything. Some of the rest of the class laughed, apparently seeing this as a sign that I was too scared to face up to Denise. I turned to Denise and asked her to come out in front of the rest of the class. She refused and said I would have to make her. I asked her again more firmly. I said I was not prepared to drag her. I continued to fix her in her eyes and she came out to the front. She faced me and before I could speak attempted to hit me in the face with her fist, and then went and sat down again. I went over to Denise and shouted at her that she could not treat people like that. I shouted there was no reason to hit me since I liked her and did not want to hurt her.

(6) At this point I resumed my efforts to start the class on their written work, before dealing with Denise. The class were all hushed in expectation at this point. Denise got up and proceeded to pick up all the paper on the rest of the class's desks and then screwed them all up and threw them on the desk at the front of the class. I asked the class to read the first act of the play whilst I left the room (I was going to find a senior member of staff to remove her from the class). As I was walking out of the room, Denise followed me and shouted at me that I could not leave the class as I was supposed to be teaching them. I replied that as a teacher I was free to leave the room when I wished. She asked me where I was going and I replied that it was none of her business and told her to return to the room. She said I was going to tell on her and then hit me in the back as I continued to walk on. The bell for the end of the lesson rang as I was crossing the playground. Denise ran up to me me and said ****. I turned to walk on and she hit me with some force in the back again. Mrs L. later dismissed the class, after discussing the incident with them (12.30).

Notice, in the above example, how the teacher tries first to secure Denise's cooperation by invoking the teacher–pupil framework of rules: I am the teacher and you are the pupil; you must do as I say. It seems, however, that Denise does not share the same basic understanding of teacher and pupil roles. She refuses to obey the teacher merely because she *is* the teacher. When attempts to control Denise by appealing to teacher–pupil roles fail, the teacher resorts to appeals on a person-to-person level: 'I don't talk to people in that way. [...] I shouted at her that she could not treat people like that. [...] Do you understand, Denise, I like you and do not want to hurt you?' These statements are attempts to convey the message, 'I am a reasonable person and so are you. Let us try to work out our differences in a more sensible and less hurtful way'. Having these personal appeals rebuffed is very painful to one's self-esteem. Not only does the teacher now feel a failure because of her inability to shift Denise on either the professional or the personal level, she is also acutely aware of having somehow made a fool of herself in front of the class: 'Some of the rest of the class laughed, apparently seeing this as a sign that I was too scared to face up to Denise.'

The notion of how a 'class hushed in expectation' adds tremendous tension to a confrontation will be discussed under the second question.

WHAT ARE THE FEELINGS EXPERIENCED BY TEACHERS DURING AND AFTER CONFRONTATIONS?

There are likely to be three main feelings aroused: anger, fear and embarrassment. There is sometimes also a feeling of sadness after a confrontation.

Anger

The teacher may begin by experiencing annoyance because one pupil is taking his time and attention which he feels ought, at that moment, to be devoted to the other 25 children in the class. Annoyance quickly turns to anger when appeals for cooperation on either the professional or the personal level fail (as in the Denise example).

Fear

There is fear of aggression and fear of losing respect. The fear of aggression is often, I feel, mistakenly only viewed as the teacher being afraid of physical or verbal abuse by the student. It is important to recognize, however, that teachers, like parents, are often afraid of their own aggressive impulses when disciplining children. Just as a parent worries that his child may have provoked him to the point where he might hit too hard or say something too hurtful and irretrievable, so too teachers are afraid of letting loose their full fury on even the most provocative pupil. Loss of temper is a double-edged sword: the teacher often fears loss of temper in himself more than in his pupils during a confrontation. This is because as a teacher one is meant to be the example-setting adult.

Teachers tend to speak about fear of losing control of the class more openly than they do about the fear of loss of self-control. There is fear of losing 'the class's respect'. To a large extent, the degree of control that a teacher is able to exert over a class is dependent on the degree of respect accorded to him by the pupils. Today, it seems, teachers are more aware than their counterparts 20 years ago that respect from the pupils needs to be earned. Perhaps this is because many of the props which supported the idea of automatic obedience to the teacher have disappeared over the past two decades. Children are increasingly aware of themselves as people with power, rights and privileges who are entitled to respect. They resent being talked down to by adults in general and by teachers and parents in particular. Teachers, however, still fear being seen as 'weak'. Therefore, when discussing a confrontation, a teacher will usually say, 'If I let the child get away with it he will try it on again', or, more commonly, 'If the class see him getting away with it then others in the class will have a go next time'.

Embarrassment

Confrontations clearly produce embarrassment for the same reasons that they produce anger and fear. When professional and personal appeals for cooperation are rebuffed, the teacher worries that this may signify a personal weakness or failing. By definition, it is impossible for the teacher to fail privately, because an essential feature of the confrontation is the audience. (The notion of public failure is, of course, equally important in understanding the *pupil's* increasing stake in the confrontation and this will be discussed later on.)

A further and less widely recognized source of embarrassment is the teacher's apprehension that someone above him in the school's hierarchy might well need to be involved, either during or after the incident. Teachers often experience acute embarrassment when they have to call a colleague out of his classroom in order to help deal with a tricky situation. But even if no other teacher needs to be summoned at the time, and even if the pupil is not sent out of his class to go to another member of staff, the teacher may feel obliged to report a serious incident to his head of department or to a senior teacher later on. Actions taken during a confrontation which seemed reasonable and imperative to take at the time are sometimes difficult to explain and to justify to colleagues *and to oneself* later on. Once the dust has settled, the events which triggered the incident may, in retrospect, seem petty, trivial or infinitely ignorable. In any case the need to involve another teacher is often construed as an admission of one's inability to cope with a class. I have found teachers in the probationary year of teaching most vulnerable to this pressure. Because probationers know that the senior staff are recording their progress, they are often unduly and unrealistically worried about having to ask for help with an unruly class. They fear that asking for help in this way will somehow go down as a black mark on their record. Further, if a probationer does call upon a senior member of staff to help handle a serious incident, for example a pupil flatly refusing to leave the classroom despite the teacher's insistence that he do so, the senior teacher sometimes appears to succeed so easily where the probationer has failed that the younger teacher finds it difficult to imagine his senior colleague ever being nonplussed by a child. What is often not realized is that the confident veteran has probably, in the past, made every mistake in the book but has learned from experience which strategies are most likely to work in certain situations; he also has the 'formal status' of his position as senior tutor, deputy head or whatever. To the probationer, however, it appears that it is only he who cannot cope.

However, it would be wrong to suggest that only young, inexperienced teachers feel embarrassment when asking a colleague for help. More often than not, a teacher with many years of teaching experience is assumed to be able to control a class. If this teacher encounters difficulty it may be embarrassing for him to admit the situation, and even more embarrassing for him to have to ask for help.

Sadness

Although less commonly experienced than anger, fear and embarrassment, many teachers have, in reflecting on confrontations, expressed feelings of sadness. There is feeling sorry for oneself, often tinged with bitterness: 'Why did I have to get landed with 3C for a double period on Friday afternoon?' Interestingly, however, a teacher may also feel sorry for the pupil after a confrontation. This usually occurs when the incident has led to the pupil being severely punished, perhaps more severely than the teacher had expected, for example suspension or expulsion. There is a feeling that, if only he had handled the situation better, the outburst and its consequence might not have occurred. A teacher may also feel sorry for a pupil when he has some intimate knowledge of the child's home background. For example, when the teacher is aware that the child receives very harsh treatment at home, the teacher may well feel that he has in some way 'let down' the pupil by acting over-punitively, just like the child's parents.

WHAT MEASURES DO TEACHERS USUALLY TAKE TO REDUCE THE UNCOMFORTABLE FEELINGS?

This is not the place to discuss the range of possible disciplinary actions available to teachers. Rather, I want to consider how teachers deal with the personal feelings of anger, fear, embarrassment and possibly sadness which are evoked by confrontations.

The most dramatic effect of a confrontation on a teacher may be avoidance of the pupil and/or the class. Teachers may refuse to have a particular class or, more likely, insist that the pupil with whom the confrontation took place 'be excused' from that class. In taking this type of action the teacher must openly ask for help from the senior staff or the headteacher. A much more difficult situation arises when the teacher takes time off 'due to illness'. I have observed the vicious circle of stress leading to time off in many schools. What happens is that a teacher who has difficulty controlling a class (or classes) succumbs to the stress by taking days off school, ostensibly because of colds or 'flu. After several such absences, however, the other teachers begin to be slightly resentful about having to cover in their 'free' lessons. The antipathy which builds up towards the absent teacher usually makes it *less likely* that he will get the support needed to cope with the difficult situation on his return. This leads to greater strain and isolation necessitating more time off, and so on. It is important, therefore, for senior staff to be sensitive to this developing situation and to intervene quickly and positively with support for the teacher, and not leave him to struggle along on his own.

By far the most common reaction to a confrontation which helps the teacher reduce uncomfortable feelings is absolving oneself by attributing the child's disobedient behaviour to 'something wrong with the child' (usually 'inside his head') or blaming the child's parents (usually referred to as 'home background'). Many schools want those children frequently involved in confrontations referred to the psychologist or psychiatrist because they 'require treatment' to enable them to return to the classroom 'cured'. Teachers are often surprised to hear that a child whom they consider 'a thorough pest' in school may be quite well behaved at home. Although children and their families may value the out-of-school support and interest shown by a psychologist, it is difficult to see how this contact will lead to dramatic and enduring behaviour change in the classroom.

In the second half of this chapter I should like to go on to discuss various strategies for preventing and defusing those situations which can prove so traumatic for teachers and pupils alike. These strategies will involve the school as a system on three levels: the class-teacher, the in-school support network and the out-of-school support services.

STRATEGIES AVAILABLE TO THE CLASS-TEACHER

From my own teaching experience and from discussions with teachers I believe that confrontations develop and progress in four, possibly overlapping, phases: a build-up, a trigger-event, a rapid escalation and a finale. The responsibility for the build-up or the trigger-event may lie with either the teacher or the pupil but both are responsible for the escalation. Consider the following account of a confrontation:

> [the headteacher writes] On December 12th, Arthur, together with two other boys, was very late for school. Mr H. saw him, sent him off to assembly and told him to report later. All three boys were given 300 words to write as an imposition.
>
> When Mr H. checked up on their records he found that Arthur and one other boy had not been late for a month and so he decided to excuse them because of their good record. When they reported he said he would excuse them from doing the writing since they had not been late for many weeks and asked them for the paper back. It then became clear that they had gone off without any intention of doing the imposition anyway because the paper was later found torn up in the school's Christmas card post box. Because of this attitude, Mr H. decided that the imposition should stand after all.
>
> Arthur refused to do this imposition. When he was told he would work in isolation to get it done in school, he refused. When he was brought before me and I told him that he would do it or be suspended, he still refused and I, therefore, have no alternative but to suspend him.

In this case the build-up is clear: coming late to school and having to report to the teacher after assembly. Although the teacher then decided to excuse Arthur from the imposition, it later became clear that Arthur had already excused himself from doing it. Was Arthur's tearing up the paper for the imposition the trigger-event? The teacher obviously thought it serious enough to warrant punishing him for his 'attitude'. On the other hand, might not one construe the teacher's action of retracting the exemption he had already given as the trigger-event? In any case, what follows is a fairly common pattern of escalating punishment, and so on. The finale is the suspension. The headmaster states that he had 'no alternative' and I believe that Mr H. would also claim that he had no alternative to the action he took. This feeling of *having no alternative* is an important feature of confrontations. In the rapid escalation phase both teacher and pupil 'stake in' more and more, thus increasing the temperature, pressure and pace of the interaction. Note that at this stage in a confrontation, 'winning' and 'losing' become increasingly important to both participants while the notions of winning and losing become more narrowly defined by them. Things reach such a pitch that the teacher can only construe winning as getting the pupil to do precisely what he says at that moment – anything less is losing. The pupil, meanwhile, defines winning as refusing to 'knuckle under' to the teacher's demands; losing is giving in and obeying the teacher. In Arthur's case, even the headteacher gets drawn into a very narrow definition of winning which, in fact, is the same as Mr H.'s definition – making Arthur do his imposition is winning and no other alternative is even considered.

What rules about preventing and handling confrontations can we derive from Arthur's case? *Rule No. 1* must be: *Decide first whether it is worth risking a confrontation over a particular incident. Has there been a breach of school rules or principles important enough to warrant intervention at that moment, or would a quiet word with the pupil later on perhaps be a better course to follow?* I am not advocating looking the other way when school rules are broken. I am advocating 'weighing up' the pros and cons of taking certain actions at certain times. In Arthur's case, the issue of lateness to school became a non-issue by the teacher's own admission. If the teacher felt that Arthur's attitude warranted punishment, why choose the same instrument of punishment – the imposition – which had already been judged by both teacher and pupil to be unfair.

Rule No. 2 is a paraphrase of Dr Benjamin Spock's well-known formula: *Leave yourself and the pupil a gracious way out.* When there are no visible outlets or graceful exits available for either the teacher or the pupil, there is pressure on both to continue escalating the confrontation. The idea of saving face, already discussed with regard to teachers, is equally important with regard to children. There is always the danger of the pupil being pushed by the audience towards greater acts of bravado and defiance. The further the confrontation develops the harder it is for both pupil and teacher to back down. Often, therefore, the best move the teacher can make is to refuse to 'stake in' during the build-up stage or to refuse to increase his stake during the escalation phase. This may sometimes require the teacher taking the lead by admitting that he was wrong. It should have been clear to Mr H. that trying to force Arthur to do the imposition would be a further escalation. An alternative strategy, still available to to Mr H. at that time, could have been to dismiss the event whilst still making his point. For instance, he might have said something to this effect: 'Arthur, you were wrong not to do the imposition I gave you but perhaps I was wrong in giving it to you in the first place. Make things easier for us both by keeping up your good record of punctuality.'

Here is another example of a confrontation:

At lunchtime today the Deputy Head reported serious trouble with a teacher over misbehaviour in the House block.

Clive was in the House area with three other boys who were from another house and shouldn't have been there. They made raucous comments in the hearing of a young teacher and then ran off. The teacher followed and found these 13-year-old boys hiding like children in lockers in a cloakroom alcove.

He told them to get out and they sauntered off in the direction of the exit. He followed them to see if they had gone out and hearing a noise in the toilets, he looked inside to see that three of the lavatory cabinets were occupied, but that Clive was waiting outside. When the teacher entered, Clive went into another toilet cabinet, sat down on the seat and made a coarse and obscene remark. The teacher told him to get out once more and had to repeat this order at least three times. Clive did not go and was quite obviously deliberately provoking a situation.

Finally the teacher had to warn him, 'If you will not go and I have to take hold of you to get you out you will regret it.'

Clive replied, 'Go on mark me, I would love that.'

Consequently the teacher had to take hold of Clive and with considerable difficulty began to lead him out of the building. By the time other staff arrived, Clive was reduced to tears of rage and frustration at not being allowed to have his own way. He continued to be loud, abusive and obscene as he was escorted from the building. When he finally left he threatened the teacher concerned with violence, saying something to the effect, 'That is the way to get your neck broken.'

The other boys admit that they were all being provocative and refer to the incident as 'aggro'.

I believe that the young male teacher involved in this incident was lured into a confrontation. The toilets, cloakrooms and locker-rooms are generally areas that adolescent pupils tend to consider their own 'ground', or at least not the teacher's ground. The teacher is usually in a 'one-down' position when trying to remove them from these areas. Note that it was the teacher, and not Clive, who first made threatening remarks about using physical force: 'If you will not go and I have to take hold of you to get you out, you will regret it.' I believe that this teacher was very fortunate not to have been assaulted by the pupil. (Referring back to the Denise incident, the reader will recall that again it was the teacher who first suggested physical force: 'I asked her whether she *wanted* me to hit her [...].

Rule No. 3 is therefore: *Remember that threats by a teacher to use physical force or the actual use of physical force will nearly always escalate a conflict very quickly and dramatically and will greatly increase the probability of the pupil reacting violently.*

A situation which is especially important to avoid is a male teacher physically handling or restraining a female pupil. Consider the example of Mary:

> At the beginning of the fifth period on a Friday, Mr S. was standing at the door of Room J20 to control the movement of the pupils out and in when Mary, holding a plastic bag, tried to push past him in order to give the bag to a friend already in J20. Mary should have been in another room and was behaving characteristically in being where she ought not to be at that particular time. The [male] teacher restrained her, intending to call over the friend to collect the bag at the door. When restrained, Mary kicked out at the teacher, hit him twice in the face, tearing off his spectacles. The teacher made no attempt to retaliate, but Mary then pulled his hair and kicked out.

Even though the impression given is that the teacher's physical contact with Mary seemed quite spontaneous and not intended to be threatening, Mary overreacted instantly. Physical handling, even something so slight as catching at the sleeve of a child's jacket, may trigger a violent response.

Rule No. 4 is: *A reasonable time after a confrontation, the teacher involved should take the opportunity to talk privately with the pupil before they are next scheduled to come into contact with one another in the classroom.* There is obviously little point in trying to have a conversation while either the teacher or the pupil is still 'high' following a confrontation and so one must allow a reasonable 'cooling-off' period. In practice, what often happens is that the pupil is sent to a senior teacher who is left to deal with the situation without further involvement by the class-teacher. Although this is a useful manoeuvre in that it allows for a cooling-off period for both teacher and child, it does little to reduce the teacher's apprehension about the next contact he will have with the child in the classroom. In a quiet moment, away from the audience, it is usually much easier for teacher and pupil to make the kind of contact in which they come over as 'themselves'. In this conversation there is little point getting hung up on the issues of who was right and who was wrong. It is better for the teacher to concede that both he and the pupil seem to get rather carried away sometimes. The message for the teacher to try to get across is: 'I regret that this happened; let us try not to force each other into a difficult position again.'

Some teachers may regard this as merely 'humouring' or 'placating' the child, when a 'firm stand' would be more correct. But desired behaviour is not brought about by confrontation: putting a child in a position he cannot move from is to confirm him in a deviant role. A child, like an adult, becomes what he does. Some children may need a good deal of humouring in this fashion but, at the very least, it enables them to keep out of a role that they would then feel they had to defend. A brief 'backstage' contact will greatly reduce the teacher's anxiety about the contact he will have with the child when both will again be 'on stage'. The personal appeals made by the teacher and rejected by the child in the heat of the confrontation are more likely to be responded to by the child later on.

The reader will recall that in defining a confrontation I stated earlier that the pupil reacted with defiance to *what the teacher considered to be a reasonable demand*. Often, however, in the aftermath, the teacher's eyes may be opened to the fact that what he considered a reasonable demand was, in fact, very *unreasonable* from a child's point of view. One dramatic example of this was evident in an account a teacher related to me. The teacher had, in his own words, 'a real dust-up' with a 13-year-old boy.

In covering a class for an absent colleague, he asked the class to read aloud from their geography books. The second boy he called upon to read was still fumbling around in his desk for the correct book. The teacher waited patiently, not wanted to let the boy off the hook by calling on someone else to read. When the boy said that he did not have his book, the teacher went over to his desk and found it for him. Feeling that the boy was 'trying it on' and testing him out, and increasingly aware of the giggles and titters from the rest of the class, the teacher demanded that the boy stand up and read immediately. At this point the boy slammed his desk shut, sat back in his chair and folded his arms in a gesture of defiance. A rapid and intense escalation followed.

Ultimately the boy was sent to wait outside the headteacher's office.

Two periods later the teacher chanced upon the boy still waiting to see the head. He asked the boy to have a chat with him in the medical room adjacent to the office. He felt that both he and the lad appeared calmer to each other. From this conversation it became apparent to the teacher that the boy had refused to read because he was almost unable to read. The boy had managed to keep his illiteracy fairly secret to all but his closest friends.

Clearly, what seemed to the teacher to be a reasonable demand for the boy to read was totally *unreasonable* and embarrassing from the boy's point of view. The confrontation had provided an effective 'smokescreen' for the boy's problem.

STRATEGIES AVAILABLE TO THE IN-SCHOOL SUPPORT NETWORK

Many schools have a specially designated pastoral-care team comprising heads of year, senior masters and mistresses and/or heads of department. Very often these staff are paid an extra allowance for their pastoral-care duties. However, a school need not necessarily have a formal pastoral-care team as such; sometimes it can even be a disadvantage. The least effective pastoral-care teams I have encountered are those that are construed by the staff as dealing exclusively with discipline problems, handing out punishment to 'troublemakers' sent to them by class-teachers and form-teachers. By contrast, the most effective senior staff, whether they are called a pastoral-care team or not, are those who make it clear to the staff that pastoral care is something worth while for all children and for all teachers. The role is one of support and guidance for pupils and staff. Matters to do with the curriculum, in-service training courses and academic standards in the school are seen to be just as much their concern as the issue of children's behaviour in the classroom. Teachers are seen to be receiving advice and back-up by the senior staff while being encouraged to take on greater responsibility for dealing with disruptive behaviour themselves rather than passing routine problems on.

Senior staff have an important role to play in the management of confrontation situations. To begin with it is essential that all the teachers know who the senior staff are and how they may be contacted at short notice. Although this may sound almost absurdly elementary, I have found several schools which were so large and with such frequent staff turnover that many of the newer teachers asked *me* – the visiting psychologist – for some kind of list or chart to clarify the staff structure of *their* school! No one had ever told them who to turn to in the complicated school hierarchy if they required help in a difficult situation. Pupils sometimes received more formal induction into the school structure than did the teachers. Senior staff need to hold regular meetings and support groups for the probationer teachers and they should include in these groups teachers who are new to the school and its particular characteristics, even though they may have had a few years of previous teaching experience.

All staff, especially the probationers, should be encouraged to ask for help from the senior staff, sooner rather than later, if they are experiencing difficulties in controlling a class. Senior staff are in the best position to explain some of the points covered in this chapter with regard to the nature of confrontations and the feelings they evoke in teachers. Many teachers have told me that it would have helped them very much if they had heard from their senior colleagues that they too sometimes experienced difficulty in controlling a class. In fact, it took them some time to find out that they were not the only ones who sometimes found it difficult to cope with a class. This discovery, really more of a revelation to many of them, was acknowledged to be greatly reassuring.

As well as a support and advisory role, senior staff need to take an intervention role. That is, they should fulfil a 'call-out' function that class-teachers can make use of if a confrontation escalates to a dangerous stage (I sometimes refer to 'calling out the cavalry'). Mark's case illustrates some useful points with regard to a teacher's summoning help during a confrontation.

When Mark came in, he immediately started to fight (not seriously) with Gary. I asked him many times, in a very quiet and friendly manner, to sit down and get to work. He continued to run around the classroom directing Kung Fu kicks at various people and jumping over the furniture. Eventually I asked him, still very quietly, to leave the room. He did leave, but returned very shortly and stood behind me. I again asked him to leave but he stopped listening to me and went and appropriated David's chair. I went over to him and tried to persuade him to leave, but all he did say was 'Piss off' and 'I'm not going'. He would not come out of the room with me and I decided not to touch him or use any force at all. I tried to phone a senior member of staff but could not contact anyone. I then went to ask Mr R. for assistance, and I had to stay to supervise his class.

Signed: Mr S. [probationer]

At approximately 14.00 hours today I was teaching 3C in D27 when Mr S. came in and said that Mark had entered his room, had hit some of the others and refused to leave. Mr S. asked me to intervene. I left him with my class and went to the class next door where Mark was sitting quietly in the far corner. I asked him to leave and his reply, as accurately as I can recall, was 'No, I'm not going to pick up any books.' This puzzled me and I said I didn't know anything of any books. I again asked him to leave and he refused. I said 'Mark, I will ask you three times to leave.' This I did and each time he refused. I then took hold of the back of his chair to turn it (he was sitting with his back to me). He stood up and lashed backwards with his foot. By accident or design he struck the chair which hit my leg. He then turned and swung a punch at my body. This I parried and he backed up against the wall. We faced each other for several moments during which I asked him several times to leave. The Senior Master then arrived and took over.

Signed: Mr R. [2-year veteran]

The class-teacher's initial handling of the situation seemed quite reasonable. He did, however, make one mistake in sending Mark out of the room without either sending him *to* someone or otherwise 'attaching' him. Just sending a child out in this manner usually invites him to stand outside the door making funny faces, much to the amusement of the class, and of course does not prevent him coming back in again to carry on the argument if he so desires. Unfortunately, in the present example, the system lets the teacher down badly, with disastrous consequences — 'I tried to phone a senior member of staff but could not contact anyone'. This should never happen. At worst, it should always be possible to contact a secretary and leave it to her to summon a senior staff member to a classroom as a matter of urgency. Or, a colleague in the next classroom could be asked to do this. Calling in a colleague who is not much more experienced than oneself (like Mr R.) will often only escalate the confrontation. There is a definite face-saving element for the pupil in being removed from the classroom by a senior member of staff and not by a junior member of staff. There is a feeling that 'anyone would go out if Mr B. ordered them to'.

A further mistake made by Mark's teacher, however, was sending his colleague next door to deal with the situation for him. If the two teachers had gone in together to deal with Mark, at least they would have had strength of numbers. Instead, Mr R. is asked to deal with the difficult situation on his own and is easily confused when he sees Mark sitting quietly in the corner; he is even more puzzled by Mark's reference to 'picking up books', about which Mr R. clearly knows nothing. Why did Mr S. feel that he needed to cover Mr R.'s class during all this?

One other point worth noting is Mr R.'s tactical error in saying to Mark, 'I will ask you three times to leave'. Less experienced teachers often fall into this trap not realising that by stating that they will ask three times, they are begging the student to defy the first two requests! Only by waiting for the third request will the pupil get the confrontation back to the stage it was already at before the first two requests were made. Usually, teachers make three requests in order to stall for time. Like Mr Micawber there is the magical hope that 'something will turn up' – a senior member of staff will suddenly materialize to help out or the bell will ring for break. Senior staff need to be available to intervene in these situations. Furthermore, they should make it clear that they would prefer to be called out *immediately* rather than have to deal with a situation that has escalated into something more serious. Probationer teachers, in particular, will need reassurance that it is reasonable to ask for help in this way: that it is better to accept help than lose control.

STRATEGIES AVAILABLE TO THE SUPPORT SERVICES

In terms of preventing and handling confrontations the educational psychologist may have a good deal to offer but only if he visits the school on a regular basis and is seen by the staff as being a useful adjunct to the in-school support network. Inviting the psychologist to attend occasional staff meetings or, more importantly, pastoral-care meetings, may often prove helpful. A psychologist who knows a school well, is familiar with its physical layout and its staff resources, is in a good position to suggest possible alternative management strategies for dealing with pupils frequently involved in confrontations. He can encourage staff to look for patterns in the confrontations; to explore such questions as:

1. Does the pupil tend to have more confrontations with male or female staff?
2. Are there more confrontations with junior staff and, if so, does the pupil's timetable show a large number of lessons with junior staff?
3. Do there appear to be more confrontations during the more formal lessons or during the more 'free-ranging' lessons such as art, PE and home economics, in which movement around the room, gym or kitchen is essential?
4. Does the class size appear to be a significant factor?

5. Is there a small group of his peers who might be providing a suitably provocative audience for the pupil in several of the classes during which confrontations take place?

6. Is there a pattern of failure or difficulty with certain subjects which might be a contributing factor to confrontations during these lessons? (Often signified by the days of the week on which the pupil poses difficulties or is absent from school.)

7. With which teacher(s) does the pupil get on particularly well in and out of the classroom? (This person, even if he or she doesn't actually teach the child, could be useful in a counselling role).

These kinds of questions may provide answers which will suggest possible management strategies. These may range from altering an individual pupil's timetable to coordinating a clear plan of action for teachers to take in the event of misbehaviour. In cases where the staff feel that counselling for a particular child may be beneficial, it is better for the psychologist not to take on the counselling himself; rather, he can offer supervision and support to a staff member with whom the child already has a good relationship if that teacher is willing to try counselling the child. The staff member need not necessarily be a member of the senior staff nor a trained counsellor. The important qualification is that he or she is the person with whom the child feels able to talk. If a teacher is willing to make this commitment, the psychologist must devote 15–20 minutes of his time on each visit to the school to conducting a private supervision session with the teacher.

It would be naïve to give the impression that schools are crying out for psychologists to work in this sort of way. Similarly, this form of intervention would not appeal to every psychologist. Some schools and psychologists still get bogged down with the idea of individual referral, assessment and treatment by the support services, and prefer a more 'traditional' approach; and clearly the psychologist must first establish his own credibility with the school staff. One way to do this is to organize in-school talks with the teachers, perhaps during the lunch hour, to cover topics *chosen by them,* for example social-skills training groups for teenagers. In this way he can make contact with all the staff, not just those senior members directly responsible for 'pastoral care' who usually liaise with outside agencies.

If this chapter has one main theme it is that of cooperation, mutual support and shared understanding in the management of behaviour problems in school. The educational psychologist is the most obvious, and the most usually available, outside agent for such a cooperative enterprise, but his role is not exclusive. An adviser, a social worker or a psychiatrist could fulfil a similar function. Shared responsibility is a characteristic of successful secondary schools: it doesn't eliminate all the problems but helps to keep them under control and, more importantly, reduces the stressful sense of isolation experienced by many teachers.

TOPICS FOR DISCUSSION

1. *Anger, fear,* and *embarrassment* are the three most likely teacher reactions to a confrontation. How might teachers best cope with these feelings?
2. Discuss the course of an actual confrontation that you or your colleagues have witnessed or experienced. To what extent is Pik's description of its progress correct? (A *build-up,* a *trigger-event,* a *rapid escalation,* a *finale.*)
3. Comment on Rule 2, *Leave yourself and the pupil a gracious way out,* as a useful and a necessary tactic in any confrontation.

SUGGESTIONS FOR FURTHER READING

1. M. Galton and T. Willcocks (1982) *Moving from the Primary Classroom,* Routledge and Kegan Paul, London. Chapter 6, 'A very Common Curriculum', and chapter 7, 'Teachers and their Specialist Subjects', provide detailed accounts of teachers' strategies for establishing control and imposing their teaching styles on pupils. The authors employ Bernstein's (1971) concepts *collection code, classification* and *framing* to identify the ways in which teachers conceive of the curriculum and organize their teaching activities. Chapter 9, 'The Primary Classroom Revisited', raises a number of interesting outcomes of teachers' organizational styles and the resultant behaviour of their pupils. For example, given the organizational strategy of *individual attention provider* on the part of a teacher, how does s/he keep the remaining children occupied when dealing with a particular child and how does s/he deal with the child who is an *attention seeker?*
2. J. Bond (1982) Pupil-tutoring: the educational conjuring trick, *Educational Review,* Vol. 34, No.3, pp 241–252. This is a fascinating account of six adolescents with records of disruptive behaviour and persistent truanting who were placed in a primary school to tutor twelve young children (5 to 8 years of age) described by their teacher as 'slow learners'. Each 15-year-old pupil-tutor (two girls and four boys) was required to attend eight two-and-a-half-hour sessions in the primary school. The author reports improvements in the pupil-tutor's attitudes to school and to teachers, in their self-concepts, their basic skills in reading and writing and in their understanding of child-rearing practices. 'The adolescents', she observes, 'turn into reliable, conscientious caring individuals who are concerned about the educational progress of their future offspring, who can sympathise to some extent with their teachers and who begin to show some insight into their problems.' The cameos of the truants' personal backgrounds (pp 250–252) lead the author to the same conclusions as most other researchers on truancy that 'these young people are more sinned against than sinning'.

3. E. Callely (1982) *Special provision for disruptive pupils – a school-based unit.* In D.P. Tattum (Ed.) (1982) Disruptive Pupils in Schools and Units, John Wiley and Sons, Chichester. One way of dealing with problem children in the ordinary school involves setting up a school-based unit which functions as an integral part of the school's pastoral system. This is an account of just such a unit within a large comprehensive school of some 1850 girls. The account contains a detailed discussion of the referral procedures and the aims and organization of the disruptive unit.

Reading 15
WHOSE SPECIAL NEEDS?
D. Galloway

INTRODUCTION

If teachers taken from a random sample in ordinary primary and secondary schools were to be asked what they knew about the Warnock Report (DES, 1978), almost all would know that it dealt with special education. If asked about the Report's conclusions and recommendations, there would probably be less confidence. Some might say that the report recommended the integration of handicapped children into the mainstream. They would, incidentally, be considerably overstating the Committee's position with respect to integration. The recommendation remembered by the largest number, however, might be that: 'one in six children at any one time and up to one in five children at some time in their school career will require some form of special educational provision'.

Before looking more critically at the evidence for this conclusion, and at its implications for teachers, it is worth considering the three broad areas of need which Mary Warnock and her colleagues had in mind. The first was the need for provision of special means of access to the curriculum. This applies mainly to children with physical, visual and hearing disabilities. A blind child, for example, will need to be taught Braille. The second and third areas were the need for 'provision of a special or modified curriculum' and 'particular attention to the social structure and emotional climate in which education takes place'.

There is no doubt that up to 20 per cent of children have diffculty coping with the ordinary curriculum at some stage in their school lives. Nor is there

D. Galloway (1985) *Whose special needs?* In D. Galloway (1985) Schools, Pupils and Special Educational Needs, Croom Helm, London

much doubt that the social structure and emotional climate in the school or classroom is a source of substantial stress to a similar proportion. The question is whether a curriculum and an emotional climate which fails to cater for up to 20 per cent of pupils can be entirely suitable for the remaining 80 per cent. In more practical terms, the relationship between the proposed special or modified curriculum and the mainstream curriculum requires elucidation. This is also true of the relationship between the social structure and emotional climate needed for children with special needs and that required for 'ordinary' pupils. Special or modified curricula, and classes with special 'social structures and emotional climates' may as frequently create special needs as meet them.

WARNOCK'S 20 PER CENT: EDUCATIONAL REALITY OR STATISTICAL FICTION?

The availability of places in special schools is unevenly distributed through the country. Marked variations can even occur between neighbouring boroughs. Thus, one London borough in 1977 placed ten times more children in schools for the maladjusted than another (DES, 1978). Consequently, special school places have never provided evidence about the numbers of children with special educational needs. To see how the Warnock Committee formed its conclusions we have to look at evidence from studies of larger groups of children.

Disturbing behaviour

The most widely quoted investigations are the National Child Development Study and those carried out by Professor Michael Rutter and his colleagues on the Isle of Wight and in an Inner London borough. The National Child Development Study included all children born between 3 and 9 March 1958. On the basis of the teacher version of Stott's Bristol Social Adjustment Guide (1963), 64 per cent of children were rated as stable, 22 per cent as unsettled, and 14 per cent as maladjusted (Davie *et al.*, 1972). The same study showed that 13 per cent of children were thought by teachers to need special educational help, but only 5 per cent were in fact receiving it.

Rutter and his colleagues asked teachers to complete a behaviour questionnaire (Rutter, 1967) on the pupils they studied. In addition they interviewed the children's mothers and, on the Isle of Wight but not in London, the children themselves. In the Inner London borough, 19 per cent of children were rated as deviant on the basis of the teacher's questionnaire results, compared with 11 per cent in the Isle of Wight. Using all the available questionnaire and interview data, 25 per cent of London's 10-year-olds were said to be showing 'clinically significant' signs of psychiatric disorder, compared with 12 per cent on the Isle of Wight. The term psychiatric disorder was used to include 'abnormalities of emotions, behaviour or relationships which are developmentally inappropriate, and of sufficient duration and severity to cause persistent suffering or handicap to the child and/or distress or disturbance to the family or community' (Rutter and Graham, 1968).

An interesting incidental observation from the Isle of Wight study was the small overlap between children whose parents were concerned about their behaviour and children whose teachers expressed concern (Rutter *et al.*, 1970). This was partly attributable to teachers reporting more behaviour problems of a broadly antisocial type, while parents tended to report a larger number of withdrawn children. Children whose parents complain about their behaviour at home may have special needs. Whether they have special *educational* needs is another question altogether.

Two explanations may be put forward for the low overlap between behaviour problems at home and at school, as reported by parents and teachers. One is that parents and teachers interpret similar behaviour in different ways. 'Quietness', for example, may be considered a virtue by some teachers who may be more concerned about openly disruptive pupils. Parents, on the other hand, may see quietness as an indication of lack of confidence or of anxiety in social situations. Another explanation is that children behave in different ways in different contexts.

Both explanations are valid. Both draw attention to the teacher's role in attributing special educational needs to a child. Teachers vary themselves in how they interpret behaviour. A healthy extrovert to one teacher can be a thoroughly noisy, disruptive nuisance to another. Similarly the child that one teacher in an open-plan class sees as quiet, but sensitive and creative, may be seen as an immature, withdrawn little baby by another. Disturbing classroom behaviour, in other words, is not a problem because of any objective criteria in the behaviour itself, but rather because of the effect it has on teachers.

All experienced teachers, moreover, will recall children whose behaviour has changed dramatically with a change of teacher. In the same way a change of school can be accompanied by a change of attitudes and of behaviour. At home, parents recognize that their children's language changes according to the company they are in; expressions and pronunciation considered unacceptable within the family may be necessary for social acceptance in the street or the playground. Thus, a teacher's statement that a child's behaviour indicates a need for special educational help has to be seen not only in terms of the teacher's own values and attitudes, but also in terms of the child's behaviour in a particular context.

An observation from a follow-up to the Isle of Wight study revealed a slight increase in the prevalence of psychiatric disorder at age 14 compared with four years earlier (Rutter *et al.*, 1976). This was not, however, attributable to any important increase in the rate of overtly disruptive behaviour of most immediate concern to teachers. More important, perhaps, just over half the pupils assessed as showing signs of psychiartric disorder had first presented problems as adolescents. Fewer than half had been disturbing their parents or teachers four years earlier. This observation has two implications. Firstly, as the Warnock Report recognized, the problems presented by many pupils are transient. Secondly, concentrating provision for pupils with special needs on the younger age-groups would be of limited value, even if all the pupils concerned could be 'treated' successfully. This is not the case, nor is there any way of identifying reliably pupils who will disturb their teachers towards the end of their school careers. Even if these pupils *could* be identified, there would be no way of telling what their educational needs would be, let alone how they should be met. We shall return later in the chapter to the confusion surrounding the concept of special educational need on account of disturbing behaviour. Firstly, though, we need to look at the prevalence of learning difficulties.

Learning difficulties

Nationally, special schools for pupils with moderate learning difficulties, formerly known as ESN(M), account for roughly 1 per cent of school-age pupils. This tells us nothing, however, about the number of children who might be experiencing learning difficulties. To see why, we need to consider the range of problems subsumed under the blanket term learning difficulties.

The 1944 Education Act and subsequent regulations (Ministry of Education, 1945) did not define criteria for ascertainment as ESN. Subsequent publications, though, made clear that special schools for ESN pupils should cater predominantly for those with a low IQ, generally assessed as below 70 or 75 (Ministry of Education, 1958, 1961). We shall return to the uses of IQ tests shortly. The point here is that the controversy was associated with two questions:

1. The way in which most IQ tests are constructed ensures that roughly 2.5 per cent of the population will obtain a score below 70.

2. Virtually all special schools for children with moderate learning difficulties have always admitted a disproportionate number of boys and a substantial minority of pupils with relatively high measured intelligence (Ministry of Education 1958). Further, they have in many areas aroused understandable anger and suspicion by admitting a disproportionate number of children of Caribbean origin (e.g. Coard, 1971). The implication is that they have been used as convenient places for problem pupils, and not simply as the most appropriate place in which to meet the needs of pupils with moderate learning difficulties.

Even without the confusion surrounding criteria for admission to a special school for children with moderate learning difficulties we would still be no nearer an idea of the prevalence of learning difficulties. The predicted figure of about 2.5 per cent scoring below 70 on an IQ test is a purely statistical artefact of the way most of these tests are constructed, a point to which we return shortly. We therefore need to look at the number of children believed to have learning difficulties in ordinary schools.

Yule *et al.* (1974) noted that 8 per cent of 10-year-olds in the Isle of Wight and 19 per cent in an Inner London borough had a reading age at least 28 months below their chronological age. In most cases the poor reading ability was associated with low measured intelligence. In other words, their reading level could be predicted from knowledge of their IQ. These pupils were regarded as backward readers. Nearly 3 per cent of the Isle of Wight pupils and 10 per cent of the London pupils were reading significantly below the level predicted by their age and IQ. These pupils with specific reading retardation overlapped with the backward group. Their special educational needs, though, were more specifically confined to reading, since they did not, on the whole, have similar problems in mathematics.

Multiple 'handicap'

The four criteria noted so far in defining learning difficulties which indicate special educational need are an IQ below 70, reading backwardness, specific reading retardation and psychiatric disorder. At least one of these conditions applied to 16 per cent of 10-year-olds on the Isle of Wight (Rutter *et al.*, 1970). More than one condition applied to a quarter of this 16 per cent, or 4 per cent of the total.

Warnock refers to these criteria as 'handicaps'. Certainly , they have been taken as evidence both in the report and in subsequent discussion as evidence of special educational need. It is therefore worth asking whether there was anything in the least surprising in the evidence that up to 20 per cent of children may have special educational needs, as defined in the report, at some stage in their school career. It is also worth asking whether the criteria themselves can meaningfully be seen as valid.

PREVALENCE OF SPECIAL EDUCATIONAL NEEDS: A CRITIQUE

Neither new, nor surprising

The first thing to be said about Warnock's conclusion on the prevalence of special educational need is that it could equally well have been reached on adequate research evidence at any time in the previous 50 years. This is true both of pupils whose behaviour disturbs their teachers and of children with learning difficulties.

As early as 1925 Haggerty had found teachers in North America reporting undesirable behaviour in more than 50 per cent of pupils. In London elementary schools teachers had reported one or more of four 'behaviour deviations' in 46 per cent of pupils (McFie, 1934). The 'deviations' listed were timidity or lack of sociability, behaviour disorders such as truancy or stealing, habit disorders such as nail-biting or incontinence, and educational problems not attributable to mental deficiency. In the private sector, teachers at five schools run by the Girls Public Day Schools Trust had put forward 17 per cent of pupils for interview on account of difficult behaviour (Milner, 1938). Other studies, in North America, had been reviewed by Uger (1938) with broadly similar results.

The position on children with learning difficulties was equally clear. Cyril Burt's (1937) book *The Backward Child,* written in his early years when his probity as a researcher remains relatively unquestioned, is regarded as a classic. In it he concluded that one child in ten above the 'educable defective' level was backward, and only one in six of the so-called educable defectives, later labelled ESN(M), was actually in a special school. These pupils, moreover, were 'lacking not so much in social capacity as in scholastic capacity, they are incompetent pupils rather than incapable citizens'. Yet even earlier than this the first Medical Inspection to the Education Department had described as 'very numerous' children requiring special education because they are 'physically and morally healthy – but backward'.

Burt himself exerted a strong influence on the deliberations between 1924 and 1929 of a committee chaired by A.H. Wood into the educational needs of the 'feeble-minded'. Excluding children with severe learning difficulties, who were then outside the education system altogether, the committee considered that existing special schools catered for only one-sixth of the estimated number of feeble-minded children in the country. These children, formerly known as ESN(M), would today be said to have moderate learning difficulties. In addition, the committee noted the special needs of children who did not formally qualify as feeble-minded, estimating that they included roughly a further 10 per cent of the population (Board of Education and Board of Control, 1929).

A statistical fiction?

Tests of intelligence and of educational attainments are designed to assess children with a wide range of ability. Most intelligence tests are designed with a mean of 100 and a standard deviation of 15. The sample on which the norms are based is assumed to be representative of the population as a whole. Hence the design of the test ensures that roughly 34 per cent of children will obtain scores between 85 and 100 (within one standard deviation below the mean), and more than 47 per cent between 70 and 100 (within two standard deviations below the mean).

Results of reading tests are more frequently described in terms of reading ages. Thus a child who has a reading age of 10 on his tenth birthday is reading 'up to' his chronological age. For statistical reasons reading quotients derived from the chronological age are misleading (Yule, 1973), particularly at the extremes.

If the way the tests are constructed ensures a wide range of scores, care is obviously necessary in using the results as evidence of special educational needs. Is it, for example, legitimate to regard as handicapped, and hence in need of special educational help, children whose low reading age is wholly predictable from evidence on their intellectual ability? The Warnock Committee could argue that a reading age 28 months below chronological age indicates a need for special help. This would be a reasonable reply, but evades an important part of the problem, that is, that the cut-off point of 28 months is an arbitrary one.

Purely from a research point of view, it is both legitimate and necessary to define some arbitrary criterion of backwardness. Without some such criterion it is logically impossible to report the number of pupils falling below the criterion. Yet in implicitly using the researchers' criterion to define special educational need, thus going further than the researchers themselves, the Committee was making an essentially moral, and political, judgement about the children that teachers in ordinary classes should, or should not, be expected to teach without additional help.

This point becomes clearer by considering different criteria the committee might have accepted. Its members could have regarded any child with a reading age more than 18 months behind his chronological age as having special educational needs. Had they done so, the proportion thought to require special help would have been much higher. Alternatively, they could have accepted 36 months backwardness as indicating a need for special help. In this case the proportion would have been considerably lower. What the Committee in effect seemed to do was to think of a percentage point and assert that any child falling below this point had special needs. The corollary, of course, was that the teachers of any child falling below the specified level needed special help in order to meet the child's needs. The wide range of scores guaranteed by the method of constructing intelligence and reading tests could then be relied on to provide educational justification for the political decision. This problem cannot be evaded by claiming that 28 months is the stage at which *teachers* think they need special help, since that depends on the average for the class, on the teachers' experience and on their expectations of what the children 'ought' to be achieving.

A similar proportion is evident in ascribing special educational need on behaviour grounds. The evidence summarized above, and by Galloway *et al.* (1982), lends no support to the widespread belief that behavioural problems are on the increase. Teachers have always expressed concern about a substantial minority of their pupils, and probably always will. In a competitive, achievement-oriented society, the lowest achievers and the least conforming pupils will inevitably be regarded as problems. The concepts of underachievement and disturbing or, more speculatively, 'disturbed' behaviour have no meaning without reference to some agreed norm. Children can be said to underachieve or overachieve with reference to their measured intelligence. The reference point cannot, however, logically be their chronological age since that would imply the logical impossibility of raising everyone to an average level — the point being that the average would change as overall standards improved. In the case of behaviour, the norm can only be the teacher's or researcher's view on what behaviour should be considered acceptable or unacceptable.

The instruments used in most of the research on children's behaviour on which the Warnock Committe based its conclusions were the Rutter A_2 Scale (Rutter, 1967) and Denis Stott's Bristol Social Adjustment Guides

(Scott, 1963, 1971). Rutter's Scale contains 26 items seen as possible symptoms of psychiatric disorder, for example 'restless, cannot remain seated for long' or 'often has temper tantrums'. The teacher has to state whether each item definitely applies, applies somewhat, or does not apply. Stott's Guides are longer, and require teachers to underline statements that apply to the child in question. Rutter's Scale is essentially a screening instrument designed to identify children who would be regarded as showing 'clinically significant' signs of psychiatric disorder in an interview with a psychiatrist. Stott's Guides aim to identify children who could be considered maladjusted and to describe the nature of their problems. They aim to give teachers more clinical information than Rutter's Scale, though their usefulness has been strongly challenged (e.g. Yule, 1976).

Both instruments depend for their popularity and their success on containing items which are familiar to teachers. If they contained problems which were *not* familiar to teachers, they would be open to criticism on at least three grounds:

1. Nil returns are of very limited interest, either to teachers or to researchers.
2. Teachers would rapidly become bored with completing the forms.
3. Teachers would quite reasonably feel that the researchers were insensitive to, or unaware of, the problems in children's behaviour which most concerned them.

Yet by including items which *are* familiar to teachers, both instruments prejudge the issue: they ensure that a substantial minority of children will be regarded as deviant, maladjusted, disturbed or just disturbing, depending on the preferred label.

Surveys of children's behaviour are therefore open to exactly the same criticism as the results of intelligence and attainment tests. Moreover the Warnock Committee's interpretation of the results is just as political. In the case of children with learning difficulties, the Committee had to decide what proportion of the children whose progress deviated from some arbitrary, and rather ill-defined, concept of normality could reasonably be considered to have special educational needs. In the case of behaviour problems the question was what proportion of children whose behaviour deviated from some equally arbitrary and equally ill-defined concept of normality could reasonably be considered to have special educational needs. Having decided on a proportion, the research evidence was at hand to justify the conclusion.

It needs to be said that there is no evidence that the Committee did in fact approach the question in the cynical way suggested here. Our analysis aims rather to demonstrate that the evidence on the prevalence of special educational needs is open to more than one interpretation. By attributing special needs to 20 per cent of the population the Committee was not simply drawing attention to the needs of a minority. As the report quite clearly recognized, drawing attention to these children's needs carried a clear implication that something should be done about them. Since the majority were, and would remain, in ordinary schools, it followed that most special educational needs would have to be met in ordinary schools. Unfortunately, there could be no guarantee that some procedures adopted to meet the alleged needs would avoid the worst faults of segregated special schools.

WHAT NEEDS?

When a teacher becomes concerned about a child's progress or behaviour an initial response is to ask whether anything in his medical history or family background throws light on the problem. As far as it goes this is reasonable. Although the overlap between behaviour problems at home and at school is small (Rutter *et al.*, 1970), it is unreasonable to expect that feelings of stress about a situation at home will have no effect on a child's progress or behaviour at school. The obvious corollary, which it is all too easy for teachers to overlook, is that stress at school may well affect a child's behaviour at home. Thus, disturbing behaviour or lack of progress at school can readily be attributed to problems at home. Yet if a parent seeks advice about behaviour problems at home, the immediate temptation may be to assume that the parent's handling of the child is at fault. In either event, parents are held responsible, implicitly exonerating teachers.

The Warnock Report referred to special *educational* needs. It makes clear, however, that teachers cannot meet these needs on their own. One chapter is devoted to cooperation with parents — 'Parents as Partners' and the question of interprofessional cooperation is dealt with at length in other chapters. The report is generally optimistic about the ability of teachers to meet their pupils' special needs. A question which it largely overlooks is whether the interprofessional cooperation which it advocates may successfully identify personal and family problems but obscure much more relevant needs created by the curriculum and in the educational climate. Before turning to the school's influence on children's behaviour and educational progress, though, we need to consider individual, family and social influences.

Children presenting behaviour problems

The children who showed 'clinically significant' signs of psychiatric disorder in the Isle of Wight and Inner London borough studies had, or presented, quite serious problems. As noted earlier their problems were 'of sufficient duration and severity to cause persistent suffering or handicap to the child and/or distress or disturbance to the family or community' (Rutter and Graham, 1968). Another way of expressing this is that the children were themselves experiencing considerable stress. Several points, though, remain unclear. Warnock regarded children who met Rutter and Graham's criterion of psychiatric disorder as having special needs. Later in the chapter we discuss the troublesome question of whose needs we are talking about. Does it make sense to talk about children having special needs when adults are distressed or disturbed by their behaviour? At this stage we need only note that many, though by no means all, children regarded as having special educational needs on account of their behaviour are themselves experiencing 'persistent suffering or handicap'. That, however, tells us little about the children under discussion.

Social class

Behavioural problems and moderate educational subnormality (maladjusted and ESN(M) pupils in the old terminlogy) were alone amongst the former categories of handicap (Ministry of Education, 1959) to have a skewed social-class distribution. In other words, children in other categories came from all social classes in roughly the proportion predicted from the general population. In contrast, children with behavioural and learning problems tended to come from working-class homes.

   Detailed discussion of research into the relationship between social class and educational achievement is beyond the scope of this chapter. Conflicting theories about social-class differences, such as those of Bernstein (1971) and Labov (1970) on uses of language, do, however, give us clues as to how working-class pupils may be disadvantaged in the school system. The fact that they are at a disadvantage, consistently performing less well than their peers from middle-class homes, is not in dispute. To the extent that factors related to social class contribute to differences in educational attainment they are relevant to an analysis of special educational needs.

Social disadvantage

In their analysis of data from the National Child Development Study,

Wedge and Prosser (1973) identified 4.5 per cent of 11-year-olds as disadvantaged. The criteria for identifying these children were that their families:

1. had only one parent and/or five or more children,
   and
2. lived in an overcrowded house or a house with no hot water,
   and
3. were in receipt of means-tested welfare benefits on account of their low income.

By the age of 16, 2.9 per cent were disadvantaged on these criteria (Wedge and Essen, 1982).

The surveys showed a strong relationship between disadvantage and educational attainment. Moreover, the relationship became more marked during adolescence. At the very least the results suggest that children living in disadvantaged circumstances are more likely than other children to meet Warnock's criteria of special educational need.

Family disadvantage

Generalizations about potentially stressful events such as parental separation or divorce invite contradiction. Thus, the effect of parental separation is likely to depend largely on what happens in the family subsequently. Rutter *et al.* (1975) showed that London children whose parents had separated or divorced were more likely to show behavioural problems than children on the Isle of Wight. This was probably because a much higher proportion of the Isle of Wight parents had married again, in most cases happily.

To take another example, illness in one or both parents is associated with a high rate of problem behaviour in the children (Rutter, 1966), mental illness appearing to be a greater risk factor than physical illness. On the other hand, in London psychiatric disorder in the mother was less frequently associated with psychiatric disorder in the child than in the Isle of Wight (Rutter *et al.,* 1975). In Sheffield Galloway (1982a) found a high rate of psychiatric disorder, mainly depression, in parents of persistent absentees from an inner-city secondary school. The relationship between performance at school and poor parental health nevertheless remains an open question.

What is not in doubt, however, is that some children live in conditions which they find acutely stressful. It does not follow that removing them from home would help them, since reception into the care of a local authority can itself be educationally and emotionally disruptive (e.g. Tutt, 1981; Sutton, 1978). Nor does it follow that disadvantage in the home will necessarily be reflected in a child's behaviour at school.

'Vulnerable' children

Children can be vulnerable by reason of adverse circumstances at home or at school. They can also be vulnerable by reason of personal factors. Slow progress can result from inadequate teaching. It can also result from low intelligence or from developmental delay in some specific area, for example certain language or perceptual skills required in the early stages of reading.

Medical or constitutional factors may also contribute to the likelihood of some pupils behaving in an antisocial manner. The relationship between temporal lobe epilepsy and behaviour problems has been investigated extensively with inconclusive results (Harris, 1978; Kligman and Goldberg, 1975). The relationship between food allergies and overactive behaviour has also attracted extensive attention, though Cantwell (1977) has argued that none of the claims has been substantiated. A sample of pupils suspended from school for disruptive behaviour were found to have had a high rate of serious illnesses or accidents compared with their siblings. These pupils were also more likely than their siblings to have been in care (Galloway, 1982b). The causal relationship is perhaps only of academic interest: they might have had illnesses and accidents and have been placed in care because they were vulnerable, or vice versa. The point is that their medical histories could, at least, be seen as associated to some extent with the problems they presented at school.

Comment

So far we have merely identified some social, family and personal characteristics commonly found in pupils regarded as having special educational needs. The list is certainly not intended to be comprehensive. Rather it aims to show that:

1. Many children have special needs, even though these may not necessarily constitute educational needs.
2. These needs arise from a range of personal, family and social circumstances.

Three further points should be made at this stage.

1. There is evidence that children can cope quite successfully with stressful situations if these are isolated (e.g. Rutter, 1978). Problems arise when stress is experienced from several sources interacting with and aggravating each other. A child may be able to cope with overcrowding, or friction between parents, or a sick parent, but not, perhaps, with all three. In Sheffield we found that persistent absentees from a secondary school came from multiply disadvantaged families compared with regular attenders of the same age and sex and from the same class in school (Galloway, 1982b).

2. The connection between social advantage and educational disadvantage is by no means straightforward. There is clearly no justification for regarding a child as having special educational needs on social grounds alone. We know that both social disadvantage and a combination of stresses within the family are associated with an increased risk of problems at school which would bring a child into Warnock's 20 per cent. Yet this tells us nothing about the ways in which a child's experiences at home may affect his behaviour and progress at school. Nor, of course, does it give any suggestion as to how experiences at school may affect his tolerance of adverse circumstances at home. The third point develops from this.

3. So far we have said nothing about the school's influence on children's behaviour and progress. If teachers themselves exert an influence over their pupils' behaviour and progress independent on the social background, it follows logically that they may have considerable responsibility for creating, or preventing, the problems associated with special educational need. Moreover, experiences of stress at school, for example through repeated failure in the curriculum, are likely to compound and aggravate experiences of stress at home. As we saw earlier, a combination of stresses has much more serious consequences than single ones. Conversely, experience of success and satisfaction at school may help a child to cope with adverse conditions at home. We must now consider this possibility.

THE SCHOOL'S INFLUENCE ON BEHAVIOUR AND PROGRESS

Underlying assumptions

The Warnock Report referred to parents as partners with teachers in their children's education. Almost all headteachers accept this view in theory but very few reflect it in practice. All too often the 'partnership' is confined to parental involvement in non-professional activities such as fund-raising, the termly or annual parents' evening, and a willingness to discuss 'problems' with parents as and when requested.

It is now well-established that parents' involvement when a child is learning to read has a major effect on the child's progress (Hewison and Tizard, 1980; Tizard *et al.,* 1982), far greater than extra or 'remedial' help from teachers at school. This research, incidentally, was carried out in a disadvantaged area of London. It is not just middle-class parents who can help their children.

Yet no more than a tiny minority of primary schools throughout the country seek parental cooperation in the planned way that has been found effective. An even tinier minority encourage parents to help in the classroom in the way that is now taken for granted in other countries such as Sweden and New Zealand. The overwhelming majority appear to believe that teaching is an activity best carried out between teachers and consenting children in the decent privacy of the classroom. If the child has problems, then this calls for extra help from the teacher professionals rather than a review of ways that professionals and parents can work together.

Insisting on the teacher's exclusive competence to teach effectively excludes the parent, or ensures that any parental help is given, at best, in parallel with that of the school. It is a short step from here for teachers to see themselves as compensating for unsatisfactory home backgrounds. Unfortunately there is a catch here.

If teachers see their own activities as being, by definition, in the child's best interests, it becomes difficult, logically, to evaluate these activities. Excellence, after all, implies, and hence does not require, evaluation. If schools are seen as compensating for inadequacies in the home, then educational failure, and related problems such as truancy and maladjustment, must also be seen as originating in the home. At best, some schools may be more effective in compensating for home background than others.

This view has been held by eminent educationists. It lay behind the Plowden Report recommendation to establish educational priority areas (DES, 1967). The rationale was that a child's progress and behaviour depended partly on the child's own intelligence and personality, largely on the family and social background, and scarcely at all on the school. Since nothing could be done about the family and social background, the only hope lay in extra 'compensatory' experience at school. At the time there seemed to be overwhelming evidence for this thesis, mainly from the Coleman Report in America (Coleman *et al.*, 1966; Jencks, 1972).

Thus, influential research in the 1960s, on which Plowden and Coleman based their findings, concluded that schools made little differences to their pupils' life chances. The methodological limitations which led to this conclusion have been discussed elsewhere (e.g. Rutter *et al.*, 1979; Reynolds, 1982). The issue here is that the message was an essentially negative one for teachers: more of the same might have some beneficial effect, but if there are no extra resources teachers will have little or no effect on their pupil's life chances. The message was seductive, placing responsibility for failure firmly on parents and on society. It was also a dangerous message for teachers, implying that their own training, attitude and competence were all of relatively little importance.

The alternative is at the same time more exciting, challenging and threatening. Schools as organizations and teachers as individuals may have an important influence on their pupils' progress and social adjustment. If so, schools themselves would exert an important influence on the prevalence of special educational needs. Two criteria for recognition as having special educational need are educational backwardness and seriously disturbing behaviour. How much effect does the school have on such factors?

Evidence

The first British study to claim that schools affected their pupils' behaviour was based on data from secondary schools in Tower Hamlets, London. Power *et al.* (1967, 1972) found large differences between schools in delinquency rates, and claimed that these differences could not be attributed to variations in the catchment areas. The teacher unions bitterly resented what they saw as an accusation that schools caused delinquency. Partly as a result, the research came to an abrupt halt. It would have been more helpful if the unions had recognized that Power's work has, however, been criticized on methodological grounds by Baldwin (1972), and other studies in London have suggested that schools with high delinquency rates tend to take pupils from catchment areas with high delinquency rates (Farrington, 1972; West and Farrington, 1973).

In support of Power's work, Gath *et al.* (1972, 1977) noted wide variations in the number of children referred to child guidance clinics, and in the delinquency rates of London schools with similar catchment areas. Children receiving supervision or treatment from a child guidance team following referral by the school could certainly be regarded as having special educational needs. Gath's work suggests that some schools may produce more pupils than others serving similar areas.

Further support for this view comes from a study of pupils suspended from Sheffield secondary schools over a four-year period (Galloway, 1980; Galloway *et al.,* 1982). We found large differences between schools in the percentage of pupils suspended for disruptive behaviour. Five of the 37 schools studied accounted for roughly 50 per cent of all suspensions. Whereas catchment area characteristics could account for much of the variation between schools in persistent absentee rates, they could *not* account for the variation in suspension rates (Galloway *et al.,* 1984). In other words, the differences reflected policy or practice within the schools concerned.

Suspension is the school's ultimate sanction. Any suspended pupil would certainly be regarded as having special educational needs, justifying referral to a special centre or unit, on the grounds that everything that had already been provided had proved inadequate. We should remember, of course, that the overwhelming majority of pupils regarded by Warnock as having special needs remain in ordinary schools. Yet the Sheffield evidence together with other evidence from an anonymous LEA (Grunsell, 1979, 1980) shows that a pupil's chances of suspension depend mainly not on personal or family factors, but rather on which school he happens to be attending.

There is further evidence that schools exert a crucial influence on their pupil's behaviour. The 10-year-olds studied by Rutter and his colleagues in an Inner London borough were followed up at the age of 14. The behaviour of the 10-year-olds, as reported by their teachers, was used to predict with statistical techniques the number of pupils whose teachers would report deviant behaviour at 14. Rutter (1977) found that some schools reported a much higher number of pupils than had been predicted, while others reported a much lower proportion. The implication is that the number of pupils who might be said to have special educational needs because of their deviant behaviour depended on pupils' experiences since entering the secondary school, not simply on their personal or family characteristics.

This work led to an influential study, carried out in London, on school influences on pupils' performance (Rutter *et al.,* 1979). Studying 12 schools, they found marked differences in the pupils' behaviour within the school, in delinquency rates, in school attendance and in examination results. Among the most interesting results was a low correlation between their measures of the pupils when they entered secondary school and behaviour within the school, as observed during the research. Thus, the implication here too is that pupils' behaviour at school may depend largely on factors within the school.

Research in secondary modern schools in South Wales also revealed notable differences between schools, in delinquency, attendance, and progress to further education. Again these differences could not satisfactorily be explained in terms of differences between the school catchment areas. The evidence suggested that factors within the school were playing an important part (Reynolds, 1976; Reynolds *et al.,* 1980; Reynolds and Murgatroyd, 1977).

Neither the London nor the South Wales studies investigated in detail the school's effect on those pupils with learning difficulties who might be regarded as having special educational needs. Rutter measured academic outcome by examination results and Reynolds by rates of entry to further education. These measures could conceal the possibility that schools exert a greater influence over the performance of their more able pupils than over that of the less able. Rutter *et al.* (1979) checked this possibility by analysing the CSE grade 4 and 5 passes (i.e. the lowest grades which they had excluded from other analyses) for the least able group of pupils admitted to the twelve schools. Again they found substantial differences between the schools, implying that the schools were exerting an important influence on their least able pupils' progress.

This view is strengthened by reanalysis of the data collected by Coleman *et al.* (1966) from 4000 American schools. These studies are discussed by Dyer (1968) and Reynolds (1982). They suggest that the schools may in fact have had a considerable influence as the pupils progressed through adolescence, but that this influence was only substantial on pupils of low ability or low social class and non-white pupils. These, of course, are precisely the pupils who are disproportionately represented in samples of children regarded as having special educational needs.

COMMENT

The argument so far can be summarized as follows:

1. The great majority of the 20 per cent of pupils regarded by Warnock as having special educational needs remain in ordinary schools.
2. The majority of these pupils present behavioural problems and/or learning difficulties; this latter group contains pupils of low measured intelligence and pupils whose attainments fall substantially below their chronological age, irrespective of their measured intelligence.

3. Schools exert a very substantial influence over their pupils' behaviour; the fact that some schools have few problems from disturbed or disturbing pupil behaviour while others are overwhelmed by problems has more to do with school factors than with factors within the catchment area.
4. Schools also exert an important influence on their pupils' educational progress.
5. This influence may be greatest on pupils who are least able intellectually and least privileged socially.

It is therefore tempting to conclude that special needs are created in school, by teachers; and that the number of pupils with special needs could be drastically reduced by improving the quality of teaching. Unfortunately the position is more complicated. Three reasons will be discussed here, the first of which is relatively straightforward.

Certainly, there are schools in which teachers have reason to regard very few pupils as having special needs because of their social adjustment or behaviour. Equally, there are schools in which few pupils give realistic grounds for concern on account of their academic progress. Any school with a mixed-ability intake, however, will contain pupils of low measured intelligence and pupils whose attainments fall below their chronological age, even though they may not necessarily be underachieving relative to their measured intelligence. Similarly, all schools with a mixed-ability intake will contain pupils requiring special attention because of personal, medical or family problems. Such pupils may be overlooked in schools with high rates of disruptive behaviour. The point is that pupils with special needs will not simply disappear because the school caters for them effectively.

Evidence that successful schools do little or nothing to reduce the range of ability among pupils is related to this. Rutter *et al.* (1979) found that the range between the most and the least able pupils was as wide in the most successful schools they studied as in the least successful. Schools, it appears, can raise the overall level of pupils' attainments, and improve the general quality of behaviour. That, however, is quite different from promoting equality. Educational equality remains a dream. However much the quality of education improves, we will still be left with the disturbing 20 per cent on an academic or behavioural continuum, or 10 per cent or 30 per cent, depending on the criterion used.

Taking this point a stage further, let us suppose that all schools could reach the standards of the most successful schools described by Rutter *et al.*

(1979). Clearly, scores on standard tests of educational attainment would rise, requiring publication of new 'norms' – that is, tables enabling an individual's score to be compared with scores of the pupils on whom the test was standardized. Yet the test could still be used to identify pupils with a wide ability range. Indeed it would be designed to do precisely that.

It follows that the concept of special educational needs as conceived by the Warnock Report is logically independent of educational standards in schools. Raising standards of attainment and of behaviour may have some slight effect on who is regarded as having special needs, but none on how many pupils are regarded as falling into this category. The reason, as indicated earlier in the chapter, is that the decision to regard 20 per cent of pupils as having special needs at some stage in their school careers is essentially both an arbitrary and a political one. It cannot in any meaningful way be said to be based on research, though the way tests and behaviour-screening instruments are constructed ensures that 'research' will always be available to justify it.

The fact remains, though, that schools vary widely in the number of pupils they appear to regard as having special needs. This does *not* imply that some schools have no pupils with special needs. Galloway (1983), Rutter *et al.* (1979) and Reynolds (1976) have all described characteristics of successful schools. The success of these schools may well disguise the existence of pupils who would be regarded as problems in other schools. Meeting special needs effectively removes pupils from the limelight.

At other schools pupils and teachers seem to be locked into a vicious cycle. Low morale amongst teachers reflects, and is reflected in, disaffected behaviour and low educational attainments in the pupils. The schools' responses to pupils' behaviour and learning difficulties can unfortunately generate further disaffection in the pupils, leading to still lower teacher morale.

REFERENCES

Baldwin, J. (1972) Delinquent schools in Tower Hamlets: 1. A critique, *British Journal of Criminology,* Vol. 12, pp 399–401.

Bernstein, B. (1971) *Class, Codes and Control,* Vol. 1, *Theoretical Studies Towards a Sociology of Language,* Routledge and Kegan Paul, London

Board of Education and Board of Control (1929) *Report of Joint Departmental Committee on Mental Deficiency,* HMSO, London

Burt, C. (1937) *The Backward Child,* Hodder and Stoughton, London

Cantwell, D. (1977) *Hyperkinetic syndrome.* In M. Rutter and L. Hersov (Eds) (1977) Child Psychiatry: modern approaches, Blackwell, Oxford

Coard, B. (1971) *How the West Indian Child Is Made Educationally Subnormal in the British School System,* New Beacon Books, London

Coleman, J.S. *et al.* (1966) *Equality of Educational Opportunity,* US Government Printing Office, Washington

Davie, R., Butler, N. and Goldstein, H. (1972) *From Birth to Seven,* Longman, London

Department of Education and Science (DES) (1967) *Children with Specific Reading Difficulties: Report of the Advisory Committee on Handicapped Children,* HMSO, London

Department of Education and Science (DES) (1978) *Special Educational Needs* (Warnock Report), Cmnd 7212, HMSO, London

Dyer, H.S. (1968) School factors and equal educational opportunity, *Harvard Educational Review,* Vol. 38, pp 38–56

Farrington, D. (1972) Delinquency begins at home, *New Society,* Vol. 21, No. 14, September, pp 495–497

Galloway, D. (1980) Exclusion from school, *Trends in Education,* ii, pp 33–38

Galloway, D. (1982a) A study of persistent absentees from school and their families, *British Journal of Educational Psychology,* Vol. 52, pp 317–30

Galloway, D. (1982b) A study of pupils suspended from school, *British Journal of Educational Psychology,* Vol. 52, pp 205–212

Galloway, D. (1983) Disruptive pupils and effective pastoral care, *School Organisation,* Vol. 3, pp 245–254

Galloway, D., Ball, T., Blomfield, D. and Seyd, R. (1982) *Schools and Disruptive Pupils,* Longman, London

Galloway, D., Martin, R. and Wilcox, B. (1984) Persistent absence from school and exclusion from school: the predictive power of school and community variables, *British Educational Research Journal*

Gath, D., Cooper, B. and Gattoni, F.E.G. (1972) Child guidance and delinquency in a London borough: preliminary communication, *Psychological Medicine,* Vol. 2, pp 185–191

Gath, D., Cooper, B. Gattoni, F. and Rockett, D. (1977) *Child Guidance and Delinquency in a London Borough,* Oxford University Press, Oxford

Grunsell, R. (1979) Suspensions and the sin-bin boom, *Where,* Vol. 153, pp 307–309

Grunsell, R. (1980) *Beyond Control? schools and suspension,* Readers and Writers, London

Harris, R. (1978) *Relationships between EEG abnormality and aggressive and anti-social behaviour – a critical appraisal.* In L.A. Hersov, M. Berger and D. Shaffer (Eds) (1978) Aggression and Anti-Social Behaviour in Childhood and Adolescence, Pergamon, Oxford

Hewison, J. and Tizard, J. (1980) Parental involvement and reading attainment, *British Journal of Educational Psychology,* Vol. 50, pp 209–215

Jencks, C. (1972) *Inequality: a re-assessment of the effects of family and schooling in America,* Basic Books, New York

Kligman, D. and Goldberg, D.A. (1975) Temporal lobe epilepsy and aggression, *Journal of Nervous and Mental Disorder,* Vol. 160, pp 324–341

Labov, W. (1970) *The logic of non-standard English.* In F. Williams (Ed.) (1970) Language and Poverty: perspectives on a theme, Markham, Chicago

McFie, B.S. (1934) Behaviour and personality difficulties in school children, *British Journal of Educational Psychology*, Vol. 4, pp 30–46

Milner, M. (1938) *The Human Problems in Schools*, Methuen, London

Ministry of Education (1945) *The Handicapped Pupils and School Health Service Regulations* (S.R. and O. No. 1076), HMSO, London

Ministry of Education (1958) *Report of the Chief Medical Officer for the Years 1956–57*, HMSO, London

Ministry of Education (1959) *The Handicapped Pupils and Special Schools Regulations*, (S.I. No. 365), HMSO, London

Ministry of Education (1961) *Special Educational Treatment for Educationally Sub-Normal Pupils*, Circular 11/61, Ministry of Education, London

Power, M.J., Alderson, M.R., Phillipson, C.M., Schoenberg, E. and Morris, J.M. (1967) Delinquent schools, *New Society*, 19 October

Power, M.J., Benn, R.T. and Morris, J.M. (1972) Neighbourhood, school and juveniles before the courts, *British Journal of Criminology*, Vol. 12, 111–132

Reynolds, D. (1976) *When pupils and teachers refuse a truce: the secondary school and the creation of delinquency*. In G. Mingham and G. Pearson (Eds) (1976) *Working Class Youth Culture*, Routledge and Kegan Paul, London

Reynolds, D. (1982) The search for effective schools, *School Organisation*, Vol. 2, pp 215–237

Reynolds, D. and Murgatroyd, S. *The sociology of schooling and the absent pupils: the school as a factor in the generation of truancy*. In H.C.M. Carroll (Ed.) (1977) Absenteeism in South Wales: studies of pupils, their homes and their secondary schools, University College Swansea Faculty of Education, Swansea

Reynolds, D., Jones, S., St Leger, S. and Murgatroyd, S. (1980) *School factors and truancy*. In L. Hersov and I. Berg (Eds) (1980) Out of School: modern perspective in truancy and school refusal, Wiley, Chichester

Rutter, M. (1966) *Children of Sick Parents: an environmental and psychiatric study*, Institute of Psychiatry, Maudsley Monographs No. 26, Oxford University Press, London

Rutter, M. (1967) A children's behaviour questionnaire for completion by teachers: preliminary findings, *Journal of Child Psychology and Psychiatry*, Vol. 8, pp 1–11

Rutter, M. (1977) *Prospective studies to investigate behavioural change*. In J.S. Strauss, H.M. Babigian and M. Roff (Eds) (1977) Methods of Longitudinal Research in Psychopathology, Plenum Publishing, New York

Rutter, M. (1978) *Family, area and school influence in the genesis of conduct disorders*. In L. Hersov, M. Berger and D. Schaffer (Eds) (1978) Aggression and Anti-Social Behaviour in Childhood and Adolescence, Pergamon, Oxford

Rutter, M. and Graham, P. (1968) The reliability and validity of the psychiatric assessment of the child: 1. Interview with the child, *British Journal of Psychiatry*, Vol. 114, pp 563–579

Rutter, M., Tizard, J. and Whitmore, K. (1970) *Education, Health and Behaviour*, Longman, London

Rutter, M., Yule, B., Quinton, D., Rowlands, O., Yule, W. and Berger, M. (1975) Attainments and adjustment in two geographical areas: III Some factors accounting for area differences, *British Journal of Psychology*, Vol. 126, pp 520–533

Rutter, M., Graham, P., Chadwick, O.F.D. and Yule, W. (1976) Adolescent turmoil: fact or fiction, *Journal of Child Psychology and Psychiatry,* Vol. 17, pp 35-56

Rutter, M., Maughan, B., Mortimore, P., Ouston, J. and Smith, A. (1979) *Fifteen Thousand Hours: secondary schools and their effects on pupils,* Open Books, London

Stott, D.H. (1963) *The Social Adjustment of Children* (2nd edn), University of London Press, London

Stott, D.H. (1971) *The Bristol Social Adjustment Guides,* University of London Press, London

Sutton, A. (1978) Theory, practice and cost in child care: implications from an individual case, *Howard League Journal,* Vol. 16, pp 159-171

Tizard, J., Schofield, W.N. and Hewison, J. (1982) Collaboration between teachers and parents in assisting children's reading, *British Journal of Educational Psychology,* Vol. 52, pp 1-15

Tutt, N. (1981) *Treatment under attack.* In B. Gillham, (Ed.) (1981) Problem Behaviour in the Secondary School, Croom Helm, London

Uger, C. (1938) The relationship of teachers' attitudes to children's problem behaviour, *School and Society,* Vol. 47, pp 246-248

Wedge, P. and Essen, J. (1982) *Children in Adversity,* Pan, London

Wedge, P. and Prosser, H. (1973) *Born to Fail?* Arrow Books, London

West, D.J. and Farrington, D. (1973) *Who Becomes Delinquent?* Heinemann, London

Yule, W. (1973) Differential prognosis of reading backwardness and specific reading retardation, *British Journal of Educational Psychology,* Vol. 43, pp 244-248

Yule, W. (1976) Critical notice (*Taxonomy of Behaviour Disturbance*, edited by D.H. Stott, N.C. Marston and S.J. Neill, London University Press), *Therapeutic Education,* Vol. 4, No. 1, pp 45-47

Yule, W., Rutter, M., Berger, M. and Thompson, J. (1974) Over- and under-achievement in reading: distribution in the general population, *British Journal of Educational Psychology,* Vol. 44, pp 1-12

TOPICS FOR DISCUSSION

1. 'The question is whether a curriculum and an emotional climate which fails to cater for up to 20 per cent of pupils can be entirely suitable for the remaining 80 per cent.' Discuss with reference to the relationship between the proposed special or modified curriculum and the mainstream curriculum.

2. Critically evaluate the Warnock Committee's interpretation of the research evidence on the proportion of children with (a) learning difficulties and (b) behavioural problems in the light of the author's statement that 'having decided on a proportion, the research evidence was at hand to justify the conclusion'.

3. 'The decision to regard 20 per cent of pupils as having special needs at some stage in their school careers is essentially both an arbitrary and a political one.' Discuss.

SUGGESTIONS FOR FURTHER READING

1. D. Galloway (1985) *Schools, Pupils and Special Educational Needs,* Croom Helm, London. In chapter 6, 'The Hidden Curriculum', the author discusses the meaning of failure and how it affects pupils' self-concepts and feelings of competence. He relates this theme to the traditional ways of ability grouping in schools and how such patterns affect both pupils and teachers. The role of counselling and pastoral care occupies the last part of the chapter.
2. S. Tomlinson (1982) *A Sociology of Special Education,* Routledge and Kegan Paul, London. Chapter 3, 'Issues and Dilemmas in Special Education', is of particular relevance to this Reading for the discussion on categorization, normative and non-normative categories, selection and the social problem classes.
3. D. Galloway (1983) Disruptive pupils and effective pastoral care, *School Organisation,* Vol. 3, pp 245–254. In this article, the author describes the characteristics of successful schools and discusses how the success of these schools may well disguise the existence of a number of pupils who would be regarded as problem children in other schools. Put another way, meeting special needs effectively removes pupils from the limelight.

Reading 16
THE SOCIAL CONSTRUCTION OF THE ESN(M) CHILD
S. Tomlinson

The category of educational subnormality was an administrative category created in 1945, one of (then) eleven possible categories of handicap, and since that time has always encompassed over half of all children designated as handicapped. Indeed recent DES statistics (DES, 1979) indicate that ESN children comprise two-thirds of all children currently in special education. In 1945 the category was extended to include children who, prewar, were known as 'defective' but educable, and a larger group of children in ordinary schools, known as 'dull and backward'. Cyril Burt was one of the first to use the term educational subnormality, and to calculate that children scoring 50–85 on mental tests should be considered as ESN (Burt, 1935). Burt was a member of the Wood Committee which reported in 1929 and

S. Tomlinson (1981) *The social construction of the ESN(M) child.* In L. Barton and S. Tomlinson (1981) Special Education: policies, practices and social issues, Harper and Row, London

recommended the creation of such a category – children with a mental score of 50–70 to be considered ESN (Board of Education and Board of Control, 1929). At this time, of course, 'intelligence' was considered to be a fixed, innate quality, measurable by tests. By 1970 children formerly known as severely subnormal were brought into education and the former ESN became known as ESN(M) (mild or moderate). The Warnock Committee, reporting in 1978, suggested that the ESN(M) and the ESN(S) (severe) categories should be merged with children currently known as 'remedial' in ordinary schools, the whole to be known as Children with Learning Difficulty (mild, moderate, severe). The 1980 White Paper on special educational needs indicated that statutory categories of handicap will be abolished, but descriptive labels, similar to the existing categories of handicap, will remain.

Since the statutory category of ESN(M) is scheduled for disappearance, it might be timely to question the status of the category and the concept of mild educational subnormality. What exactly is, or was, an ESN(M) child? One initial point that can be made is that it is most certainly a non-normative category. That is, while there can be some external agreement, by relatively objective measurement, about categories such as blindness, deafness or epilepsy, there can and has been disagreement over what constitutes mild educational subnormality. It would seem sociologically important to question the category, since a major feature of children who come to be categorized as ESN(M) is that they are almost entirely the children of manual working-class parentage – and since the arrival of West Indian families in Britain, black children have been overrepresented in ESN(M) schools. Sociologists of education have traditionally been preoccupied with the comparative underachievement of working-class children in education, and from the point of view of the acquisition of qualifications and credentials, ESN(M) education can be regarded as total non-achievement. Why is it that relatively powerless groups in society, working-class and black parents, are more likely to have their children assessed as ESN(M)? (And, of course, the creation of the CWLD will encompass even more working-class and black children, as they comprise a majority of children in remedial classes in ordinary schools.)

The criteria by which children are referred, assessed and placed in ESN(M) schools or classes has traditionally been decided on a discretionary basis by groups of professional people (educationalists, educational psychologists and medical officers) using professional judgements and supposedly objective testing procedures. These procedures lead to placement in a non-credentialling type of schooling which leads only to semi- or unskilled employment or unemployment. Moreover, the historical development of schooling for the mildly subnormal, linked in the earlier twentieth century to crime, poverty and moral depravity (Tredgold, 1908), has meant that there is a stigma attached to this type of special education – to be ESN(M) has indeed meant a 'label for life' (Omar, 1971) and a disqualification from full social acceptance.

A study in a large city in 1976–77 attempted to explore the criteria professionals used to designate children as ESN(M), using both phenomenological and structural perspectives (Tomlinson, 1981). Forty children were followed through the process of their referral and assessment and placement (in 28 cases) in ESN(M) schools, and all the 120 professionals and others who had made a decision about the children were asked how they 'accounted for' (Scott and Lyman, 1968) ESN(M) children. The phenomenological perspective used in this study was that developed most systematically by Berger and Luckman in their book *The Social Construction of Reality* (1966). From their perspective, social categories such as ESN(M) are not fixed, objective categories, they are socially created artefacts which, however permanent they appear to be, may be redefined and changed. The assessment of children as ESN(M), and their being officially recorded as such, creates the category ESN(M). The professionals who refer and assess children – headteachers, educational psychologists, doctors and others – see themselves, quite reasonably, as solely concerned with 'doing a job', but they are also engaged in constructing a 'reality'. The ESN(M) category can be regarded as a social construct which comes into existence through the judgements and decisions of professional people. The construction of the category is influenced by the values, beliefs, and perceived interests of the professionals who have vested career interests in assessing and defining ESN(M) children. The more children who are candidates for assessment, the more work for the professionals. In addition, if professionals feel they are 'overworked' it becomes a good reason for arguing for the expansion of the profession.

ACCOUNTS OF EDUCATIONAL SUBNORMALITY

Professionals who make judgements about educational subnormality and profess to distinguish between the normal and the 'not normal' can provide apparently logical, rational accounts of subnormality. Their accounts appear to be natural, because they are held to be grounded in nature. For example, mild educational subnormality is seen by some to be an intrinsic quality – a child 'is ESN(M)' yet at the same time the intrinsic quality is made up of negative qualities – a child 'cannot benefit' from normal education because he or she lacks certain attributes. In the literature on ESN(M) children, and between practitioners and professionals, there is actually little consensus as to which accounts are more important in describing an ESN(M) child. In the study of 1976–77 it was possible, from initial interviews, professional journals, prescriptive books written to assist practitioners, government acts and circulars, and so on, to abstract a series of analytic accounts of ESN(M) children. Table 16.1 illustrates the account.

The most popular account of ESN(M) children is in terms of function. An ESN(M) child is unable to perform certain tasks that it is implicitly understood that a 'normal' child of that age can. The key concept in functional accounts is that of attainment – children who cannot obtain a given level of skill or competence in comparison to other children may be subnormal. Functional definitions of ESN(M) children predominate in the literature written for practitioners.

> In theory the term ESN(M) could be applied to a large group of children who are very backward in their school work, ranging from those who are barely capable of responding to schooling, to others who apart from their backwardness are capable of following much in the normal school curriculum. (Gulliford, 1966, p. 40)

Thus, functional accounts tend to be descriptive, depending on the notion that a child cannot perform or attain at a variety of levels.

From 1945 functional accounts have created some confusion by their failure to distinguish between official definitions of ESN(M) (Ministry of Education, 1946; DES, 1972) and children known as backward, remedial, or slow-learning in normal schools. The extension of the category into CWLD is a logical solution to a dynamic twentieth-century educational problem – 'What do we do with children who cannot or will not learn?' (Berger and Mitchells, 1978, p. 15). Because functional accounts tend to be descriptive they are usually accompanied by other accounts which purport to be explanatory. One of the most popular accompanying accounts is statistical – a low IQ explains 'ESN(M)-ness'. The assumption is made that IQ tests are accurate, scientific, measuring instruments which can place a child's mental attributes in relation to other children. Teachers, in particular, consider that an IQ score explains a child's attainment (Squibb, 1977), and rely on educational psychologists to confirm this. Statistical accounts of ESN(M) children have popularly followed Cyril Burt's judgement, and the Wood Committee's recommendation, that an IQ score

Table 16.1 Accounts of educational subnormality

1. *Functional*	1. Child cannot do X (X may be social, educational, technological, but is usually connected to 'learning' or intellectual functioning).
	2. Child cannot communicate adequately.
2. *Statistical*	1. Child has a 'low' IQ as measured on standardized tests.
	2. Child falls into lowest 1 per cent (or 20 per cent) of school population in school achievement.
3. *Behavioural*	1. Child is disruptive, troublesome, uncontrolled.
	2. Child exhibits bizarre, odd, nonconformist behaviour.
	3. Child is unable to behave 'appropriately'.
4. *Organic*	Child has:
	1. Genetic disorder or 'innate capacity'.
	2. Prenatal or birth 'damage'.
	3. Organic or metabolic disorder.
	4. Medically demonstrable 'illness' or 'condition'.
5. *Psychological*	Child is 'emotionally disturbed'.
6. *Social*	Child has:
	1. Family with low socio-economic status; father semi- or unskilled.
	2. Family 'disorganized' – poor maternal care, single parent, working mother, etc.
	3. Poor or different socialization techniques.
	4. Adverse material factors – poor housing, bad physical environment.
	5. Cultural deficiency – poor cultural milieu; poor preparation for school.
7. *School*	1. Unsatisfactory school conditions.
	2. Normal school rejects child.
	3. Child rejects school, i.e. truants.
8. *Statutory*	Child may be 'certified' as in need of special education.
9. *Intuitive*	Child has 'something wrong with him'.
10. *Tautological*	Child is in need of special educational treatment.

of between 50 and 70 or 75 'is ESN(M)', and this has given rise to debates over whether children with higher IQs should be placed in ESN(M) schools or classes. This kind of argument demonstrates the ease with which accounts became reified. IQ is itself a very problematic concept – it has often been used to legitimate political decisions (Kamin, 1977; Block and Dworkin, 1977) – and yet, as the research reported here demonstrated, it is still relied on by a variety of professionals and practitioners to account for children as ESN(M).

Behavioural accounts of ESN(M) children are often presented in conjunction with functional accounts, but there is little consensus as to whether an ESN(M) child is badly behaved or not. Professionals sometimes referred to a 'true ESN(M) child', by which they meant a dull but conforming child. This mythical figure was sometimes used to invoke the description of a child as 'not ESN(M)'. However, one of the reasons for the creation of special schools in the late nineteenth century was that children who were difficult to teach, and interrupted the system of payment by results, should be removed from normal school classes; and the subsequent history of ESN(M) referral indicates a tendency for schools to refer children who exhibited troublesome, disruptive or nonconformist behaviour. The artificial simplification attempted by the 1945 Handicapped Pupils regulations – that backward children were to go to ESN schools, and badly behaved children were to go to maladjusted schools – was never very successful. In practice, teachers preferred to get rid of children who were both learning and behaviour problems by ESN referral and it was the ESN(M) category which expanded most rapidly postwar. A decline in referrals during the 1970s was paralleled by the development of a new type of special education – disruptive units – which were a much quicker route to the removal of children with behaviour problems from the normal classroom, and in new legislation children termed disruptive will officially be brought within special education.

Organic accounts of ESN(M) children, which include 'innate' accounts implicitly referring to some inherited attributes, are also used as explanations for ESN(M) children. Indeed, the 1946 Ministry of Education guidelines on the handicapped spoke of 'retardation due to limited ability [...] which was likely to be permanent' (Ministry of Education, 1946). Traditional medical domination in the assessment process for special education (doctors claiming early on that only they were qualified to detect 'weak-mindedness' – Pritchard, 1963) made it likely that doctors would give organic accounts of ESN(M) children, but interestingly, doctors have been at some pains to stress that mild educational subnormality, or mild mental retardation as the doctors usually put it, seldom has an organic cause (Stein and Susser, 1960; Court Report, 1976). It is the medical profession who stress social accounts of ESN(M) children, and a tautological factor is sometimes introduced in that children ascertained as having other 'handicaps' are often also designated as educationally backward.

Psychological accounts of ESN(M) children are not particularly prevalent in the literature although the 1946 Ministry guidelines did suggest that one cause of educational subnormality might be 'psychological maladjustment'. Some writers have suggested that emotional disturbance and/or poor family relationships can account for educational backwardness (Davies, 1961; Hunt, 1975).

The most popular accounts of ESN(M) children have always been social. It was in elementary schools for working-class children that children unsuitable for education in these schools were first 'discovered', and it was in the London School Board's poorest districts that the first schools for special instruction were set up during the 1890s. The influence of the eugenics movement in the early twentieth century linked the lower social classes to a variety of social evils, including crime, poverty, unemployment and mental subnormality (Report of the Royal Commission on the Care and Control of the Feebleminded, 1908) and reinforced popular beliefs that mental subnormality and educational retardation were a prerogative of the lower social classes. Despite some assertions that the middle and upper classes did have dull and defective children, but were able to provide for them privately (Tredgold, 1908), the belief has persisted that there is a natural relationship between the working class and educational subnormality. Postwar research in the sociology of education, while demonstrating the social factors which impinge upon the intellectual development of children, probably also reinforced popular and professional belief in the 'natural' lower educational capacities of lower working-class children. The kind of environment factors used to account for relative working-class 'failure' at normal schools are also used to account for ESN(M) children, for example low socio-economic status, cultural and linguistic deficiency and disadvantage, poor socialization techniques and preparation for school, adverse material factors and disorganized families. Much of the literature on ESN(M) children stresses social causation (Stein and Susser, 1960; Williams and Gruber, 1967; Gulliford, 1969). The Warnock Report, which purported to eschew causal explanations for handicapped children, noted that, 'many children with educational deficiencies may suffer from familial or wider social deficiencies' (DES, 1980, p. 4), reinforcing the popular notion that it is largely the 'deficient' working class who produce the educationally backward children. Social accounts have, historically, been so persistent and persuasive that their plausibility as an account of 'ESN(M)-ness' is seldom questioned. It is taken for granted that lower social class attributes are natural factors in accounting for ESN(M) children and that one function of special ESN(M) schools is to help children overcome the deficiencies of their environment (Williams, 1965). The notion that normal schools can be held accountable for a child's educational subnormality is not popular in the literature, nor with practitioners, although again, the 1946 guidelines mentioned 'unsatisfactory school conditions' as a possible causal factor of backwardness. It would, however, seem unrealistic to suppose that practitioners would criticize their own institutions when a variety of other accounts of ESN(M) children are available.

Statutory accounts are likewise seldom referred to but can be discovered in the relevant government acts and circulars. In statutory terms an ESN(M) child is one who can be legally designated as such under Section 35(5) of the 1944 Education Act and by a 'certification procedure' through which a child can be compelled to attend a special school or class. No change in 'enforceable procedures' is envisaged for children requiring special education who are 'recorded' (DES, 1980).

Intuitive accounts of ESN(M) children are usually offered by parents. The parents 'know there is something wrong' but the intuitive speculations of parents have to be confirmed by professional opinion, whose judgements confirm of deny the speculation (Booth, 1978).

Tautological accounts of ESN(M) children are quite common among professionals and in the literature. The whole concept of 'special educational needs', on which future legislation is to be based, is tautological as far as ESN(M) children are concerned. An ESN(M) child (or a CWLD) is described as a child in need of special education. This presupposes that there is a consensus on how such children can be recognized, but in the literature, and in the research reported here, no such consensus could be deduced. It must surely be logically dubious to prescribe for a 'need' without a causal account of how the need came into existence.

The accounts and explanations of ESN(M) children to be discovered in the literature and from professionals are in fact problematic. They are often contradictory, and they are by no means as 'natural' as common sense would have them be.

SOCIAL CONSTRUCTION AND SMOOTH TEAMWORK

It is, nevertheless, the judgements of professionals, working within the complex referral and assessment processes, which continue to create the category of ESN(M) and to ensure for a particular group of children what Sharp and Green (1975) have called the 'social transmission of ignorance'. At the time of the 1976–77 study local education authorities were engaged in developing the new referral and assessment procedure suggested in the government Circular 2/75 (DES, 1975) and the professionals were beginning to record their opinions and decisions on the new SE (special education) forms, rather than the old HP (handicapped pupils) forms. The 'ideal' procedure envisaged by 2/75 is illustrated in Table 16.2.

Table 16.2   'Ideal' referral and assessment procedure suggested by Circular 2/75

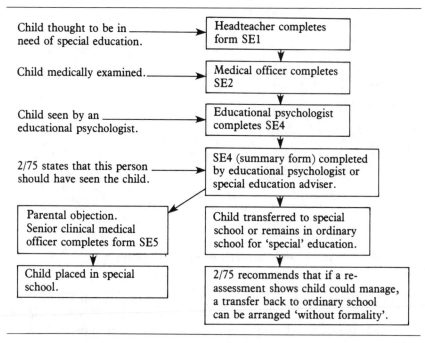

The official picture of the construction of the category ESN(M) is that of 'smooth teamwork' – cooperation and agreement between professionals on the 'needs' of particular children. Teachers, headteachers of referring and special schools, educational psychologists, medical officers, and a variety of other people who may be involved – social workers, psychiatrists, assessment centre staff, education welfare officers, etc. – are all supposed to work in close cooperation, documenting in writing a series of formal decisions which will produce a consensus on the educational future for particular children. In practice 'smooth teamwork' remains very much an ideology – accounts differ and conflict, and there are a variety of other conflicts, anxieties, and communication difficulties between professionals.

How, in fact, did the various professionals account for ESN(M) children? In order to demonstrate the accounts visually, the percentage of replies given by each group of the professionals in this study were calculated out of the total replies given, and shown in histogram form. In this way it is possible to see at a glance the different kinds of accounts offered by referring heads, educational psychologists, medical officers, special school heads and parents, and to compare the accounts.

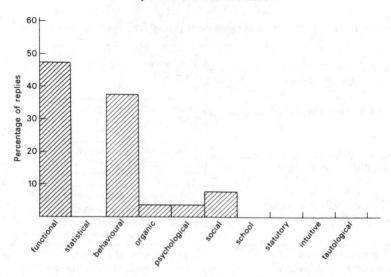

Figure 16.1   Referring heads' accounts of ESN(M) children

Thus, Figure 16.1 shows that headteachers overwhelmingly use functional and behavioural criteria when accounting for ESN(M) children. The heads are the people who begin the construction of possible ESN(M) children, usually after a class-teacher has noted a child: 'The teacher tells one if a child is dull, not talking or reading – we take it from there.' 'Once a year I send a card to all teachers asking about children with problems – down to being backward or smelly.'

In the study, referring heads felt they could make a distinction between ESN(M) children and those who were 'merely backward' on an intuitive basis. However, the selection, by heads, of potentially ESN(M) children did depend to a significant degree on disruptive or nonconformist classroom behaviour. One head, in accounting for his referral of an 8-year-old West Indian boy, said: 'He's disruptive and constantly seeks attention – he makes class teaching a misery.'

Heads were not particularly concerned to offer causal explanations of their descriptive accounts of learning and behaviour problems; identification rather than explanation was their most pressing problem. It did appear that the tipping point at which a child became potentially ESN(M), rather than 'remedial', was the behaviour he or she exhibited in the classroom. Heads' accounts of ESN (M) children were very much like the kind of accounts offered by normal schools in the 1890s, when the first candidates for special schools were being selected. Children who cannot, or will not, be 'educated' in a controlled, orderly environment may be candidates for a 'special' education.

In the study, referring heads sometimes viewed psychologists with antipathy, regarding them as people with considerable power, including the power to frustrate the initial referral; and indeed, psychologists did seem to be crucial figures in the construction of the ESN(M) child. It is the educational psychologist, working within a 'scientific' testing model and using skills which the schools do not possess, who may or may not legitimate the schools' judgement that a child 'is ESN'. One potential source of conflict was that the psychologists' accounts of ESN(M) children differed considerably from the headteachers', as Figure 16.2 demonstrates. Psychologists did account for ESN children in functional terms: 'The major thing would be attainment – that's what it's all about – intellectual functioning.' But one psychologist qualified this by commenting that: 'Our special schools are full of – no, have a percentage of – children who have scored low on some verbal IQ tests – a test which does not put working-class kids in a favourable situation.'

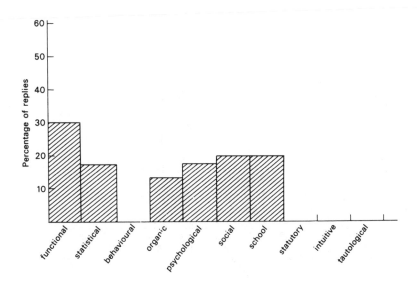

Figure 16.2 Educational psychologists' accounts of ESN(M) children

Psychologists also tended to accompany functional accounts with statistical accounts – low intellectual functioning was partly accounted for by a 'low IQ'. But although 36 out of the 40 children in the study had been tested (on the Stanford-Binet revised test) most of the psychologists did not place the kind of reliance on tests that psychologists in the 1930s would have done: 'People think if a child is assessed as ESN he's ESN for ever more. [...] we've got to get away from heredity, teachers and administrators are working with a psychology that's twenty years out of date.'

The psychologists did not regard potential ESN(M) children as behaviour problems, and it was here that their differences with headteachers arose, particularly as they saw themselves as being able to circumvent the referral process. One psychologist remarked that 'normal schools often refer children they want to be rid of', and another said: 'In the past schools used to be anxious about children with behaviour problems; there are still a few rogue schools where the children's feet don't touch the floor if they cause problems.' But psychologists do not have to agree with the headteacher's view: 'We may have to say – I'm sorry this child is a nuisance, but what he needs is more appropriate teaching.' And they do not see themselves as able to turn the referral back and thus not continue the 'construction' of the ESN(M) child.

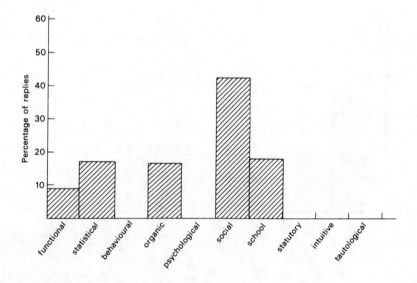

Figure 16.3   Doctors' accounts of ESN(M) children

Psychologists also account for children who do become ESN(M) in social terms; they may be 'culturally disadvantaged' and *also* partially disadvantaged by organic and psychological problems. But it was the doctors who, interestingly, tended to use social accounts of ESN(M) children the most (see Figure 16.3).

The doctors thought that ESN(M) children were likely to be of lower social class origins and, as one doctor put it, 'to be a rough child'. They appeared to operate upon the tautological assumption, expressed in the Court Report (1976), that an ESN(M) child is essentially a lower-class child, and that mild educational subnormality (or mental retardation as the doctors tended to put it) is a characteristic of lower social-class children. Like the educational psychologists, doctors do not account for ESN(M) children in behavioural terms; their image of the ESN(M) child is that of the dull but conforming child, who may have 'defects in make-up' or may have been 'failed by his normal school'. Two doctors offered genetic accounts in terms of a child's 'innate dimness' but they did not think that ESN(M) children suffered any particular medical pathologies – indeed the administrative category was regarded almost as a pathology in itself. The doctors also demonstrated that there was some conflict with other professionals during the construction of the ESN(M) child, despite the ideology of smooth teamwork. There was some resentment that psychologists particularly had been 'taking over' what they had formerly regarded as their area of competence – and the autonomy and status of the medical profession conflicted with the notion that they were part of a team.

Headteachers of special schools are also important figures in the social construction of the ESN(M) child, given that the final decision to admit a child to his or her school rests with the head. Indeed, if an ESN(M) child is literally one who has attended an ESN(M) school, the public image of educational subnormality can largely be shaped by the judgements they make on the kind of children they admit, and on what happens in the school. Thus, in one suburban ESN(M) school, a head rejected 'violent' children and the local image of the ESN(M) child was that of a dull, slow child. In an inner-city ESN(M) school, where the head felt he could deal with 'difficult' children and a high proportion of black children were also admitted, the local image of ESN(M) children was of disturbed children who were also often black children. Figure 16.4 illustrates the special school heads' accounts of ESN(M) children.

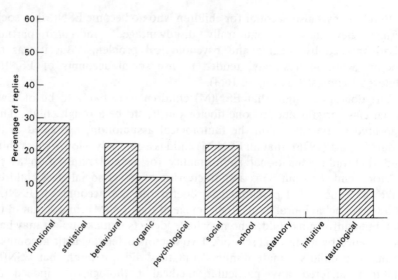

Figure 16.4 Special school heads' accounts of ESN(M) children

Heads of special schools do use functional and behavioural accounts to explain why a child 'is ESN(M)' in their school, but their behavioural accounts are much milder than those offered by referring heads – children are 'deeply disturbed' rather than 'disruptive' or 'vicious'. Some special school heads also accounted for the children in their schools in terms of the rejection by normal schools. One head said, 'My school is a dumping ground of the problem children in the city.' They used social accounts too, stating that ESN(M) children came from disorganized or disadvantaged families, and tautological accounts of some children whom they described as being 'not ESN' despite the fact that they had been accepted into an ESN(M) school.

Intuitive accounts of ESN(M) children tended to be most often used by parents. Parents do not, of couse, officially 'construct' the ESN(M) child, nor are they involved or consulted too closely in the process, despite official statements that they 'should' or 'ought to' be involved (DES, 1980, p. 7). Parents gave functional accounts of their children: 'He's a bit slow – he doesn't make progress.' But such accounts were often given after the head of the referring school had 'sent for and told them' that their child had learning problems. They then followed this by intuitive accounts, either positive or negative: 'we knew there was something wrong with her' or a decisive 'there's nothing wrong with him, despite what the flipping school says'.

The parents were very dependent on the referring head's presentation of what was wrong and how the special school would 'help', and this dependency probably eased the head's self-appointed task of persuading parents to cooperate in the construction of their child as 'ESN(M)'. If a parent does not agree, and is not threatened with legal sanctions, it is possible for the referral to be dropped and the child never officially becomes 'ESN(M)' (this happened with the one middle-class family in the study). Figure 16.5 illustrates parental accounts of ESN(M) children. Despite the referring schools' preoccupation with behavioural accounts, not many parents accounted for their children 'being ESN' in behavioural terms.

Of the children placed in special schools in this study, the parents had been involved in the process for almost two years. It is difficult to imagine selection procedures in any other area of education taking this length of time, or being tolerated by parents – and it is certainly difficult to imagine articulate middle-class parents accepting a lengthy process where they are 'sent for and told' or 'persuaded' to accept a stigmatized type of schooling for their children.

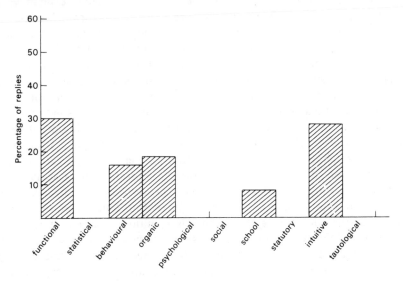

Figure 16.5   Parental accounts of their (potentially) ESN(M) children

The notion that only working-class families produce 'ESN(M)' children, or, as the Court Report put it, the 'socially disadvantaged [...] or the socially incompetent are at special risk of having children who are mildly mentally retarded' (Court Report, 1976, p. 24), is thus reinforced during the process of constructing the ESN(M) child. Although Tredgold in 1908 was able to note that 'many of our feeble-minded are gentlefolk [...] able to enter into the social amusements of their class' (p. 175), the middle and upper classes in the later twentieth century simply do not allow, or need, their children to be socially constructed as ESN(M).

ESN(M) AND SOCIAL STRUCTURE

While it is possible, using phenomenological perspectives, to ask why and how the category of ESN(M) comes to be socially constructed, it is almost impossible to generate propositions about education in complex societies from phenomenological perspectives. A phenomenological analysis of the social construction of the ESN(M) child could be accused of doing no more than documenting the obvious – that professionals have social power to construct categories in which their decisions continually place children who are deemed 'less intelligent' or 'in need' of a particular kind of non-credentialling education. A structural perspective is needed to explain what the social uses of the ESN(M) category are and why this form of education is accorded only to lower social-class (and black) children. In the study reported in this chapter the structural perspective adopted was that articulated by Bourdieu and Passeron (1977). Their work has attempted to illuminate the subtle relationships between the class structures and the education systems of industrial societies by pointing out that the development of education systems is closely related to changes in the socio-economic structure. Modern societies perpetuate the conditions of their own existence partly through the transmission of varying kinds and amounts of schooling. Education selection has replaced real capital as a seemingly more democratic currency for the reproduction of social-class relationships, and educational advancement or exclusion is based on ostensibly fair testing and selection procedures. But Bourdieu and Passeron argue that the education system demands a cultural competence which it does not itself provide. Advantage is given to those who possess cultural 'capital' and can pass it on to their children. The families of children who come to be categorized as ESN(M) have neither cultural capital nor economic capital to pass on. Indeed the 'cultural disadvantage' of the families of ESN(M) children is a recurring theme in the literature. The study reported here suggests that this literature can be turned back to front, since, by withdrawing children from normal education and offering them a stigmatized education which fits them only for low status in society, the reproduction of a part of the lower social class is ensured. There is little possibility that children other than those of low socio-economic status will find their way to ESN(M) schools – the upper and middle classes have cultural, and often economic, capital to pass on to their dull children, who do not need to be controlled or legitimated as do those of low status.

The development of this type of special education may have served two functions in society. First, by removing potentially troublesome children who upset the smooth running of the normal education system, order within that system was better ensured. ESN(M) education may have functioned more as a 'safety-valve' of the normal education system than anything else. In the later twentieth century the recognition that more and more children are troublesome to the system has led to more subtle ways of transferring children out. Secondly, the development of ESN(M) education has been one way of solving the perennial problem of social order in class-structured industrial societies, by selecting out and controlling, through a stigmatized type of schooling, potentially troublesome social groups.

The category of ESN(M) is socially constructed by the decisions and beliefs of professional people, but it also serves a wider purpose in the social structure. It is in the interests of all those concerned with special education to be clearer about the categorization of any children out of the normal education system, particularly those in the non-normative categories of ESN(M), Child with Learning Difficulty, disruptive and maladjusted, whether these categories are statutory or merely descriptive. The development of categories must be understood within a wider historical, social and political context than has so far been the case.

REFERENCES

Berger, A. and Mitchells, G. (1978) A multitude of sin-bins, *Times Educational Supplement,* July

Berger, P. and Luckman T. (1966) *The Social Construction of Reality,* Penguin, Harmondsworth

Block, N. and Dworkin G. (1977) *The IQ Controversey,* Quartet Books, New York

Board of Education and Board of Control (1929) *Report of Joint Departmental Committee on Mental Deficiency* (Wood Report), HMSO, London

Booth, T. (1978) From normal baby to handicapped child, *Sociology,* Vol. 12, No. 2

Bourdieu, P. and Passeron, J.C. (1977) *Reproduction in Education Society and Culture,* Sage, London

Burt, C. (1935) *The Sub-Normal Mind,* Oxford University Press, Oxford

Court Report (1976) *Fit for the Future – Report of the Committee on Child Health,* HMSO, London

Davies, D.R. (1961) A disorder theory of mental retardation, *Journal of Mental Sub-Normality,* No. 7

Department of Education and Science (DES) (1972) *The Health of the School Child 1969–72– Report of the Chief Medical Officer to the* DES, HMSO, London

Department of Education and Science (DES) (1975) *The Discovery of Children Requiring Special Education and the Assessment of their Needs,* Circular 2/75, HMSO, London

Department of Education and Science (DES) (1978) *Special Educational Needs* (Warnock Report), Cmnd 7212, HMSO, London

Department of Education and Science (DES) (1979) *Statistics in Education,* Vol. 1, HMSO, London

Department of Education and Science (DES) (1980) *Special Needs in Education* (White Paper), Cmnd 7996, HMSO, London

Gulliford, R. (1966) Special education for the ESN, National Association for Special Education, Conference Proceedings, July, HMSO, London

Gulliford, R. (1969) *Backwardness and Educational Failure,* Routledge and Kegan Paul, London

Hunt, S. (1975) *Parents of the ESN,* National Elfrida Rathbone Society, Liverpool

Kamin, L. (1977) *The Science and Politics of IQ,* Penguin, Harmondsworth

Ministry of Education (1946) *Special Educational Treatment,* Pamphlet No. 5, HMSO, London

Omar, B. (1971) ESN children – labelled for life, *Race Today,* January

Pritchard, D.G. (1963) *Education and the Handicapped, 1760–1960,* Routledge and Kegan Paul, London

Royal Commission on the Care and Control of the Feeble-Minded (1908) Report, 8 volumes, HMSO, London

Scott, M. and S. Lyman (1968) Accounts, *American Sociological Review,* Vol. 33, No. 1

Sharp, R. and Green, A. (1973) *Education and Social Control,* Routledge and Kegan Paul, London

Squibb, P. (1977) Some notes towards the analysis of the less-able or backward child, *Journal of Further and Higher Education,* Vol. 1, No. 3

Stein and Susser (1960) Families of dull children, Part III, *Journal of Mental Science,* Vol. 106, No. 445

Tomlinson, S. (1981) *Educational Sub-Normality: a study in decision making,* Routledge and Kegan Paul, London

Tredgold, A.F. (1908) *A Text-Book of Mental Deficiency,* Bailliere, Tindall and Cox, London

Williams, P. and Gruber, E. (1967) *Response to Special Schooling,* Longman, London

Williams, P. (1965) The ascertainment of ESN children, *Educational Research,* Vol. 7, No. 1

TOPICS FOR DISCUSSION

1. With reference to Table 16.1, discuss the fallibility and limitations of the ways in which professions make judgements about children.
2. What are the social factors which have constructed the picture of the ESN(M) child?
   or
   'Social accounts have, historically, been so persistent and persuasive that their plausibility as an account of "ESN(M)-ness" is seldom questioned.' Discuss.
3. 'The official picture of the construction of the category ESN(M) is that of "smooth teamwork" - cooperation and agreement between professionals on the 'needs' of particular children.' How does the author's research demonstrate this not to be the case?

SUGGESTIONS FOR FURTHER READING

1. S. Tomlinson (1982) *A Sociology of Special Education',* Routledge and Kegan Paul, London. In chapter 2, 'The Social Origins of Special Education', the author examines the development of special education with particular reference to prevailing social, economic and professional interests rather than in terms of ideological considerations of humanitarian progress. She traces the expansion of vested interests in the field of special education showing that 'provision' developed to cater for the needs of ordinary schools, the interests of the wider industrial society and the specific interests of professionals.
2. T. Dessent (1983) *Who is responsible for children with special needs?* In T. Booth and P. Potts (Eds) (1983) Integrating Special Education, Basil Blackwell, Oxford. The author examines some of the major issues involved in the development of integrated facilities for children with special needs, claiming that the issues relate to the question of responsibility - administrative, professional and personal responsibility for handicapped and difficult-to-teach children. His argument is that the tendency to segregate responsibility for children with special needs is both cause and effect of a segregated special education system.
3. P. Potts (1983) *What difference would integration make to the professionals?* In T. Booth and P. Potts (Eds) (1983) Integrating Special Education, Basil Blackwell, Oxford. Potts discusses the ways in which professionals may impede

integration, showing how their patterns of work and training tend to sustain a segregated special education system, and how the kinds of relationships that commonly exist between professionals and their clients often preclude the full participation of clients in important decisions.

Reading 17
THE EXPANSION OF SPECIAL EDUCATION
S. Tomlinson

Special education in Britain, as in other advanced technological societies, is expanding. In changed forms and rationalized by changed ideologies, notably the ideology of special needs, it is becoming a more important mechanism for differentiating between young people and allocating some to a future which, if not as stigmatized as in the past, will be characterized by relative powerlessness and economic dependency. It is expanding primarily as part of a political response to a crucial dilemma facing education systems in late twentieth-century technological societies. This dilemma is centred round restructuring the education–training system to deal with the increasing number of young people who are defined as being unable or unwilling to participate satisfactorily in a system primarily directed towards producing academic and technical elites. Adequate achievements in normal school education or educational training are becoming more important in gaining any sort of employment or income above subsistence level, or exerting any influence on the wider society. The expansion of special education is linked to the question of what sort of education – or preparation for future life-style – can or should be offered to a larger social group who are likely to be partially or permanently non-employed and who thus, in traditional industrial-society understandings, are not economically profitable or 'useful'. As special education expands it is likely to provide both a rationale and a justification for the economic and social position of at least a part of this social group. Although presented in ideological terms as catering for the 'needs' of pupils, the expansion of special education is

S. Tomlinson (1985) The expansion of special education, *Oxford Review of Education,* Vol. 11, No. 2, pp 157–165

the result of rational action on the part of those who control and direct education and training, to restructure the education system to fit the perceived needs of a post-industrial, technologically based society.

This article examines evidence for the claim that special education is expanding and discusses three reasons for the expansion – professional vested interest, comprehensive school dilemmas and the declining youth labour market – and asserts that the ideology of 'special needs' directs attention away from the social, economic and political concerns which have led to the expansion.

EVIDENCE FOR EXPANSION

Legally, special education is defined as the curriculum and pedagogy offered to pupils who pre-1981 had a 'disability of body or mind' calling for special educational treatment, and post-1981 have a learning difficulty which calls for special educational provision. The number of such children rose from nil in the early 1870s – at the beginning of compulsory state education – to some 1.5 million in 1981.[1] This argues that a subsystem of special education has been successfully established and has become an important structural component of the educational system. The expansion can be largely accounted for by the number of children who have no physical or sensory handicap, but who are educationally defined as being incapable of participating or unwilling to participate in what is currently defined as the 'normal' curriculum, and being incapable of 'adequate achievements' via this curriculum. Such children have, over the past 100 years, been variously described as feeble-minded, educable defective, educationally sub-normal, those having moderate learning difficulties, dull and backward, remedial, and maladjusted and disruptive.

The expansion is linked to enhanced definitions of 'achievement'. There is increasing pressure on schools to raise standards and to credential more and more pupils. This has led to pressures on schools to devise more and more courses leading to lower-level credentials and to seek ways of separating out those who are unable or unwilling to achieve even these lower-level qualifications. In this way the subsystem of special education appears capable of indefinite expansion. For example, the number of pupils considered to have a disability of body or mind in 1946 was 2 per cent with a further 8-9 per cent likely to be unable to achieve adequately in schools (Ministry of Education, 1946, pp 22-23). In 1978 the number in need of special provision was considered by the Warnock Committee to be 20 per cent of the school population. By 1982 the Secretary of State was expressing his concern about the less able 40 per cent and a DES-sponsored programme for lower-attaining pupils was instigated. The ideological differences between the 20 per cent of pupils needing special provision owing to learning difficulties and the learning difficulties of the bottom 40 per cent are problematic, and in practice the programme appears to fill a gap between school definitions of 'special needs' and 'CSE material' (NFER, 1984). In Scotland the system may be expanding faster. A Scottish Inspectorate comment on learning difficulties in 1984 noted that since 'there is a whole range of difficulties faced by very many pupils in the lower half of the ability range [...] the progress report was thinking in terms of up to 50%.' Accurate numbers of those in special education provision, or 'in need' of this kind of provision, have always been difficult to quantify. One reason for this has been the changing definitions of special education. Another reason is that LEAs have always differed in the kinds and amount of special provision they offered. Perhaps of more interest are the proportional and percentage increases.

Postwar, Booth has worked out that, in 1950, 2402 pupils per million were categorized as ESN(M); by 1977 the proportion had risen to 5763 per million. Similarly, in 1950, 93 pupils per million were officially maladjusted, by 1977 this had risen to 1416 per million (Booth, 1981, p. 295). In another entertaining comparison Squibb (1981, p. 47) estimated that in 15 years (1961–76) there was an increase of 150 per cent in pupils classed as ESN, a 237 per cent increase for those classed as maladjusted, a 1332 per cent increase for those classed as speech defective and an infinite increase (from no pupils in 1961 to 951 in 1976) in those classed as autistic. As Squibb has noted, 'we may all be autistic soon' (1981, p. 48). Further evidence of percentage increases of pupils segregated into special schools and classes under the pre-1981 system of classification by handicap has been provided by Swann (1984), who worked out that, despite assumptions that integration was occurring and fewer pupils were being physically removed from mainstream schooling, the proportion of pupils segregated in special schools actually increased by 4.8 per cent between 1977 and 1982, and he particularly noted the increased segregation into ESN(M) and maladjusted provision.

From its beginnings special education was concerned to take in those with obvious and definable physical and sensory handicaps and behaviourally troublesome pupils, but from 1889 the most likely candidates for inclusion in an expanding system were those originally classed as feeble-minded or educable defectives – their heirs being the dull and backward, educationally sub-normal, remedial, moderate learning and behavioural difficulties, the less able and so on. I have argued (Tomlinson, 1982) that the persistent connection of this expanding group – and of learning and behavioural problems – with the children of the manual working class is perennially resilient. The 'social problem' class that worried Cyril Burt continues to worry educationalists from the Secretary of State downwards. Connections between lack of intelligence, inability to learn, bad behaviour, low socio-economic status and a variety of undesirable social attributes continue to ensure that it is largely the children of the lower working class and the unemployed who are candidates for the expanding special education sector. The story of Bill and Daisy included by A.F. Tredgold (1914) in his *Text-Book of Mental Deficiency* may still be pertinent:

Bill, we will suppose, had been a pupil in a special [educationally sub-normal] school up to the age of 16 [...] and has since been employed in a number of jobs, starting as an errand boy and graduating to simple machine-minding in a factory. Daisy went to an ordinary school but was very backward and like Bill, is scarcely able to read and write. Daisy, before her marriage to Bill, has held a variety of jobs mainly assembling or varnishing small electrical parts.

After joining a gang for acceptance and a sense of importance Bill was [...] impelled to seek a girl friend, but was so unprepossessing that his only chance would be with a girl equally unattractive who might be available. Daisy was unattractive but simple and compliant and an easy date. Between the pair a bond of sympathy grew up. They each provided for the other what had been lacking all the years – comfort and appreciation.

[Daisy became pregnant and they married and went to live in an attic room in an overcrowded house – going down four flights of stairs for water and six for the WC. Daisy had to give up her job, the couple lacked foresight and planning.]

After the baby's birth, Daisy went out cleaning, Bill lost his job – they had another baby but fear of further pregnancies led Daisy to fail to give Bill comfort and solace. Bill took to staying away from home and he became ripe for any criminal exploitation that might come his way. The children will have a natural backwardness at school, will play truant and delinquent practices will follow. Thus history will have repeated itself. (p. 394)

Tredgold's documentation of two ESN school-leavers who found semiskilled work, married and had a family could be read as a eugenist's warning, or as a libel on a couple who lacked an adequate wage, decent housing and contraceptive advice.

EXPANSION AND PROFESSIONAL INTERESTS

Much of the expansion of special education has been ascribed to accident, spontaneous adjustment, progress and benevolence. These explanations have always proved a stumbling block to the analysis of the emergence and expansion of a special subsystem of education. Archer's (1979) contention that educational structures are the result of the *interests* of those social groups who manage, as a result of conflicts, to achieve educational control, is a more useful starting point. The development and expansion of special education is the result of a variety of conflicting interest groups, both inside and outside education. Indeed, an understanding of the competition and alliances among interest groups in special education is crucial to understanding its expansion.

Pre-1945 (as I have documented in Tomlinson, 1982), educationalists, psychologists and medical practitioners all had vested interests in expanding the numbers of pupils in special education, and government had an interest in the control and direction of numbers of pupils who might prove 'troublesome' in the post-school careers in a variety of ways (principally by unemployment, crime or by requiring resources). Ordinary teachers' interests in the removal of special pupils – who originally interfered with payment-by-results and filled the standard 'O' classes – has proved an enduring and crucial force behind expansion. Then, as now, the public status of ordinary teachers was dependent on their ability to 'raise standards', which called for the removal of defective and troublesome children. This removal coincided with the interests of the new subprofession of special school teachers who had a vested interest in obtaining clients for their schools. It also coincided with the interests of the eugenists who were concerned to identify and isolate defectives who threatened the 'racial stock'. Psychologists had a crucial interest in developing the tools of assessment for special education, which have proved to be so important in their professional development and claims to specialist expertise. The enduring medical influence in special education has also been well documented (Pritchard, 1963) and the recorded conflicts of educational and medical personnel over the control of access to special education post-1908 provides a good example of the strategic power-play that ultimately determines control of the education system (see Royal Commission on the Care and Control of the Feeble-Minded, 1908).

Post-1945, medical and psychological interests took precedence over education in vying for control of assessment processes for special education, psychologists partially reaching parity of esteem by 1975 and certainly by 1981. However, by this time all professional interests were becoming united by a suspicion that central and local administrators had annexed control of special education via distribution of resources, control of assessment procedures, parental appeals and decisions on provisions. The 1981 Act did, however, place more control of the expanding sector of special education in the educationalists' area, as its major location became the ordinary school. In particular the expanding subprofession of 'special needs' heads of departments, teachers and support staff in ordinary schools now have power to shape and control large sectors of special education and in particular to decide who the special clients in the ordinary school will be and what sort of 'special' curriculum and pedagogy they will be offered. The ideology of 'special needs' is currently penetrating the secondary school curriculum and conflicts of interest are developing between 'special needs' specialists and their colleagues. In addition it was not to be expected that teachers in special schools would willingly give up their special expertise or clients as the location changed, and there are currently conflicts of interest between special and ordinary schools over the retention or movement of pupils, particularly in areas where segregated provision was well established.[2] But by the 1970s 'special' teachers in both segregated and integrated provision had, to some extent, realized that their common interest lay in enhanced professional claims to special expertise. These claims are currently being strengthened and the expansion of special education has created the opportunity for more expert special teachers, support staff, advisers and inspectors to be employed.

COMPREHENSIVE SCHOOL DILEMMAS

The expansion of special education cannot be understood without reference to developments and changes in the whole education system, particularly changes since the establishment of state comprehensive education during the 1970s. A common school, underpinned by egalitarian ideologies and attended by middle- and working-class children, was envisaged by comprehensive supporters, but comprehensive education is now dogged by a series of dilemmas. One dilemma which was slowly realized during the 1970s was that, if selection by ability was inadmissible, so was selection by disability or inability. The 100-year-old principle of segregation gave way to notions of integration and comprehensive schools were expected to incorporate many nonconformist and troublesome children who would previously have been candidates for exclusion. Other dilemmas included the promise to offer equality of opportunity, while explaining away unequal outcomes in what Shaw has termed 'our incorrigibly competitive and hierarchical society' (1983, p. 37); the pressure to raise standards and credential more pupils by expanding the examination system while offering a suitable curriculum to the 'less able'; and the pressure to incorporate a subject-oriented traditional grammar-school-type curriculum while incorporating secondary-modern-type pupils.

Reynolds and Sullivan (1979) have argued that initially comprehensives were left relatively free to develop their own curriculum, pedagogies and forms of control with little outside interference, and one response to dilemmas posed by the 'less able' and the 'unwilling' (pupils with learning and behavioural problems), whose numbers increased after 1973 and the raising of the school-leaving age, was to segregate them internally within the schools. The rapid development of large remedial departments created an unofficial expansion of special education in secondary schools. This expansion was noted by the Warnock Committee which recommended that 'children previously regarded as disruptive' and 'children who have hitherto been seen as requiring remedial rather than special education' should be deemed candidates for special education (DES, 1978, p. 47). Thus the unofficial expansion was given official recognition. Up to the beginning of the 1980s there was little evidence that comprehensive schools had solved the dilemma of providing a curriculum for the 'less able' or the 'remedial-special'. Evidence (HMI, 1979; Reid *et al.,* 1981) indicated that most comprehensives preferred streaming, setting and banding to mixed-ability teaching, and their curriculum for the less able was narrow and inappropriate. Given the pressures to concentrate on the able and the examinable this is perhaps not surprising.

The incursion of the new vocationalism and MSC activities into secondary schooling and the blurring of the education–training divide have created more dilemmas for comprehensive schools – one of which is how far 'special needs' pupils will be incorporated into technical and vocational courses, or how far they will be offered watered-down palliatives of 'work experience' and 'social and life skills'.

THE DISAPPEARING YOUTH LABOUR MARKET

While the comprehensive school curriculum has increasingly become a matter for pressures from political and economic interest groups outside school, a major focus has been on the curriculum for the 'less able'. The DES 14–16 'lower attaining pupils programme', for example, is a direct but little publicized political incursion into this curriculum. DES criticism of the inappropriate curriculum offered to the less able up to the early 1980s was largely a criticism of the apparent slowness of schools to realize the social and political consequences of the disappearance of the youth labour market for less able and special leavers. The pupils at whom the DES and other vocational and educational programmes for the less able are aimed at those who, up to the mid-1970s, could be minimally motivated to learn and behave at school by means of the carrot of possible employment. Programmes designed for the less able and special adolescents are part of a political response to the problem of dealing with larger numbers of young people who, despite new vocational initiatives, will probably never acquire employment. The expansion of special education to embrace larger numbers of young people, particularly at post-16 level, may provide both a rationale and a justification for the subsequent economic position of this group. I suggested in 1982 that 'to have received a special education – with its historical stigmatic connotations, even a non-recorded special education in an integrated setting, may be regarded unfavourably by potential employers' (Tomlinson, 1982, p. 177). However, this kind of assertion now needs much more careful elaboration. The role of special education in preparing large numbers of young people for a workless future, or at least one of sporadic, low-skilled employment, needs research and analysis.

Any discussion of the relationship between the expansion of special education and the economic situation must start from the premise that to have 'special needs' is not an individual characteristic; it is the product of interaction between individuals and their social environment. It has been an underlying theme of this article that special education expands, not because of intrinsic qualities or lack of qualities in pupils, but because of the social or educational criteria currently being applied. *Similarly, whether or not the handicapped or the special find employment depends on the current economic conditions rather than on the possession of suitable abilities or skills.* Thus, while the economy was in need of low-skilled labour, the majority of special school leavers found employment, even though their mental or physical capacities were judged to be low. It has been an enduring characteristic of the 'handicapped', as Barnett (1984) has recently elaborated in an interesting discussion of the economics of mental retardation, that they have often been considered retarded or problematic at school, but not outside school, particularly in employment. In Britain one careers officer wrote in 1974 that in his experience 'the majority of special school leavers found jobs with comparative ease [...] these included polishing, assembling, building, painting, canteen work and even office work' (City of Birmingham, 1977). A major task of special education has always been to prepare pupils for routine manual work, and some employers came to prefer special school leavers who were often more docile, obedient and punctual than others (see Collman, 1956; Atkinson, 1981). By 1975, however, the same careers officer was noting that 'many special school leavers are affected by the recession and those requiring routine or semi-skilled work found most difficulty'.

In this, of course, special school leavers were joined by the less able and also leavers with school-leaving certificates. In 1974 80,000 under-20-year-olds were unemployed; by 1981 this number was 532,000 (although 360,000 were in government schemes or work experience programmes). The kind of work those who had received a special education formerly undertook has now virtually disappeared, except for some low-skilled manufacturing or service jobs which may continue to be available for them. Although the question of 'specially educated for what?' can only be answered by empirical investigation of the post-school careers of those leaving special education, an examination of some post-16 college courses for special needs students suggests that for those pupils with severe sensory, physical or mental handicaps traditional supervised provision, usually at adult training centres, is envisaged after they have undertaken college courses to the age of 19 or 21. For those with moderate learning difficulties (as the description now runs) further special courses, including special YTS schemes, transfer to a normal YTS place, or even low-skilled employment is the aim, while for more able but handicapped students transfer to mainstream college courses, YTS or particular kinds of employment is the aim. The courses usually include a large component of 'social and life skills', 'coping and independent living' and 'adult responsibility' as well as college or employer-based introductions to basic manual skills. The expansion of special education may have brought more young people into its orbit but the aims of special education may not have changed too drastically over 100 years. Training for self-sufficiency and controlled social behaviour, and training for low-skilled productive work are traditional aims in special education. The major future difference may be that disappearance of low-skilled work will lead to more and more extensive special courses and more carefully planned supervision for those who will never achieve work. The next expansion of special education will undoubtedly be into 'adult special needs' courses.

THE IDEOLOGY OF SPECIAL NEEDS

To study ideology, as J. Thompson (1984) has recently pointed out, is to study the ways in which the meanings of particular words or ideas serve to sustain relations of domination. The concept of 'special needs' has become an ideological rationalization for those who have the power to shape and define the expanding special education system and have vested interests in this expansion. Those who can define the 'needs' of others and give or withhold provision have great power, yet the benevolent image with which the notion of 'catering for special needs' has become imbued precludes discussion of the supposed needs, or criticism of provision and practice. This, however, is the purpose of ideology – 'ideology is, as it were, the linguistic legislature which defines what is available for public discussion and what is not' (J. Thompson, 1984, p. 85).

The concept of special needs began to be applied to particular groups of pupils in the 1960s – most notably to ethnic minority pupils whose language and cultural needs were 'special', and to 'disadvantaged pupils'. The liberal child-centred pedagogies of the 1960s focused on children's supposed needs, as did egalitarian programmes to compensate for social disadvantages. The concept was applied to special education in 1965 when a DES report described such education as 'education that is specially well adapted to meet a child's needs'. The Warnock Committee (DES, 1978) adopted the concept both as a rationale for an expanded system of special education ('broader provision', p. 36) and as a more positive description of the clients of special education than description by handicap or disability. While the concept appears to have done the former – all sorts of expansion is now taking place with no further justification than 'the pupil has special needs' – the descriptive problem has not been overcome. The child with special educational needs has become the SEN or the SNARC pupil who needs a SNAP![3] The extension of the concept to cover 'gifted' pupils, or indeed *all* pupils, has led Mary Warnock (1982, 1983) to repudiate the use of the concept for those pupils her report had dealt with.

The whole concept of special needs is ambiguous and tautological. It has become part of a rhetoric that serves little educational purpose. While it does mainly focus on negative psychogenic properties of individual pupils – their difficulty, disability, incapacity or lack of intelligence – it does not provide any mechanism for deciding who has these properties. The current desperate search for improved assessment procedures is an indication that the concept of special needs is no actual help in deciding who the clients of special education should be. At the same time the concept, with its humanitarian overtones, precludes discussion of the needs and interests actually being served by the expansion of special education. Those who find difficulty in moving beyond humanitarian rhetoric, and insist that 'all children have special needs', still have to explain why a whole subsystem of special education has developed and expanded which is backed by legal enforcement and caters largely for the children of the manual working class. To do this, attention must turn from the psychogenic focus on individual 'needs' to the social interest groupings, the educational, political and economic 'needs' which an expansion of special education is serving. At the present time the ideological obfuscation provided by the focus on the 'child's special needs' prevents an adequate analysis of this expansion.

NOTES

1. In 1981 approximately 200,000 pupils were excluded from mainstream education in special schools and classes plus those unofficially counted and excluded in disruptive units. The Warnock Report's suggestion that remedial and disruptive pupils be officially counted as needing special provision – implicitly accepted by the 1981 Act – and that 1 in 5 children may need special provision, brought the number to 1.5 million in 1981 – a fifth of the (then) 8 million pupils in education.
2. See, for example, the conflicting evidence offered to the Fish Committee, set up in 1984 to examine segregated special provision in the Inner London Education Authority.
3. Some schools now have Special Education Needs (SEN) departments, at least one school has a Special Needs and Remedial Children (SNARC) department, and many schools are adopting the Special Needs Action Programme (SNAP) produced in Coventry.

REFERENCES

Archer, M.S. (1979) *The Social Origins of Educational Systems,* Sage, London
Atkinson, P., Shone, D. and Rees, T. (1981) *Labouring to learn? Industrial training for slow learners.* In L. Barton and S. Tomlinson (Eds) (1981) op. cit.
Barnett, W.S. (1984) *The Economics of Mental Retardation.* Ph.D. Dissertation, State University of Utah
Barton, L. and Tomlinson, S. (Eds) (1981) *Special Education Policies, Practices and Social Issues,* Harper and Row, London
Booth, A. (1981) *Demystifying integration.* In W. Swann (Ed.) (1981) The Practice of Special Education, Open University Press, Milton Keynes
Collman, R.P. (1956) The employment success of ESN pupils, *American Journal of Mental Deficiency,* Vol. 60, pp 247–251
Department of Education and Science (DES) (1978) *Special Educational Needs* (Warnock Report), Cmnd 7212, HMSO, London
Her Majesty's Inspectorate (HMI) (1979) *Aspects of Secondary Education: an HMI survey,* HMSO, London
Ministry of Education (1946) *Special Educational Treatment,* Pamphlet No. 5, HMSO, London

National Foundation for Educational Research (NFER) (1984) *Lower Attaining Pupil Programme Newsletter,* November, NFER, Slough

Pritchard, D.E. ((1963) *Education of the Handicapped 1760–1960,* Routledge and Kegan Paul, London

Reid, M.I. *et al.* (1981) *Mixed Ability Teaching: problems and possibilities,* NFER, Slough

Reynolds, D. and Sullivan, M. (1979) *Bringing school back.* In L. Barton and R. Meighan (Eds) (1979) Schools: pupils and deviance, Nafferton, Driffield

Royal Commission on the Care and Control of the Feeble-Minded (1908) Report, Vol. 1, HMSO, London

Shaw, B. (1983) *Comprehensive Schooling: the impossible dream,* Blackwell, Oxford

Squibb, P. (1981) *A theoretical, structuralist approach to special education.* In L. Barton and S. Tomlinson (Eds) (1981) op. cit.

Swann, W. (1984) Statistics of segregation, *Childright* No. 8, pp 18–19

Thompson, J. (1984) *Studies in the Theory of Ideology,* Polity Press, London

Thompson, J.H. (1984) The concept of special educational needs. Paper given to the Conference on Special Educational Needs, Dundee, February

Tomlinson, S. (1982) *A Sociology of Special Education,* Routledge and Kegan Paul, London

Tredgold, A.F. (1914) *Text-Book of Mental Deficiency* (2nd edn), Bailliere, Tindall and Cox, London

Warnock, M. (1982) Personal column, *Times Educational Supplement,* 12 November, p. 72

Warnock, M. (1983) Personal column, *Times Educational Supplement,* 11 November, p. 64

TOPICS FOR DISCUSSION

1. 'The ideology of 'special needs' directs attention away from the social, economic and political concerns which have led to the expansion [of special education].' Discuss.
2. 'Special education expands, not because of intrinsic qualities or lack of qualities in pupils, but because of the social or educational criteria currently being applied.' Discuss.
3. 'The whole concept of special needs is ambiguous and tautological. It has become part of a rhetoric that serves little educational purpose.' Discuss.

SUGGESTIONS FOR FURTHER READING

1. P. Squibb (1981) *A theoretical, structuralist approach to special education.* In L. Barton and S. Tomlinson (Eds) (1981) Special Educational Policies, Practices and Social Issues, Harper and Row, London. From a 'structuralist' perspective the author argues that one feature of modern educational thought has been to persuade us that much which is essentially social in origin has come to be seen and acted upon as though it were 'natural', so that children are often labelled, categorized and treated as though their characteristics were natural when in fact they are socially posited and socially maintained.

2. D.J. Gavine, (1985) Special educational needs – fact or friction? *Scottish Educational Review,* Vol. 17, No. 1, May pp 14–22. The author argues that, while the concept of special educational need may be useful in day-to-day decision making, it is too vague and value-laden to sustain the formal operational structure laid down by legislation in the Education (Scotland) Act 1981. Gavine maintains that the smooth operation of implementing the legislation centres round various assumptions about the concept 'need', and that *none* of these assumptions hold in practice.

3. P. Atkinson, D. Shone, and T. Rees, (1981) *Labouring to learn? Industrial training for slow learners.* In L. Barton and S. Tomlinson (Eds) (1981) Special Education Policies, Practices and Social Issues, Harper and Row, London. The authors show how the growth in youth unemployment has been matched by an increase in state intervention to manage the 'social problems' thought to be an inevitable and direct consequence. The chapter examines one such intervention strategy to do with the process of work socialization. The client group consists of *slow learners* and the project describes overt attempts to inculcate certain industrial skills designed to make the slow learners more marketable whilst at the same time instilling in them a range of social skills which are considered important and appropriate in a 'good worker'. The authors argue that increasingly such interventions 'have shifted in emphasis from allowing the experience itself to be the formative factor in work socialization to more overt instilling of "right" attitudes'.

Reading 18
EDUCATIONAL SYSTEMS FOR DISRUPTIVE ADOLESCENTS
K.J. Topping

CURRICULUM

There is substantial evidence that learning difficulties are frequently found in children with behavioural difficulties, and it is generally accepted that the former may cause the latter just as frequently as vice versa. Thus schools with under-resourced remedial departments, or who try to impose a highly academic curriculum on children from homes that place more value on practical skills, can expect a higher than average incidence of behavioural problems, other things being equal. However, a pre-existing, adequately resourced, well-balanced and appropriate curriculum will be assumed in

K.J. Topping (1983) *Educational Systems for Disruptive Adolescents,* Croom Helm, London pp 125–140

discussion of the following studies, which largely refer to the effectiveness of additions to such a curriculum. It goes without saying that attempts to deal with behaviour problems resulting from massive dysjunction in the curriculum by throwing in a mini-course on pupil self-management are unlikely to meet with much success. Further, as Docking (1980) points out, curriculum content has to be determined on grounds of educational value rather than on just whether reductions in disruptive behaviour result therefrom. No doubt high pupil interest and involvement might be gained from lessons in guerrilla warfare and safe-cracking, but few teachers would consider that an adequate reason to adopt such an approach. Docking further points out that disruptive behaviour may not result so much from what is taught, but from the way it is taught.

An interesting attempt to provide a curriculum for children with difficulties in school is described by P.H. Chard (personal communication, 1980) and Rendell (1980), whose Individual Studies Department operates not by the espousal of a particular curriculum structure which is believed to be generally 'therapeutic', but by offering the flexibility in individual curriculum programming that many secondary schools find so difficult to achieve. The Department provides the security of a fixed base, relationships with fewer and more pastorally oriented teachers, regular attention to basic skills, the opportunity to take CSE examinations in 13 subjects, work experience and a wide range of non-academic, community-oriented activities which are available once the day's academic targets have been met. The Department has been found helpful with low-ability, low-motivation and disruptive children. Although it is noted that disruptive behaviour and absenteeism have decreased very substantially, this may be due to factors in addition to the establishment of the Department, and no harder evaluative data are available. However, teachers will find Rendell's paper very interesting.

Webb and Cormier (1972), in an intervention of greater specificity and smaller scale, withdrew 22 disruptive junior high students from maths classes and gave them a specific academic programme where all teaching was geared to specific behavioural objectives, and students were rewarded with free time when their daily assignments were completed. Increased task-related behaviour and reduced disruptive behaviour resulted, and this effect was maintained when the students returned to ordinary classes. That success is not automatic, however, was demonstrated by Ahlstrom and Havighurst (1971), whose 400 socially maladapted urban boys were divided into two groups, one to follow an ordinary classroom programme and one to follow a modified curriculum involving work experience. Both groups were monitored for six years, but the 'experimental' group did not make any better subsequent adjustment to working life. However, this latter is a very stringent criterion, and most studies of disruptive behaviour in school have been content to evaluate in terms of improved behaviour within that specific environment.

Other researchers have looked at the effectiveness of more restricted and specific curricular inputs which had the intention of reducing disruptiveness. Garibaldi (1979) describes School Survival Courses integrated with the timetable which give the children strategies for becoming better learners, techniques for staying out of trouble, and practice in gaining insight into the consequences of the behaviour of themselves and others. One high school offers a mini-course for pupils on dealing with assaults and disruptive behaviour, which includes definitions of deviance, explication of the range of consequences for misdeeds, and suggested steps for reporting attacks and assaults.

Few studies detailing the teaching of behavioural methods to pupils as part of the regular curriculum came to light. Perhaps behavioural techniques are considered too powerful to be made generally available to children. The major exception is the study of Lovitt (1973), who describes the teaching of self-management skills as part of the curriculum. Lovitt had his 'behavioural disability' students taught to do their own scheduling and programming, take responsibility for assignment completion, evaluate their own work, plot their own progress, and set their own contingencies and rewards. This had the advantage of taking a substantial organizational burden off the class-teacher, and the children were well, motivated by the scheme. However, evaluation results are bitty.

Other curricular inputs can be more sweeping and less immediately pragmatic. The DES (1978) mention a 'personal development course', and 'education for personal relationships' and 'social education' seem to be growth areas in schools, as is 'health education'. Ojemann's (1967) review paper is cited as something of a classic in this area. Rather than have pupils go through 'group awareness exercises', Ojemann preferred the specific teaching of psychological concepts via discussion of example scenarios. He cites observational evidence from ordinary lessons (albeit on rather obscure dimensions) that his experimental groups became less extrapunitive and judgemental as a result of understanding more about human motivation and behaviour. Trained groups have demonstrated greater understanding of human behaviour on post-course tests than non-trained groups, and there is some evidence that 'insecure and unstable' children can benefit quite as much as their better adjusted comrades. Many of the studies cited by

Ojemann have unfortunately relied on paper-and-pencil tests, but the results of those that have not are encouraging, although there is no suggestion that such techniques are particularly effective with disruptive children. This also applies to the studies of Sprinthall (1974) and Long (1970, 1974).

In the UK, Manchester Education Committee (1974) describe a Social Education Project with an emphasis on group awareness and group work method. The intention seems to be to help pupils develop insights into, and involvement with, various aspects of society, but 'the method of work takes precedence over the content'. Unfortunately, the 'evaluation' section of the report is disappointing.

The overall results from these curriculum innovations are thus not particularly solid or encouraging, but curriculum specialists would doutbless argue that, where such projects are tailored for a wide cross-section of the school, it would be unrealistic to expect a specific and lasting effect on that small proportion of pupils who are consistently disruptive. There is, of course, the contrary view that the surest way to kill children's interest in something is to include it in the curriculum.

SUMMARY

In addition to the body of general aetiological evidence which suggests that failure to cater for learning difficulties can result in disruptive behaviour, there is some evidence that where a school is able to be highly flexible in devising individual curricula for disruptive pupils, disruption and absenteeism are reduced. Giving pupils specific work targets and free time on target achievement has reduced disruptiveness in adolescents. Teaching children psychological concepts can produce more understanding and tolerance of the behaviour of others, but effects on disruption remain unevaluated. The work in this area is full of interesting ideas but limited in hard evaluative data.

ROUTINE SANCTIONS

In the 'best-practice' sample of schools visited, the DES (1978) noted that all sanctions were traditional. In the main they appeared to depend for their effect on the respect of the pupil for the teacher administering punishment, on their irksomeness to the pupil, or on an appeal to communal responsibility. A 'dressing-down' could still be effective, if the pupil respected the teacher. Referral to a senior teacher might lead to various courses of action, such as exclusion from a frequently disrupted class or part of the timetable, with work set and done under the supervision of senior staff. General misbehaviour or absenteeism might be met by being 'put on report', involving every lesson teacher's signature or comments being shown to a senior teacher at regular intervals.

Such treatment was felt to be irksome for many pupils, and effective only for some. Some children *liked* being on report as it provided security and attention from teachers. In some schools recalcitrant pupils were attached to senior staff and had to follow them throughout the day. This too proved agreeable to some pupils. Detention also had its hazards, in that transport home could prove very difficult, and this caused some anxiety, particularly in the case of girls during the winter months.

Maughan and Ouston (1979) noted from their more detailed research that levels of punishment varied considerably between schools, but seemed to have little bearing – either positively or negatively – on outcomes for the children. Two exceptions were unofficial physical punishment and very frequent tellings-off in lessons, which were actually associated with *worse* behaviour. By contrast, all kinds of rewards, from praise in lessons to more public commendations or formal reward systems, did seem to result in better outcomes. The overall picture for rewards 'provided a sharp contrast with the results on punishment'. The more immediate forms of positive feedback showed the strongest association with good outcome. Maughan and Ouston (1979) comment: 'the contrast became even more striking when we found that in all schools punishments tended to be more frequent than praise – in the ratio of two or three to one'.

Rutter *et al.* (1979) noted that, where a 'disciplinary' as distinct from a 'welfare' attitude to pupils was adopted by teachers, better behaviour resulted, but that schools where a lot of punishment was *used* enjoyed no better behaviour than schools where little was used. The consistent setting of widely known standards of behaviour resulted in better behaviour, but high levels of corporal punishment (official or unofficial) were strongly associated with worse behaviour.

It is clear that what is prescribed as punishment may often prove not to be punishing. Madsen *et al.* (1968) demonstrated experimentally that the more teachers said 'sit down', the more children stood up. Thomas *et al.* (1968) demonstrated that systematic variation of the teacher's classroom behaviour directly affected the amount of disruption, and that increases in 'punishment' could actually produce increased disruption. Nor are rewards free from unexpected effects. McCullough (1972) showed that praise can be punishing to some older pupils if delivered too publicly.

The most frequently used 'punishment' is undoubtedly the verbal reprimand. McAllister *et al.* (1969) present one of the few studies demonstrating that verbal reprimand can work at all. In this case it was coupled with praise for the whole group when everyone was behaving well. The reprimands were very brief, directive and stern and included the pupil's name. In a class of 25 16–19-year-olds, disruption was reduced and study behaviour increased by this method.

However, Rutter *et al.* (1979) report that *frequent* reprimands alone by teachers result in worse behaviour. O'Leary *et al.* (1970) noted that, with elementary children, quiet reprimands were usually more effective in reducing disruptive behaviour than loud reprimands. Kazdin and Klock (1973) draw attention to the non-verbal component of reprimands and praise, and in their study they found that non-verbal expressions of approval from the teacher (smiles, nods, gestures, etc.) were effective on their own in improving student attention.

Turning to another time-hallowed favourite, 'detention', it is noteworthy that Rutter *et al.* (1979) found no association between the use of detention and behavioural outcomes (i.e. it made no difference). The same applied to giving 'lines' or extra work impositions. Docking (1980) gives a useful discussion of the practical problems inherent in the use of detention, not the least being that, if children are given extra academic work as a punishment, this is unlikely to improve their attitude to such work at other times, while penalties unrelated to the offence are likely to be resented. Hall *et al.* (1971) report on various studies which have utilized carefully structured 'detention' schemes to good effect. A study with 16-year-olds where low marks in lessons resulted in extra *tuition* after school to remedy the difficulty led to much higher marks being achieved in normal lessons. In another study, 10 children in a special class for disruptive children received five minutes' detention for every out-of-seat behaviour. This dramatically reduced the incidence of this behaviour. Unfortunately, in both studies the experimental period was short, and to what extent the effectiveness of the punishments was due to their novelty value is not clear.

The third punishment in the traditional 'trinity' is, of course, corporal punishment. We have already noted that Rutter *et al.* (1979) found high levels of corporal punishment (official or unofficial) associated with *worse* behaviour. Clegg (1962) and Reynolds and Murgatroyd (1977) present evidence which supports this finding. Many schools claim that corporal punishment is hardly ever used, but in the 1977 National Children's Bureau Study of a large sample of children born in 1958, it was found that 80 per cent of the 16-year-olds were in secondary schools where corporal punishment was still used. Musgrave (1977) found no evidence from examination of punishment books that the use of corporal punishment in elementary schools had fallen between 1900 and 1939. A survey by the Inner London Education Authority (1978) found little evidence of change in the incidence of corporal punishment over the previous three years, and a substantial minority of schools resorted to this measure frequently. ILEA has since, of course, abolished the practice.

The DES (1978) noted that schools were inconsistent in their use of corporal punishment even within themselves, citing one school where one 'house' used the cane three times more frequently than another of the same size. The DES further comment: 'some schools reported that many children were so accustomed to severe beating at home that they were impervious to corporal punishment at school, and indeed, that some children claimed to prefer it to other more inconvenient punishments'. This is supported by the work of Sallows (1972), who studied a sample of normal and a sample of deviant children at home, and reported that, while the normal sample's parents used almost entirely verbal punishment, the deviant sample's parents used a substantial amount of physical punishment – with less effect.

The British Psychological Society (1980) reviewed all the available evidence on the effectiveness of corporal punishment, and concluded: 'We can find no evidence which shows that corporal punishment is of value in classroom management. We have found evidence of its disadvantages, although such evidence is not of the highest scientific rigour.' This report also notes that children often express a preference for corporal punishment. The BPS note that 'the use of C.P. in schools has long since been officially abandoned in the majority of Western European countries as well as throughout the communist bloc', and that nearly all the professional organizations concerned with the welfare of children favour the abolition of corporal punishment. The report comments: 'in order that physical punishment may be optimally effective a number of conditions have to be observed that obtain in a normal school setting'.

The BPS report that there is evidence that, where corporal punishment has been abandoned, an improvement in behaviour is often reported, and this is supported by Munro's (1981) account of recent research in Scotland. No school which had abolished corporal punishment had considered reintroducing it.

The amount of research evidence against the practice of corporal punishment is vast. The Society of Teachers Opposed to Physical Punishment (STOPP) publish a reading list (1979) of 225 items in support of abolition, of which many are solid, reliable, respectable, objective research studies, in sharp contrast to the subjectivism which tends to characterize the retentionists.

The view that, even if corporal punishment is ineffective with frequent offenders, it serves to deter others, is frequently put forward, and there is some research evidence to support this view. Walters *et al.* (1965) found that, where children observed a peer punished for a misbehaviour, the probability of the observers' committing those behaviours was reduced. There is no evidence as to the duration of this effect. However, many people might find the prospect of public flogging purely *pour encourager les autres* not particularly acceptable, particularly if they were parents themselves.

A fourth type of sanction is 'deprivation of privileges'. That this is less frequent in usage may be suggestive that school children enjoy few privileges of which they can be deprived. The method of time-out can of course be construed as deprivation of the privilege of remaining in the classroom. Clarizio (1976) has reviewed research in the area of privilege deprivation. It is clear, though perhaps not immediately obvious, that the effectiveness of this form of punishment will depend on how much the pupil values what he or she is threatened with losing, *and* on how clearly the way to regain the privileges is shown.

Many studies of deprivation of privileges have been conducted within a behaviourist framework, where the system is usually referred to as 'response cost'. The behaviour resulting in loss of reward, the reward lost, and the means of regaining the reward are carefully specified *in advance*. This enables extremely consistent application of the system. Provided it is well structured, the scheme can be effective, but you do have to have something you can lose. The previously cited studies of Hall *et al.* (1971) could also be construed as 'response cost' systems. Broden *et al.* (1970) found a system of 'minus' points accumulating to an after-school detention (which could be 'bought off' by plus points gained by good behaviour), effective with 13–15-year-olds.

Many sanctions in secondary schools have been in use so long that they have entered into the folk rituals of the teaching profession. There is substantial evidence that the children's perceptions of the effectiveness of various sanctions is considerably at variance with the teachers' perceptions, yet many teachers proceed on the assumption that 'teacher knows best'. Burns (1978) asked 785 11–15-year-olds and their teachers to rank 12 rewards in terms of preference and believed effectiveness. The teachers thought praise from themselves was the most powerful reward, but the children were lukewarm about this. Within school, the children thought receiving prizes would be a powerful incentive, although the best thing would be a favourable report home. The teachers were indifferent re these latter.

The references to prizes must be qualified by the findings of Rutter *et al.* (1979), who found good behaviour associated quite strongly with public praise, but not with the award of prizes, although *academic* improvement was associated with the latter. However, we have already referred to the need to make a careful distinction between public and private praise for some pupils. Indeed, Burns (1978) found that boys valued private praise more highly than girls, and this doubtless relates to Davie's (1972) finding that girls are more anxious for parental approval, boys for peer approval.

The high effectiveness reported by pupils of good or bad reports home is confirmed by the studies of Davies and Thorne (1977) and Highfield and Pinsent (1972). Of course it may be argued that disruptive pupils frequently have uncooperative or anti-school parents whose response to such reports is unlikely to be helpful, but this is an empirical question on which no specific data seem to be available. Davies and Thorne also found that children regarded the rewards of 'time off lessons' and 'extra time at favoured lessons' as highly desirable; much more desirable than teacher praise. Again, pupils became more ambivalent to public praise the older they were. The most effective punishments were considered to be 'a letter home about bad behaviour' and 'parents asked to come to school'. Older pupils were generally more sceptical about the effectiveness of punishments than younger pupils, and were particularly unimpressed by 'extra work' and 'detention'. On the whole, rewards were endorsed as effective much more strongly than punishment, and the involvement of parents in both received strong support.

In the Davies and Thorne (1977) study, corporal punishment was considered quite effective, although not as effective as home contact. Munro (1981) reports that in Scotland pupils are divided on the effectiveness of the belt, but there is a clearer consensus on the effectiveness of parental involvement. Scottish children also seem to find detention more effective than English children.

A more subtle inquiry has been conducted by O'Hagan and Edmunds (1983), who explored pupils' perceptions of different teacher styles of response to disruptive behaviour. A total of 120 13- and 14-year-old pupils were asked to rate six teacher control 'styles' along six evaluative dimensions. The six styles were: 'reactive hostile' (teacher only punishes when the class are not behaving properly); 'initiatory instrumental' (teacher punishes occasionally at random to demonstrate purposefulness in maintaining peace and quiet); 'pro-social' (teacher punishes a pupil for being unpleasant to a peer); 'initiatory hostile' (teacher picks on and punishes pupils for selfish pleasure); 'reactive instrumental' (teacher reluctant to punish and only does it when the class misbehave); and 'non-aggression' (teacher never punishes irrespective of class behaviour).

The pupils felt that the 'pro-social' style was the most justifiable, followed by the 'reactive instrumental' style. They had little time for the totally non-aggressive style. The 'initiatory hostile' style was felt likely to be the most effective form of containing disruptive behaviour, but it was also felt likely to result in a lot of truancy from such lessons. The 'reactive instrumental' style was felt likely to result in maximum pupil application to work, good behaviour from the class as a whole and low truancy rates. Interesting interaction effects according to sex of pupil and teacher were reported. O'Hagan and Edmunds conclude that 'apparently successful attempts to control disruptive conduct by intimidatory practice may have deleterious consequences in other ways'. Neither person nor situation variance predominated in the results, and it is noted that this suggests that in the ordinary school it is as important to be aware of potentially disturbing situations as it is to be aware of potentially disruptive pupils.

There is a great deal of research literature on the effectiveness of punishment which is not necessarily related to the school environment. Reviews of this are provided by Church (1963), Solomon (1964), Azrin and Holz (1966), and Mayer *et al.* (1968). Wright (1973) presents an overview directly related to schools. From these and other reviews referred to below, guidelines on how to use punishment effectively may be drawn. However, as the BPS (1980) has already pointed out, the requisite conditions for effective use may not always pertain in schools – in these circumstances, teachers would need to demonstrate professionalism and not carry on punishing for want of consideration of alternatives.

Various interesting pointers emerge from the more academic research. Rotter (1966) reviewed a number of studies and found that 'rewards' and the experience of success were not always reinforcing. There was evidence that the extent to which a child saw these as reinforcing depended on whether the child saw the rewards or success as achieved by his own skill and effort rather than by sheer luck or chance. This would seem to imply that providing pleasant experiences for disruptive pupils might make them happier, but is not likely to make them better behaved, unless the pleasant experiences are made contingent upon good behaviour.

Parke (1969) studied the effectiveness of various punishment conditions on 6- and 7-year-old boys. There were variations in timing of punishment, intensity of punishment, relationship between agent and recipient of punishment, and amount of rationale given for punishment. Parke found that the provision of 'high cognitive structure' (rationale and explanation of offence and punishment) was effective, and that it modified the operation of the other factors. High-intensity punishment was more effective than low-intensity when no 'cognitive structure' was given, but not when 'cognitive structure' was given. Similarly, early punishment was more effective than late punishment under low cognitive structure, but not under high cognitive structure, under low- but not high-intensity punishment, and under good relationship but not weak relationship conditions. Finally, children with prior good relationships with the punisher were more resistant to deviation than children where this did not apply, but only under low cognitive structure conditions.

To summarize:

1. Rationalization/explanation/clarification is effective.
2. Rationale and mild sanction has same effect as severe sanction.
3. Early sanction without rationale = late sanction with rationale.
4. Early better than late for mild sanctions.
5. Early better than late where relationships good.

Unfortunately, for our purposes, Parke's study was conducted with primary-aged children in a very artifical laboratory situation. The punishments were loud noises of varying intensity. Whether these results are generalizable to disruptive adolescents is an empirical question which necessitates further study. However, Parke and other authors (Presland, 1980; Heron, 1978; Macmillan *et al.,* 1973), having reviewed the extant literature on the effectiveness of various forms of punishment, suggest that *implications* for classroom practice may be drawn, even from research on infra-human subjects in some cases.

Parke (1969) notes that five studies have demonstrated that the more delayed punishment is after the offence, the less effective it becomes. Research with infra-human subjects generally demonstrates that the more intense the punishment, the greater the suppressive effects thereof. However, as Parke's own (1969) study shows, the situation with human subjects is considerably more complex, although the generalization *per se* still holds some validity for human applications. Thirdly, Parke notes that several studies with children have shown that punishment from a nurturant agent with whom the child has a good relationship is considerably more effective than punishment from a non-nurturing agent. It is perhaps worth noting that much of the classical research work on punishment is based on the notion that punishment arouses anxiety which generalizes to other situations when the punishing agent is not present, thus achieving widespread inhibition of undesired behaviour. However, experience suggests that, while this may be true of the majority of children, for those identified as severely disruptive it does not appear to apply, almost by definition. And, as Parke's valuable study shows, there are complex interactions between the general trends in the ways punishment affects its subjects.

Heron (1978) notes that the effectiveness of response-cost procedures with 'emotionally disturbed' boys was demonstrated in two studies, whereby each rule infringement resulted in the loss of a preset amount of break or free time. Similar results were achieved with other populations of schoolchildren in four further studies.

From his review of the literature, Heron generates a list of 'guidelines' for the use of punishment:

1. Aversive punishment usually suppresses, but only temporarily.
2. This short-term effect can reinforce teachers into using more and more aversive punishment, with less and less effect.
3. Aversive punishment may have undesirable side-effects, e.g. escape behaviour, emotional reaction, suppression of *wanted* behaviours, developing tolerance of increasing intensity of punishment or tolerance of a particular type of punishment, etc. Just as inhibition of undesired behaviour can generalize to other children as a result of observing punishment of such behaviour in others, so can these damaging side-effects generalize.
4. Early punishment is more effective than delayed punishment. Just as positive reinforcement is more effective when the teacher has 'caught them being good', so punishment is more effective when administered directly upon their being 'bad'.
5. Remember that punishment merely suppresses undesired behaviour; it does not teach new behaviour.
6. Teachers utilizing aversive punishment should remember that they are serving as models for the rest of their pupils, who may adopt similar techniques for use on fellow-pupils or teachers.

Macmillan *et al.* (1973), in a pro-punishment review of the research literature available at the time, reiterate the point that there are no universally effective punishments. However, they suggest that teachers require techniques other than extinction (ensuring non-reinforcement) of disruptive behaviour to couple with the accepted technique of reinforcing desired behaviour. The point is made that, with disruptive children, the conditions for effective extinction of undesired behaviour can be difficult to arrange. However, Macmillan *et al.* certainly do not assume that punishment alone is effective. They do appear to assume that the conditions for *effective* punishment are easier to arrange in schools than the conditions for extinction, and this is perhaps debatable.

Concerning intensity of punishment, Macmillan *et al.* note that intense aversive punishment is only more effective than less intense punishment where the situation provides clearly discriminable alternatives for the children. Where children are confused about what they have done wrong and what they should be doing instead, more intense punishment may serve only to confuse and disturb them further. Macmillan *et al.* also note that there is some evidence that an initial fairly intense punishment is more effective than starting with a very mild aversive and gradually increasing the intensity of punishment. However, the evidence on this point is far from conclusive.

Macmillan *et al.* also address themselves to the question of consistency of punishment, a particular problem in secondary schools, where children are exposed to a large number of different teachers with different expectations and different management styles. It is noted that disruptive pupils have often received poor social training and been subject to erratic and inconsistent management at home, making the need for consistent management in the educational situation a prerequisite for even the slowest social relearning. In some cases disruptive behaviour at school may be positively approved of out of school and there is considerable evidence that the association of both reward and punishment with the same behaviour renders the behaviour much more resistant to extinction. Learning theory, of course, heavily emphasizes the systematic and consistent implementation of programmed action.

Macmillan *et al.* concur with Heron (1978) on children's satiation with, and tolerance of, much-used punishments, and on the question of variation of punishment effectiveness according to the child's relationship with the punishing agent. In conclusion, they support the use of certain types of punishment as a means of increasing the effectiveness of a positively oriented programme of social training, when used in conjunction with such. As they point out, in the normal wear and tear of classroom management, teachers must ensure that the positive outweighs the negative, and particularly guard against 'holding grudges' which prevent them from positively reinforcing 'good' behaviour as soon as it occurs after a misdemeanour.

Presland (1980), although not taking an exhortatory pro-punishment stance, concurs with the conclusion of Macmillan *et al.* (1973) and his paper particularly deals with English secondary schools. Presland, too, emphasizes that the use of punishment should be planned and systematic, rather than an *ad hoc,* routine or despairing response to disruptive behaviour. Consistency and predictability are emphasized, as is clarity about the specific undesired behaviour *and* desired alternative behaviour.

Presland suggests a system of allocating various points to a range of offences, punishment being delivered when points have accumulated to a pre-specified level. (This system operates with footballing and driving offences, of course.) In addition, presumably a variety of punishments could be 'offered', each absorbing a different number of accumulated points. The specification of the latter would, of course, need to vary from pupil to pupil. However, the establishment of a systematic punishment system of this kind in a school would still prove largely ineffective if positive reinforcement for good behaviour were not also available, and to a greater degree than punishment. Presland's paper is particularly recommended to teachers for its brevity, simplicity and clarity.

Some teachers might argue that a positive rewards system would be unwieldy, time-consuming, inappropriate and ineffective. However, there is massive research evidence as to the effectiveness of positive reinforcement, and Milburn (1980) describes the use of such a scheme in a 2000-strong split-site comprehensive school. Practical details of the operation of a merit and demerit scheme are provided, and Milburn notes that the scheme can be easily adapted to suit the needs of any school. Also relevant here is a reminder of the work of Ayllon and Roberts (1974), whose demonstration that disruptive behaviour can be reduced by reinforcing incompatible behaviour, that is, academic performance should serve to encourage us not to dwell excessively or solely on 'the problem of disruptive behaviour', but to see it in the context of the functioning of the school as a whole.

SUMMARY

Rewards systems are much more effective in producing good behaviour than punishment, which often makes little difference. Nevertheless, punishment is usually much more frequently employed in schools than rewards. What teachers intend to be punishing may not be so perceived by pupils, and increased disruption can result therefrom.

Verbal reprimands are useless if too frequent and can actually reinforce disruption. They can work if brief, specific, directive, stern and coupled with group praise for good behaviour. Quiet reprimands may be more effective than loud ones. Non-verbal displays of disapproval can be as effective as verbal reprimands.

Detention and 'lines' as usually operated make no difference to pupils' behaviour, and this is confirmed by the pupils themselves, except in Scotland. Carefully structured and systematic behavioural studies involving the loss of free time have shown much better effectiveness. These 'response-cost' procedures can apply to deprivation of other privileges, but the pupils have to have some privileges to be deprived of.

Despite the existence of massive research evidence that corporal punishment is at best ineffective and at worst damaging, there is no evidence that its use is declining other than very slowly. Such punishment is often used inconsistently, and there is evidence that the use of unofficial, physical punishment is particularly likely to result in worse behaviour. To some extent its use may serve to deter other children from offending, but there are ethical objections here, and the children themselves do not consider it particularly effective. Disruptive children are in any case likely to be the most resistant to such punishment. There is no evidence that behaviour deteriorates in schools where corporal punishment is abandoned.

On the whole, the children regard punishments involving contact with their parents as the most effective. Older pupils are generally more sceptical about the effectiveness of all punishments.

In general, punishment may sometimes suppress behaviour, but only briefly, and this can result in overuse of punishment by teachers. No one punishment is effective for all pupils. Punishment shows more effectiveness where: (1) it is immediate (especially with mild sanctions); (2) the recipient regards the punisher as 'caring', and has a good relationship with him/her (especially with immediate sanctions); (3) it is consistent, systematic and predictable; (4) the undesired behaviour is not positively reinforced elsewhere; (5) there is clear specification of undesired and desired alternative behaviour, and attempts are made to train towards the latter as well as punish the former; (6) the punishment is intense and has commenced at a fairly high level of intensity, but only where (5) also applies; and the interaction can be complex. The damaging effects of punishment can include escape behaviour, adverse emotional reaction, suppression of desired behaviours, development of tolerance of punishments of increasing intensity, satiation with oft-repeated punishments, and copying of punishing behaviour by pupils.

There is massive research evidence that reward systems result in better outcomes than punishment, and schoolchildren agree with this finding although teachers usually do not. Children regard rewards involving parents as the most effective, and also favour time off lessons and extra preferred lessons. Rewards are likely to be effective where pupils see they are earned by good behaviour, rather than distributed randomly. Early reward is more effective than delayed reward. Verbal praise from teachers can be an effective reward, but public praise tends to be reacted to adversely by some older pupils, especially boys. Non-verbal approval can be as effective as verbal praise.

Children quite favour prizes as rewards, but the evidence suggests this to be more effective with academic achievement than behaviour. However, reinforcing academic performance can result in a decrease in incompatible disruptive behaviour in some pupils.

Clear and specific behavioural requirements, consistently and systematically applied, are associated with better behaviour.

REFERENCES

Ahlstrom, W.M. and Havighurst, R.J. (1971) *400 Losers,* Jossey-Bass, San Francisco

Ayllon, T.A. and Roberts, M.D. (1974) Eliminating discipline problems by strengthening academic performance, *Journal of Applied Behavioural Analysis,* Vol. 7, pp 71–76

Azrin, N.H. and Holz, W.C. (1966) *Punishment.* In W.K. Honig (Ed.) (1966) Operant Behaviour: areas of research and application, Appleton-Century-Crofts, New York

British Psychological Society (BPS) (1980) Report of a Working Party on Corporal Punishment in Schools, BPS, Leicester

Broden, M. *et al.* (1970) Effects of teacher attention and a token reinforcement system in a junior high school special education class, *The Exceptional Child,* Vol. 36, pp 341–349

Burns, R.B. (1978) The relative effectiveness of various incentives and deterrents as judged by pupils and teachers, *Educational Studies,* Vol. 4, No. 3, pp 229–243

Church, R.M. (1963) The varied effects of punishment on behaviour, *Psychological Review,* Vol. 70, pp 369–402

Clarizio, H.F. (1976) *Towards Positive Classroom Discipline* (2nd edn) Wiley, New York

Clegg, A.B. (1962) *Delinquency and Discipline,* Council and Education Press

Davie, R. *et al.* (1972) *From Birth to Seven,* Longman, London

Davies, B. and Thorne, M. (1977) What pupils think, *Times Educational Supplement,* 23 December

Department of Education and Science (DES) (1978) *Truancy and Behavioural Problems in Some Urban Schools,* HMSO, London

Docking, J.W. (1980) *Control and Discipline in Schools,* Harper and Row, London

Garibaldi, A.M. (Ed.) (1979) *In-School Alternatives to Suspension: Conference Report,* Department of Health, Education and Welfare for National Institute of Education, Washington DC

Hall, R.V. *et al.* (1971) The effective use of punishment to modify behaviour in the classroom, *Educational Technology,* Vol. 2, No. 4, pp 24–26

Heron, T.E. (1978) Punishment: a review of the literature with implications for the teacher of mainstreamed children, *Journal of Special Education,* Vol. 12, No. 3, pp 243–252

Highfield, M.E. and Pinsent, A. (1972) *A Survey of Rewards and Punishments in School,* Newnes for NFER, London

ILEA (1978) *Survey of Corporal Punishment in ILEA Secondary Schools,* ILEA, London

Kazdin, A. and Klock, J. (1973) The effect of non-verbal teacher approval on student attentive behaviour, *Journal of Applied Behavioural Analysis,* Vol. 6, pp 71–78

Long, B.E. (1970) A model for elementary school behavioural science as an agent of primary prevention, *American Psychology,* Vol. 25, pp 371–374

Long, B.E. (1974) Increasing depth of self-perception in children through a course in psychology, *Counselling and Values,* Vol. 18, No. 2, pp 117–22

Lovitt, T.C. (1973) Self-management projects with children with behaviour disabilities, *Journal of Learning Disabilities,* Vol. 6, pp 138–50

McAllister, L.W. *et al.* (1969) The application of operant conditioning techniques in a secondary school classroom, *Journal of Applied Behavioural Analysis,* Vol. 2, No. 4, pp 277–285

McCullough, J.P. (1972) An investigation of the effects of model group size upon response facilitation in the high school classroom, *Behaviour Therapy,* Vol. 3, pp 561–566

Macmillan, D.L. *et al.* (1973) The role of punishment in the classroom, *The Exceptional Child,* Vol. 40, pp 85–96

Madsen, C.H. *et al.* (1968) *An analysis of the reinforcing function of 'sit down' commands.* In R.K. Parke (Ed.) (1968) Readings in Educational Psychology, Allyn and Bacon, Boston

Manchester Education Committee (1974) Social Education Project. Unpublished Paper

Maughan, B. and Ouston, J. (1979) Fifteen thousand hours: findings and implications, *Trends,* Vol. 4, pp 18–24

Mayer, G.R. *et al.* (1968) The use of punishment in modifying student behaviour, *Journal of Special Education,* Vol. 2, pp 323–328

Milburn, C.W. (1980) *A positive rewards system.* In G. Upton and A. Gobell (Eds) (1980) Behaviour Problems in the Comprehensive School, Faculty of Education, University College, Cardiff

Munro, N. (1981) Belt ban has not led to worse classroom behaviour, *Times Educational Supplement,* 9 October

Musgrave, P.W. (1977) Corporal punishment in some English elementary schools: 1900–1939, *Research in Education,* Vol. 17, pp 1–11

O'Hagan, F.J. and Edmunds, G. (1983) Pupils' attitudes towards teachers' strategies for controlling disruptive behaviour, *British Journal of Educational Psychology*

Ojemann, R.H. (1967) Incorporating psychological concepts in the school curriculum, *Journal of School Psychology,* Vol. 5, pp 195–204

O'Leary, K.D. *et al.* (1970) The effects of loud and soft reprimands on the behaviour of disruptive students, *Exceptional Children,* Vol. 36, pp 145–155

Parke, R.D. (1969) Effectiveness of punishment as an interaction of intensity timing, agent nurturance, and cognitive structuring, *Child Development,* Vol. 40, No. 1, pp 213–235

Presland, J.L. (1980) *Behavioural modification and secondary schools.* In G. Upton and A. Gobell (Eds) (1980) Behaviour Problems in the Comprehensive School, Faculty of Education, University College, Cardiff

Rendell, B. (1980) *The Individual Studies Department, Whitecross School, Lydney, Glos.* In G. Upton and A. Gobell (Eds) (1980) Behaviour Problems in the Comprehensive School, Faculty of Education, University College, Cardiff

Reynolds, D. and Murgatroyd, D.S. (1977) *The sociology of schooling and the absent pupil: the school as a factor in the generation of truancy.* In H.C.M. Carroll (Ed.) (1977) Absenteeism in South Wales, Faculty of Education, University College, Swansea

Rotter, J.B. (1966) Generalised expectancies for internal versus external control of reinforcement, *Psychological Monographs,* Vol. 80, No. 1

Rutter, M., Maughan, B., Mortimore, P., Ouston, J. and Smith, A. (1979) *Fifteen Thousand Hours: secondary schools and their effects on children,* Open Books, London

Sallows, J.O. (1972) Responsiveness of deviant and normal children to naturally occurring consequences, *Dissertation Abstracts International,* 6092–B, p. 266

Society of Teachers Opposed to Physical Punishment (STOPP) (1979) *Reading List,* STOPP, Croydon

Solomon, R.L. (1964) Punishment, *American Psychology,* Vol. 19, pp 239–253

Sprinthall, N.A. (1974) A cognitive developmental curriculum – the adolescent as psychologist, *Counselling and Values,* Vol. 18, No. 2, pp 94–101

Thomas, D.R. *et al.* (1968) Production and elimination of disruptive classroom behaviour by systematically varying teachers' behaviour, *Journal of Applied Behavioural Analysis,* Vol. 1, pp 33–45

Walters, R.H. *et al.* (1965) Timing and punishment and observation of consequences to others as determinants of response inhibition, *Journal of Experimental Child Psychology,* Vol. 2, pp 10–30

Webb, A.B. and Cormier, W.H. (1972) Improving classroom behaviour and achievement, *Journal of Experimental Education,* Vol. 41, pp 92–96

Wright, D. (1973) *The punishment of children.* In B. Turner (Ed.) (1973) Discipline in Schools, Ward Lock, London

TOPICS FOR DISCUSSION

1. 'The overall picture for rewards provided a sharp contrast with the results on punishment.' Discuss.
2. 'The underlying problems may derive from or be influenced by the regime and relationships in schools, and many children may simply be reacting to these' (Warnock, 1978). Discuss.
3. Discuss the proposition that disruptive behaviour may not result so much from what is taught, but from the way it is taught.

SUGGESTIONS FOR FURTHER READING

1. J.L. Presland (1981) Modifying behaviour long-term and sideways. *Journal of the Association of Educational Psychologists,* Vol. 5, No. 6, pp 27–30. This is a useful paper about the long-term and wider effects of using behaviour modification techniques in changing unwanted classroom behaviour. Although the changes obtained by behaviour modification often appear specific to the circumstances, there is evidence of what can be termed *generalization,* that is to say, changes that spread to different classrooms, different teachers, different times of the day and different behaviour. The evidence that *generalization* can occur offers the possibility that we can do something that allows the discontinuation of the full rigour of a behaviour modification programme. The author sets out suggestions in terms of things that teachers can do by way of maintaining the beneficial effects of changed behaviour and extending such change to other areas of classroom activities.

2. F.E. Merrett (1981) Studies in behaviour modification in British educational settings, *Educational Psychology,* Vol. 1, No. 1, pp 13–38. This useful review of British studies shows that, at the time of writing, more studies were reported from junior schools than from secondary, with roughly equal numbers being carried out in 'ordinary' and special school settings. All of the experimental and case studies reported took place in the natural environment rather than the laboratory.

    Overall, the review concludes that:

    (i)   the efficacy of the behavioural approach is demonstrated;
    (ii)   the more teachers know about behavioural methods, the more favourably inclined they are to their use in classrooms;
    (iii)   there is a need for more research into the usefulness of behavioural methods in 'ordinary' schools;
    (iv)   more efforts are needed to discover the best ways of teaching both parents and teachers about behavioural methods and techniques of monitoring their effects.

    The review is particularly interesting because of the many brief cameos of behavioural modification programmes in classrooms and child guidance clinics.

3. D. Olweus (1980) Familial and temperamental determinants of aggressive behaviour in adolescent boys: a causal analysis, *Developmental Psychology,* Vol. 16, No. 6, pp 644–660. This somewhat technical paper identifies factors in the personalities and the home backgrounds of two representative groups of 13-year-old and 16-year-old boys that relate to their habitual levels of aggressive behaviour as rated by their peers. Four factors were found to contribute in an additive way to the development of an aggressive reaction pattern. They were: (1) *mother's negativism,* (2) *mother's permissiveness for aggression,* (3) *father's use of power-assertive methods,* and (4) *boy's temperament.* Of the four associated factors, the first two were found to have the greatest causal impact; that is to say, according to the degree to which the mother's basic attitude to the boy during the first four or five years of life was characterized as hostile, rejecting, cold and indifferent, and the degree to which the mother was lax and permissive of the child's aggressive behaviour during those early years.

INTEGRATION IN PRACTICE

INTRODUCTION

The last section of the sourcebook contains four readings which provide accounts of various ways in which integration programmes have been initiated. All of the readings deal, in a very practical way, with the issues which directly affect the working life of the teacher coping with the numerous problems involved. Reading 19 suggests that every teacher's requirements for support will differ, depending upon the nature of the pupils in the group and the teacher's own training and experience. The article reviews support mechanisms which many mainstream staff have found helpful, particularly those concerned with the encouraging of liaison and sharing of ideas and expertise. The suggested further readings have been chosen for their 'practical' consideration of many of the ideas raised in the main reading.

Reading 20 is an account of the 'initiatives' taken by a group of headteachers of special and ordinary schools in Oxfordshire between 1971 and 1981 who sought ways to 'normalize' the educational experience of children who were streamed out into special education. In this paper, Jones identifies and discusses a number of markers which illustrate developing principle and practice. He considers three approaches: first, the 'unit' strategy, where children are located in 'units' on the campus of ordinary schools but where their educational experience will not be very different from that which obtains when they are in special schools. This approach also goes by the name of the 'limpet' model, for children are attached as a group to a school, like a limpet to a ship, in the hope 'that some of the waves of normality will wash over them'. The second strategy of persuading ordinary schools to mainstream children with handicaps the author refers to as 'stretching' – since in the present climate of financial constraints it is hoped that such schools 'will have something to stretch'. The last approach is that of starting with the ordinary school and looking at the way the school, and everything it embraces, is managed. The author discusses in detail a mode of management advocated to overcome some of the difficulties involved in integration – the 'resources' model – and illustrates this approach with reference to a number of schools in Oxfordshire. The suggestions for further reading include a case study directly related to Reading 20 and a report by Lowden of a 'units' approach to integration.

Reading 21 is a very useful 'offshoot' of the research project which resulted in *Record Keeping in Primary Schools* (1981). Clift and his colleagues found that many teachers in ordinary schools were concerned in obtaining relevant and reliable information about those pupils in their classes who displayed disabilities of various kinds. The article considers the types of information desired, the use of anecdotal records, and explores the problem of the insensitivity of customary methods of assessment in relation to the often inherently slow progress of handicapped children. The author offers particularly relevant advice on the use of anecdotal records, observations, inventories and rating scales. The suggested readings 'back up' Clift's suggestions by reporting on various forms of arrangements which schools make for monitoring children's progress. Hegarty and Pocklington with Lucas deal comprehensively with formal and informal means of gathering information and recording it, and with constructing records as well as other means of monitoring the progress of handicapped pupils.

The last reading in this section, Reading 22, examines the curriculum on offer to pupils with special needs in ordinary schools. Hegarty and Pocklington with Lucas find considerable diversity in the offerings. The diversities are illustrated with concrete examples and the authors outline a model of curriculum provision. The article also discusses the principles by which the curriculum is determined in integration programmes and details the various ways in which children are assigned to programmes of work. This comprehensive account of various arrangements and practices is supported by readings which discuss the 'objectives approach', a strategy which has tended to gain ground in recent years in the planning of programmes for the handicapped. Because this is a very controversial approach and not without its critics, we have included in the reading the paper by Swann criticizing the way the conception of the curriculum as teacher plans, and the tendency to specialization are combined in the current emphasis afforded to the use of 'behavioural objectives' as a basis for the special curriculum. Booth takes a broader perspective suggesting that progress towards integration depends, in part, on counteracting the forces and arguments which promote segregation.

Reading 19
SUPPORTING THE MAINSTREAM TEACHER
L. Clunies-Ross

Two major outcomes of the 1981 Education Act are the increase in educational experiences provided for children and young people with special educational needs in ordinary schools and the new challenges presented to those who teach them in integrated settings. In this regard, aspects of classroom organization and a variety of teaching strategies have been explored in an earlier article; here, consideration is given to the teacher's need for support, advice and assistance. At present, the majority of staff in mainstream schools have received no initial or in-service training for teaching pupils with special needs and many take on their new role with considerable trepidation.

Support for the teacher can derive from a variety of sources. Additional classroom helpers, back-up teaching, specialist equipment and resource materials are readily identifiable; less tangible but no less valuable, however, is the support provided by information gained from specialist or peripatetic staff, from teaching colleagues and from in-service training. The importance of the latter, the gathering and exchange of information from other educationists, requires emphasis as there is still a tendency to assume that integration will take place provided the right 'mix' of resources, staffing and children is achieved.

This is not so. There is a world of difference between merely locating a child with special needs in a school and educating him there together with his peers. Many ordinary teachers teaching children with special needs in integrated settings have found that it is of immense value to have that extra support and confidence which come from a knowledge of the educational implications of a child's special needs, an understanding of individual specific medical requirements, together with information about how to acquire – and how and when to use – particular resources and items of equipment.

CLASSROOM HELPERS

Teachers can gain support from adults as well as from other pupils. Adult helpers typically include other teachers, classroom ancillaries and welfare

L. Clunies-Ross (1984) Supporting the mainstream teacher, *Special Education : Forward Trends*, Vol. 11, No. 3, pp 9–11

assistants, while help from classmates and, in a few schools, sixth-form volunteers, can also be organized.

Several points arise regarding the presence of a second adult in the classroom. First, many teachers are unused to having a second adult in the room and can take some time to adjust to this new situation. (This is particularly applicable in secondary schools.) Secondly, it is essential to establish a clear role definition so that each individual has a correct understanding of his or her own role and that of the other adult. Thirdly, personality factors should never be overlooked; two people who work together so closely must be able to 'get on' with one another, and teachers stressed the importance of being able to establish rapport with support staff who joined their class group.

Examples which worked well involved a teacher joining the class to help one or more pupils with special needs and, if time allowed, to assist others in the group who wanted help. Without exception the class or subject teacher was 'in charge' of the classroom and the second teacher played a responsive rather than a leading role. It was found helpful if the two staff had been able to meet before the lesson to discuss content and to identify possible problem areas but, even where time did not permit this, the assistance given by the support teacher allowed the class or subject teacher to continue with the planned lesson without major deviations or unscheduled pauses. Where the support teacher was a specialist, there was the added bonus of an element of in-service training, as the teacher could see how the specialist approached a particular topic, concept or problem area with a given pupil.

In one secondary school, specialist teachers of the deaf joined mainstream lessons. They ensured that hearing-impaired pupils had understood the set tasks and, particularly in the initial stages of integration, assisted with a few small problems of communication which arose between pupils and teacher as they became used to the new situation and to each other. Most importantly, however, they enabled the class-teacher to continue with the planned lesson while at the same time allowing hearing-impaired pupils to take a full part. For example, when pupils read aloud round the class, the support teacher pointed to the words in the text so that hearing-impaired pupils did not lose their place. Support staff checked that homework was properly understood and also carried out back-up work with pupils after the lesson.

In one junior school, where several visually impaired pupils were on roll, a team-teaching approach was adopted, with one specialist staff member appointed to each team. In this way, special provision for blind and for partially sighted pupils was built in at the start of each topic, ensuring their full participation in class activities. This scheme also gave class-teachers valuable in-service training; over time, their own awareness of pupils' individual needs grew and their knowledge of how to prepare materials for visually impaired pupils increased, and also their confidence in teaching pupils with differing visual handicaps.

Ancillary helpers, sometimes known as welfare assistants, provided valuable aid to teachers in many schools and constituted a major staffing resource. Although LEA and school policy regarding their appointment varied considerably, they could provide a level of classroom support which effectively freed teaching staff to concentrate on teaching; for example, ancillaries helped pupils with mobility problems move around the school, they carried equipment, collected resources and acted as 'scribes'. In some schools, ancillary helpers held qualifications such as NNEB or SEN but, in all, personality factors were perceived to be vitally important – together with sensitivity and adaptability. Ancillaries were expected to observe pupils' needs and meet them within the framework of the teacher's lesson and without actually doing the work for the pupil with special needs. Some pupils, particularly those with more severe physical handicaps, were allocated their own personal ancillary helper. At the start of integration, the ancillary would remain with the pupil throughout each lesson, giving support and encouragement and noting the pupil's responses. Subsequently, after discussion with the class or subject teacher, the ancillary might leave the pupil for periods of time – in order to encourage independence and interaction with the peer group.

Teachers favoured the employment of ancillary helpers for pupils with special needs and would, in general, like to see more of them in classrooms where such pupils are taught, particularly in lessons with a practical element such as physical education, science, cookery and craft. The only reservation came from one or two staff who felt unsure just when and how they should check up on the progress of a pupil who worked closely with an ancillary. The answer seemed to lie in establishing close cooperation between ancillary and class-teacher.

Some assistance of a voluntary nature was provided in certain schools by 'buddies' or 'peer tutors' or by older, sixth-form students. Help given centred on the setting up of equipment such as table lights, typewriters and other resources, and in interpreting and 'filling out' lesson content in terms of notes and explanation. While pupil helpers obviously reduced demands on teacher time, they also promoted social and academic integration as the pupil was drawn into the activities of the class group. In some primary schools, a 'rota' of helpers was organized; in others, individual friendships grew up within which some of a pupil's practical needs were met. (Some reservations occurred in secondary schools, where staff were concerned that pupils should not fall behind in their work as a result of helping a friend with special needs.) Sixth-form students helped hearing-impaired pupils with note taking in subjects with a high written content, where a one-to-one situation was helpful for discussion and clarification.

SUPPORT OUTSIDE THE CLASSROOM

Occasionally, pupils were given help outside the classroom, a mechanism which provided a less direct kind of support for the teacher but which was nevertheless recognized as helpful.

The main aim of back-up teaching was to provide pupils with a sufficient level of competence in basic skills to enable them to take a full part in mainstream lessons. Additionally, it was found necessary to give some pupils subject-specific tuition such as reinforcement of new concepts or special vocabulary. This kind of support may well operate best from a unit or resource base, as pupils' individual needs are so varied. For some pupils, for example, a need for additional help arose largely from the use of a specific resource or teaching mode; for others more regular back-up was needed to sustain progress in the mainstream.

Pre-lesson teaching worked best where subject and support staff liaised closely and decided on the concepts and vocabulary which were to be introduced to the pupil before the mainstream lesson. In one school, details of subject work plans were given to the teacher in charge of a unit for hearing-impaired pupils, together with copies of the mainstream texts. The teacher identified new words and key concepts and introduced them to hearing-impaired pupils before they were first presented to the whole mainstream group. Although expensive in terms of teacher time, it was found that this did much to increase pupils' confidence and participation in mainstream lessons, and effectively reduced their immediate demands on the teacher for individual attention and explanation.

In another school, a weekly meeting arranged between all the subject and specialist staff who taught maths to a blind pupil gave time for work to be prepared in Braille, for tactile aids to be located and for potential problem areas to be identified. This timetabled meeting was organized in response to the maths teacher's request for additional support in teaching a blind pupil. (Ancillary in-class support was also provided.)

Alternative tuition during lesson time sometimes took the form of teaching support provided elsewhere in the school, when a pupil left the class for a while, for example in order to type or to dictate answers in a test situation, or to use the CCTV or other specialist equipment, returning as soon as the task was complete. This support requires that the teacher and pupil have an understanding of each other's needs and that the support staff liaise closely with the mainstream teacher who is to be involved.

Back-up teaching after a lesson was the most usual kind of extra-classroom support provided for pupils with special needs, relying for its success on cooperation between subject and support teachers as regards content, resources and subject-specific vocabulary. The usual pattern was for the support teacher to work closely with individual pupils, discussing the mainstream lesson, ascertaining what had been covered, reinforcing concepts, revising vocabulary and checking that the content had been fully and correctly understood. For example, in one secondary school most back-up lessons were timetabled against French as only rarely did hearing-impaired pupils take a second language. Mainstream work was brought to the partially hearing unit, where the specialist teacher checked over what had been done in class each day and focused attention on homework tasks, ensuring that these were properly understood and that the pupil was equipped to carry them out. Another school, in which pupils with specific learning difficulties were catered for, used material from class lessons in a specialist unit in order to give pupils practice in writing and spelling problem words.

In a small number of schools the effort was made to provide support before *and* after lessons in an integrated way. An example comes from a school where a deaf fifth-year pupil previewed films and filmstrips which were shown in lead lessons. The humanities department worked in teams, introducing each new topic with an audio-visual presentation to several classes at once, a situation in which it was not always possible to check what the deaf pupil had understood. Follow-up work was done by the specialist teacher of the deaf who attended all lead lessons. This example highlights the importance of close consultation between specialist and mainstream staff at every stage of an integration programme: from the planning stage when content, materials and methodologies are first discussed, through the teaching stage when special resources or support mechanisms are often required, and on to the review and evaluation stage when assessments of pupils' achievements are made. The subject teacher and the specialist teacher have much to learn from one another, and by working together they can tailor a learning programme to the developing and changing needs of the pupil.

SPECIALIST EQUIPMENT

Aids which individual pupils use to help their learning, communication skills or their mobility around the school are too numerous to list here, but any items of equipment which enable them to participate more easily in mainstream education support both pupil and teacher. In this specialist area, teachers welcomed advice from the peripatetic and advisory services concerning, for example, the availability and uses of bookstands, low vision aids, radio microphones, slant boards, non-slip plastics and so on. Information about technical and electronic equipment also provided support. For example, teachers appreciated that, by using an overhead projector and facing the class, lip-reading was helped; they found it useful to pass OHP transparencies on to pupils with visual impairment or with learning difficulties for more detailed study. Computers have enabled teachers to run individual learning programmes for certain pupils, while others have benefited from using equipment such as tape-recorders, video loops or the enlarging facility of a CCTV.

DESIGNATED TEACHER

The appointment of a member of staff who acted as a source of information about pupils with special needs, who could liaise with outside agencies, and who also took charge of the additional paperwork and could organize and/or provide school-based in-service training was welcomed by teachers as a source of support of paramount importance.

The difference such an appointment can make is exemplified by one middle school which had on roll a number of pupils with a range of physical and sensory handicaps. Mixed-ability classes typically comprised some 35 pupils and the sole source of expertise came via the peripatetic teaching service, which provided individual tuition on a withdrawal basis for a number of pupils each week. Unfortunately, time did not permit class-teachers to meet with peripatetic staff and teachers felt that a potentially valuable source of information and expertise was not being fully utilized. They wished to know more about the pupils' handicaps, about ways and means of meeting special needs in the classroom and how best to obtain items of equipment to aid their teaching.

The appointment of a teacher who had responsibility for pupils with special needs did much to resolve these problems. This teacher met with peripatetic staff and relayed information on appropriate teaching strategies and resources to class-teachers and gave classroom assistance and advice on follow-up teaching.

The role of a teacher with designated responsibility for pupils with special needs is of necessity multifaceted and emphasis will vary from school to school depending upon pupils' needs and teachers' requirements and requests. The following examples illustrate some of the ways in which designated teachers supported mainstream staff.

In one secondary school, the teacher in charge of a resource room for pupils with visual handicap offered classroom support and advice to mainstream staff, assisted with the production of tactile teaching aids, organized case conferences, supervised the acquisition of Braille texts and assisted with the overwriting of pupils' Braille work so that ordinary teachers could then mark it. Teachers appreciated the opportunity for consultation and in-service training which arose as a result of classroom support being given by this specially trained member of staff, and derived benefit from the regular case conferences at which written comments from all mainstream staff who taught a particular pupil provided a basis for discussion.

In other schools, the designated teacher met with mainstream staff on a weekly or less frequent basis, in order to discuss lesson plans and content, so that certain concepts and vocabulary could be presented to pupils before they were introduced to the class as a whole. The designated teacher could also prepare specific teaching and learning materials for the class-teacher to use, such as enlarged texts, tapes and tactile aids. In some secondary schools this teacher reviewed the wording of internal examinations, revising the carrier language as necessary, so that all pupils could sit the same paper.

In some schools, in addition to giving in-class help, the designated teacher offered extra support to mainstream staff by withdrawing one or two pupils for individual tuition in a small group or unit setting. For this to take place, close cooperation was necessary but such schemes had the effect of utilizing the skills of both specialist and subject teachers and promoted liaison and cooperation.

The giving of information about pupils with special needs to class and subject teachers was another important supportive function carried out by designated teachers. The acquisition of some information about a pupil's medical condition and the way in which this was likely to affect educational potential or progress gave class-teachers more confidence in devising appropriate programmes and planning lessons. Similarly, an understanding of the educational implications of particular kinds of special needs was found helpful: to realize the fatigue engendered by lengthy periods of lip-reading, to appreciate the time some pupils required to complete apparently straightforward tasks and to understand the need for periods of rest, for example, all helped teachers to cater in a more realistic way for pupils with a variety of special needs.

Such information could be given personally to each teacher or in part of a staff meeting reserved for pupils with special needs; it could take the form of a written summary or a discussion. One helpful system involved the teacher in charge drawing up brief notes on each of the hearing-impaired pupils in the school, comprising suggestions on the best seating position, level of lip-reading skill and the degree of hearing loss. Displayed beside a photograph of each pupil, these staffroom notes provided a ready reference for any member of staff who taught the pupil and could be used as a basis for further discussion.

IN-SERVICE TRAINING

Very few mainstream staff were specially trained to teach pupils with special needs and many were anxious to widen their skills in order to approach their new role with greater confidence and understanding. Short, school-based in-service courses were perceived as offering much in the way of support, as these could be tailored to specific needs.

For example, in one school, specialist staff from a unit for hearing-impaired pupils ran a 12-week course for all teachers new to the school. Teaching techniques and aspects of classroom management were covered, and information on different kinds of hearing loss provided. Reference booklets on hearing impairment were available from the unit for all mainstream teachers. A primary school organized and planned a series of meetings on a range of special needs over two terms before the first special pupils were enrolled. This course, included lectures, discussions and visits to special schools, and teachers found it a most helpful introduction to teaching pupils with special educational needs.

The benefits that accrue from this kind of cooperative enterprise are well illustrated by a small primary school where two specialist teachers of the deaf were appointed to the staff one term before the first pupils arrived. During this period they worked as ordinary teachers, at the same time building up resources and providing in-service training for all staff in preparation for the arrival of the hearing-impaired pupils. Certainly the ethos of the open-plan school plus the integrated day had resulted in teachers being particularly flexible and ready to accept a new challenge, but the way in which the preparations were made gave the programme an excellent start. Both specialist staff continued to teach in mainstream mixed-ability groups, where they felt it was helpful to teachers to see how a teacher of the deaf talked to hearing-impaired pupils and in particular how vocabulary could be explained – techniques best learnt by example.

CONCLUSION

Every teacher's requirements for support will differ, depending upon the nature of the pupils in the group and the teacher's own training and experience. In this brief review of support mechanisms which many mainstream staff have found helpful, key themes would appear to be the encouraging of liaison and the sharing of ideas and expertise. In this way pupils' educational opportunities can be maximized with the combined support and cooperation of adults and peers.

TOPICS FOR DISCUSSION

1. Discuss some of the major problems which might ensue from the assumption that 'integration will take place provided the right "mix" of resources, staffing and children is achieved'.
2. Discuss the role of ancillary helpers (welfare assistants) in supporting the mainstream teacher.
3. What advantages might result for teachers and schools from the appointment of a designated teacher for pupils with special needs?

SUGGESTIONS FOR FURTHER READING

1. A. Hodgson, L. Clunies-Ross and S. Hegarty (1984) *Learning Together: teaching pupils with special educational needs in the ordinary school,* NFER–Nelson. In chapter 7, 'Teachers, Ancillaries and Liaison', the authors suggest that coping effectively with special needs entails changing the roles and deployment of staff. They discuss the implications of such changes with respect to designated teachers and ancillary staff and concentrate on the problems of liaison when many staff have dealings with individual pupils.
2. S. Pollock, (1982) *Blueprint for increasing integration in an infant school.* In T. Booth and J. Statham (Eds) (1982) The Nature of Special Education, Open University Set Book, Croom Helm–Open University Press, London and Milton Keynes. The author assesses the work done in her school with 'maladjusted' and 'non-communicating' children, and the improvements that might be made in incorporating such pupils into the general life of the school.
3. S. Hegarty and K. Pocklington with D. Lucas (1981) *Educating Pupils with Special Needs in the Ordinary Schools* NFER-Nelson, Windsor. In chapter 6, 'Specialist Teachers and Ancillaries in Integration', working from the premiss that specialist teachers and ancillary staff are the major resources for an integration programme, the authors examine the various roles of staff in integration schemes.

Reading 20
AN INTEGRATIVE APPROACH TO SPECIAL
EDUCATIONAL NEEDS
N.J. Jones

The term integration – derived from the Latin word *integrare,* meaning to make whole – refers to the process of enabling children with special educational needs to maximize their opportunities, potential and personal fulfilment, in their families, school and the wider community. Set within the principle of 'normalization' (Nirje, 1969) which recently gave rise to a United Nations Bill of Rights for the Handicapped, it is part of the change process in society aimed at 'deinstitutionalizing' handicapped persons back into normal society, a process that in America over the past decade has become known as 'mainstreaming' (Meisgeier, 1976). In educational terms it is not just the opportunity (in Warnock terminology) to be locationally, socially and functionally integrated, all of which is open to very wide interpretation (Hegarty and Pocklington with Lucas, 1981, 1982), but a personal right to have as open access to a normal school curriculum as would any other school-age child.

What is described below may be referred to as initiatives, mainly on the part of Oxfordshire heads of special and ordinary schools, who between 1971 and 1981 sought ways to 'normalize' the educational experience of children who under the present system are streamed out into special education. It was a period that, first, saw the 'recovery' of some 34,000 severly intellectually handicapped children back into education from Health Authorities through the 1970 Education (Handicapped Children) Act; secondly, the reorganization of local government boundaries bringing together Oxford City, the old County, and part of North Berkshire, to form the new administrative County of Oxfordshire; thirdly, the setting up and report of the Committee of Enquiry into the Education of Handicapped Children and Young People (DES, 1978); and finally, the anticipated enactment of provisions related to special education in the 1981 Education Act.

Those working in the field of education are well aware that from myriad discussions, conferences and individual initiatives in education it is not always possible to decide from whom, and at what point in an innovation, a particular idea has sprung, particularly when for its implementation there

N.J. Jones (1983) An integrative approach to special educational needs, *Forum,* Vol. 25, No. 2, pp 36–39

are so many levels of decision making. The purpose of this paper is not to pin-point individual endeavour, or indeed that of a particular school or department of the LEA, but to identify some markers which illustrate developing principle and practice. Very many schools practice integration (Tuckwell, 1982), sometimes just for an individual child; those mentioned below are a selection to illustrate where an integration initiative can be seen in practice, albeit in some approximate form to the ideal. First, some general principles and approaches.

The term integration, and the current debate about it, focuses sharply on those children who are now in special schools but for whom the intention is to return them at least minimally to be integrated on the campus of ordinary schools. Where this is being tried, the strategy in principle is of two kinds: first, that children will be located in 'units' on the campus of ordinary schools but their educational experience will not be so far from that which obtains when they are in special schools (the 'unit' model is discussed more fully below). This has been referred to as the limpet model of integration whereby children are attached as a group to a school, like a limpet to a ship, in the hope that some of the waves of normality will wash over them (Jones, 1983). Secure and cosseted in their special educational life-belts, they float around ordinary schools as observers to the mainstream scene. The second strategy is to persuade ordinary schools to take into mainstream classes a number of handicapped children, sometimes on a promise of extra resourcing. This is known as 'stretching' the system in the hope that schools, in these days of economic siege, will have something to stretch.

There is a third approach: that of starting with the ordinary school and looking at the way the school, and everything that it embraces, is managed. It has to be remembered that ordinary schools are presently structured on the assumption that children with extremes of need, whatever these are, will receive their education elsewhere, in special schools or private schools. To ask ordinary schools to extend their jurisdiction, or simply make the principle of comprehensiveness a reality, is to do more than make a humanitarian appeal: the schools themselves, teacher skills, classroom management, attitudes toward disability, pupil–teacher ratios, styles of curriculum, types of additional support and so forth will need to change. John Sayer, Principal of Banbury School, drew attention to this revolution in concept, yet to be realized in practice, when he wrote that 'the Warnock Report has quietly unleashed a revolution which is of much greater consequence to the educational process than all the structural transmogrifications which over the past two decades we have described as comprehensive education' (1981).

The aim in Oxfordshire has been to move away from the polarization of handicap – those who are handicapped and those who are not. All children, at some stage in their educational development, have potentially a claim to something extra and individual. Warnock has suggested that this might apply to as many as 20 per cent of children in ordinary schools. But few children are handicapped in the same degree of severity, in all areas of growth and development, in all circumstances of everyday living. How then can we approximate the management of these educational needs so that we respond to what has been called 'the continuum of need' from minimal to severe, and meet needs at the points where the handicap constitutes an educational problem? How can we avoid educating such children in a totally handicapped environment? The old system of classifying children according to the Department of Education and Science list of recognized disorders did precisely this. The new 1981 Education Act retains the segregated notion, previously special and ordinary, but now 'statemented' and 'non-statemented': a mode of management advocated to overcome some of these difficulties is known as the 'resources' model.

THE 'RESOURCES' MODEL

The 'Resources' model, developed mainly in the United States in the early 1970s, embraces the idea of different 'levels of intervention' in a child's education while it attends ordinary school. There are some lessons where the child with a handicap requires no additional assistance; others where the child could remain in the ordinary class providing some extra support, sometimes a teaching aid, classroom ancillary, or welfare assistant, or even advice for the ordinary class-teacher, is made available. A third level is where the child needs to be withdrawn to a 'resource' room, individually or to join a small group, for additional specialized training, to cover a subject not possible to take in the larger mainstream class, or to study some alternative lesson, all of which goes to sustain both an individualized programme of work and *in toto* a viable education for the child. (Deno, 1970).

A 'resources' approach begins with ordinary classroom teachers, plus the normal tutor in secondary schools, and extends out according to individual needs. It is an approach being adopted in Oxfordshire in both primary and secondary schools where 'resource' rooms are coming into being staffed by school-based special needs teachers. It is a model that is superceding the 'unit' style of management and is replacing, therefore, procedures where children are classified into groups, often retained for the majority of their education in such groupings, and where the ethos of their educational experience can so easily become handicapping.

The move towards a 'normalized' system of care does not stop with the children and mainstream schools. If the 'institution' of special education is to change in any way, so that fewer and fewer children are removed from a normal school environment, there must be changes wherever the concept of segregated and separate provision operates. A reorganization of the County Administrative staff in Oxfordshire has taken a big step towards this: all the area education officers, as part of their normal duties, now also cover those aspects of special administration which previously had been covered by an area education officer with special responsibilities for special education. Where a special administrator was possibily required to administrate a system that was separate, and different from ordinary schooling in its principles of policy and practice, for children attending special schools, this makes little sense once a local authority turns its attention to integrating ordinary children with special needs in ordinary schools. The issues that then arise, for administrators, are not 'special' *per se*, but all those factors that currently preoccupy those responsible for the management of ordinary schools.

In the Banbury Special Needs Project, described briefly below, one group of schools, that of Banbury School itself and its primary schools, have opted for a policy of 'normalizing' the work of all their support personnel. Falling rolls have partly created the accommodation to achieve this. The specialist teachers work from the ordinary school, some to a specific school, others to the group of schools in the sector group, some across the primary-secondary phase; and the school counsellor and educational psychologist also find their accommodation and rations within the ordinary school, in this case, the comprehensive school. There is, therefore, a close daily link between all members of the support services, heads, and their staff.

SPECIAL SCHOOL INITIATIVES

The period following the publication of the Warnock Report was a time of consternation for special school heads with rumour rife that special schools would soon shut down. Some Oxfordshire heads of special schools came together to look at what a 'resources' model could mean for their special schools. It was not long before innovations began to take place: these now vary in style and the degree to which an integration programme operates.

One school for maladjusted children, Northern House, unable to retain its children beyond the age of 13 years, places children in ordinary schools and provides from its own staffing a support teacher to work in the ordinary class on a basis of team teaching. A school for the severely mentally handicapped places children in primary schools with special school staff acting in a consultancy role. Another school, Bishopswood, has placed in an ordinary school its complete reception class together with teachers from the special school. A school for the physically handicapped, the Ormerod, having pioneered a scheme for the total integration of a group of physically handicapped adolescents into a comprehensive school, has extended its scheme by making links with a local primary school, and for both primary and secondary schools provides support with teachers from the special school staff.

PRIMARY SCHOOLS

Integration in Oxfordshire primary schools may be seen from two angles: the experience of the individual child and the question of overall management and resourcing. The first blends into the second the more handicapped children there are in any given school when the management tolerances of the school become increasingly tested. This does not mean, however, that for any individual child the question cannot be asked as to whether an integrated experience actually pertains: it is, however, necessary to look and see for yourself. Accounts of integration that do not embrace individual observation of what a child does all day, what he experiences, what real openings there are for learning, come nowhere near to answering the questions that underlie the integration concept as these relate to ordinary schools. It is not that heads or teachers have wrong perceptions. It is that the concept of integration is a many-coloured coat and, like all innovations in education, capable of being lightly worn; some heads genuinely believe that what they practise is integration.

The awareness of needs in children is never so far away from those who are not aware that there is more to learn. Oxfordshire has attempted to increase such awareness through its programme of Handicap Awareness Courses for teachers, lasting five consecutive days (Jones, 1981). What is in question is how far in-service training that does not take place *within* the school where the teachers work, and arise from day-to-day problems, really does more than sensitize. Teachers' willingness to integrate children into their classrooms has been shown to increase with in-service courses (Stephens and Braun, 1980), but opportunity to take part in school-based workshops on methods and techniques, to observe children in normal classroom situations, and to interact with 'resources' staff maximizes learning and the carry-over into the classrooms (Shotel *et al.,* 1972).

In a carefully monitored study of a special resources department in an Oxfordshire secondary school Elizabeth Jones found that all teachers needed assistance to (1) identify factors that were handicapping to the child (some other than the handicap itself), (2) to establish realistic goals for learning for the handicapped, and (3) to develop methods and materials to implement and evaluate educational objectives (Jones, 1980). She concluded that the in-service training for those working with handicapped children needed to relate to *all* aspects of teaching and curriculum in an ordinary school.

Where the primary school is large, and the numbers of children with special needs substantial, a primary resources 'centre' makes sense. At Queensway Primary School in Banbury a whole suite of rooms is used. Having set it up first as a 'unit' for language-delayed children and the partially hearing, the head and staff quickly moved to a more flexible way of working. The school draws pupils for their particular handicaps from a wide area and returns them when appropriate to their normal catchment schools, providing the supportive expertise and consultation. Such a school can make a response on three levels: first, to its own special need children; secondly, to the group of primaries within its sector group; and thirdly, to a group of sectors where it is inappropriate to set up highly specialized provision in each primary school. While the children from Queensway, or other primary schools, are attending the resource centre every effort is made to ensure that they also participate in ordinary lessons in the main school. This work is now being extended to other types of need in such areas as specific learning disabilities and giftedness.

COMPREHENSIVE SPECIAL NEEDS DEPARTMENTS

These began to come into being in Oxfordshire in 1969 when a 'unit' for slow-learning children opened in Cooper School, Bicester, and quickly moved to a 'resources' style of working (Garnett, 1976). Some years were to pass before the 'policy' of developing resource departments in all comprehensive schools was adopted – this was to await a Report and Discussion Document prepared as a result of the monitoring programme being carried out at the newly opened Special Resource Department at Carterton Comprehensive School (Jones and Jones, 1980). Here the physical and staffing resources comprised a suite of rooms, three special needs teachers, and two ancillary workers (Jones and Berrick, 1980). It was from the Discussion Document, and discussions held with heads in the County, that the Chief Education Officer decided to promote the Banbury

Special Needs Project. In the last two years many secondary heads have been looking at ways to develop their 'resource' departments (and in the process the old remedial classes have begun to disappear) catering for a wide range of children with special needs who can be managed in more flexible ways of working.

THE BANBURY SPECIAL NEEDS PROJECT

Integration was no new thing to some of the schools in the Banbury community. Banbury Comprehensive School had already taken into its fold a segregated department catering for the mildly mentally handicapped. These children are now part of normal tutor groups and withdrawn to 'resource' rooms for specialized teaching.

The purpose of the Banbury Project is for a group of schools, primary, secondary and further education, to examine their styles of organization and to ask what would be necessary for them to make an effective response to all children who live in Banbury and its environs irrespective of the severity or nature of their special needs. It is the 'wholeness' concept of education outlined by John Sayer, Principal of Banbury School, in his paper 'Down and up the line to integration' (1981). The rationale of the Project is that of the 'resources' model, initiated through a 'levels-of-intervention' programme, within a structure of management embracing the notion of sectors (being a comprehensive and its associated primaries) and a management executive representative of all sector heads, LEA administration, psychology services, and special advising staff.

Banbury was chosen for this Project for a number of reasons: its social mix had been well documented by Margaret Stacey (1960, 1975); the town contained a good cross-section of large and small primary and secondary schools, some urban some rural, both Catholic and non-sectarian; the special needs of its children were already well documented following a survey by the County Psychological Service immediately following the publication of the Warnock Report; research projects of this dimension had already been carried out in *The Banbury Enquiry* on mixed-ability teaching and other DES research-promoted projects; embryo special needs departments already existed in many schools; and, most important, the heads and their staff were enthusiastic about the kind of innovations being proposed.

Once the structure of consultation between schools, and with the LEA administration, had been set up, the first task was to look at existing resources in the area and to see how some County input of resources, obtained through a reduced out-County budget of boarding placements but with extra teachers for main-school work, could be best allocated. One sector, that of Banbury School, has opted as policy for maximizing the numbers of its *school-based* support staff. A second stage was to see how a better use could be made of those resources which now lie outside ordinary schools, especially the resource of specialist teachers, and to bring these within the orbit of a 'normalized' style of management. Preliminary discussions are taking place about school-based in-service training and meetings are beginning to be organized. The aim is to implement the Warnock proposals as these affect separate remedial provision, and to link salary enhancement with qualifications and experience instead of through special schools allowances.

A project like this brings to the surface a range of problems which relate to the needs of individual children: how one resolves the tensions when one style of working is changing over to another – the issue of parallel management; the changing role of expectations of heads of ordinary schools – where they develop their additional knowledge and expertise; new ways of working for support services such as psychologists; how examination-dictated curriculum currently affects the less able; LEA policy and practice – centralized or school-based; how to utilize segregated resources; parent involvement and governor responsibilities; a new style of financing with 'significant discretion at Head and Governor level'; how to attract research funds for initiatives on special education in ordinary schools when this money is tied up for studying 'special' segregated provision. These problems are not unrelated to the fact that we have 'segregated' LEA advisory services, university departments of special education, specialist HMI and a special branch of the Civil Service, in other words, a special educational pyramid that sustains segregation at ordinary school level: so where is the meeting point between all the different pyramids in education? If there is some coming together within a group of schools – from nursery through to adult education – then some progress has been made.

REFERENCES

Deno, E. (1970) Special education as development capital, *Exceptional Children,* Vol. 37, No. 3, pp 229–237

Department of Education and Science (DES) (1978) *Special Educational Needs* (Warnock Report), Cmnd 7212, HMSO, London

Garnett, J. (1976) Special children in a comprehensive school, *Special Education,* Vol. 3, No. 1

Hegarty, S. and Pocklington, K. with Lucas, D. (1981) *Educating Pupils with Special Needs in the Ordinary School,* NFER-Nelson, Windsor

Hegarty, S. and Pocklington, K. with Lucas, D. (1982) *Integration in Action,* NFER-Nelson, Windsor

Jones, E.M. (1980) The Carterton Project: a monitored account of the way a comprehensive school responded to children with special educational needs. Unpublished M.Ed. Thesis, University of Birmingham

Jones, E.M. and Berrick, S. (1980) Adopting a resources approach, *Special Education,* Vol. 7, No. 1

Jones, E.M. and Jones, N.J. (1980) Special education in Oxfordshire in the 1980s. A Discussion Document Report to the Chief Education Officer, Oxfordshire

Jones, N.J. (1981) Oxfordshire looks towards the future, *Special Education,* Vol. 8, No. 2

Jones, N.J. (1983) *The management of integration in Oxfordshire.* In T. Booth and P. Potts (Eds) (1983) Integrating Special Education, Blackwell, Oxford

Meisgeier, C. (1976) *A review of critical issues underlying mainstreaming.* In L. Mann and D.A. Sabatino (Eds) (1976) The Third Review of Special Education, JSE Press, Philadelphia

Nirje, B. (1969) *The normalisation principle and its human management implications.* In R.B. Kugel and W. Wolfensberger (Eds) (1969) Changing Patterns in Residential Services for the Mentally Retarded, President's Committee on Mental Retardation, Washington DC

Sayer, J. (1981) Down and up the line to integration, *Education,* 17 July

Shotel, J.R., Iano, R.P. and McGettigan, J.F. (1972) Teacher attitudes associated with the integration of handicapped children, *Exceptional Children,* Vol. 38, No. 9, pp 677–683

Stacey, M. (1960) *Transition and Change,* Oxford University Press, Oxford

Stacey, M. (1975) *Power, Persistence and Change,* Routledge and Kegan Paul, London

Stephens, T.M. and Braun, B.L. (1980) Measurement of regular teachers' attitudes towards handicapped children, *Exceptional Children,* Vol. 46, No. 4, pp 292–294

Tuckwell, P. (1982) *Integration in practice: a small rural school.* In T. Booth and J. Statham (Eds) (1982) The Nature of Special Education, Croom Helm–Open University Press, London and Milton Keynes

TOPICS FOR DISCUSSION

1. 'The Warnock Report has quietly unleashed a revolution which is of much greater consequence to the educational process than all the structural transmogrifications which over the past two decades we have described as comprehensive education' (Sayer, 1981). Discuss.

2. What are the essential differences in integration strategies between the 'limpet' model, the 'stretching' strategy and the third approach suggested by the author? Discuss each approach with reference to teacher skills, classroom management, attitudes towards disability, pupil-teacher ratios, styles of curriculum and types of additional support.

3. What are the advantages claimed for a 'resource' model as opposed to a 'unit' style management in catering for pupils with special educational needs?

SUGGESTIONS FOR FURTHER READING

1. C. Meisgeier, (1976) *A review of critical issues underlying mainstreaming.* In L. Mann, and D.A. Sabatino (Eds) (1976) The Third Review of Special Education, J.S.E. Press, Philadelphia, pp 245–269. This article provides an interesting comparative perspective of the problems inherent in the change process in society aimed at 'deinstitutionalizing' handicapped persons back into normal society and establishing their personal rights to have as open access to a normal school experience as would any other pupil.

2. G. Lowden, (1985) The 'units' approach to integration, *British Journal of Special Education,* Vol. 12, No. 1, March, pp 10–12. The article reports the results of a survey of Welsh units for children with learning difficulties. The author demonstrates that the way in which a school approaches the problem of integrating children with special educational needs is likely to reflect the 'philosophy' of the head and staff. Lowden found that most mainstream teachers preferred not to teach slow learners – they thought that these children should be the responsibility of the unit teachers and that, although all schools subscribed to an official policy of integration, only one in five appeared to have planned a strategy for progressively extending integration.

3. T. Booth, and C. Pym, (1982) *Some aspects of special education in Oxfordshire: innovation and change.* In T. Booth, and J. Statham (Eds) (1982) The Nature of Special Education, Croom Helm-Open University Press, London and Milton Keynes, pp 423–442. This case study (directly related to Reading 20) documents the background problems of policy and implementation underlying the attempts to develop programmes for children with special educational needs in Oxfordshire. Of particular relevance is the discussion of the resources approach and the roles of the Special Resources Department.

Reading 21
KEEPING THE RECORDS STRAIGHT
P. Clift

In the two years spent working on the *Record Keeping in the Primary Schools* project (Clift *et al.,* 1981), we met many teachers who vigorously asserted that for most children only minimal records need be kept, if any at all. Pressed, they would justify this by pointing out that the majority of their charges were neither geniuses nor fools; knaves nor angels; made about a year's progress every year; grew up with reasonable grace. Towards

P. Clift (1982) Keeping the records straight, *Special Education: Forward Trends,* Vol. 9, No. 4, pp 14–16

the end, we put the question in a rather more systematic way, asking project teachers to rank in order of importance the information potentially offered by previous teachers. At the top of their collective list, immediately following essential demographic information (name, address, particular family circumstances), they put:

1. health handicaps which may affect progress in school;
2. quality of hearing;
3. quality of sight;
4. specification of any learning difficulty;
5. results of referral to educational psychologist;
6. the nature of remedial treatment being given;
7. reading: stages reached in a named reading scheme;
8. personality factors which may affect progress in school;
9. mathematics: stage reached in a named mathematics scheme;
10. noteworthy abilities;
11. various, mainly attainment, kinds of information followed, with 'study skills' deemed least important.

TYPES OF INFORMATION DESIRED

This ranking suggests that, in conformity with the informal views expressed earlier in the project, it is information about *exceptional* children which is valued by teachers, and more particularly information about those with *disabilities*: the ones in fact for whom some form of special educational provision is implied. Post-Warnock, such provision is increasingly likely to have to be made in the child's neighbourhood school (though for most such children, this has always been so).

Casting themselves in the role of potential *recipients* of school records about handicapped children, the project teachers placed much stress on their need for relevant and reliable information. Sadly, when the roles are reversed, they often display the very reluctance to admit to difficulties posed by handicapped children and the tender-mindedness over recording poor attainment which lead to the unreliable and irrelevant records about which they often complained.

In part, the root of the problem lies in the insensitivity of customary methods of assessment in relation to the inherently slow progress of handicapped children and, in part, in teachers' anxiety over a perceived lack of objectivity in ways of assessing and recording the development of pupils' personal qualities. Class tests and examinations place them constantly at the bottom of the rank order. Standardized tests fail to reflect their generally minimal progress. Indeed many handicapped children find the whole notion of 'being tested' difficult to understand and ultimately disagreeable. What are needed are alternative ways of assessing and recording the development, cognitive and personal, of such children.

Criterion-referenced testing linked to precision teaching is one possibility *vis-à-vis* cognitive development. In practice, very few published tests of this type are available, and their production by teachers is time consuming and requires considerable skill. Such testing offers no help in the assessment of personal qualities. In this article an alternative approach which makes use of teachers' observations is described.

Teachers are constantly assessing pupils informally, making intuitive, unstructured and sometimes mistaken use of the multitude of signs, verbal and non-verbal, however minimal, by which developing skills, knowledge, understanding and attitudes are revealed. This process can be formalized to produce records about handicapped children which are reliable and relevant to the needs of next teachers.

ANECDOTAL RECORDS

The least structured of deliberate observational techniques for assessment are *anecdotal* records. When a pupil is observed to do something considered to be *significant* by the teacher, the teacher writes a paragraph describing what has occurred, including such contextual information as he feels necessary, then adds his interpretation of the incident.

This approach to the recording of the development and progress of pupils with learning disabilities was frequently seen in schools visited during the project. The emphasis was on *personal* rather than cognitive development. Regrettably, we all too rarely encountered the rich, cumulative picture of a pupil's characteristic ways of responding to schooling which anecdotal records are potentially able to provide. Like all the other skills of teaching, this too has its ground rules. Paraphrasing Gronlund (1976) these are as follows:

1. Decide in advance what behaviour to observe. Concentrate on the behaviours which could not be effectively evaluated by any other method and on looking for only a few specific kinds of behaviour at any given time. It is also important to be on the lookout for any unusual behaviour which may be particularly valuable in understanding the pupil and which could otherwise be overlooked.
2. The situation in which the behaviour occurs should also be observed and recorded so that the behaviour recorded can be correctly

interpreted by later readers as well as you. Watching the activities of all other children involved and the setting in which the behaviour takes place could throw light on the meaning of the behaviour. An aggressive action, like one child pushing another, may express boisterous fun, attention seeking, overreaction to being provoked or a tendency to extremely strong hostility.

3. Make notes about the incident as soon as possible after you have observed it, even if there is time only for a few lines during the remainder of the school day. The longer the delay in recording your observations, the more risk there is that something important will be forgotten. The writing of all the records can be completed after school.

4. Be brief and concise in discussing each incident. This will save time in writing and in reading the account later.

5. Separate the facts from the interpretation. The incident should be described objectively and accurately, avoiding subjective judgements like 'lazy' or 'hostile'. When interpretations are given, they should be clearly distinguishable from factual description.

6. Positive incidents should be recorded as well as negative ones. There is a temptation to include more of the disturbing and distracting behaviours and to neglect those which indicate that the child is learning and developing in positive ways. Make a conscious effort to record positive behaviour which may be less easy to detect, and superficially less 'newsworthy'.

7. Do not jump to conclusions about the pupil on the basis of a single incident which can sometimes be misleading. The child needs to be observed on several occasions in a variety of situations before reliable conclusions can be drawn about what is his typical behaviour.

8. Get practice in record writing before beginning to make and use anecdotal records regularly. Choosing significant incidents, observing them dispassionately and recording them objectively are difficult at first. A good way to begin is to look at the pupil's habits at a time when you are not actively involved with the class and when there is more time to watch and record significant behaviour. A colleague will be able to help by assessing the quality of the records, highlighting any deficiencies in technique.

Probably the most important advantage of records of this kind is that they provide a description of actual behaviour in a natural situation – 'actions speak louder than words' – in a way which enables the recipient to make his own judgements as opposed to merely accepting those of the writer. Their major drawback is the time they take. This probably prohibits their use with *all* the pupils in a class, in respect of *all* aspects of development. Anecdotal records are thus more appropriate to use where children with learning difficulties are integrated into 'normal' classes, and where such records would be kept only in respect of those children. Obviously even in such situations the teacher has to exercise some selectivity over what is recorded or the system becomes overwhelming.

OBSERVATION INVENTORIES

Next teachers, as the audience for the information, may regret the inherent long-windedness and lack of structure of anecdotal records and prefer the relative parsimony of observation inventories. Essentially these are *specifications* for assessment in which the source of the information is teachers' *accumulated,* retrospective observations. Figure 21.1 shows three examples taken from teacher-produced inventories found in use in schools visited during the project.

The first two examples merely require the teacher to agree or disagree with the statement, after first reflecting upon his perceptions of the pupil. The third allows for graduations of assessment within a five-point scale, though it must be supposed that in practice the extremes of 'Always' and 'Never' could hardly ever legitimately be used!

A number of observation inventories have been produced by professional researchers. Two strongly contrasting examples which we frequently found in use in schools are *Match and Mismatch* (Harlen *et al.,* 1977) and *A Children's Behavioural Questionnaire* (Rutter, 1967). The former focuses teachers' attention on observable aspects of pupil behaviour which indicate progress in mastering scientific concepts, the latter on personal/social adjustment to school.

In direct contrast with anecdotal records, observation inventories require teachers to pre-specify the particular aspects of pupil development they intend to assess and record. Reliable assessment, and its subsequent accurate interpretation by others, depends on the precision of the wording of this pre-specification. As with anecdotes, there are ground rules for this, paraphrased this time from Thorndike and Hagen (1969).

1. Each inventory item should refer to observable pupil behaviour, not to learning activities or to the teacher's intentions. A good example would be 'Can compare objects in terms of the properties of height, length, weight, density, etc. etc.'

Figure 21.1 Three examples of observation inventories

Arithmetic/Mathematics Basic Scheme: Preliminary Stage

Name	1st Year	2nd Year	3rd Year
1. Knows cardinal numbers and can count-number of objects in a set			
[2, 3, 4, 5,]			
6. Has a concept of a set and numbers of a set (classifying, sorting, matching)			
[7, 8, 9, etc.]			

Language Inventory

Name .... Date of birth ....

Speech
Articulates clearly
[...]
Can understand teacher's language structure
[...]
Delivers a simple message
[...] etc ...

What Are We Aiming For?

Name	Always	Usually	Sometimes	Seldom	Never
1. Cooperates well with teacher [2, 3,] 4. Thinks for himself [5 to 19] 19. Exercises self-control [20, 21, etc]					

2. Each item should include an *active* verb, to indicate the behaviour to be observed in respect of what is being assessed. Table 21.1, taken from Thorndike and Hagen, illustrates the dos and don'ts in this.
3. Each item should refer to only *one* unit of assessed behaviour, e.g. 'Throws a cricket ball accurately, distances up to 70 metres'. If the item contains two or more units, e.g. 'Can recognize coins, 1p, 2p, 5p, 10p, 20p, 50p', how is *partial* success to be recorded or interpreted?
4. Linked with rule 3 above, each item should be stated at an appropriate level of *generality,* otherwise the inventory will become a vastly long list of atomistic pieces of behaviour. Thus the item concerning coins might be expressed as 'Can recognize British decimal coins'. The key to applying this rule is deciding what *is* the *appropriate* level of generality: not so global as to be meaningless, like 'Can spell in English', or so narrow and specific as to transform the educational process into isolated bits and pieces such as 'Can spell *it'*, 'Can spell *and'*.

Table 21.1 The wording of observation inventories

Do not use:	Recommended for use:
Understands ...	Defines ...
Appreciates ...	Gives examples of ...
Thinks critically about ...	Compares ...
Is aware of ...	Describes ...
Feels the need for ...	Classifies ...
Is growing in ability to ...	Summarizes ...
Becomes familiar with ...	Applies in a new situation ...
Grasps the significance of ...	Solves problems in which ...
Is interested in ...	Expresses interest in ...
Feels the need for ...	States what he would do if ...

5. Each item should represent the likely outcomes of the curriculum (including the 'hidden' curriculum). Thus, if the pupil has been learning about addition, items on addition may legitimately be included; if the way in which the class has been organized is designed to encourage pupils to collaborate with one another, collaboration may legitimately be included.
6. Each item should reflect reasonable expectations of the capacities of the pupils. There is little point in cluttering observation inventories (which tend in their nature to be rather long) with items which are not realistic in relation to teaching objectives and the characteristics of the pupils being assessed.

Most of the rules are aimed at increasing the precision, hence the reliability, of observation inventories. Their *validity*, that is the degree to which they depict what they set out to depict (e.g. adjustment to school, attainment in mathematics, progress in science), lies in the choice of items: each must represent a learning intention; collectively they must adequately cover, or sample, the overall intentions or aims of what is being assessed.

RATING SCALES

It is worth noting that, although items may be expressed in terms of absolutes such as 'defines, describes, solves, states', almost invariably the concern is rather with the *extent* to which pupils are able to do these. The use of rating scales provides for this. Three- and five-point scales were typical amongst the inventories we found in use. One example was: ' "Tends to be fearful or afraid of new things or new situations." Doesn't Apply, Applies Somewhat, Certainly Applies' (Rutter, 1967).

Where teachers had been at a loss to find suitable words with which to rate pupils, they frequently had adopted the following very useful graphical alternative.

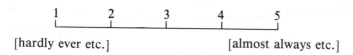

[hardly ever etc.]   [almost always etc.]

The choice of words to put at opposite poles is obviously determined by what is being assessed.

As with anecdotal records, it is best to develop observation inventories in collaboration with colleagues, seeking their aid in avoiding both ambiguity (rules 1, 2, 3) and overspecificity (rule 4).

Observation inventories lack the contextual information which characterizes anecdotal records. They more than compensate for this by their relative brevity and structure and the way in which they make explicit their originators' underlying intentions for their pupils' development. Since assessment using observation inventories does not involve the participation of the pupil, they:

1. can be used frequently and repeatedly;
2. can be used for individuals as necessary without arousing the curiosity of others;
3. do not take up time from, or directly interfere with learning activities;
4. do not disturb pupils or make them anxious.

Potentially, anecdotal records and observation inventories provide valuable means of assessing and recording the progess of pupils with learning difficulties. Both were found widely in use in primary schools at the time of the record-keeping project (1976–78). The latter were the more popular, probably because, once formulated, they are much less time consuming to implement. Regrettably, almost all of the examples of both approaches which we saw were flawed to a greater or lesser extent, in ways likely to reduce their value to later teachers. Practice at writing, collaboration over formulation, and the observance of simple rules set out here would help teachers to produce less flawed systems in the future.

A more detailed discussion of these (and other) approaches to assessment and record keeping can be found in *Measuring Learning Outcomes* (Open University, 1982), and in the record-keeping project report (Clift *et al.*, 1981).

REFERENCES

Clift, P.S., Weiner, G.G. and Wilson, E.L. (1981) *Record Keeping in Primary Schools,* Macmillan Education-Schools Council, London

Devon County Council (1981) 3–5. *A Handbook of Guidance.* County Council Education Department, Exeter, Devon

Gronlund, N. (1976) *Measurement and Evaluation in Teaching,* Macmillan, New York

Harlen, W., Darwin, A. and Murphy, M. (1977) *Match and Mismatch: Raising questions,* Oliver and Boyd, Edinburgh

Open University (1982) Course E364: Curriculum Evaluation and Assessment in Educational Institutions, Block 4: *Measuring Learning Outcomes,* Open University Press, Milton Keynes

Rutter, M. (1967) A children's behavioural questionnaire for completion by teachers: preliminary findings, *Journal of Child Psychology and Psychiatry,* Vol. 8, pp 1–11

Thorndike, R. and Hagen, E. (1969) *Measurement and Evaluation in Psychology and Education* (3rd edn), Wiley, New York

TOPICS FOR DISCUSSION

1. Teachers tend to look at record keeping from two points of view: first, their perception of the *purpose* of keeping school records and, secondly, what these records are supposed to *do*. Discuss with reference to children with special educational needs.
2. Many handicapped children 'find the whole notion of "being tested" difficult to understand and ultimately disagreeable'. What *alternative* ways might there be of assessing and recording the cognitive and personal development of such children?

3. Critically evaluate the reasons the author puts forward for his contention that anecdotal records are more appropriate to use where children with learning difficulties are integrated into 'normal' classes and where such records would be kept only in respect of these children.

SUGGESTIONS FOR FURTHER READING

1. A. Hodgson, L. Clunies-Ross and S. Hegarty (1984) *Learning Together: teaching pupils with special educational needs in the ordinary school,* NFER–Nelson, Windsor. Chapter 12, 'Monitoring Progress', is concerned with evaluating the teaching process and reports on the various arrangements which schools make for monitoring the progress of pupils with special needs. The authors discuss the problems and complexities of monitoring progress in relation to the mainstream curriculum, and the importance of having clear lines of responsibility for overseeing the progress of children with special educational needs.

2. P.S. Clift, G.G. Weiner, and E.L. Wilson, (1981) *Record Keeping in Primary Schools,* Macmillan Education–Schools Council, London. An extremely useful and comprehensive account of all aspects of record keeping and monitoring progress. Much of the material in this book is especially suitable for teachers of pupils with special educational needs. Of particular relevance to the first topic for discussion is chapter 3, 'The Functions and Purposes of School Records: teachers' views.

   For a very thorough account of the use of anecdotal records, see also, N. Gronlund (1976) *Measurement and Evaluation in Teaching,* Macmillan, New York.

3. S. Hegarty and K. Pocklington with D. Lucas, (1981). *Educating Pupils with Special Needs in the Ordinary School,* NFER–Nelson, Windsor. Chapter 16, 'Monitoring and Recording Progress', considers the problems involved in monitoring progress in the context of integration. The chapter deals very comprehensively with formal and informal means of gathering and recording information and discusses the uses of other means of monitoring progress (drawing on teachers' tacit knowledge of their pupils; holding case conferences and assessment meetings; and engaging in focused discussion). The chapter concludes with a very useful discussion of the problems involved in constructing records.

Reading 22
THE CURRICULUM IN INTEGRATION
S. Hegarty and K. Pocklington with D. Lucas

The purpose of education for all children is the same; the goals are the same. But the help that individual children need in progressing towards them will be different. (Warnock Report)

The pursuit of educational goals is the prime function of schooling. This is as true of pupils with special needs as it is of their peers. This is not to say that all pupils should engage in the same learning activities or that all are to be taught in the same way. The curriculum available to pupils and the specific programmes of work selected from it must match their needs, as well as take account of the educational environment in which they find themselves.

In this chapter we examine the curriculum on offer to pupils with special needs in ordinary schools. There is considerable diversity in practice. We illustrate this with concrete examples and outline a model of curricular provision. We discuss the principles by which the curriculum is determined in integration programmes and detail ways in which pupils are assigned to programmes of work.

A first consideration is to clarify the sense in which we speak of the curriculum in integration. The aims of education refer to the promotion of individual development through growth in knowledge and understanding, sensitivity and moral sense, through the acquisition and exercise of skills, and through becoming an active, responsible member of society. Many children and young people make only limited progress toward these goals but we now accept that nobody is ineducable, no matter how ineffective our teaching, and the general goals must remain for all. When educational programmes for individual pupils are being planned it is necessary to break down the general goals into specific objectives – use a knife and fork, sort objects into different sets, imitate words, reach a certain standard in reading. The curriculum then comprises the formal activities devised by the school to achieve these objectives. Since both the objectives and the means by which they are achieved vary from pupil to pupil, it follows that the school's curriculum will reflect the nature of its pupils and their special needs. For example, blind and sighted pupils will share the same goal of

S. Hegarty and K. Pocklington with D. Lucas (1981) *The curriculum in integration*. In S. Hegarty *et al.* (1981) Educating Pupils with Special Needs in the Ordinary School, NFER–Nelson, Windsor, pp 305–333

developing their musical awareness but the objectives into which this goal is broken down will vary – as they do for sighted pupils anyway. If they share a common objective, for example to develop a competence in sight reading, the means by which it is achieved may also be different.

It is worth emphasizing that these considerations – of objectives and means toward them – are the ones that come into play when different curricula are being devised. Pupils are not to be taught differently from their peers simply because they are blind, physically handicapped or whatever. A given pupil will require to be treated differently from peers because of special needs that dictate different objectives (based on common goals) and different routes toward them. These special needs may or may not be related to physical condition or to handicap as conventionally defined. Physical handicap, for instance, is associated with a very wide range of special teaching needs but none of them is necessarily prescribed by a given physical condition.

This helps us see why the curriculum in integration assumes distinctive character. It rests on the two foci of particular objectives, based on pupils' special needs, and the means of achieving these objectives, based on many factors but especially the nature of the school. Pupils' special needs will, broadly speaking, be the same whether they are in a special school or an ordinary school, so that the objectives will be the same. The means by which objectives are achieved may vary considerably, however, and lead to rather different curricula. The changes come from both the opportunities the ordinary school presents and the constraints it imposes. Thus ordinary secondary schools can offer a wider range of options and specialist teachers than most special schools, but they may not be able to maintain a highly structured linguistic environment such as might be required by hearing-impaired or communication-disordered pupils, or set tight limits on behaviour in a way that might benefit pupils exhibiting behavioural disturbances.

EXAMPLES OF CURRICULAR PROVISION

We begin with some examples of the curricula on offer in the integration programmes we studied. These vary in the extent to which they are 'integrated' curricula. Some are no different, other than in scale, from the curriculum that a special school dealing with comparable pupils would provide, while others draw on the resources of the main school in an integral way to offer a distinctive set of learning opportunities.

The first example comes from a large comprehensive school which, in addition to the usual complement of slow learners and some pupils with specific learning difficulties, has 60 pupils with moderate learning difficulties. The school has a Basic Studies Department which has primary curricular responsibility for the latter and provides remedial support for the former. Of necessity, the department's curriculum offerings are differentiated as between the different groups. The two guiding aims are mastery of the basic skills of literacy and numeracy and general enrichment through supplementary options (art, social studies, etc.) provided within the department or in main school. These aims are fundamental to curriculum planning within the department though the balance between them may vary; in the case of slow learners from the main school, for instance, the department's sole curricular responsibility is to provide remedial work.

Pupils with moderate learning difficulties follow programmes of work that are split between the department and the main school. In the first three years they follow a common core of lessons in the main school alongside mainstream peers. This comprises drama, music, PE/games, design, art and library (first year only). Occasionally a pupil who displays a particular aptitude in another subject area (e.g. science, maths) may be integrated slightly more. 'We operate on the basis of a continuum of special needs, whereby a pupil will attend as many mainstream lessons as offer him educational value and help satisfy his needs' (head of department). Within the department there is 'Basic Studies Curriculum' comprising: literacy (reading and writing), numeracy, social studies (subdivided into 'the self' and a local geographical/historical component), science, woodwork, art, home management, rural studies and additional sport.

The programme within the department operates in a self-contained way without particular reference to the main school. This is particularly true of work on literacy and numeracy. Where reading is particularly weak the SRA Distar and Racing to Read schemes are drawn on, as well as the department's own phonics resource kit, supplemented by a wide range of cassettes, workbooks and reading books. Most pupils are given structured practice in order to acquire a word-building skills. Here the department's own reading scheme comes into play. This was developed by the head of department because he considered that existing commercial schemes were insufficiently structured for this type of pupil. The scheme is in two parts: a phonics-based programme, and a section that concentrates on comprehension. It is based on the principles of programmed learning. Pupils work on those aspects of the scheme which relate to their specific area(s) of difficulty. There is a wide array of learning resources (workcards, worksheets and language masters). Pupils whose spelling does not match their reading ability either follow a commercial scheme (Blackwell's Spelling Workshop) or a course specially structured for them, drawing upon a spelling resource kit developed within the department and designed to facilitate self-help skills in spelling. Once literacy has been attained (defined as reading at the 9–10–year-old level), a range of associated skills are taught, increasingly with a view to the needs of adult life. By the time pupils are in their fourth year the concern is almost exclusively with such aspects of the adult world as writing letters, filling forms and completing job applications.

The department has also developed its own number scheme. Here the primary aim is competence in money and time. If and when these have been mastered, pupils go on to deal with weight, area and capacity. The scheme can encompass all stages on the achievement continuum.

Those pupils still at the pre-numeracy stage (very few) will concentrate on such topics as sorting, matching and recording. The next stage is based upon Fletcher Maths, supplemented with specially prepared workcards and materials intended to make this scheme suitable for the older pupil. Further progress leads the individual on to developing more complex arithmetic skills as well as being introduced to problem solving.

In years IV and V an options system comes into play. Midway through each pupil's third year, staff consult with pupils and their parents, and possibly outside agencies, to help determine choice. A booklet goes out to all parents which describes the various courses offered over these two years. Pupils are free to choose five of the ten courses they are required to take. Mandatory courses are: English, maths, 'core' (games, plus a choice from RE, health education, music and careers), human studies and science. These may be provided within the department or in main school. The department itself offers specific courses in the following areas: a specially devised leavers' programme, social studies, child care/home management, literacy and numeracy. There are additional extracurricular activities in woodwork, photography and car maintenance. Staff of the department maintain that the supplementary art, craft or home economics that they provide for many pupils is an essential part of their education: 'Rightly or wrongly special educationists advocate more practical education for special children, these are the subjects the less able can achieve in.'

A second example also comes from a large comprehensive school where a special department caters for some 15 pupils with severe learning difficulties and 60/70 pupils with moderate learning difficulties, as well as functioning as the school's remedial department. Again, there is considerable differentiation of curriculum, with pupils with severe learning difficulties being educated entirely within the department, pupils with moderate learning difficulties having some work in the main school, and slow learners or those with specific learning difficulties being withdrawn for specific remediation.

For pupils with severe learning difficulties, the emphasis is on the basic skills of literacy and numeracy (though many remain at pre-reading and pre-number levels) and on social competence. The latter is addressed in particular to equipping pupils for optimum independence in adult life and includes exposing pupils to a variety of real-life situations: using the telephone, borrowing books from the library, obtaining assistance from the emergency services. The aim is to provide 'a mental preparation for leaving' by encouraging self-reliance, developing problem-solving skills, and giving practice in making decisions. As pupils get older, this becomes of increasing importance and has indeed been the subject of specific curricular development, along the lines outlined in the following chapter.

Emphasis on basic skills work is also a strong feature of the curriculum for pupils with moderate learning difficulties. About 50 per cent of the timetable is devoted to number, language and social studies, all provided by staff from the department in a special class setting. Subject specialists from main school supply the remainder of the curriculum, teaching either classes comprised exclusively of pupils with moderate learning difficulties (e.g. for science, music) or mixed-ability groups which contain some pupils with moderate learning difficulties (e.g. art and craft, PE). For remedial pupils or the pupil with a specific learning difficulty the specialized attention forthcoming from the department is more particularized. Remedial pupils, for example, receive additional help with their maths and/or English; pupils who experience difficulty in writing attend a handwriting clinic which is convened once weekly over a term, and so forth.

A third example comes from a set of five special classes for preschool and infant-age children with severe learning difficulties. While there are considerable differences between the classes, the common aim underlying their curricular provision is to offer an enriched version of nursery and infant teaching practice: an abundance of learning resources; a stimulating learning environment; and individual attention – in relation both to children's general difficulties in learning and to specific difficulties (e.g. developing speech and language). A few children receive individual speech programmes prepared by a visiting speech therapist. Another aspect that is strongly emphasized is music and movement, provided by a peripatetic teacher. The classes are self-contained for teaching purposes, and the work children do owes little or nothing to the main school curriculum.

Each teacher will typically draw up termly aims for every child in each of the following areas: self-management; pre-number; pre-reading; speech and language; constructive and creative. Teachers aim to cover the basics – reading, writing, number and language – every day with each child. Other activities such as painting, shop and playing with large, wheeled toys take place twice weekly. Reading begins with the children's own names, progressing to matching words using flash cards. Children may produce their own books, the teacher or ancillary writing a sentence which the children have to copy and make a suitable drawing for. Number work begins with counting objects, recognizing numbers, using songs and finger plays. Children also learn to sort, count and recognize numbers. Language work is particularly emphasized. It is strongly individualized, with children encouraged to name objects by pointing to them and saying the appropriate word. Teachers do not use specialized language schemes such as the Peabody Language Development Kit or Distar Language.

Given the severity of these children's difficulties, instruction must extend beyond the customary classroom activities and opportunities for teaching them must be sought throughout the day. For instance, toileting sessions can be captialized upon for teaching the various parts of the body, lunchtime is an opportunity for teaching socially acceptable eating habits, and so on. The close supervision which a generous staffing ratio permits is important since staff need to spend a good deal of time with these children. As one participant wrote, 'It is not enough to provide and encourage participation in (for example) play situations; the adults must be on hand to exploit with the individual child the first glimmer of a materializing association, be it visual, aural or kinaesthetic.'

The examples to date have referred to provision for pupils with learning difficulties. Different considerations come into play with provision for communication-disordered children. The working philosophy common to the language units visited was one of concentrated individual or small-group teaching based upon good infant or junior school practice plus specific therapy and remediation geared to the individuals' language disorders. The latter varied greatly, encompassing specific reading and writing disabilities, sequencing difficulties, poor short-term memory, laterality problems and so on.

A balance is maintained between the normal school curriculum and specialist language work. These are the primary responsibility respectively of the teacher and the speech therapist. The former follows the normal infant curriculum as much as possible, as well as carrying out speech or language exercises devised by the speech therapist. The latter conducts detailed assessments, devises or assists in devising programmes of work, and provides individual treatment. The assessment covers language comprehension, expressive language and the intelligibility of speech. This provides the basis for both programmes of work and treatment, which typically have a twofold focus: promoting language development where it has been lacking, and remedying inappropriate learning.

We studied two contrasting provisions for hearing-impaired pupils, one involving special centres attached to ordinary schools, the other based on individual integration. While teachers in both cases followed established practice in British deaf education with its concentration on oralism, the difference in organization made for curricular differences as well.

The first comprised special centres at each of infant, junior and secondary stages of schooling. Naturally the particular curriculum content varies according to the age and special needs of the pupils. Broadly speaking, the overriding emphasis at infant level is upon developing language. Good infant practice is closely followed. Apart from the area of reading, specialist teachers adhere to the curriculum of the parent school, allowing for any necessary simplification of linguistic content. Plans of work are presented half-termly to the teacher in charge or headteacher. A particular theme is followed for a whole term with basic number and written work arising from it. The centre has its own reading scheme (Link Up), grounded in the everyday lives of the hearing impaired. Deliberate teaching of speech, based upon work carried out by Ling and Ling (1978), was introduced into the curriculum midway through our study.

At junior level the emphasis is on language consolidation, together with introducing a rather more rigorous approach to teaching basic literacy and numeracy. For much of our study there was limited contact with the parent school and in consequence few links with its curriculum. At secondary level the concern is to develop further and consolidate basic skills. Contact with the main school curriculum is limited and is confined to art, drama, PE and games. In the first three years hearing-impaired pupils spend about 20 per cent of their time taking these subjects in main school alongside hearing peers. For the older pupil specific preparation for adult life becomes important; this was being provided by means of a leavers' programme and a design-for-living course.

All pupils in the individual integration programme follow the normal school timetable of their classmates. There will be some modification to this, on two main grounds: first, the need for some form of specialist teaching (e.g. auditory training, speech improvement) or for additional 'back-up' work where some part of the curriculum is proving difficult;

secondly, when it is felt that a pupil is unlikely to derive much benefit from a particular subject or activity and that his or her time might be better spent on other activities. (These curricular modifications are the responsibility of teachers of the deaf or specially appointed support teachers.) Thus, one pupil was placed into a lower-band English group. His support teacher withdrew him for one English lesson each week and supported within the classroom during other English periods. He did not appear to be making much progress, however, so his support teacher withdrew him altogether from these lessons, providing content that she felt would be more relevant to his everyday experience.

The content of the specialist teaching and reinforcement work can be illustrated with a few examples. Alexis is a partially hearing boy attending a junior school. A teacher of the deaf visited him for a half-hour speech and language session three times weekly. Typically, she would spend time on speech improvement, hold a conversation, requiring that he listen, lip-read, comprehend and respond, and finish with some reading. In addition, a support teacher spent some five hours with him each week. The latter described what she sought to do with Alexis: 'I have to back up what the class is doing but I have (also) to see he has a much wider understanding of things.' This can sometimes mean 'doing a lot of the things that aren't on the curriculum or (are) not what the class is doing'. (Support teachers have to diverge from the timetable at their own discretion.)

In general, pupils drop one or more subjects as they move through secondary school, particularly where they are considered to be deriving little benefit. This is partly to enable adequate support to be provided. Thus, Jimmy had followed a full timetable initially. History quickly proved problematic and was dropped at the end of the first year. All other subjects, including science, were retained until the end of his third year, although, despite being quite extensively supported, some had to be taken with lower-ability pupils. In the fourth and fifth year an 'options' system is introduced. Jimmy retained his strong subjects, generally the more practical ones (technical drawing, engineering, geography, social studies – which he dropped midway through his final year – and mathematics) with specific remediation/speech and language work in addition. His command of language was very poor. Accordingly, one-seventh of his timetable was taken up with language work provided by the teacher of the deaf. His support teacher, even when supporting in specific subjects, also put considerable emphasis upon general language work.

The various examples outlined so far all involve special curricula or substantially modified ones. In many cases, however, there is need of only minor modifications to the curriculum. Thus, one primary school catering for some 14 visually impaired pupils had them following the same 'balanced curriculum of academic, creative and physical activities' that all pupils followed. The visually impaired work on the same tasks and with the same materials as their sighted peers. Some of them are taught Braille or typing and many receive extra help with physical education or practical subjects. Likewise, many physically handicapped pupils follow the same curriculum as their able-bodied peers with minor modifications necessitated by poor handwriting or fine motor control. Physical education may need to be modified and supplemented with specific exercises. It should be noted that some physically handicapped pupils *did* experience a modified curriculum, usually a restricted one because of ignorance or lack of awareness on the part of teachers. This occurred when teachers had unduly low expectations of them, did not know how to get round their physical limitations or were overly cautious in making demands of them or letting them take risks. Thus, some physically handicapped pupils were virtually deprived of physical education while others were subjected to unnecessary constraints in science and craft.

A MODEL OF PROVISION

We have suggested elsewhere that the range of special educational provision could be thought of as a continuum from segregated special schooling to full attendance in a normal class, and that different forms of provision could be seen as different points along that continuum. Here we propose a parallel account in order to describe the range of curricular provision available to pupils with special needs. This too can be viewed as a continuum running from a special curriculum with little or no reference to work being done by age peers to an unsupported normal curriculum. A tentative outline of this might looks as follows:

1. special curriculum;
2. special curriculum plus;
3. normal curriculum, significant reductions;
4. normal curriculum, some modifications;
5. normal curriculum, little or no modification.

Curricula cannot be viewed simply along this one axis of course, and there is overlap between the different categories; nevertheless it is a useful way of conceptualizing the variety of special provision.

1. Special curriculum

By special curriculum here we mean a curriculum that has little or no reference to work being done by age peers. Such curricula are unlikely to find a place in integration programmes and are increasingly being called into question as offering a valid approach to special education. This is not to say that they have not been widespread in the past or, indeed, that they have disappeared. Dunn (1973), reviewing American provision in the 1950s and 1960s for 'trainable' children (with moderate and severe learning difficulties), noted that the educational goals for them were different not only from the goals held for normal children but even from those held for the mildly retarded. The emphasis was on developing the minimal skills needed to live and work in sheltered environments. So, the goals were threefold: self-help; socialization; and oral communication. Very little academic work or vocational training was included.

Special curricula arise in other ways too, as when quite distinctive techniques such as the Doman-Delecato method or conductive education are being used or when a highly structured programme is being implemented in a controlled environment. The Doman-Delecato method is essentially a programme of motor training where children are systematically taken back and patterned through the developmental stages – rolling over, crawling, creeping and walking (Delecato, 1966). It enjoyed a vogue in ESN(S) schools in this country in the early 1970s. Swann (1981) describes visiting a school where it was in use: 'Limp little bodies were being manipulated by a determined group of teachers and volunteers. The children, lying prone on a table had their arms and legs moved back and forth in imitation of crawling. [...] this patterning of movement, not to be confused with physiotherapy, along with exercises performed with the forced use of only one hand or one eye is designed to achieve hemispheric dominance.'

One might also include here highly specialized short-term programmes, such as are used with emotionally disturbed or developmentally delayed children, though with the difference that such programmes would usually be geared explicitly to facilitating participation in mainstream activities, at least in the long term. These differ from normal school work through being intensive and highly structured, often based on behaviourist principles. They may entail setting up an artificial environment where behaviour is tightly monitored and controlled.

2. Special curriculum plus

With the growing realization that all children are educable and that it is important to focus on similarities as well as differences, special curricula have become less isolated from mainstream curricula and have moved toward them in various way. Thus, a common curricular pattern is 'basic skills' plus general enrichment' or 'basic skills plus other subjects'. This is probably a fair description of the curriculum in many special schools and certainly applies to several of the integration programmes in our study. The broader curriculum was not neglected but it was clearly secondary to basic skills or specialist language work.

Even when some form of work in basics predominates, we have seen from the examples above that the extent of other work can vary considerably. In the case of some hearing-impaired pupils, for instance, general enrichment and work in subjects other than the basics occupied as little as 20 per cent of the week and was attributed far less importance than specialist language work. On the other hand, pupils with moderate learning difficulties followed a basic curriculum that was itself enriched and comprised far more than literacy and numeracy for at most 50 per cent of their time, and otherwise followed lessons alongside peers in the main school.

3.   Normal curriculum, significant reductions

Though the essence of a continuum is the absence of qualitative change and gradual movement from one point to the next, there is a clear shift in emphasis and approach from the previous category to this one. There the focus is still on how pupils with special needs are different; the priority is on meeting their special needs and *then* seeing in what ways they can join in with their peers. Here the emphasis is on what pupils with special needs have in common with their peers; they follow a normal curriculum as far as possible, with omissions or modifications made so that their special needs can be met. The difference can be illustrated by reference to the two hearing-impaired programmes described above. The programme involving special centres tended toward a special curriculum whereas the individual integration programme – dealing with pupils whose hearing losses were no less severe – based itself on the normal curriculum, modified or reduced as necessary. Thus, pupils were withdrawn from normal lessons for auditory training, speech work and other specialist language work as well as for reinforcement of lesson content. The amount of withdrawal could mean that they were missing parts of subjects or, indeed, had to drop some subjects entirely. Even when extensive withdrawal was necessary and several subjects had to be dropped, the approach to the curriculum is clearly different from one where the starting point is pupils' special needs.

4.   Normal curriculum, some modifications

Some pupils with special needs follow essentially the same curriculum as their peers with some omissions and possibly supplementary or alternative activities. Thus, partially sighted pupils were precluded from taking part in certain aspects of art and craft; instead, they concentrated on sculpture and other activities dependent on tactile senses. In addition, blind pupils were taught Braille. Some physically handicapped pupils likewise did the same work as their peers with the exception of physical education, which they did separately to a programme worked out by a physiotherapist, and possibly domestic and life skills where specific instruction and practice were necessary in some instances.

Some of the provision for pupils with mild or specific learning difficulties could be included here also. Thus, in one school pupils with mild learning difficulties were withdrawn to the special centre for two to four periods a week but otherwise followed normal lessons. In several schools, individual programmes of work were devised for pupils with specific learning difficulties; these too were implemented on a withdrawal basis but at time selected to give minimal disruption to the main school curriculum.

5.   Normal curriculum, little or no modification

Many pupils with special needs in our study followed the same curriculum to all intents and purposes and in the same teaching groups as their peers. This was especially so in the case of physically handicapped pupils but applied to others as well. Younger physically handicapped pupils were often withdrawn for management purposes – toileting, transfer to and from wheelchairs – while handwriting difficulties made for a slight modification with older pupils, but quite a number were following a full normal timetable. This was also true of some partially sighted and hearing-impaired pupils; the school's teaching arrangements and the amount of support available made it possible for them to participate fully in the school's normal curriculum.

DETERMINING THE CURRICULUM

We have seen that schools offered the pupils in our study a wide range of options from full participation in the normal curriculum to what was virtually a distinct special curriculum. Such diversity may be taken for granted in a system that seeks to meet pupils' needs flexibly. It is not always clear, however, that the diversity is justified or that it constitutes a planned response to perceived needs. In order to examine this, we look in this section at the principles underlying curriculum selection, and in the following section at the allocation of pupils to individual programmes of work.

Two principles turned out to be central to curriculum selection in the integration programmes we studied, viz. 'normalization' and special action to meet special needs. Indeed, the rationale underlying curriculum development in the vast majority of cases could be summarized in terms of a compromise between these two principles. Teachers sought to expose pupils with special needs to the same work as their peers and at the same time to ensure their special needs were being met. The tension arising from these conflicting principles is a familiar one in special education. Nowhere, perhaps, is it clearer than in deaf education. Sign language provides hearing-impaired people with a means of communication that for many greatly excels the combination of speech and lip-reading, but it cuts them off from the majority of people who do not know sign language. For this reason many teachers of the deaf are strongly opposed to the use of sign language: it shuts more doors than it opens by reducing competent speech and by locking hearing-impaired youngsters into the world of the deaf.(This view is not universally held and, indeed, writers such as Conrad, 1979, argue that the *concept* of language that develops from using a signing system is an important aspect of speech and language development in hearing-impaired people.)

There is a sense of course in which normalization and special action to meet special needs are not opposed to each other. Sometimes normality is only to be achieved by pursuing special measures. Thus, the visually impaired miss out on certain experiences that others take for granted, and will need specific training and compensation in order to win an appreciation of the normal and carry out ordinary domestic and life skills. Again, many pupils need specific training in independence before they can even approximate to the norm for their age group. Despite these links, however, the differences at the level of practice can be considerable. Regardless of whether they are directed to achieving normality or not, the pupil's *actual* educational experiences may be far from normal.

A more substantial problem in examining the tension between normalization and special provision is the lack of precision surrounding the principles themselves. So a first step is to clarify what is meant by normal and special curriculum respectively. It is well to realize in doing so that the state of curriculum development is far from advanced. The curriculum in schools is rarely worked out from first principles. It is the outcome rather of an amalgam of existing practice, ideas in currency, tasks assigned to the school by society (both formally and informally), staff and resources available, and perception of pupils' needs and abilities. In recent years there has been greater concern for the theoretical basis of the curriculum and a spate of documents and manifestos have appeared. (The production of curriculum documents would seem to be one of the few growth areas in education.) Attempts to formulate an agreed theoretical framework for systematic curriculum planning are, however, still in their infancy, and much classroom practice and overall school planning continues to rest on precedent and rule of thumb.

Traditional school subjects have been the mainstay of curricular differentiation. This conception of the curriculum as a series of distinct, albeit overlapping, subjects is most apparent at secondary level where individual subjects can easily be distinguished. Even though subjects may be grouped in non-traditional ways (humanities, environmental science and so on) or taught in team contexts the subject approach continues to dominate in many schools. It provides an unsatisfactory basis for systematic planning, however, on account of the relative arbitrariness and lack of theoretical coherence of school subjects. It is also open to criticism, particularly in the special education field, for its emphasis on transmitted knowledge and for underplaying the significance of firsthand experience for the learner.

Two alternatives have been posed, one based on skills, the other on forms of knowledge or areas of experience. While a given subject will entail the exercise of certain skills, it is possible to give an account of skills which cuts across subject boundaries. This could be done for example, in terms of the traditional 'basics' of literacy and numeracy, broader communication skills, personal and social skills, physical skills, skills of discrimination and judgement, and so on. Such an approach could have particular relevance for pupils with special needs since so many skills which others acquire naturally have to be taught deliberately.

Forms of knowledge as outlined by Hirst (1974) or areas of experience as detailed by HMI (DES, 1977) refer to the structurally different ways in which we apprehend the world. Hirst proposes that all knowledge and understanding is logically locatable within the domains of mathematics, the physical sciences, knowledge of persons (including the human sciences and history), literature and the fine arts, morals, religion and philosophy. HMI sees the essential areas of experience to which pupils should be introduced during the period of compulsory schooling as the following: aesthetic and creative, ethical, linguistic, mathematical, physical, scientific, social and political, and spiritual. Such lists do not in themselves constitute actual curricular programmes. By differentiating human consciousness into distinguishable cognitive structures, they offer a map within which different activities can be located and curriculum choices made in a balanced and reflective way.

Underlying these various approaches – subjects, skills, forms of knowledge – there is also the 'hidden curriculum': the lessons taught and the opportunities for learning set up by the way the school is run, how staff relate to pupils and each other, how discipline is exercised and over what, how decisions are taken, what the effective priorities are. This has much to do with values and attitudes. While the considerations raised are important in all education, they are especially so where pupils with special needs are concerned, since once again formal teaching may be necessary to inculcate what others acquire indirectly.

Curriculum planning in the mainstream, then, is not an exact affair. It is a multifaceted process that responds to prevailing ideas and practices and to individual situations in a highly complex way. So when we speak of 'the normal curriculum' this is at best a loose description.

It must not be supposed that there is any greater consensus over how to meet special educational needs. The variety of special curricula which are quite distinct from mainstream curricula was indicated in the previous section. It may be instructive here to take an overview of the curriculum for slow learners. Brennan (1974) noted two key orientations underlying traditional curriculum planning for slow-learning pupils: (a) because they were perceived as capable of learning very little, teachers pared down the normal curriculum to its absolute essentials, leading to much repetition of 'the basics'; (b) the limited life opportunities open to pupils after leaving school resulted in a stress on practical activities with a strongly utilitarian basis.

With time their supposed future needs as adults came to exert increasing influence on the nature of the curriculum – to the point where it has challenged the primacy of the 'watered-down' mainstream curriculum which had hitherto prevailed. Segal (1963), for example, organized his curriculum for secondary-age slow learners around the following components: applied basic skills; citizenship; safety; health and hygiene; religious and moral education; leisure pursuits; vocational guidance; and science. Tansley and Gulliford (1960), dismissing the watered-down academic curriculum approach as 'a travesty of special educational treatment', identified a central core of language and number supplemented by additional knowledge concerning the environment, creative and aesthetic activities and practical interests. This was taken further by Brennan (1974) in his formulation of the twin concepts of 'education for mastery' (implying a central core of objectives which must be mastered) and 'education for awareness' (implying less central objectives where familiarity or awareness is appropriate).

Brennan was subsequently (1979) to classify approaches to the curriculum for slow learners under seven headings:

1. sensory training (influenced by the writings of Montessori);
2. the watered-down academic curriculum;
3. concrete use of basic subjects;
4. core programmes emphasizing social competence and occupational efficiency;
5. units of experience, designed to secure interest and motivate through their concern with contemporary problems closely related to pupils' developmental levels;
6. broad subject fields such as communication, literacy, social competence and so on, stressing the interaction between learning and use of knowledge and skills;
7. education of special groups, concerned with specific programmes geared to factors such as brain injury, perceptual difficulties and so on.

More recently, the objectives approach, as described for example by Ainscow and Tweddle (1979), has gained ground. This concentrates entirely on those classroom factors which can be controlled by the teacher in the classroom and ignore – for teaching purposes – other factors such as brain damage, poor home or low IQ. The approach rests on defining teaching goals, breaking them down into precisely stated and carefully sequenced behavioural objectives, and monitoring pupils' progress on them through continuous systematic assessment.

This, then, is the context within which curriculum options are selected or developed in integration programmes. The two principles of normalization and special action to meet special needs, and the tension between them, become rather more problematic when viewed against this background. If both the normal and the special are imprecisely defined, the effort to reach a balance between them is far from easy. In point of fact, there was very great diversity in the ways in which the principles were combined. This reflected in part the nature and complexity of pupils' special needs but there was more to it than that. Pupils with comparable special needs were dealt with quite differently from each other and were exposed to curricula that either stressed special provision or were oriented to the main school curriculum. The contrasting provision described above for hearing-impaired pupils is a case in point. Numerous similar examples could be cited.

In the following section we look at these differences in terms of how pupils were allocated to individual programmes of work. In general terms, it can be noted here that the variations reflected (1) individuals' commitment to either normalization or special provision and (2) their awareness of alternative possibilities. The two are interrelated since a knowledge of what is possible can lead to a commitment to integration, but they are independent since a person can be committed to integration for many reasons. Indeed, the process can work in reverse: an abstract commitment to normalizing the experience of pupils with special needs can lead to a search for new practical possibilities. This was evident in several programmes that we studied in regard to both general organization of provision and specific curricular provision. Thus, a group of visually impaired pupils in a special centre attached to an ordinary primary school were receiving a traditional education geared exclusively to the educational consequences of visual impairment and with considerable emphasis on social training (the latter carried out in isolation from the natural situation of the main school). This was in marked contrast with the individualized approach based on projects, workcards and so on that prevailed in the main school. The head of the school was strongly committed to integration, however, and was unhappy about the isolation of the visually impaired pupils. In spite of initial objections from the specialist teacher in visual impairment, she insisted on incorporating them into the main school teaching arrangements and exposing them to the same curriculum provision as their peers.

The importance of the working philosophy of the headteacher or teacher in charge must not be ignored. One approach is illustrated by the teacher who said: 'Borderline M and S children's basic need is for four years of special education [...] they've not been diagnosed as needing integration but as needing special education.' The emphasis in the special centre in question was in fact on pupils' special needs: they had failed in the ordinary system so 'we can't just put them back in ordinary classes'. A similar example came from a junior school which housed a special centre for hearing-impaired pupils. For most of our fieldwork the centre operated on fairly separate lines, the emphasis being on providing a deaf education with pupils spending most of their time in the special centre. The arrival of a new headteacher with a strong commitment to integration led to a transformation of curricular practice – and much else besides. The school's academic organization was revised and team teaching initiated. The intention was that the hearing impaired and their teachers would be gradually absorbed into this arrangement. Hearing-impaired pupils would be fully integrated for the whole of the curriculum and withdrawn only for specialist work.

ALLOCATING PUPILS TO PROGRAMMES OF WORK

In order to see what this means in practice it is necessary to look at what pupils actually do in the classroom. The school or special department may have a carefully worked out curriculum but this signifies little until it is translated into practice. What matters to the individual pupil is the selection from the curriculum to which he or she is exposed. Thus, science is an important part of the curriculum in secondary schools but it is not available in any effective sense to many pupils with special needs. So in this section we outline the principles by which pupils are allocated to different programmes of work. Five areas of consideration may be noted:

1. characteristics and needs of the individual;
2. nature of the subject matter and the learning activities to be engaged in;
3. maintaining a balance;
4. pedagogical considerations;
5. factors arising out of the particular local situation.

It may be noted at the outset that these considerations did not apply for some pupils. Though 'special' in the sense of having a recognized hearing loss, speech disorder or physical impairment of some kind, they were not affected as far as educational functioning was concerned. The curriculum of the school was as available to them as to their peers and they followed programmes of work selected from it in just the same way. Minor accommodations may have been necessary on occasion, but for them meeting their special needs meant ensuring access to the normal curriculum of the school.

1. Individual characteristics and needs

The programme of work followed by a pupil clearly must reflect that pupil's characteristics and needs in various ways. There were three considerations here in the integration programmes we studied. First, staff sought to compensate for deficiencies or overcome pupils' disadvantages. Secondly, pupils were excluded from taking part in certain activities because of difficulties or perceived dangers associated with their handicapping condition. Thirdly, there was the concept of limited gain – if there was little likelihood of benefit from a subject or activity then there was no point in exposing a pupil to it.

The first of these had to do with efforts to overcome the disadvantages associated with their handicapping conditions. In many ways this was the central consideration. Thus, for a pupil who experiences learning difficulties – moderate or severe or of a specific kind – a prime consideration was to provide structured teaching designed to ensure mastery of the 'basics' of numeracy and literacy or to overcome the specific disability. Depending on the severity of the learning difficulty, certain social skills which the normal pupil would pick up incidentally were deliberately taught. For the hearing impaired and communication disordered the primary emphasis was on the medium of communication. Specialist speech and language work – 'special' in regard of both content and form of delivery – was provided directly (e.g. through deliberate teaching of speech) as well as being introduced throughout other learning activities. Pupils suffering from a sensory impairment were sometimes taught social skills which their impairment prevented them from acquiring naturally. Visually impaired pupils in particular need orientation and mobility training. Pupils with very severe sensory impairment were introduced to another working medium entirely: manual communication for the deaf and Braille for the educationally blind. Physically handicapped pupils commonly have difficulty with fine or gross motor coordination so they may experience problems with writing. In some cases a physiotherapist devised special exercises to develop hand control or hand/eye coordination. Where gross motor movement was defective the therapist was able to advise the teacher or classroom ancillary on modifying the PE programme or providing appropriate alternative experiences when classmates were engaged in PE.

For older pupils a particular need was to give preparation for adult living. This can take many forms. In some cases pupils' entire programmes of work in the later years of school were directed toward preparing them for life after school. In other cases there were specific timetable slots or a general orientation running through their other work.

Moving on to the second consideration, there were a number of exclusion principles in operation. Thus, pupils did not take part in certain activities which were assumed to be beyond their capacities. Pupils with severe vision impairment were steered away from taking geography because of the practical difficulty that fieldwork would present; few teachers would recommend that a severely or profoundly deaf pupil with limited oral capacity should study a foreign language; and physically handicapped pupils were excluded from subjects such as biology, chemistry and metalwork on the grounds of inadequate fine motor skills or slowness. Safety was a further consideration. Physically handicapped pupils were denied the opportunity to engage in certain craft activities, practical science or physical education on the grounds that the risk was too great. The same was sometimes advocated for pupils with severe vision impairment. A further excluding factor usually associated with the physically handicapped was their physical stamina. One girl suffering from spina bifida opted for a full timetable at the end of her third year in secondary school. Though academically able it became apparent that this was too much for her. The pace of the work combined with mobility and physical care problems left her quite exhausted. In the event, she dropped two subjects in order to keep up with the remainder of her programme.

Finally, pupils were withdrawn or excluded from certain subjects because of failure to adjust to their situation in some respect. Again, this was a particular feature of pupils who were physically handicapped. It was most evident at the time of transfer to secondary school, when the move to a much larger school – which in itself can be a difficult experience – is compounded with the trauma of early adolescence. One 18-year-old who had contracted polio spent less time in mainstream lessons than a straightforward educational or intellectual assessment would suggest simply because she had not come to terms with her physical condition: 'She feels it totally blocks her life. [...] She uses her handicap to put a block on everything.' Whereas this girl's reaction has been to withdraw and display very little motivation for any task set, other pupils reacted in a grossly extrovert way and had to be withdrawn from mainstream lessons because of the difficulty of containing them.

The third consideration, the concept of limited gain, was in evidence when a programme of work was drawn up to take account of a pupil's strengths and ignored or played down his weaknesses. If little benefit was likely to be gained from the study of a particular subject, this would be ignored and others where success was more likely would be substituted in its place. This principle could never be applied in more than a partial way since certain activities were deemed essential and were persevered with regardless of pupils' difficulties with them. It was widely used, however, in deciding on pupils' allocation of time between a special centre within a school and mainstream lessons: pupils stayed within the special centre for core subjects since they were more likely to benefit from the individualized instruction that could be provided there. It was associated in some teachers' eyes with the view that integration was for social benefit primarily: pupils could integrate for subjects where academic progress was less important; if in the event little academic progress was made, the placement could be justified in terms of the presumed social benefits.

Some teachers were well aware of the danger inherent in this principle. It was all too easy to assume that a pupil would not gain from taking certain subjects, when in fact good progress could be made given appropriate presentation and teaching. Rather than working to *a priori* exclusion principles, their approach was to give pupils a trial at subjects and only withdraw them when difficulties became too great. Thus, an educationally blind girl on entering secondary school was allowed to take maths and science, even though it was thought probable that she would meet difficulties at a later stage. A profoundly deaf boy followed the same subjects as his peers throughout the first year of secondary school. His progress was monitored closely and at the end of the first year it was decided he would drop history because of difficulties he had with it. He retained all the remaining subjects until the end of the third year.

2. Subject matter and learning tasks

The nature of the subject matter and learning activities engaged in led to a further source of differentiation in programme allocation. Three pointers may be noted: concentration on the basics; emphasis on practical subjects; and the cumulative nature of some subjects.

We have seen above that pupils' learning difficulties led to their spending considerable time in reaching a basic competence in literacy and numeracy. Quite independently of any learning difficulties, however, this tendency was reinforced by the importance attached to literacy and numeracy. Being able to read and write and cope with simple number concepts were seen as important in their own right and in providing a basis for further learning. Literacy especially was seen as opening the door to much of the rest of the curriculum, and work on developing the associated skills was regarded as laying the groundwork for other work. (In practice, basic skills often became an end in themselves, and pupils were spending a great deal of time in mastering them without going on to a broader curriculum.)

It was common to find a stress on practical working where dependence on literacy was less important or, at certain levels of working, could be dispensed with entirely. This resulted in a predisposition toward the practical subjects. Art and craft, domestic science and, for some, PE/games were widely regarded as particularly appropriate activities for pupils with special needs. This was especially apparent when integration was at issue. Practical subjects tended to be taken because pupils' deficiencies were less in evidence, there was the possibility of joining in group activities, and less was at stake since these subjects were less important. (This latter view was not universally held. In several cases, practical work allied to domestic and life skills was seen as a central part of the older pupil's curriculum. This was too important to be left to the chance of mainstream lessons and was provided in a structured way within the special centre.) Thus, hearing-impaired pupils in one programme joined mainstream lessons in art, craft and games and remained in the school for the deaf for all other subjects. Again, it was common for pupils with learning difficulties to join mainstream lessons for craft subjects but not for English or maths.

Integration possibilities were affected in some instances by the cumulative nature of some subjects or the way in which they were taught. If a class is following a syllabus – as often in languages, maths and science – where work builds up cumulatively and later content refers in a specific way to what has gone before, it will not be possible for pupils to join a class in midstream or to join it on a part-time basis. This restricted the integration that was possible in some cases.

3. Maintaining a balance

A related consideration was the need to maintain a balance in the programme of work a pupil followed. This came up in various ways. It was a corrective, for example, to the undue preoccupation with the basics that sometimes prevailed. It drew attention to pupils' needs arising out of being pupils or young adults in addition to those consequent on their handicapping conditions; special steps might be necessitated by the latter but a pupil's entire programme of work could not be constructed around them. Balance had to be found between the academic and the practical and, as pupils got older, between education and specific preparation for adult living.

In practical terms, the balance can be sought in one of two ways. Either teachers consider what must be provided for pupils' special needs to be met and then add to this by selecting from the mainstream options, or their starting point is what the mainstream can offer and they then supplement any deficiencies relative to their pupils. Thus, in one school adopting the latter approach the aim was 'to balance up with things they haven't got from (the main school)' – notably, home economics and physical education/games.

4. Pedagogical considerations

Pupils' work programmes can be affected by the teaching implications of integration. Consider the need for reinforcing lesson content for example. Pupils can sometimes follow mainstream lessons if they get additional help. This may be provided within the lesson but more often outside. Time has to be found for this, possibly at the expense of another subject. Thus, hearing-impaired pupils who were integrated on an individual basis were able to do so only because of considerable support provided within the lesson and on a withdrawal basis. (This encompassed auditory training and specific language work as well as reinforcing specific lesson content.) In order to make time for this it was necessary in some cases to restrict a pupil's programme by dropping certain subjects.

The considerations here overlap with the notion of limited gain referred to above, and the need to use the time available to pupils' best advantage. Working priorities must be established that will determine what is to be included and what omitted. A minority of teachers indeed felt that the time taken up by integration could be put to more effective use by specialist teachers: 'Time is so precious, [...] we are well qualified, so is it fair on the children to put them in with teachers who can't give them very much attention and don't understand their problems?'

We encountered several examples where pupils' programmes of work were restricted through pedagogical considerations of this nature. Thus, one profoundly deaf girl began her third year at comprehensive school taking seven subjects. During the autumn term her support teacher found that more and more of her time was taken up going over new vocabulary and explaining increasingly more sophisticated concepts – mostly from humanities lessons – to the detriment of other equally important activities (e.g. practising speech). Accordingly, at the end of term it was decided to withdraw the girl from this particular subject, not just because of the difficulties she was experiencing with it, but also because of the amount of support time it was taking up. In another instance, a 15-year-old suffering from spina bifida was obliged to drop science and geography after two years of secondary schooling in order to allow greater concentration on 'life skills' (notably cookery plus a little needlework), typing and walking exercises. A third example concerns a physically handicapped sixth-former who could not write. Despite her undoubted intelligence – she began her sixth-form career by taking three subjects at A level – she was obliged to drop one of these subsequently because of the amount of time she took over dictating or typing lesson notes and doing homework assignments.

5. Local factors

Pupils' programmes of work reflect the particular opportunities and constraints of the school they attend. If the school has a strong musical tradition, it is likely that their musical education will benefit, and so on. Here we are concerned to look at some of the ways in which local factors constrained the opportunities open to pupils. In particular, we look at access, teachers' lack of awareness and timetabling difficulties.

Access   Being denied access to particular subjects or activities because they take place in areas of the school physically inaccessible to them is a potential difficulty that the physically handicapped may expect to meet in integration. What disadvantages were found in practice? In one programme involving physically handicapped pupils, they were effectively restricted to the ground and first floors of the senior part of this school. A number of specialist laboratories and classrooms were on the second floor, and pupils either did not take these options or took them under less favourable conditions. For example, because of the presence of a girl in a wheelchair, one class was obliged to vacate a properly equipped biology laboratory and move to a Portakabin which was too small and had inferior facilities. It was particularly unfortunate that, while the subject proceeded here, a biology lab stood empty. In another location a pupil suffering from spina bifida could not obtain access to a language laboratory. Furthermore, she sometimes had to join different forms in order to take certain subjects because of the difficulty of access to the first floor of the main part of the school.

A more substantial limitation arose from the fact that specialist rooms such as science and language laboratories or rooms equipped for geography or other subjects had to be vacated by subject teachers. They were then faced with taking their lessons under makeshift conditions: sometimes overcrowded teaching areas, inappropriate for use by pupils in wheelchairs, and above all lacking their collection of special equipment and resources.

Lack of awareness   There were various instances where limitations in a pupil's programme of work could be traced back to a failure among ordinary teachers to realize that the individual could not easily cope or that the programme was inappropriate in some respect. More often, necessary components were missing because their relevance had not been appreciated. Such disadvantages are more likely to be found under programmes of individual integration, particularly where specialist advice and guidance are not readily forthcoming, but it is not a problem exclusive to this particular organizational format and did occur elsewhere, often when there was insufficient cooperation between specialist and ordinary teachers.

John is an 8-year-old with cerebral palsy. He has very considerable educational problems: his speech is very poor, his reading ability is well behind his chronological age; and his writing is 'spidery' as a consequence of very poor hand control. Despite all this he is following the same programme of work as his classmates. No speech therapy, no special exercises to develop fine motor control, no individual programme to help with reading, have been forthcoming.

Timetable difficulties This turned out to be less of a problem than might have been expected. There was only one programme, where physically handicapped pupils from a special school attended a neighbouring comprehensive on a part-time or full-time basis, where timetabling constraints meant that pupils were not always receiving the special educational help they needed. This was manifest in two respects. First, there was the problem of providing physiotherapy in the limited time left over from an intensive integration programme that could not be rearranged to suit the therapist's availability. A physiotherapist noted that she faced a constant dilemma of cutting down on the physiotherapy exercises that a pupil really needed so that his or her presence in integrated lessons would not be jeopardized, either through having to miss them or because of sheer physical exhaustion. Secondly, staff experienced difficulty in preparing older pupils for postschool life, most especially in arranging opportunities for work experience. Those who attended the comprehensive had individual timetables and it has proved virtually impossible to find times during the school week when they could all reassemble in the special school for specific preparation for adult living geared to their particular concerns and problems.

CONCLUSION

In conclusion, the central importance of curricular considerations in integration programmes may be noted. Special schools developed at least in part because ordinary schools were failing to educate certain groups of pupils. If these pupils are to return to ordinary school there must be some certainty that their special *educational* needs will be met there at least as well as in segregated special schools. This is not to suggest a comparison between curricular provision in special schools and in ordinary schools since that would miss the point. Meeting special educational needs in an ordinary school is a different enterprise from meeting them in a special school and operates under different constraints and opportunities. Success must be seen in terms of circumventing these constraints and capitalizing on the opportunities, not in reproducing the educational environment of the special school.

We have seen here some different ways in practice whereby ordinary schools set about developing a curriculum for pupils with special needs. Finding a balance between exposing them to the same or similar curricular experiences as their peers and ensuring that their special needs were met was far from easy and led to great diversity in practice. This can be examined in concrete terms by looking at the programmes of work that pupils follow and the principles by which they are allocated to them.

REFERENCES

Ainscow, M. and Tweddle, D.A. (1979) *Preventing Classroom Failure*, John Wiley and Sons, Chichester

Brennan, W.K. (1974) *Shaping the Education of Slow Learners*, Routledge and Kegan Paul, London

Brennan, W.K. (1979) *Curricular Needs of Slow Learners*, Routledge and Kegan Paul, London

Conrad, R. (1979) *The Deaf School Child: language and cognitive function*, Harper and Row, London

Delecato, C.H. (1966) *Neurological Organization and Reading*, Charles C. Thomas, Springfield, Ill.

Department of Education and Science (DES) (1977) *Curriculum 11-16* (Working Papers by HM Inspectorate), HMSO, London

Dunn, L.M. (Ed.) (1973) *Exceptional Children in the Schools: special education in transition*, Holt Rinehart and Winston, New York

Hirst, P.H. (1974) *Knowledge and the Curriculum*, Routledge and Kegan Paul, London

Ling, D. and Ling, A.H. (1978) *Aural Habilitation: the foundations of verbal learning in hearing impaired children*, Alexander Graham Bell, Washington DC

Segal, S. (1963). *Teaching Backward Pupils*, Evans, London

Swann, W. (1981) *A Special Curriculum?* Open University Press, Milton Keynes

Tansley, A.E. and Gulliford, R. (1960) *The Education of Slow Learning Children*, Routledge and Kegan Paul, London

TOPICS FOR DISCUSSION

1. The authors identify two principles which appear to underlie curriculum selection in integration programmes (viz. 'normalization' and 'special provision'). In what ways might these principles conflict with each other?

2. Critically evaluate the curriculum orientations for children with special educational needs suggested by Brennan (1979), and Ainscow and Tweddle (1979.)
3. Discuss the implications of the authors' finding that 'pupils with comparable special needs were dealt with quite differently from each other and were exposed to curricula that either stressed special provision or were oriented to the main school curriculum'.

SUGGESTIONS FOR FURTHER READING

1. M. Ainscow and D.A. Tweddle (1979) *Preventing Classroom Failure,* John Wiley and Sons, Chichester. An example of the 'objectives approach' which has tended to gain ground in recent years. The 'objectives approach' concentrates solely on those classroom factors which are under the control of the teacher and ignores – for teaching purposes – other factors such as low IQ, debilitating home environment or brain damage. Essentially, the approach depends on the careful defining of teaching goals (aims), breaking them down into precisely stated and sequenced objectives (strategies), and monitoring children's progress on them by means of continuous and systematic assessment.

2. W. Swann (1983) *Curriculum principles for integration.* In T. Booth and P. Potts (Eds) (1983) Integrating Special Education, Basil Blackwell, Oxford. In chapter 7 the author examines the way the conception of the curriculum as teacher plans and the tendency to specialization are combined in the current emphasis afforded to the use of behavioural objectives as a basis for the special curriculum. Swann argues that it is commonly asserted that behavioural objectives are especially important for pupils with learning difficulties because such children do not learn 'incidentally' or 'spontaneously'; they require highly structured and planned learning experiences. The article critically examines this assertion, showing it, in effect, to be a contradiction in terms, and argues that the process of specifying behavioural objectives is no guarantee of appropriate teaching. Indeed, the author asserts, the approach tends to direct attention towards a small part of children's experiences at school, and away from many potent effects of segregation.

3. T. Booth, (1985) *Prospects for integration.* In P. Gurney (Ed.) (1985) Special Educational Needs in the Ordinary School, Perspectives 15, School of Education, University of Exeter. The author examines the idea that integration in education has to be understood as part of a wider scheme for the participation of excluded and disadvantaged groups in society – so that, in a broad sense, integration becomes a programme for the education system as a whole. Booth suggests that progress towards integration depends, in part, on counteracting the forces and arguments which promote segregation (the *overt* and *hidden curriculum* of segregation), and discusses examples of such curricula.

AUTHOR INDEX

Bibliographical details will be found on those page numbers printed in *italic*.

SUBJECT INDEX

352

planning 333–9; curriculum provision 102–4, 109–10, 322–30; curriculum provision model 330–3; planning 65, 101–2, 108–16; structural/organizational factors 64–5, 94–107; work programme allocations 339–46

integrative approach 303–4; Banbury Project 309–10; comprehensive special needs departments 308–9; primary schools 307–8; 'resources' model 305–10; special school initiatives 306–7

intellectual performance 3, 53, 55, 56; *see also* educational achievement

intelligence tests 183, 185–7, 189, 191; for ESN(M) 241–2, 244–5, 251–2; as evidence of needs 221–2, 224

interagency cooperation 11–12, 19, 23–7, 30, 31, 100–1; *see also* health services; social service departments

interest groups xxii, 21, 23, 29–31, 37–9, 41, 141; expansion of special education and 198, 261, 264–5; progressive focussing 32, 33–4

intermediate objectives 73, 74

intuitive accounts (ESN) 245, 248, 255–6

knowledge ix, xv; broad-based approach 81–5; core-periphery model 80–1; differential learning 85–90; forms of 335–6; instructional approach 78–9

labelling 47–8; deviance 174–7, 196, 219–23; statutory categories 40–1; theory 141, 174–7, 190–2; theory (case studies) 177–90

language 125, 269, 327–9, 332, 334–6; deafness and xxii, 140, 143–6

learning difficulties xx–xxi, 77–8, 221; significant 67–9

learning experiences 73

legislation: design and implementation 16–17; enabling nature xvii, 3, 14, 20–1; Norway 131, 132; passage of (case study) 2, 13–34; *see also individual Acts*

lighting (adequacy) 115, 145

limpet model *see* unit system

'lines' 277, 286

local education authorities: accountability 12, 23, 25–6, 29; decision-making 22, 30–1; integration practices 45, 171–2; parents and 4, 10, 11, 12, 29; response to legislation xvii–xix, 12, 17–18, 20–2, 24, 27–8, 31–4, 43; *see also* appeals procedures; inter-agency cooperation; statement procedure

locational integration 44

low achievers: alternative provision 65, 123–6; current provision 65, 117–22; heterogeneity of 118, 122–3

mainstreaming 45, 46, 175–7, 303; support mechanisms 292, 294–302; *see also* integration

maladjusted pupils 134: curriculum design for 69–71; *see also* ESN(M) and maladjusted children

medical models x, xii, 37–9

micro-sociology (segregation) 141, 174–90

mixed-ability teaching 72, 79, 133, 179, 236; for low achievers 65, 117, 118, 120–1, 125

'mixed motive' interaction 30

mobility problems 152, 153–4, 166, 345; access and 114–16, 345; curriculum design for 66–7

'moral career' 180

motivation (integration) 2, 46–9

multidimensional models 17, 18

multiple handicap 71–2, 134, 222–3

muscular dystrophy 157

'named person' 7, 8, 10, 191

National Child Development Study 219, 228

National Children's Bureau 277

National Federation of the Blind and Association of Blind and Partially Sighted Teachers and Students 164–5

National Foundation for Educational Research 44–5, 94–107, 150–7

negotiation processes 29–31

noise levels 115, 144, 147

normal curriculum 332–4, 336, 337–8

normative and non-normative categories xiii, 43–4, 242, 257–8

Norway 130, 131–4

numeracy 324–8, 332, 335–6

objectives model 64, 73–6, 77, 92, 293, 337

observation inventories 316–20

OECD 45–6, 130

open curriculum 80

operational assessment 77

ordinary schools: hearing impairment in, 142, 143–8; physical handicap in 140, 150–7; resource centres 124–5, 133, 136, 164–7, 170, 171; resources model 292, 304, 305–10; special needs provision 64–5, 94–107; 'stretching' 292, 304; support in *see* support systems; units *see* unit system; visual handicap in 160–5, 170–3

organic accounts (ESN) 245, 246

organizational structure xii; for hearing-impaired 140, 143–4; influence on